P9-BZB-544

Praise for
When Corporations Rule the World

66 This is a 'must read' book—a searing indictment of an unjust international economic order, not by a wild-eyed idealistic leftwinger, but by a sober scion of the establishment with impeccable credentials. It left me devastated but also very hopeful. Something can be done to create a more just economic order."

Archbishop Desmond M. Tutu
Nobel Peace Laureate

66 Required reading for women who want to peek behind the curtain of the global economy and figure out how to save ourselves and respond to the global SOS. Korten describes a nightmarish system out of control. . . . So overwhelming is corporate control that even the men who pull the levers seem powerless to stop the wheels of destruction—even if they wanted to."

Bella S. Abzug
Cochair, Women's Environment &
Development Organization (WEDO)

66 Probably the most important economics book to come out since *The Wealth of Nations*."

David Rivard
President, Steel Reinforcing Inc.,
and Cofounder, California World
Foundation

66 From the vantage point of the year 2000, this may well be judged the most important book of the 1990s. It is an eye-opener, which, in a nerve-touching way, clearly depicts the role of business in a changing world. Every business leader should read it."

Rolf Österberg
Former Chairman, Swedish
Newspapers Association, and
Author of *Corporate Renaissance*

" I recommend this book to any business executive as a 'must read.' It deals with one of the most important questions we can ask these days: What is the future role of business on the planet? The book is tough-minded, hard-hitting, and right on the money. It might at first glance strike some readers as anti-business, but it is not. It is just pro-people and pro-planet."

Willis Harman
President, Institute of Noetic
Sciences

" A wise, learned, and inspiring book about the challenge of the new world economy. Korten's impressive analysis of global corporations is essential reading for anyone who places a higher value on the welfare of human beings than on money. The book is indispensable help in the search for a more hopeful path into the twenty-first century."

Richard J. Barnet
Coauthor of *Global Dreams: Imperial
Corporations and the New World Order*

" If you work in a business, or know someone who does, this book is required reading. Korten defines the business agenda for the next twenty years, and he does it thoughtfully and from the heart."

Peter Block
Author of *Stewardship* and
The Empowered Manager

" A revealing portrait of the effects of corporations on the global scene along with proposals for a transformation that will bring the massive global economy into tune with human values. Highly recommended."

In Context magazine

" David Korten's book is an important tool for social movement activists who are trying to get a handle on the new system of corporate rule that is undermining democracy throughout the world today."

Tony Clarke
Former National Chair, Action
Canada Network

"Never in history has there occurred the economic gamble that is taking place today in the form of economic globalization. David Korten's important work begins the critical process of economic reformation that will surely follow this universal loss of sovereignty, self, and community."

Paul Hawken
Author of *The Ecology of Commerce*

"Korten is an honest witness to the disastrous betrayal of common people and future generations that is being carried out by corporations, governments, and multilateral banks. He cuts through the loud rhetoric of economic growth and global economic integration to the facts of increasing poverty, inequality, and dependence. I hope that this book is widely read."

Herman E. Daly
Senior Research Scholar,
University of Maryland

"David Korten is an eloquent critic of globalization that is untempered by either compassion or vision. He will move you to profoundly rethink our collective direction, and to take steps towards redirecting your own life."

Joe Dominguez and Vicki Robin
Coauthors of *Your Money or Your Life*

"If you can read only one book on how to understand and address the enormous challenges of our time, this is it. . . . Korten weaves together a devastating critique of the tyranny of the global economy with an arsenal of well-argued alternatives that combine vision and practicality to offer an empowering agenda for change."

John Cavanagh
Fellow, Institute for Policy Studies,
and Coauthor of *Global Dreams*

"Taking us beyond the myths and illusions of the global economy, Korten's proposals for change bear careful consideration by all who care about the future we leave to our children."

Doug Tompkins
Cofounder and ex-CEO, Esprit

" The world system is not working for most people. In this courageous volume David Korten confronts the illusions of unlimited growth and domination of global corporations. He describes an alternative to a global system rooted in participatory communities, spiritual values, and mutual respect. A compelling vision."

John A. Lapp
Executive Secretary, Mennonite
Central Committee

" The transnational corporations that control the global economy are working hard to assure that nothing interferes with their short-term interests. In this masterful book, David Korten spells out the dramatic implications and shows why our greatest priority today must be to bring economic activities once more under democratic control."

Teddy Goldsmith
Founding Editor of *The Ecologist*
and recipient of The Right
Livelihood Award, commonly
known as the Alternative Nobel
Prize

" Hard-nosed and idealistic, Korten challenges corporate and financial leaders as intensively as grassroots community organizers. Korten's wide-ranging and controversial views enrich the dialogue among those who must address the widening gap between the rich and the poor and the future of the planet—that is the dialogue among all of us."

Claire L. Gaudiani
President, Connecticut College

" *When Corporations Rule the World* spells out the reality and consequences of a corporate-dominated globalization process and how it is undermining democracy. It sets forth an agenda for regaining citizen sovereignty that is an important starting point on the long road back to democracy."

Maude Barlow
National Chairperson, Council of
Canadians

When
Corporations
Rule
the World

When Corporations Rule the World

David C. Korten

A Copublication of
Kumarian Press, Inc.,
and Berrett-Koehler Publishers, Inc.

Berrett-Koehler Publishers

Kumarian Press

When Corporations Rule the World. Copublished 1995 in the United States of America by Kumarian Press, Inc., and Berrett-Koehler Publishers, Inc.

Kumarian Press, Inc., 14 Oakwood Avenue,
West Hartford, Connecticut 06119
(860) 233-5895

Berrett-Koehler Publishers, Inc. 155 Montgomery Street,
San Francisco, California 94104
(415) 288-0260

Copyright © 1995 PCDForum. All rights reserved.

No part of this book may be reproduced or transmitted in any form or by any means, electronic or mechanical, including photocopy, recording, or information storage and retrieval system, without prior permission of Kumarian Press, Inc.

Production supervised by Jenna Dixon
Copyedited by Linda Lotz *Proofread by Beth Richards*
Text designed by Jenna Dixon *Typeset by Ultragraphics*
Index prepared by Barbara DeGennaro

Printed in the United States of America on recycled acid-free paper by Edwards Bothers, Inc.

Library of Congress Cataloging-in-Publication Data
Korten, David C.
    When corporations rule the world / David C. Korten.
        p.   cm. — (Kumarian Press books for a world that works)
    Includes bibliographical references and index.
    ISBN 1-887208-00-3 (hard cover : alk. paper)
    1. Corporations—Political aspects. 2. Industries—Environmental aspects.
3. Industrialization—Social aspects. 4. Big business. 5. Power (Social sciences).
6. Business and politics. 7. International business enterprises. 8. International
economic relations. 9. Sustainable development. I. Title.   II. Series.
HD2326.K647   1995
322'.3—dc20   95-18853

04 03 02 01 00 99 98 97 96   10 9 8 7 6 5 4 3 2

To two great teachers,
Professors Robert North and Willis Harman,
who taught me to question conventional wisdom
and opened my eyes to possibilities that changed my life.

And

To my life partner, Dr. Frances F. Korten,
who shares the incredible journey
on a road less traveled.

Contents

Acknowledgments

This book is the product of an international collaboration involving many wonderful colleagues. I am especially indebted to Tony Quizon, Sunimal Fernando, Bishan Singh, Chandra de Fonseca, Felix Sugitharaj, and Sixto Roxas, with whom I shared a ten-day retreat in Baguio, Philippines, in November 1992. This book is to a large extent an elaboration of the collective report we produced as a result of that retreat.

Krishna Sondhi and Ian Mayo-Smith of Kumarian Press, which published many of my previous books, unrelentingly prodded me to undertake this project and gave me extraordinary support to make it happen. They commissioned Henry Berry as editorial and marketing consultant to help me make the transition from writing for a specialized development audience to writing for a broader trade audience. They also developed a unique copublication partnership with Berrett-Koehler Publishers that brought this project to the creative talents of Steve Piersanti and his colleagues.

Frances Korten helped shape the book's core arguments through many hours of dinner table conversation and with great love, devotion, and an unrelentingly critical eye read and edited every chapter—several times. An editorial advisory board of Anwar Fazal, Robert Gilman, Willis Harman, Stanley Katz, and Donella Meadows provided ideas, inspiration, and advice throughout. Michelle Beesten and Claudia Radel provided voluntary research and editorial assistance.

In addition, extensive critical input and feedback was provided by Nancy Alexander, Robin Broad, John Cavanagh, Walter Coddington, Sandy Cohen, Herman Daly, Richard Douthwaite, Neva Goodwin, Jonathan Greenberg, Ross Jackson, Elizabeth Kramer, Mark Leach, Jerry Mander, and Marilyn Mehlmann. Other colleagues who made special contributions to the underlying ideas and analysis include Fatma Alloo, Gar Alperovitz, Roy Anderson, Winifred Armstrong, Patricia Bauman, Walden Bello, David Bonbright, Jeremy Brecher, Beth Burrows, Ruth Caplan, Robert Cassani,

Mary Clark, Clifford Cobb, Harriet Crosby, Joëlle Danant, Joe Dominguez, Duane Elgin, Bill Ellis, Linda Elswick, Gustavo Esteva, Joyce Gillilan-Goldberg, Edward Goldsmith, Alisa Gravitz, Nathan Gray, Leanne Grossman, Richard Grossman, Ted Halstead, Wendy Harcourt, Paul Hawken, Judy Henderson, Noeleen Heyzer, Janet Hunt, Tom Keehn, Danny Kennedy, Martin Khor, Andy Kimbrell, Alicia Korten, Smitu Kothari, Sigmund Kvaloy, Kathy Lawrence, Michael Lerner, Tina Liamzon, Peter Mann, Atherton Martin, Michael McCoy, Luis Lopezllera Méndez, Victor Menotti, John Mohawk, Ward Morehouse, David Morris, Shierry Nicholsen, Helena Norberg-Hodge, Michael Northrup, Sharlye Patton, David Perrin, George Porter, William Rees, David Richards, Mark Ritchie, Neil Ritchie, James Robertson, Vicki Robin, Atila Roque, Isagani Serrano, Vandana Shiva, Michael Shuman, Greg Thompson, Sally Timpson, Edgardo Valenzuela, Steve Viederman, Paul Wachtel, Lori Wallach, and Paul Wangoola. The extraordinary musical creations of Jeff Clarkson—friend and colleague, New Zealand composer, synthesizer artist, and environmental activist—created a relaxed and reflective mood during the long periods of writing.

The book was prepared as a project of the People-Centered Development Forum (PCDForum). Specific financial support for this project was provided to the Forum by the Jenifer Altman Foundation. Additional support for this and other Forum projects was provided by the Batir Foundation, the Bauman Family Foundation, the Deep Ecology Foundation, the New Road Map Foundation, the Charles Stewart Mott Foundation, the Directors' Discretionary Fund of the Jessie Smith Noyes Foundation, the Rockefeller Foundation, the Rockwood Fund, the Sierra Club, and the Uniterra Foundation. Individual contributors included Andrès Carothers, Harriett Crosby, Margaret Korten, Maryanne Mott, and Edgardo Valenzuela.

The PCDForum is a purely voluntary organization that pays no salaries. I have received no personal compensation from any source for the preparation of this book, and all royalties from book sales will go to the PCDForum. Further information on the PCDForum is available at either of the two following Internet addresses:

URL: gopher//wn.apc.org/sangonet/PCDF
(maintained by SangoNet South Africa)

HTTP://iisd1.iisd.ca/devideas
(maintained by the International Institute for Sustainable Development Canada)

The views expressed in this book are mine and do not necessarily represent those of the PCDForum and its contributors. I extend my deepest appreciation to all who helped make this book possible.

Prologue: A Personal Journey

> *I think there are good reasons for suggesting that the modern age has ended. Today, many things indicate that we are going through a transitional period, when it seems that something is on the way out and something else is painfully being born. It is as if something were crumbling, decaying and exhausting itself, while something else, still indistinct, were arising from the rubble.*
>
> —*Václav Havel, president of the Czech Republic*[1]

My personal journey of the past several years has brought me into contact with people of widely diverse backgrounds in countries as different as the Philippines, Hungary, New Zealand, Bangladesh, Brazil, South Africa, Thailand, and the United States. Everywhere I travel, I find an almost universal sense among ordinary people that the institutions on which they depend are failing them. Many are increasingly fearful of a future that seems to offer declining prospects for themselves and their children. In the United States and elsewhere, that fear is creating a growing sense of political frustration and alienation that is finding current expression in falling voter turnouts, a taxpayer revolt, and the rejection of political incumbents. Yet the real issues go far deeper than a simple rejection of big government.

Although politicians and the press play to the public's frustrations over governmental failure, they display little understanding of the root causes of the conditions of

1

rising poverty and unemployment, inequality, violent crime, failing families, and environmental deterioration which lead so many people to foresee a dark future. Our leaders seem to be unable to move beyond blaming their political opponents and promoting the same old ineffectual solutions—accelerating economic growth through deregulation, cutting taxes, removing trade barriers, giving industry more incentives and subsidies, forcing welfare recipients to work, hiring more police, and building more jails.

It is often the people who live ordinary lives far removed from the corridors of power who have the clearest perception of what is really happening. Yet they are often reluctant to speak openly of what they believe in their hearts to be true. It is too frightening and differs too dramatically from what those with more impressive credentials and access to the media are saying. Their suppressed insights may leave them feeling isolated and helpless. The questions nag: Are things really as bad as they seem to me? Why don't others seem to see it? Am I stupid? Am I being intentionally misinformed? Is there anything I can do? What can anyone do?

I have been struggling for a number of years with the same questions, at first with a similar sense of isolation, but increasingly with an awareness that there are millions of others bringing their insights to bear on these same questions. Even so, each time I prepare to speak to a new group I invariably have a nervous feeling that what I have to say will be rejected out of hand in a world committed to growth, big business, and deficit financing. Yet the usual response is an outpouring of affirmation from people who express their relief and pleasure at the unusual experience of having their own experience affirmed in a public forum. Getting the difficult and unpleasant truth out on the table for discussion is a necessary first step toward action. Whereas fear of the unknown may immobilize us, the truth empowers us to act.

Roots of the Inquiry

For me, each book I write is a new step in a continuing intellectual journey, an opportunity to engage in a conversation with many readers on issues about which I care deeply. As we embark on this present journey, it may be helpful for you to know something about the experiences that led me to the views I now hold and that I share in the following pages. The history of these experiences also provides an overview of the central arguments of *When Corporations Rule the World*.

I was born in 1937 into a conservative, white, upper-middle-class family and grew up in Longview, Washington, a small timber industry town of some 25,000 people. Assuming that one day I would manage the family's retail music and appliance business, I had no particular interest in international affairs or in venturing beyond the borders of the United States. As a psychology major at Stanford University, I focused on musical aptitude testing and the uses of psychology to influence buying behavior. Then in 1959, during my senior year, a curious thing happened.

For reasons that I cannot now recall, I took a course on modern revolutions taught by Robert North, a professor of political science. I was stunned. Poverty was fueling revolutions the world over—a threat to the American way of life I held so dear. One of those rare life-changing educational experiences, this course sparked a decision. I would devote my life to countering this threat by bringing the knowledge of modern business management and entrepreneurship to those who had not yet benefited from it.

I prepared myself with an MBA in international business and a PhD in organizational theory from the Stanford Business School. Three years in Ethiopia setting up a business school with the help of my newly wed life partner Frances Korten provided my apprenticeship. I did my obligatory military service during the Vietnam War as a captain in the U.S. Air Force, fulfilling staff assignments at the Special Air Warfare School, the Office of the Secretary of the Air Force, and the Office of the Secretary of Defense. I then signed up for what turned out to be a five-and-a-half-year tour on the faculty of the Harvard University Graduate School of Business.

For three of my Harvard Business School years I served as the Harvard advisor to the Nicaragua-based Central American Management Institute (INCAE), a graduate business school catering to the established business families of the Central American and Andean countries. After returning to Boston, I taught for two more years at the Business School and then moved to the Harvard Institute for International Development and the Harvard School of Public Health. At the beginning of 1978, Fran and I joined the Ford Foundation staff in the Philippines and remained in Southeast Asia for the next fourteen years. While Fran stayed with Ford, I moved on to spend eight years as a senior advisor on development management to the U.S. Agency for International Development (USAID), the official U.S. foreign aid program.

I share this detail to establish the depth of my conservative roots. The more interesting part of my story, however, has to do with my gradual awakening to the conclusion that the conventional development practice espoused by most conservatives and even liberals is a leading cause of—not the solution to—a rapidly accelerating and potentially fatal human crisis of global proportions.

The first step toward my awakening came with the course on modern revolutions, which opened my eyes to the fact that the development benefits I enjoyed were not widely shared. In 1961, a summer in Indonesia immersed me in the realities of underdevelopment and brought me into contact with the heroic struggles, spiritual grounding, and generosity of people who live in desperate poverty. It was an aspect of the human experience with which I had had little experience.

While at INCAE in the early 1970s, I wrote a number of Harvard Business School–style management cases for a course I was teaching on the management of change. They were based on Latin American experiences, and many involved efforts by government, business, and voluntary agencies to improve the conditions of the urban and rural poor. Many of these cases carried a disturbing message: externally imposed "development" was seriously disrupting human relationships and community life and causing significant hardship for the very people it claimed to benefit. By contrast, when people found the freedom and self-confidence to develop themselves, they demonstrated enormous potential to create a better world. I became fascinated with the challenge of transforming development programs to support these kinds of self-led, grassroots processes. During our INCAE and Harvard years, Fran and I also became involved in efforts to improve the management of family-planning programs. This brought us into contact with many local initiatives, including those of poor people who were trying to gain control of their lives on a declining resource base.

When Fran and I left Harvard to join the Ford Foundation staff in Manila, Fran inherited a portfolio of grants that included a small grant to the Philippine National Irrigation Administration (NIA). It was intended to strengthen the NIA's ability to assist small farmer-owned and -operated irrigation systems. This led to a long-term cooperation between the NIA and the Ford Foundation that ultimately transformed the NIA from an engineering- and construction-centered organization that dictated to farmers to one that worked in partnership with farmer organizations and encouraged a substantial degree of local self-governance.

We were able to see at work the powerful energies that people and communities can mobilize on their own behalf when development initiatives are actually centered in people. We saw firsthand how foreign-funded development projects commonly overwhelm such efforts—even many projects that seek to embrace them. However, we also learned how foreign funding can be used to debureaucratize large centralized public agencies and strengthen control of local resources by local people. USAID invited me to help it apply the lessons of this experience to its programming in Asia. I focused on this task for eight years, only to conclude that USAID was too big and bureaucratic to be effective as a catalyst in helping other development agencies debureaucratize.

These experiences left me with a deep conviction that real development cannot be purchased with foreign aid monies. Development depends on people's ability to gain control of and use effectively the real resources of their localities—land, water, labor, technology, and human ingenuity and motivation—to meet their own needs. Yet most development interventions transfer control of local resources to ever larger and more centralized institutions that are unaccountable to local people and unresponsive to their needs. The greater the amount of money that flows through these central institutions, the more dependent people become, the less control they have over their own lives and resources, and the more rapidly the gap grows between those who hold central power and those who seek to make a living for themselves within local communities.

I came to see the difference between those things that increase economic growth and those that result in better lives for people. This difference raised a basic question: what would development look like if instead of being growth centered—with people treated only as a means of achieving growth—it were people centered—with people being both the purpose and the primary instrument? In 1984, I edited the anthology, *People-Centered Development*, published by Kumarian Press. In 1986, I edited another Kumarian anthology, *Community Management*, that focused on the importance of getting resource control in the hands of people.

The more I saw development's presumed beneficiaries struggling to maintain their dignity and the quality of their lives in the face of the systemic attack by the development agencies and projects that were colonizing their resources, the more alienated I became from mainstream development thinking. In 1988, I left USAID but remained in Southeast Asia.

Having become disillusioned with official development agencies, I immersed myself in the world of nongovernmental organizations (NGOs) and soon found myself among NGO colleagues who were asking basic questions about the nature and process of development. I became a synthesizer and scribe of the collective insights emerging from an increasingly dynamic dialogue within the NGO community. It was a period of intense personal learning that led to my next book, *Getting to the 21st Century: Voluntary Action and the Global Agenda*, published by Kumarian Press in 1990. That book focused on the threefold human crisis of deepening poverty, environmental destruction, and social disintegration, and it traced the roots of the crisis to models that made growth the goal of development and treated people as mere means. It concluded that since the dominant institutions of modern society are creations of a growth-centered development vision, the leadership for change must necessarily come from voluntary citizen action.

Embracing this argument to recast my own commitments, I joined a number of colleagues to found the People-Centered Development Forum (PCDForum), a global citizen network engaged in advancing the articulation of a people-centered vision of the future and redefining development practice in line with that vision. The PCDForum has given particular attention to examining the role of national- and global-level structures and institutions in depriving people and place-based communities of the power to meet their own needs in responsible, sustainable ways. This explains what some people may see as a paradox: although I talk of the need for local empowerment, much of my attention is focused on the transformation of global institutions. I am among those who seek to transform the global to empower the local.

In November 1992, I went to Baguio, a Philippine mountain resort town, to meet with the leaders of several Asian NGOs. We engaged in a ten-day reflection on Asian development experience and its implications for NGO strategies. We were concerned that Asia's economic success is dangerously superficial. Beneath the surface of dynamic competitive economies lies a deeper reality of impoverishment and spreading disruption of the region's social and ecological foundations. Our discussions turned to the need for a theory that would explain and provide guidance in addressing the deeper causes of the crisis. Without a theory, we were like a pilot without a compass. Late one night in a small Chinese restaurant, our discussions began to converge on two fundamental insights. First, it was not an alternative theory of development that we needed as our guide. Rather, we needed a theory of sustainable societies that would apply to Northern and Southern countries alike. Second, the theory must go beyond the sterile formulations of economics to explain why human societies have become so alienated from natural processes.

As we continued our discussion over the next few days, the pieces began to fall into place. The Western scientific vision of a mechanical universe has created a philosophical or conceptual alienation from our own inherent spiritual nature. This has been reinforced in our daily lives by the increasing alignment of our institutions with the monetary values of the marketplace. The more dominant money has become in our lives, the less place there has been for any sense of the spiritual bond that is the foundation of community and a balanced relationship with nature. The pursuit of spiritual fulfillment has been increasingly displaced by an all-consuming and increasingly self-destructive obsession with the pursuit of money—a useful but wholly substanceless and intrinsically valueless human artifact.

It seemed evident from our analysis that to reestablish a sustainable relationship to the living earth, we must break free of the illusions of the world of money, rediscover spiritual meaning in our lives, and root our economic institutions in place and community so that they are integrally connected to people and life. Consequently, we concluded that the task of people-centered development in its fullest sense must be the creation of life-centered societies in which the economy is but one of the instruments of good living—not the purpose of human existence. Because our leaders are entrapped in the myths and the reward systems of the institutions they head, the leadership in this creative process of institutional and value re-creation must come from within civil society.

It was in many ways an unremarkable insight. What we had accomplished was little more than to rediscover the ancient wisdom that a deep tension exists between our spiritual nature and our economic lives and that healthy social and spiritual function depends on keeping the two in proper balance and perspective. Nor was there anything new in recognizing the importance of civil society, which has always been the foundation of democratic governance. Yet we felt that we had deepened our own insights into the practical relevance of these ideas for the crisis that imperils contemporary societies. We devoted the remainder of our time in Baguio to fleshing out our insights in a paper entitled "Economy, Ecology, & Spirituality: Toward a Theory and Practice of Sustainability."[2]

Returning Home

In the summer of 1992, shortly before the Baguio retreat, Fran and I left Southeast Asia to return to the United States. We had announced our decision to friends and colleagues in our Christmas letter with the following explanation:

> We were drawn to these far-away regions in the early 1960s by a belief that they were the locus of the development problems to which we had decided as young university students to dedicate our careers. We began these careers challenged by a mission—to help share the lessons of America's success with the world—so that "they" could become more like "us."
>
> Development as we understood it thirty years ago, and as it is to this day vigorously promoted by the World Bank, the IMF [International Monetary Fund], the Bush administration, and most of the world's powerful economic institutions, isn't working for the majority of humanity. And the roots of the problem are not

found among the poor of the "underdeveloped" world. They are found in the countries that set global standards for wasteful extravagance and dominate the global policies that are leading our world to social and ecological self-destruction.

Now thirty years older and hopefully a good deal wiser, Fran and I have come to realize the extent to which America's "success" is one of the world's key problems. Indeed, the ultimate demonstration of this assertion is found in America itself.

From our vantage point in Asia we have watched in horror as the same policies the United States has been advocating for the world have created a Third World within its own borders as revealed in its growing gap between rich and poor, dependence on foreign debt, deteriorating educational systems, rising infant mortality, economic dependence on the export of primary commodities—including its last remaining primary forests—indiscriminate dumping of toxic wastes, and the breakdown of families and communities.

While we have been away from home, the powerful have consolidated the nation's wealth in their own hands and absolved themselves of responsibility for their less fortunate neighbors. Labor unions have withered as American workers desperate to keep their jobs have been forced to compete with the even more desperate unemployed of Mexico, Bangladesh, and other Third World countries by negotiating for wage cuts with corporations that may still bear American names but honor no national allegiance.

We feel that our own education has been the primary product of our years abroad and that it is now time to return home to face up to our responsibilities to confront the problem at its geographical source. New York, a major center of economic power manifesting all the qualities of a contemporary Third World city— including wandering armies of the homeless juxtaposed with the extravagant lifestyles of the rich and famous, incapacitated government, and indiscriminate violence—seemed an appropriate choice. So we are moving to the belly of the beast, bringing the perspectives gained from our thirty years of learning about the causes of these conditions.

We had set out to solve for others the problems we perceived to reside in them by making them more like us. We now came back home to help our own compatriots better understand the ways in which we have contributed to placing the world—ourselves included—on a self-destructive course. Only when we are prepared to assume responsibility for changing ourselves will others be able to fully reclaim the social and environmental space we have appropriated from them and recover their ability to meet their own needs within a just, democratic, and sustainable world of cooperative partnerships.

Disclosure Statement

As the issues discussed in these pages are inseparable from basic questions of values, I believe that it is appropriate to disclose the underlying political and spiritual values I bring to the exchange. With regard to political values, I remain a traditional conservative in the sense that I retain a deep distrust of large institutions and their concentrations of unaccountable power. I also continue to believe in the importance of the market and private ownership. However, unlike many contemporary conservatives, I have no more love for big business than I have for big government. Nor do I believe that possession of wealth should convey special political privilege.

I share the liberal's compassion for the disenfranchised, commitment to equity, and concern for the environment and believe that there are essential roles for government and limits to the rights of private property. I believe, however, that big government can be as unaccountable and destructive of societal values as can big business. Indeed, I have a distrust of any organization that accumulates and concentrates massive power beyond the bounds of accountability. In short, I align with those who are defining a new path that is more pragmatic than ideological and who cannot be easily pigeonholed within the conventional conservative–liberal spectrum of political choice.

I first encountered economics in college when I chose it as my undergraduate major. I soon found it mechanistic, boring, and detached from reality, so I switched to the study of human behavior and organization. I've since come to realize that economic systems are the dominant systems for organizing behavior in modern societies and are most appropriately studied as behavioral systems.

Although this book takes a harshly critical look at the institution of the corporation and the system within which business functions, I have never been, and am not now, antibusiness. An efficient system of industry and commerce is essential to human well-being. As an MBA student, I believed that global corporations might offer an answer to the problems of poverty and human conflict. I have since concluded, however, that the systemic forces nurturing the growth and dominance of global corporations are at the heart of the current human dilemma. I now believe that to avoid collective catastrophe we must radically transform the underlying system of business to restore power to the small and local. I further believe that accomplishing the needed transformation will require the cooperative efforts of those within the system—including those who head our major corporations and financial institutions—in addition to the efforts of citizen movements working from outside it.

With regard to spiritual values, I was raised in the Protestant Christian faith but find wisdom in the teachings of all the great religions. I believe that we have access to an inner spiritual wisdom and that our collective salvation as a species depends, in part, on tapping into this wisdom from which the institutions of modern science, the market, and even religion have deeply alienated us. Through this rediscovery we may achieve the creative balance between market and community, science and religion, and money and spirit that is essential to the creation and maintenance of healthy human societies.

I hope that this introduction will help you approach this book as you would an active conversation with a valued friend. In reading this book, you are in fact engaging in an exchange with many friends who have had important roles in shaping the analysis and the vision it presents. If you are not already involved in the larger conversation on these issues, I hope that this book will encourage you to become so engaged.

If you are among those who work within the system of business, I urge you to step out of your business role while reading *When Corporations Rule the World*. Read it from the perspective of your role as a citizen and as a parent concerned for the future of your children. This may make it easier and less painful to hear and assess the book's underlying message objectively and to consider its invitation to join in the movement to transform the system.

Please read what follows actively and critically. Bring your own perspectives and insights to bear. Question. Challenge. Consider the implications for the way you want to live your life. Discuss it with friends. Tell them where you agree, where you disagree, what new insights you gained, where you find it incomplete. Get their thoughts. Explore new avenues together. Take the conversation to a new level. And act.

Although the general direction we must travel becomes clearer with each passing day, no one has yet been where we must go. If we seek a well-marked road, we will look in vain. To borrow from the title of a book of conversations between Myles Horton and Paulo Freire, two of the great social activists of our time, we set our sights on a destination beyond the distant horizon and then "we make the road by walking."

The Argument

Part of our inability to come to terms with institutional systems failure stems from the fact that television reduces political discourse to sound bites and academia organizes intellectual inquiry into narrowly specialized disciplines. Consequently, we become accustomed to dealing with complex issues in fragmented bits and pieces. Yet we live in a complex world in which nearly every aspect of our lives is connected in some way with every other aspect. When we limit ourselves to fragmented approaches to dealing with systemic problems, it is not surprising that our solutions prove inadequate. If our species is to survive the predicaments we have created for ourselves, we must develop a capacity for whole-systems thought and action.

Whole-systems thinking calls for a skepticism of simplistic solutions, a willingness to seek out connections between problems and events that conventional discourse ignores, and the courage to delve into subject matter that may lie outside our direct experience and expertise. In taking a whole-systems perspective, this book covers a broad territory with many elements. To help you keep in mind how the individual arguments that are developed and documented throughout the book link together into a larger whole, the overall argument is summarized here. I don't ask you to accept these many arguments on face value—only to keep an open mind until you have had the opportunity to examine the reasoning and documentation underlying each of them. At that point, I trust that you will exercise your own independent critical judgment and eventually build your own synthesis that may or may not correspond with mine. Always bear in mind that we are all participants in an act of creation, and none of us can claim a monopoly on truth in our individual and collective search for understanding of these complex issues.

The point of departure of *When Corporations Rule the World* is the evidence that we are experiencing accelerating social and environmental disintegration in nearly every country of the world—as revealed by a rise in poverty, unemployment, inequality, violent crime, failing families, and environmental degradation. These problems stem in part from a fivefold increase in economic output since 1950 that has pushed human demands on the ecosystem beyond what the planet is capable of sustaining. The continued quest for economic growth as the organizing principle of public policy is accelerating the breakdown of the ecosystem's regenerative capacities and the social fabric that sustains human community; at the same time, it is intensifying the competition for resources between rich and poor—a competition that the poor invariably lose.

Governments seem wholly incapable of responding, and public frustration is turning to rage. It is more than a failure of government bureaucracies, however. It is a crisis of governance born of a convergence of ideological, political, and technological forces behind a process of economic globalization that is shifting power away from governments responsible for the public good and toward a handful of corporations and financial institutions driven by a single imperative—the quest for short-term financial gain. This has concentrated massive economic and political power in the hands of an elite few whose absolute share of the products of a declining pool of natural wealth continues to increase at a substantial rate—thus reassuring them that the system is working perfectly well.

Those who bear the costs of the system's dysfunctions have been stripped of decision-making power and are held in a state of confusion regarding the cause of their distress by corporate-dominated media that incessantly bombard them with interpretations of the resulting crisis based on the perceptions of the power holders. An active propaganda machinery controlled by the world's largest corporations constantly reassures us that consumerism is the path to happiness, governmental restraint of market excess is the cause our distress, and economic globalization is both a historical inevitability and a boon to the human species. In fact, these are all myths propagated to justify profligate greed and mask the extent to which the global transformation of human institutions is a consequence of the sophisticated, well-funded, and intentional interventions of a small elite whose money enables them to live in a world of illusion apart from the rest of humanity.

These forces have transformed once beneficial corporations and financial institutions into instruments of a market tyranny that is extending its reach across the planet like a cancer, colonizing ever more of the planet's living spaces, destroying livelihoods, displacing people, rendering democratic institutions impotent, and feeding on life in an insatiable quest for money. As our economic system has detached from place and gained greater dominance over our democratic institutions, even the world's most powerful corporations have become captives of the forces of a globalized financial system that has delinked the creation of money from the creation of real wealth and rewards extractive over productive investment. The big winners are the corporate raiders who strip sound companies of their assets for short-term gain and the speculators who capitalize on market volatility to extract a private tax from those who are engaged in productive work and investment.

Faced with pressures to produce greater short-term returns, the world's largest corporations are downsizing to shed people and functions.

They are not, however, becoming less powerful. While tightening their control over markets and technology through mergers, acquisitions, and strategic alliances, they are forcing both subcontractors and local communities into a standards-lowering competition with one another to obtain the market access and jobs that global corporations control. The related market forces are deepening our dependence on socially and environmentally destructive technologies that sacrifice our physical, social, environmental, and mental health to corporate profits.

The problem is not business or the market per se but a badly corrupted global economic system that is gyrating far beyond human control. The dynamics of this system have become so powerful and perverse that it is becoming increasingly difficult for corporate managers to manage in the public interest, no matter how strong their moral values and commitment.

Driven by the imperative to replicate money, the system treats people as a source of inefficiency and is rapidly shedding them at all system levels. As the first industrial revolution reduced dependence on human muscle, the information revolution is reducing dependence on our eyes, ears, and brains. The first industrial revolution dealt with the resulting unemployment by colonizing weaker peoples and sending surplus populations off as migrants to less populated lands. People in colonized countries fell back on traditional social structures to sustain themselves. With the world's physical frontiers largely exhausted and social economies greatly weakened by market intrusion, few such safety valves remain. Consequently, the redundant now end up as victims of starvation and violence, homeless beggars, welfare recipients, or residents of refugee camps. Continuing on our present course will almost certainly lead to accelerating social and environmental disintegration.

It is within our means, however, to reclaim the power that we have yielded to the institutions of money and re-create societies that nurture cultural and biological diversity—thus opening vast new opportunities for social, intellectual, and spiritual advancement beyond our present imagination. Millions of people the world over are already acting to reclaim this power and to rebuild their communities and heal the earth. These initiatives are being melded into global alliances that form the foundation of a powerful political movement grounded in a global consciousness of the unity of life.

When Corporations Rule the World outlines a citizens' agenda to enhance these efforts by getting corporations out of politics and creating localized economies that empower communities within a system of global cooperation. Having reached the limits of the materialistic vision of the scientific and industrial era ushered in by the

Copernican Revolution, we are now on the threshold of an ecological era called into being by an Ecological Revolution grounded in a more holistic view of the spiritual and material aspects of our nature. This revolution now calls to each of us to reclaim our political power and rediscover our spirituality to create societies that nurture our ability and desire to embrace the joyful experience of living to its fullest.

1 Cowboys in a Spaceship

1 From Hope to Crisis

People who celebrate technology say it has brought us an improved standard of living, which means greater speed, greater choice, greater leisure, and greater luxury. None of these benefits informs us about human satisfaction, happiness, security, or the ability to sustain life on earth.

—Jerry Mander[1]

The last half of the twentieth century has been perhaps the most remarkable period in human history. Scientifically we have unlocked countless secrets of matter, space, and biology. We have virtually dominated the planet with our numbers, technology, and sophisticated organization. We have traveled beyond our world to the moon and reached out to the stars. A mere fifty years ago, within the lifetime of my generation, many of the things we take for granted today as essential to a good and prosperous life were unavailable, nonexistent, or even unimagined. These include the jet airplane and global commercial air travel, computers, microwave ovens, electric typewriters, photocopying machines, television, clothes dryers, air-conditioning, freeways, shopping malls, fax machines, birth-control pills, artificial organs, suburbs, and chemical pesticides—to name only a few.

This same period saw the creation of the first consequential institutions of global governance: the United

Nations, the International Monetary Fund, the World Bank, and the General Agreement on Tariffs and Trade (GATT). Western Europe was transformed from a conflictual continent of warring states into a peaceful and prosperous political and economic union. The superpower conflict between East and West, and its dark specter of nuclear Armageddon, already seems a distant historical memory, eclipsed by a rush of business deals, financial assistance, and scientific and cultural exchanges. There has been a dramatic spread of democracy to nations formerly ruled by authoritarian governments. We have conquered many once devastating illnesses such as smallpox and polio, increased life expectancy in developing countries by over a third in the past thirty years, and cut their infant and under-five mortality rates by more than half.[2]

One of the most significant human commitments of the last half of this century has been to economic growth and trade expansion, and we have been spectacularly successful in accomplishing both. Global economic output expanded from $3.8 trillion in 1950 to $18.9 trillion in 1992 (constant 1987 dollars), a nearly fivefold increase. This means that, on average, we have added more to total global output *in each of the past four decades* than was added from the moment the first cave dweller carved out a stone axe up to the middle of the present century. During this same period, world trade soared from total exports of $308 billion to $3,554 billion (1990 dollars)—an 11.5-fold increase, or more than twice the rate of increase of total economic output. More than a billion people now enjoy the abundance of affluence.

These are only a few of the extraordinary accomplishments of the last half century. We have arrived at a time in history when it seems that we truly have the knowledge, technology, and organizational capacity to accomplish bold goals, including the elimination of poverty, war, and disease. This should be a time filled with hope for a new millennium in which societies will be freed forever from concerns of basic survival and security to pursue new frontiers of social, intellectual, and spiritual advancement.

A Threefold Human Crisis

The leaders and institutions that promised a golden age are not delivering. They assail us with visions of wondrous new technological gadgets, such as airplane seats with individual television monitors, and an information highway that will make it possible to fax messages while we sun ourselves on the beach. Yet the things that most of us really want—a secure means of livelihood, a decent place to live, healthy and uncontaminated food to eat, good education and health care for our children, a clean and vital natural environment—seem to slip further from the grasp of most of the world's people with each passing day.

Fewer and fewer people believe that they face a secure economic future. Family and community units and the security they once provided are disintegrating. The natural environment on which we depend for our material needs is under deepening stress. Confidence in our major institutions is evaporating, and we find a profound and growing suspicion among thoughtful people the world over that something has gone very wrong. These conditions are becoming pervasive in almost every locality of the world—and point to a global-scale failure of our institutions.

Even in the world's most affluent countries, high levels of unemployment, corporate downsizing, falling real wages, greater dependence on part-time and temporary jobs without benefits, and the weakening of unions are creating a growing sense of economic insecurity and shrinking the middle class. The employed find themselves working longer hours, holding multiple part-time jobs, and having less real income. Many among the young—especially of minority races—have little hope of ever finding jobs adequate to provide them with basic necessities, let alone financial security. The advanced degrees and technical skills of many of those who have seen their jobs disappear and their incomes and security plummet mock the idea that unemployment can be eliminated simply by improving education and job training.

In countries both rich and poor, as competition for natural resources, space, and waste dumps grows, those people who have supported themselves with small-scale farming, fishing, and other resource-based livelihoods find those resources being expropriated to serve the few while they are left to fend for themselves. The economically weak find their neighborhoods becoming the favored sites for waste dumps or polluting smokestacks.

Small-scale producers—farmers and artisans—who once were the backbone of poor but stable communities are being uprooted and transformed into landless migrant laborers, separated from family and place. Hundreds of thousands of young children, many without families, make lives for themselves begging, stealing, scavenging, selling sex, and doing odd jobs on the streets of great cities in Asia, Africa, and Latin America. There are an estimated 500,000 child prostitutes in Thailand, Sri Lanka, and the Philippines alone.[3] Growing millions migrate from their homes and families in search of opportunity and a means of survival. In addition to the 25 to 30 million people working outside their own countries as legal migrants, there are an estimated 20 to 40 million undocumented migrant workers—economic refugees without legal rights and with little access to basic services. Some, especially women, are kept in confinement and subjected to outrageous forms of sexual, physical, and psychological abuse.[4]

The world is increasingly divided between those who enjoy opulent affluence and those who live in dehumanizing poverty, servitude, and economic insecurity. While top corporate managers, investment bankers, financial speculators, athletes, and celebrities bring down multi-million-dollar annual incomes, approximately 1 billion of the world's people struggle in desperation to live on less than $1 a day. One need not go to some remote corner of Africa to experience the disparities. I see it daily within a block of my apartment in the heart of New York City. Shiny chauffeured stretch limousines with built-in bars and televisions discharge their elegantly coiffed occupants at trendy, expensive restaurants while homeless beggars huddle on the sidewalk wrapped in thin blankets to ward off the cold.

Evidence of the resulting social stress is everywhere: in rising rates of crime, drug abuse, divorce, teenage suicide, and domestic violence; growing numbers of political, economic, and environmental refugees; and even the changing nature of organized armed conflict. Violent crime is increasing at alarming rates all around the world.[5]

The seemingly impossible dream of millions of young people in the United States is simply to have a stable family and survive to adulthood. More than half of all children in the United States are being raised in single parent families.[6] On an average day in the United States, 100,000 American children carry guns with them to school, and forty of them are wounded or killed. Rare is the city, or even small town, in which people feel truly secure in their property and persons. Private security guards and systems have become a major growth industry around the world.

In developing countries, an estimated one-third of wives are physically battered. Of every 2,000 women in the world, one is a reported rape victim. There may be as many as 9,000 dowry-related deaths of women in India each year.[7]

In the era of "peace" that began in 1945 with the end of World War II, more than 20 million people have died in armed conflicts. Only three of the eighty-two armed conflicts between 1989 and 1992 were between states. The remainder were wars in which the combatants were killing those of their own nationality. Ninety percent of war casualties at the beginning of this century were military combatants. As the century ends, 90 percent are civilians.[8]

The increase in the number of internal wars is a primary cause of an alarming increase in the number of refugees in the world. In 1960, the United Nations listed 1.4 million international refugees. By 1992, the number had grown to 18.2 million. An additional 24 million people were estimated to be displaced within the borders of their own countries.[9]

Environmentally, although there have been important gains in selected localities in reducing air pollution and cleaning up polluted rivers, the deeper reality is one of a growing ecological crisis. The ever-present threat of nuclear holocaust has been replaced by the threat of increasing exposure to potentially deadly ultraviolet rays as the protective cover of the ozone layer thins. The younger generation lives with the question of whether they may be turned into environmental refugees by climate changes that threaten to melt the polar ice caps, flood vast coastal areas, and turn fertile agricultural areas into deserts.

Even at present population levels, nearly a billion people go to bed hungry each night. Yet the soils on which we depend for food are being depleted faster than nature can regenerate them, and one by one the world's once most productive fisheries are collapsing from overuse. Water shortages have become pervasive, not simply from temporary droughts but also from depleted water tables and rivers taxed beyond their ability to regenerate. We hear of communities devastated by the exhaustion of their forests and fisheries and of people much like ourselves discovering that they and their children are being poisoned by chemical and radioactive contamination in the food they eat, the water they drink, and the earth on which they live and play.

As we wait for a technological miracle to resolve these apparent limits on continued economic expansion, some 88 million people are added to the world's population every year. Each new member of the human family aspires to a secure and prosperous share of the planet's dwindling bounty. In 1950, the year I entered high school, the world population was 2.5 billion people. Since then it has more than doubled to 5.5 billion, and the United Nations estimates that it will double again in the next thirty-five years. Bear in mind that population projections are produced by demographers using mathematic models based only on assumptions about fertility rates. They take no account of what the planet can sustain. Given the environmental and social stresses created by current population levels, it is likely that if we do not voluntarily limit our numbers, famine, disease, and social breakdown will do it for us well before another doubling occurs.

Taken together, these manifestations of institutional systems failure constitute a global threefold human crisis of deepening poverty, social disintegration, and environmental destruction. Most elements of the crisis share an important characteristic: solutions require local action—household by household and community by community. This action can be taken only when local resources are in local hands. The most pressing unmet needs of the world's people are for food security, adequate shelter, clothing, health care, and education—the lack of which defines true deprivation. With rare exception, the basic resources and capacity to meet these needs are already found in nearly every country—if those who control the resources would make meeting basic needs their priority. The natural inclination of local people is usually to give these needs priority. If, however, control lies elsewhere, different priorities usually come into play.

Unfortunately, in our modern world, control seldom rests with local people. More often it resides either with central governmental bureaucracies or with distant corporations that lack both the capacity and the incentive to deal with local needs. The result is a crisis of confidence in our major institutions.

Loss of Institutional Legitimacy

Public-opinion polls reveal a growing sense of personal insecurity and loss of faith in major institutions all around the world. Particularly telling is the public attitude in the United States, the country that defines for many of the world's people their vision of prosperity, democracy, and high-tech consumerism. Here the polls tell us that the real dream of the vast majority of Americans is not for fast sports cars, fancy clothes, caviar, giant TV screens, and country estates, as the popular media might lead one to believe. Rather, it is for a decent and secure life[10]—which American institutions are failing to provide. Today, the single greatest fear of Americans is job loss.[11] Only 51 percent of America's nonmanagement employees now feel that their jobs are secure—down from 75 percent ten years ago. A similar drop has occurred in the sense of job security among management employees.[12] Fifty-five percent of adult Americans no longer believe that one can build a better life for oneself and one's family by working hard and playing by the rules.[13]

The Louis Harris polling organization's annual index of confidence in the leaders of twelve major U.S. institutions fell from a base level of 100 in 1966 to 39 in 1994. At the bottom of the list were the U.S. Congress (8 percent of respondents expressed great confidence), the executive branch of government (12 percent), the press (13 percent), and major companies (19 percent). Meanwhile, the Louis Harris "alienation index"—which taps feelings of economic inequity, disdain about people with power, and powerlessness—rose from a low of 29 in 1969 to 65 in

1993. A Kettering Foundation report captured the mood of the American electorate: "Americans . . . describe the present political system as impervious to public direction, a system run by a professional political class and controlled by money, not votes."[14] International polls generally report similar results for other industrial countries.[15]

Confidence in our major institutions and their leaders has fallen so low as to put their legitimacy at risk—and for good reason. On the threshold of the golden age, these institutions are working for only a fortunate few. For the many, they are failing disastrously to fulfill the promise that once seemed within our reach.

2 End of the Open Frontier

If current predictions of population growth prove accurate and patterns of human activity on the planet remain unchanged, science and technology may not be able to prevent either irreversible degradation of the environment or continued poverty for much of the world.
—Royal Society of London and
U.S. National Academy of Sciences[1]

[I]t is impossible for the world economy to grow its way out of poverty and environmental degradation. . . . As the economic subsystem grows it incorporates an even greater proportion of the total ecosystem into itself and must reach a limit at 100 percent, if not before.
—Herman Daly[2]

What has gone wrong? Why is the dream that should be in our grasp turning to a nightmare? The fundamental nature of our problem was dramatically articulated in 1968 by Kenneth Boulding's classic essay "The Economics of the Coming Spaceship Earth."[3] Boulding suggested that our problem results from acting like cowboys on a limitless open frontier when in truth we inhabit a living spaceship with a finely balanced life-support system.

Cowboys and Astronauts

How different the lives of the cowboy and the astronaut. The cowboys of earlier frontier societies, such as the great American West, lived in a world of sparsely populated expanses blessed with seemingly inexhaustible material resources. Except for the presence of indigenous peoples who felt that they had rights to the land, everything was free for the taking, to be used and discarded at will for the earth to absorb and the restless winds to scatter. The opportunities for those willing to work seemed limitless, and anyone who presumed that the gain of one must be the loss of another was rightly dismissed as shortsighted and lacking in vision. Let each person compete in search of his or her fortune with the expectation that the gains of each will in the end be the gain of the community as well.

Astronauts live on spaceships hurtling through space with a human crew and a precious and limited supply of resources. Everything must be maintained in balance, recycled; nothing can be wasted. The measure of well-being is not how fast the crew is able to consume its limited stores but rather how effective the crew members are in maintaining their physical and mental health, their shared resource stocks, and the life-support system on which they all depend. What is thrown away is forever inaccessible. What is accumulated without recycling fouls the living space. Crew members function as a team in the interests of the whole. No one would think of engaging in nonessential consumption unless the basic needs of all were met and there was ample provision for the future.

Boulding's analogy conveys a basic truth. Modern societies are practicing a *cowboy economics* in what has become a *spaceship world*. We still treat nature's bounty and waste-disposal services as free for the taking; we honor the strong and equate progress with never-ending increases in the rates of our consumption. As we surmise that ancient Egyptians measured themselves in part by the size of their pyramids, a future civilization may look back on our era and conclude that we measured our progress by the size of our garbage dumps. Living like cowboys in a spaceship world has tragic consequences:

- It overburdens the life-support systems, resulting in their breakdown and a decrease in the level of human activity they can ultimately sustain.
- It creates intense competition between the more powerful and weaker members of the crew for a shrinking pool of life-support services. Some crew members are deprived of a means of basic sustenance, social tensions mount, and the legitimacy of governance structures erodes—creating significant potential for social breakdown and violence.

To address the crisis, we must come to terms with a basic reality: we have passed over the historic threshold from an open frontier to a spaceship world. *Our lives depend on the life-support systems of the natural world, and that world is now full.* We must adjust ourselves to the principles of a life-centered spaceship economics.[4] On our current course, we are at once plundering our planet and tearing apart the fabric of nonmarket social relationships, which are the foundation of human civilization. It is a direct consequence of a misperception of the human relationship to natural systems.

From Open Frontiers to Full World

Throughout most of human history, the aggregate demand placed on the planetary ecosystem by human economic activities has been inconsequential compared with the enormous regenerative capacity of those systems, and we have not taken the issue of resource limits seriously. When industrialization caused countries to exceed their national resource limits, they simply reached out to obtain what was needed from beyond their own borders, generally by colonizing the resources of nonindustrial people. Although the consequences were sometimes devastating for the colonized people, the added impact on the planetary ecosystem was scarcely noticed by the colonizers.

Thus, Europe's industrialization was built on the backs of its colonies in Africa, Asia, and Latin America. For the United States, this same need was met largely by colonizing its western frontiers at the expense of the Native Americans who inhabited them, and by expanding its economic domain to embrace Central America and the Caribbean. Japan, a more recent colonizer, used a sophisticated combination of aid, foreign investment, and trade to colonize the resources of its neighbors in East and Southeast Asia. Asia's newly industrializing countries, South Korea and Taiwan, are now reaching out in a similar manner, as are Thailand and Malaysia.

So long as only a small portion of the world was industrialized, environmental frontiers were available for exploitation through settlement, trade, and traditional colonization. Similarly, frontier territories served as a social safety valve to absorb surplus population from industrial societies. Between 1850 and 1914, economic conditions in Britain prompted an outward migration of over 9 million people from a country with an average population of 32 million, mainly to the United States.[5]

The era of colonizing open frontiers is now in its final stage. The most readily available frontiers have been exploited, and the competition for those few that remain in such remote locations as Irian Jaya, Indochina, Papua New Guinea, Siberia, and the Brazilian Amazon is intensifying.

It is relevant to our current inquiry to note that the out-migration from Britain in the late nineteenth and early twentieth centuries suggests that the commonly held idea that colonialism benefited the people of the colonizing countries is largely myth. The situation was more ambiguous and has much in common with the new corporate colonialism of economic globalization. For the most part, its benefits went to the monied classes, not to the average citizen. A recent study of the British colonial experience by two American historians found that although wealthy investors profited from investments in the colonies, the middle class received only the tax bills that supported the vast military establishment required to maintain the empire. They concluded, "Imperialism can best be viewed as a mechanism for transferring income from the middle to the upper classes."[6] Economic globalization is largely a modern form of the imperial phenomenon, and it carries much the same consequence.

The bottom line for our species is that because of population growth and the fivefold economic expansion since 1950, the environmental demands of our economic system now fill the available environmental space of the planet. This has brought us to a historic transitional point in the evolutionary development of our species from living in a world of open frontiers to living in a full world—in a mere historical instant (see Figure 2.1). We now have the option of adjusting ourselves to this new reality or destroying our ecological niche and suffering the consequences.

The first environmental limits that we have confronted, and possibly exceeded, are not the limits of nonrenewable resources such as oil and copper, as many once anticipated, but rather the limits of renewable resources and the environment's ability to absorb our wastes—referred to by ecologists as "sink functions." Evidence of our encounter with these limits is everywhere. Acid rain has damaged 31 million hectares of forest in Europe alone. At the global level, each year deserts encroach on another 6 billion hectares of once productive land, the area covered by tropical forests is reduced by 11 million hectares, there is a net loss of 26 billion tons of soil from oxidation and erosion, and 1.5 billion hectares of prime agricultural land are abandoned due to salinization from irrigation projects. Per capita grain production has been falling since 1984. Five percent of the ozone layer over North America, and probably globally, was lost between 1980 and 1990. There has been a 25 percent increase in atmospheric carbon dioxide in the past 100 years.[7]

There is now a vast literature and much debate assessing the data with regard to whether a particular limit has been exceeded already or will be passed by the end of the century. Such exactness, however, is far less important than coming to terms with the basic truth that we

Figure 2.1   Transition to a Full World

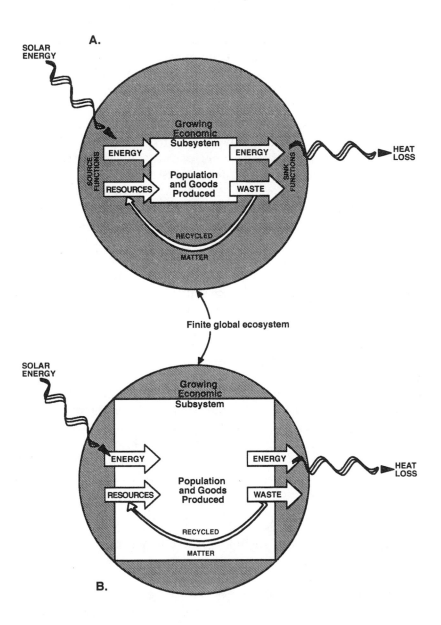

Source: Robert Goodland, Herman E. Daly, and Salah El Serafy, *Population, Technology and Lifestyle: The Transition to Sustainability* (Washington, D.C.: Island Press, 1992), p. 5.

have no real option other than to re-create our economic institutions in line with the reality of a full world.

The countries that are consuming beyond their own environmental means control the rule-making process of the international economy. They adjust the rules to ensure their own ability to make up their national environmental deficits through imports—often without being mindful of the implications for the exporting countries. The pattern is most clearly revealed by looking at the export side of the equation:

> El Salvador and Costa Rica . . . grow export crops such as bananas, coffee, and sugar on more than one fifth of their cropland. Export cattle ranches in Latin America and southern Africa have replaced rain forest and wildlife range. At the consumer end of the production line, Japan imports 70 percent of its corn, wheat, and barley, 95 percent of its soybeans, and more than 50 percent of its wood, much of it from the rapidly vanishing rain forests of Borneo. . . . [In the Netherlands] millions of pigs and cows are fattened on palm-kernel cake from deforested lands in Malaysia, cassava from deforested regions of Thailand, and soybeans from pesticide-doused expanses in the south of Brazil in order to provide European consumers with their high-fat diet of meat and milk.[8]

The lands used by Southern countries to produce food for export are unavailable to the poor of those countries to grow the staples they require to meet their own basic needs. The people who are displaced to make way for export-oriented agriculture add to urban overcrowding or move to more fragile and less productive land that quickly becomes overstressed. The grains that many Southern countries import from the North in exchange for their own food exports are used primarily as feedstocks to produce meat for upper-income urban consumers. The poor are the losers on both ends.

These dynamics are invisible to Northern consumers, who—if they do raise questions—are assured that this arrangement is providing needed jobs and income for the poor of the South, allowing them to meet the food needs more cheaply than if they grew the basic grains themselves. It makes for a plausible theory, but in practice, the only certain beneficiaries of this shift of the food economy to trade dependence have been the transnational agribusiness corporations that control global commodities trade.

Just as wealthy countries import resources when their demands exceed their own limits, they export their surplus wastes. Indeed, waste-disposal practices reveal with particular clarity the relationship between power and the allocation of environmental costs. Polluting factories and waste-disposal sites are so consistently located in poor and minority neighborhoods or communities that we might use them as proxy indicators of the geographical distribution of political power.

Adding insult to injury, the rich commonly point to the miserable environmental conditions in which the poor sometimes live as proof that the poor are less environmentally responsible than themselves. Such claims draw attention away from two important realities. First, most environmental stress is a direct function of human consumption, and rich people unquestionably consume far more than do poor people. Second, although it is true that poor people are far more likely to be found living next to waste dumps, polluting factories, and other scenes of environmental devastation than are wealthy people, this doesn't mean that it is their wastes filling those dumps or that they are major consumers of the products produced in those factories. Nor does it mean that they wouldn't prefer to live in more environmentally pristine settings. It simply means that wealthy people have the economic and political power to make sure that pollutants and wastes are dumped somewhere other than in their neighborhoods and to ensure that their neighborhoods are not stripped bare of trees to become the sites of polluting factories. Poor people do not. What we are seeing is purely a consequence of income inequality, not a difference in environmental awareness and concern. It can be corrected only by equalizing power.

Economic globalization has greatly expanded opportunities for the rich to pass their environmental burdens to the poor by exporting both wastes and polluting factories. This has been a particularly common practice among Japanese companies—with nearby Southeast Asia being a major recipient. The figures are striking. Japan has reduced its domestic aluminum smelting capacity from 1.2 million tons to 140,000 tons and now imports 90 percent of its aluminum.[9] What this involves in human terms is suggested by a case study of the Philippine Associated Smelting and Refining Corporation (PASAR). PASAR operates a Japanese-financed and -constructed copper smelting plant in the Philippine province of Leyte to produce high-grade copper cathodes for shipment to Japan. The plant occupies 400 acres of land expropriated by the Philippine government from local residents at give-away prices. Gas and wastewater emissions from the plant contain high concentrations of boron, arsenic, heavy metals, and sulfur compounds that have contaminated local water supplies, reduced fishing and rice yields, damaged the forests, and increased the occurrence of upper-respiratory diseases among local residents. Local people whose homes, livelihoods, and health have been sacrificed to PASAR are now largely dependent on the occasional part-time or contractual employment they are offered to do the plant's most dangerous and dirtiest jobs.

The company has prospered. The local economy has grown. The Japanese people have a supply of copper at no environmental cost to themselves. The local poor—the project's professed beneficiaries—have lost their means of livelihood and suffered impaired health. The Philippine government is repaying the foreign aid loan from Japan that financed the construction of supporting infrastructure for the plant. And the Japanese are congratulating themselves for the cleanliness of their domestic environment and their generous assistance to the poor of the Philippines.[10]

There is nothing particularly special about this case, other than the fact that it has been documented. There are thousands of such stories illustrating the realities of corporate colonialism that economic globalization is advancing around the world. *The Economist*, an ardent globalization proponent, has argued that those who criticize such toxic dumping practices would deprive the poor of needed economic opportunities.[11]

Although an open trading system is sometimes advocated as necessary to make up for the environmental deficits of those who have too little, it more often works in exactly the opposite way—increasing the environmental deficits of those who have too little to provide a surplus for those who already have too much. Furthermore, an open trading system makes it easier for the rich to keep the consequences of this transfer out of their own sight. The farther out of sight those consequences are, the easier it is for those who hold power to ignore or rationalize them.

Perhaps the ultimate resource limit is the available input of solar energy, the one truly renewable and nonpolluting energy source. The significance of this limit is highlighted by the difference between plant life and animal life. Plants have the ability to capture and store solar energy through photosynthesis. Animals—including humans—do not. Thus animals, even those that are meat eaters, ultimately depend on this distinctive capability of plant life for their food.

The amount of energy potentially available from photosynthesis for the support of animal species, after deducting what is consumed by the respiratory processes of the plants themselves, is known as net primary production (NPP). A 1986 study concluded that humans were already using directly, co-opting, or displacing nearly 40 percent of the potential annual NPP of the earth's land surfaces. This leaves less than 60 percent for other species, for improving the lives of the 80 percent of humanity that enjoys only 20 percent of the wealth, and for meeting the needs of increasing human numbers. If current patterns of consumption are maintained, the doubling of the earth's human population that is projected to occur within the next thirty-five years would require some 80 percent of NPP just to maintain living standards at current unequal levels. Only 20 percent of NPP would be available to support all other nonplant life.[12]

Consumption, Population, and Equity

We have endured far too many debates in which the representatives of rich countries condemn the population growth of the poor and refuse to discuss overconsumption and inequality, and the representatives of poor countries condemn overconsumption and inequality and refuse to discuss population growth. In a full world, consumption, population, and equity are inseparably linked, and we must deal with them holistically. One reason we fail to do so is that we have failed to develop accounting systems for sustainable resource use. I have found three studies to be particularly instructive in illuminating what such systems might monitor and what they would tell us.

The first is a study by William Rees, an urban planner at the University of British Columbia. Rees estimates that four to six hectares of land are required to maintain the consumption of the average person living in a high-income country—including the land required to maintain current levels of energy consumption using renewable sources. Yet in 1990, the total available ecologically productive land area (land capable of generating consequential biomass) in the world was only an estimated 1.7 hectares per capita.[13] The deficit of the industrial countries is covered in part by drawing down their own natural resource stocks and in part through trade that allows them to expropriate the resources of lower-income countries.

Among the industrial countries, per capita resource consumption is generally highest in the United States and Canada. However, since Europe and Japan have higher population densities, the case can be made that they are living even further beyond their own ecological means. Rees estimates that the population of the Netherlands, for example, consumes the output equivalent of fourteen times as much productive land as is contained within its own borders.[14] The deficits are made up through international trade.

A study by Friends of the Earth Netherlands took such an analysis a step further, asking: what would the allowable annual levels of consumption of environmental resources and waste-absorption services be for the average Dutch person in the year 2010 if (a) resource consumption levels are equal among all people living on the earth at that time and (b) the global level of resource consumption is sustainable? The results are sobering. The researchers found that in almost every area of consumption, the average person in the Netherlands is consuming far beyond his or her means and is thereby depriving people in poorer countries of the ability to meet their basic needs.[15]

Friends of the Earth USA applied the Dutch estimates to the United States and reached a similar conclusion.[16] For example, current annual per capita carbon dioxide emissions are 19.5 tons in the United States and 12 tons in the Netherlands. To meet suggested targets for the reduction of global warming, world per capita carbon dioxide emission levels from fossil fuel use must be brought down to 4 tons by 2010. If the burden of achieving this target were shared equitably, each person would be reduced in 2010 to consuming no more than one liter of carbon-based fuel per day. "A Dutch person will be given the choice of traveling 24 km (15.5 mi) by car, 50 km (31 mi) by bus, 65 km (40 mi) by train or 10 km (6.2 mi) by plane per day. A flight from Amsterdam to Rio de Janeiro can probably be undertaken only once every twenty years!"[17]

For those whose only transportation option is walking, such standards may seem luxurious. They are sobering indeed, however, for those of us accustomed to spending much of our lives in cars, planes, buses, and trains. It is even more sobering when we note that our allowance of one liter of fossil fuel a day is our allowance not only for direct personal travel but for the fuels used to produce, transport, and market the things we consume as well—burdens we place on the environment but never see and tend to neglect.

The allowable timber usage, based on an assumption that there will be no further logging of primary forests and that existing nonprimary forestlands will be used on a sustained-yield basis, would be 0.4 cubic meters per person per year—including wood used for paper. To bring consumption in line with equitable sustainable use, the Netherlands would have to reduce its timber consumption by 60 percent, the United States by 79 percent.

The Friends of the Earth studies were based on simple sector-by-sector estimates of the availability of environmental services and took projected population growth as a given. A third study, reported in a paper presented at the annual meeting of the American Association for the Advancement of Science by Cor-nell University professor David Pimentel and his colleagues, asked similar questions but also looked at interactions among sectors and took population as a variable. For example, it took into account that although we might cultivate more land, doing so would require using more water. We could get more of our energy from the sun, but only by using more land. Each hectare of agricultural land could produce higher yields, but only by using more energy inputs.

The Cornell researchers also took into account that although we continue to bring new land under cultivation, 10 million hectares of productive arable land are already being abandoned each year due to severe degradation. These abandoned lands must be replaced simply to maintain existing levels of food consumption. An additional 5 million hectares of new land must be put into production to feed the annual net addition to the world population—before making any dent in reducing existing malnutrition. Most of this new agricultural land comes from clearing forests.[18]

In conclusion, they posed a fundamental question: "Does human society want 10 to 15 billion humans living in poverty and malnourishment or one to two billion living with abundant resources and a quality environment?"[19] They argue for a population of 1 to 2 billion, which by their calculations would allow a level of consumption roughly equivalent to the current per capita standard for Europe. They note that "a drastic demographic adjustment to one to two billion humans will cause serious social, economic, and political problems, but to continue rapid population growth to 12 billion or more will result in more severe social, economic, and political conflicts plus catastrophic public health and environmental problems."[20] What they do not mention is that in a world of 10 to 15 billion humans, there will be no place for other forms of animal or plant life that are not immediately essential to human survival.

Such calculations are at best preliminary approximations based on controversial assumptions and the use of fragmented and often unreliable data. They are, however, the kinds of analyses that are fundamental to any realistic discussion of sustainability, and they bring into clear perspective what we are otherwise inclined to ignore—the inescapable relationship in a full world between consumption, population size, and equity. This virtually forces us to take a whole-systems perspective on these fundamental issues. It becomes abundantly clear that if the earth's sustainable natural output were shared equally among the earth's present population, the needs of all could be met. But it is equally clear that it is a physical impossibility, even with the most optimistic assumptions about the potential of new technologies, for the world to consume at levels even approximating those in North America, Europe, and Japan. Furthermore, each time the world's population doubles, the allowable per capita consumption share is reduced by half.

If we take seriously the implications of studies such as those cited above, we have little real choice other than to give the highest priority to efforts to simultaneously end overconsumption, population growth, and inequality. They are inextricably linked, and no one, rich or poor, could possibly want the consequences that we will all bear if we do not achieve each of these outcomes in the very near future. It is of utmost importance that we develop adequate resource-use accounting systems, embodying concepts from the above-mentioned studies, to provide ourselves with adequate tools for monitoring progress toward bringing our lives into balance with the earth—household by household, locality by locality, and country by country. It is also essential that we break free of the myth that economic growth is the foundation of human progress.

3 The Growth Illusion

To address poverty, economic growth is not an option: it is an imperative.

—*Mahbub ul Haq,
former World Bank vice president*[1]

Economic growth provides the conditions in which protection of the environment can be best achieved.
—*International Chamber of Commerce*[2]

Perhaps no single idea is more deeply embedded in modern political culture than the belief that economic growth is the key to meeting most important human needs, including alleviating poverty and protecting the environment. Anyone who dares to speak of environmental limits to growth risks being dismissed out of hand as an antipoor doomsayer. Thus most environmentalists call simply for "a different kind of growth" although it is seldom evident what kind it would be.

Nobel laureate economist Jan Tinbergen and his distinguished colleague Roefie Hueting point out that there are basically two ways for an economy to grow by our current mode of reckoning. One is to increase the number of people employed. The other is to increase the labor productivity—the value of output per worker—of those already employed. Historically, increases in labor productivity have been the most important source of growth. About 70 percent of this productivity growth has been in the 30 percent of economic activity accounted for by the petroleum, petrochemical, and metal industries; chemical-intensive agriculture; public utilities; road building; transportation; and mining—specifically, the industries that are most rapidly drawing down natural capital, generating the bulk of our most toxic wastes, and consuming a substantial portion of our nonrenewable energy reserves.[3]

Furthermore, the more environmentally burdensome ways of meeting a given need are generally those that contribute most to the gross national product (GNP).[4] For example, driving a mile in a car contributes more to GNP than riding a mile on a bicycle. Turning on an air conditioner adds more than opening a window. Relying on processed packaged food adds more than using natural foods purchased in bulk in reusable containers. We might say that GNP, technically a measure of the rate at which money is flowing through the economy, might also be described as a measure of the rate at which we are turning resources into garbage.

We could expend a lot of effort on the probably unrealistic goal of making GNP go up indefinitely without creating more garbage. But why not instead concentrate on ending poverty, improving our quality of life, and achieving a balance with the earth? These are achievable goals—if we can free ourselves from the illusion that growth is *the* path to better living.

A Disillusioned Economist

In 1954, R. A. Butler, the British chancellor of the Exchequer, made a speech to a Conservative Party conference in which he pointed out that a 3 percent annual growth rate would double the national income per capita by 1980 and make every man and woman twice as rich as his or her father had been at the same age. The speech proved to be a turning point in British life. Previously, national goals had been set in terms of specific targets, such as building 300,000 houses a year or establishing a national health service. Henceforth, the primary goal would be economic growth. The ideological debate between Left and Right as to how a fixed pie would be distributed was largely defused. Attention centered on how to increase the size of the pie.

In 1989, Irish economist Richard Douthwaite set out to document the benefits of the subsequent doubling of Britain's per capita income. In his own words:

> Problems only arose when I attempted to identify what they [the benefits] were, especially as it quickly became apparent that almost every social indicator had worsened over the third of a

century the experiment had taken. Chronic disease had increased, crime had gone up eight fold, unemployment had soared and many more marriages were ending in divorce. Almost frantically I looked for gains to set against these losses which, in most cases I felt, had to be blamed on growth.

. . . [E]ventually . . . I gave up. The weight of evidence was overwhelming: the unquestioning quest for growth had been an unmitigated social and environmental disaster. Almost all of the extra resources the process had created had been used to keep the system functioning in an increasingly inefficient way. The new wealth had been squandered on producing pallets and corrugated cardboard, nonreturnable bottles and ring-pull drinks cans. It had built airports, supertankers and heavy goods lorries, motor ways, flyovers and car parks with many floors. It had enabled the banking, insurance, stock brokering, tax-collecting and accountancy sector to expand from 493,000 to 2,475,000 employees during the thirty-three years. It had financed the recruitment of over three million people to the "reserve army of the unemployed." Very little was left for more positive achievements when all these had taken their share.[5]

We might apply a similar test to the fivefold increase in global output since 1950. The advocates of growth persistently maintain that economic growth is the key to ending poverty, stabilizing population, protecting the environment, and achieving social harmony. Yet during this same period, the number of people living in absolute poverty has kept pace with population growth: both have doubled. The ratio of the share of the world's income that went to the richest 20 percent and that which went to the bottom 20 percent poor has doubled. And indicators of social and environmental disintegration have risen sharply nearly everywhere. Although economic growth did not necessarily create these problems, it certainly has not solved them.

The Limits of Growth

Few would dispute that there has been real and consequential human progress over the past several centuries and that advances in technology and the consequent productivity increases have resulted in real gains in human well-being. At the same time, as this chapter elaborates, there is little basis for assuming that economic growth, as we currently define and measure it, results in automatic increases in human welfare. As British economist Paul Ekins points out, it is possible to conclude that a particular instance of growth has been a good thing only by:

- Showing that the growth has taken place through the production of goods and services that are inherently valuable and beneficial;
- Demonstrating that these goods and services have been distributed widely throughout the society; and
- Proving that these benefits outweigh any detrimental effects of the growth process on other parts of society.[6]

Our measures of GNP make no such distinctions. Indeed, a major portion of what shows up as growth in GNP is a result of:

- Shifting activities from the nonmoney social economy of household and community to the money economy—with the consequent erosion of social capital;
- Depleting natural resources stocks—such as forests, fisheries, and oil and mineral reserves—at far above their recovery rates; and
- Counting as income the costs of defending ourselves against the consequences of growth, such as disposing of waste, cleaning up toxic dumps and oil spills, providing health care for victims of environmentally caused illnesses, rebuilding after floods resulting from human activities such as deforestation, and financing pollution-control devices.

Standard financial accounting deducts from income an allowance for the depreciation of capital assets. The economic accounting systems by which economic growth is measured make no comparable adjustment for the depletion of social and natural capital. Indeed, economic accounting counts many costs of economic growth as economic gains, even though they clearly reduce rather than increase our well-being. The results are sometimes ludicrous. For example, the costs of cleaning up the *Exxon Valdez* oil spill on the Alaska coast and the costs of repairing damage from the terrorist bombing of the World Trade Center in New York both counted as net contributions to economic output. By this distorted logic, disasters that are tragic for the people and the environment are often counted as good for the economy.

In their book *For the Common Good*, Herman Daly and John Cobb Jr. reconstruct the national income accounts for the United States from 1960 to 1986, counting only those increases in output that relate to improvements in well-being and adjusting for the depletion of human and environmental resources. The result is an index of economic welfare rather than gross output. Their index reveals that, on average, individual welfare in the United States peaked in 1969, then remained on a plateau and fell during the early and mid-1980s. Yet from 1969 to 1986, GNP per person went up by 35 percent, and fossil fuel consumption increased by around 17 percent. The main consequence of this growth has been that most of us are working harder to maintain a declining quality of life.[7]

Often, how the economic pie is allocated is more important to our well-being than its absolute size. Studies done by the United Nations Development Programme (UNDP) show that it is *not* necessary to have particularly high levels of economic output in order for a country to meet the basic needs of its people. In fact, some countries with relatively modest levels of economic output do better in this regard than other countries with much higher GNPs. Saudi Arabia's literacy rate is lower than Sri Lanka's, despite the fact that its per capita income is fifteen times higher. Brazil's child mortality rate is four times that of Jamaica, even though its per capita income is twice as high.[8]

Obviously, some minimum level of economic output is essential to meet basic needs, and this required level is probably a good deal higher than the current output of the world's poorest countries. However, for most of the world's people, the question of whether their basic needs are met depends less on the absolute level of per capita income than on how productive output is allocated. If the priority in the allocation of that output is to provide people with a good diet, shelter, clothing, clean water, health care, basic transport, education, and other essentials of good living, then it is within the means of most countries to do so and thus alleviate human deprivation within their existing levels of productive output. In many instances it would require little more than reallocating the resources now devoted to military purposes.

Clean water and proper sanitation are perhaps the most important contributors to good health and long life. Experience in places such as the state of Kerala in India prove that such necessities can be provided at quite modest income levels. By contrast, countries with high income levels are experiencing increases in rates of cancer, respiratory illnesses, stress and cardiovascular disorders, and birth defects, as well as falling sperm counts. A growing body of evidence links all these phenomena to the by-products of economic growth—air and water pollution, chemical additives and pesticide residues in food, high noise levels, and increased exposure to electromagnetic radiation.[9]

Suburbanization, greater dependence on the automobile for mobility, and increased use of television for entertainment are also associated with economic growth. Each has reduced the normal human contacts and interactions that used to be a regular part of village and urban life as people met on paths and sidewalks, created family and community entertainment, and congregated in local shops and coffee stalls.

Rapid economic growth in low-income countries brings modern airports, television, express highways, and air-conditioned shopping malls with sophisticated consumer electronics and fashion labels for the fortunate few. It rarely improves living conditions for the many. This kind of growth requires gearing the economy toward exports to earn the foreign exchange to buy the things that wealthy people desire. Thus, the lands of the poor are appropriated for export crops. The former tillers of these lands then find themselves subsisting in urban slums on starvation wages paid by sweatshops producing for export. Families are broken up, the social fabric is strained to the breaking point, and violence becomes endemic. Those whom growth has favored then need still more foreign exchange to import arms to protect themselves from the rage of the excluded.

Growth and the Poor

Any mention of the need to end growth elicits protests that this would condemn the poor to perpetual deprivation. Ironically, the argument that the well-being of the poor depends on economic growth comes mainly from professional development workers, economists, financiers, corporation heads, and others who have no problem putting food on their tables. When the poor speak for themselves, they more often talk of secure rights to the land and waters on which they live and from which they obtain their livelihoods. They seek decent jobs that pay a living wage. They want health care and education for their children. In a world in which all things come to those with money, they may as well say, "We need money." But rarely, if ever, do they say, "We must have economic growth."

They have good reason, as it is all too common for the deprivation of the poor to increase during periods of rapid economic expansion and decrease during periods of economic contraction. The reason is simple: the policies that favor economic expansion commonly shift income and assets to those who own property at the expense of those who depend on their labor for their livelihood. Although growth itself does not necessarily cause poverty, the policies advanced in its name often do.[10] Consider, for example, the following policy outcomes typically associated with economic growth:

- Increasing the rate of depletion of natural resources provides financial gains for the economically powerful at the expense of people whose livelihood base is disrupted.
- Shifting activities from the social (nonmoney) economy to the money economy increases the dependence of the working classes on money and thereby on those who own assets, provide professional services, and control access to jobs.
- Shifting control of agricultural lands, forests, and fisheries from those engaged in creating subsistence livelihoods to property owners engaged in investing for profit adds to measured economic output, redistributes the ownership of these assets to the capital-owning classes, expands the pool of low-cost wage labor, and pushes wages downward.

For centuries, the indigenous Igorot ("people of the mountains") of Benguet province, Philippines, have engaged in small-scale "pocket mining" of the rich gold veins found on their ancestral lands. The men dig small round caves into the mountain. Women and children hammer the gold-bearing rocks into nuggets the size of corn kernels.[11] Their lands are now dominated by huge open-pit mines operated by the Benguet Corporation—owned in approximately equal shares by wealthy Filipinos, the Philippine government, and U.S. investors—to produce gold for export. Dozens of bulldozers, cranes, and trucks cut deep gashes into the mountain, stripping away the trees and topsoil and dumping enormous piles of rocky waste into the riverbeds. The local people tell visitors how, with their water sources destroyed, they can no longer grow rice and bananas and must go to the other side of the mountain for water to drink and bathe. Even their own mining grounds are threatened, their rights ignored.[12]

Instead of using water to separate the gold from the rock, as the Igorot do, the mining company uses toxic chemicals, including cyanide compounds, and flushes them down the river, poisoning the water and killing the cattle that drink it. Downstream, rice farmers in the affected area of Pangasinan province are losing an estimated 250 million pesos a year as the mine tailings cover their irrigated fields and cause sharp declines in yields, resulting in a net population exodus. Still farther on, fisherfolk in the gulf report substantial reductions in their catch as tailings smother the coral reefs. It's good for growth. Benguet and the other major mining companies involved earn combined net profits of 1.1 billion pesos a year—a massive resource transfer from the poor to the rich.[13] Countless such stories are told wherever mining companies operate.

The poor suffer similar consequences when timber companies move in to strip their forests bare, usually without regard for the rights of local people. As a young peasant woman in a remote community of San Fernando in the southern Philippine province of Bukidnon explained to visitors, "Without trees there is no food and without food, no life." An old man explained that before the logging trucks came to his village, "There was plenty of fish, plenty of corn, and plenty of rice." People went on to describe how their rivers have changed shape, turned muddier, shallower. During the monsoons, the river now overflows its banks and swallows adjacent fertile fields in formerly flood-free areas. Creeks that once nourished the fields during the dry season have disappeared; landslides have become common during the rainy season. The rat population, which previously found food in the forests and was kept in check by forest predators, now ravages farmers' fields at night. In a once prosperous community, more than four out of five children suffer some degree of malnutrition.[14]

In the name of promoting economic growth, such devastation is often heavily supported by public subsidies. For each ton of mine tailings they produce, the Philippine mining companies described above earn 96.73 pesos and pay 0.5 pesos in taxes.[15] In the United States, the government gives away mining rights to federal lands for $12 a hectare or less. Adding insult to injury, miners are able to take a tax deduction of 5 to 22 percent of their gross income as a "depletion allowance" to compensate them for the depletion of these federal lands—after deducting their costs of exploration and extraction. In Japan, the government offers loans, subsidies, and tax incentives for domestic mineral exploration and development.[16] Infrastructure costs associated with mining and timber extraction by Japanese companies in Southern countries are commonly funded by loans disbursed under the Japanese foreign aid program.

As opportunities for industrial employment have declined in high-income countries, economists have looked to the service economy to pick up the slack. Little note is taken of the fact that much of the expansion of the service economy results from a colonization of the social economies of households and communities. These social economies once productively engaged more than half the working hours of the adult population, mostly women, in meeting many of the basic needs of families and carrying out the countless neighborly functions essential to the maintenance of healthy, caring communities. Indeed, there was a time when social economies engaged both women and men in carrying out most of the productive and reproductive activities through which people met their basic needs for food, shelter, clothing, child care, health care, care of the elderly, housekeeping, education, physical security, and entertainment. Social economies are by nature local, nonwaged, nonmonetized, and nonmarket. They are energized more by love than by money.

As productive and reproductive functions such as child care, health care, food preparation, entertainment, and physical security are transferred from the social economy to the market economy, they show up as additions to economic output and thus contributors to economic growth—though they do little, if anything, to improve the quality of the services we receive. This shift also increases the demand for economic overhead functions, which are counted as additions to economic output although they are actually an enormous source of economic inefficiency. Consider that when family and community members worked directly with and for one another, there were no tax collectors, managers, government regulators, accountants, lawyers, stockbrokers, bankers, middlemen, advertising account executives, marketing specialists, investment brokers, or freight haulers collecting their share of the output of those who did the actual productive work. The full value of the goods and services produced was shared and exchanged within the family and the community, among those who actually created the value.[17] The result was an extraordinarily efficient use of resources to meet real needs.

Many people find that the market economy's overhead costs have become so high that, even with two wage earners and longer work hours, they cannot adequately meet needs that they once met quite satisfactorily on their own. Parents—or more often a single impoverished female parent—are left with little time, energy, or encouragement to do more than function as income earners and night guardians. The modern urban home has become little more than a place to sleep and watch television. Fewer people find time to participate in the vast array of community activities and services that once made neighborhoods more than a physical address. The dense fabric of relationships based on long-term sharing and cooperation that social economies once maintained comes unraveled. High rates of deprivation, depression, divorce, teenage pregnancy, violence, alcoholism, drug abuse, crime, and suicide are among the more evident consequences in both high- and low-income countries.[18]

Because such shifts have given women new opportunities, they are often hailed as a victory for women's equality. Yet rather than promoting new partnerships that involve men more fully in family and community as women expand their participation in the workplace, the change has more often simply increased the burden on women. This has placed heavy stresses on family relationships and left communities dependent on paid professional staff to perform functions that neighbors once provided for one another. Many children grow up in commercial day-care centers or are left at home or in the streets without any adult supervision. Many women who started working as an expansion of their options now find themselves tied to poorly compensated and unfulfilling jobs on which their families have become dependent.

Economists applaud the economic growth that results from creating new highly paid professional classes and new opportunities for the health care, social services, and security services industries. The net costs to societies—and especially to the poor, for whom the money economy provides inadequate opportunities—are ignored.

The displacement of the poor from the lands on which they live and obtain their livelihoods has been a long historical process. Time after time, the consequence has been economic growth for the strong and deprivation for the weak. Economists estimate that between 1750 and 1850, Britain's per capita income roughly doubled, but the quality of life for the majority of people steadily declined. Before 1750, travelers to the British countryside reported little evidence of deprivation. For the most part, people had adequate food, shelter, and clothing, and the countryside had a prosperous appearance. Most farming was done on open fields, with families holding the rights to farm small and scattered strips of land. Even those without such rights were able to provide for themselves from the common lands, which provided grazing for their animals, rabbits to eat, and wood for their fires. A few industrious souls managed to consolidate larger properties through exchange, rental, and purchase and to hedge or wall them off from the rest—a process commonly referred to as enclosure—but this was a slow and cumbersome process.[19]

Then landed interests chose to speed up the process through the introduction of legislation that made enclosure a requirement. As enclosure progressed, the poor were increasingly deprived of access to the lands from which they once derived their living. With no other source of livelihood, they were forced to work as laborers for the larger farmers. The resulting surge in the labor pool depressed wages and increased the profits of the larger landowners. The introduction of land taxes forced many smaller farmers to sell the bits of land they held. The result was a major consolidation of landholdings and a continuing flow of labor from the countryside to the city to supply the factories of the industrial revolution with workers—many of them women and young children—who were willing to accept employment in factories that "were viler than prisons.... So appalling were these conditions that British factory employees in the early nineteenth century were probably worse off than the slaves on American plantations."[20]

In contrast to their experience during this early period of "economic expansion," conditions for ordinary people in Britain improved from 1914, the year World War I began, through the end of World War II, including the years between the wars, when there was no overall growth in Britain's national income. As explained by Douthwaite, the wars made it politically necessary to control the forces of capitalism. The government introduced heavy taxes on top incomes and controlled wages. Although it held wage increases below the level of inflation, more people were employed, and their work was steady. As a consequence, the real purchasing power of most wage-earner households improved. Furthermore, when the government sanctioned wage increases, it frequently authorized the same absolute increase for everyone. Thus the raises for unskilled workers were proportionately higher than for skilled workers. The overall result was a massive shift of income from the rich to the poor.[21]

Following World War I, a reduction of the workweek from fifty-four hours to forty-six to forty-eight hours to absorb the influx of returning military personnel kept unemployment low and wages high. Those without jobs were protected by the national employment insurance scheme introduced in 1911. Paid for by the substantial taxes on high incomes, it systematically transferred income from wealthier taxpayers to those most in need.

World War II resulted in much the same consequence for the poor. The benefit came not from the growth in output that accompanied the war effort but from a combination of a high demand for labor, the erosion of wage differentials, government control of profits, and the implementation of a highly progressive tax structure. Income equality increased dramatically, and the enforced saving that resulted from rationing left an enormous pent-up demand following the war, easing the transition to a peacetime economy.

Similar patterns were experienced in the United States. The imperatives of the depression of the 1930s and World War II galvanized political action behind measures that resulted in a significant redistribution of income and built the strong middle class that came to be seen as the hallmark of America's economic strength and prosperity. The resulting structure of relative equity and shared economic prosperity remained more or less intact until the 1970s, when a combination of economic competition from East Asia, labor unrest, inflation, and a rebellious youth culture mobilized conservative forces to reassert themselves. An all-out political attack on labor unions, social safety nets, market regulation, and trade barriers realigned the institutional forces of American society behind the big-money interests. In the 1970s and 1980s, the percentage of working Americans whose wages placed them below the poverty line increased sharply, and the society became increasingly polarized between haves and have-nots with respect to employment opportunities and earnings.[22]

Those who call for expanding the economic pie as the answer to poverty overlook an important reality. Whether or not a person has access to the resources required for survival depends less on absolute income than on relative income. In a free-market economy, each individual is in competition for access to the limited environmental space, and the person with the most money invariably wins.

As we have seen above, economic growth often raises the incomes of the wealthy faster than those of the poor. Even if all incomes were to increase at the same rate, the consequence would be much the same—the absolute gap between rich and poor would increase. It is simple arithmetic. Take the uniform annual 3 percent global increase in per capita income that the Brundtland Commission on the Environment and Development proposed as the answer to global poverty and environmental problems. That would translate into a first-year annual per capita increase (in U.S. dollars) "of $633 for the United States; $3.60 for Ethiopia; $5.40 for Bangladesh; $7.50 for Nigeria; $10.80 for China and $10.50 for India. By the end of ten years, such growth will have raised Ethiopia's per capita income by $41—hardly sufficient to dent poverty there—while that of the United States will have risen by $7,257."[23] The per capita *increase* in purchasing power for the United States would thus be 177 times that of Ethiopia.

Without concurrent redistribution, an expanding pie brings far greater benefit to the already wealthy than to the poor, increases the absolute gap between rich and poor, and further increases the power advantage of the former over the latter. This advantage becomes a life-and-death issue in a resource-scarce world in which the rich and poor are locked in mortal competition for a depleting resource base.

If the prophets of illusion who promote growth as the answer to poverty are really concerned with the plight of the poor, let them advocate measures that deal directly with increasing the ability of the poor to meet their basic needs—not tax breaks for the rich.

Growth in the Name of Development

Many development economists believe that moving a country on the path to industrialization requires that labor be forced off the farm and into the cities so that agriculture can be modernized and an urban industrial labor pool can be created. The parallels to the enclosure process in Britain are striking. Costa Rica provides a particularly egregious contemporary example.

Before the International Monetary Fund (IMF) and the World Bank restructured Costa Rica's economic policies in the name of easing its foreign debt problems, Costa Rica was widely known as a society that was more egalitarian than its neighbors. It had a strong base of small farmers and few of the large landholdings characteristic of other Latin American societies. The policies imposed by the IMF and the World Bank shifted the economic incentives away from small farms producing the things that Costa Ricans eat toward large estates producing for export. As a consequence, thousands of small farmers have been displaced, their lands have been consolidated into large ranches and agricultural estates producing for export, and Costa Rica's income gap is becoming more like that of the rest of Latin America. An increase in crime and violence has required sharp increases in public expenditures on police and public security. The country is now dependent on imports to meet basic food requirements, and the foreign debt that structural adjustment was supposed to reduce has doubled. As outrageous as the consequences of their policies have been, the IMF and the World Bank point to Costa Rica as a structural adjustment *success* story because economic growth has increased and the country is now able to meet its growing debt service payments.[24]

In Brazil, the conversion of agriculture from smallholders producing food for domestic consumption to capital-intensive production for export displaced 28.4 million people between 1960 and 1980—a number greater than the entire population of Argentina.[25] In India, large-scale development projects have displaced 20 million people over a forty-year period.[26] In 1989, ongoing World Bank projects were displacing 1.5 million people, and projects in preparation threatened another 1.5 million. Bank staff were unable to point to a single bank-funded project in which the displaced people had been relocated and rehabilitated to a standard of living comparable to what they enjoyed before displacement.[27] A conference on Asian development sponsored by Asian nongovernmental organizations working at the grassroots on environmental and poverty issues revealed an aspect of Asia's development experience that the gushing reports in World Bank reports and business periodicals never mention:

> In Thailand, ten million rural people face eviction from the land they live on to make way for commercial tree farms. Ground water is depleted and mangroves are continually destroyed by export oriented shrimp farms. Tribal people struggle for recognition of

ancestral land rights in the forests of Eastern Malaysia and Indonesia. In the Philippines, the government's land reform program is systematically eroded by the conversion of prime agricultural lands into industrial estates and other non-agricultural uses—even as the country needs to spend its scarce foreign exchange on rice imports. Agricultural chemicals and toxic industrial wastes, including those brought to the region by foreign corporations and agencies under the guise of international assistance continue to poison us. Dams and geothermal projects displace people and destroy agricultural and forest lands to meet the energy demands of export-oriented industries. Slum dwellers are evicted to make way for industries and shopping centers that benefit others. Destructive fishing practices, commonly supported by corporate interests serving foreign markets, deprive our fisherfolk of their livelihoods and threaten the regenerative capacities of our oceans.[28]

Urban development plans in Bangkok, Thailand, call for the eviction of 300,000 people for highway and other urban development projects. Low-income families that resist find their water and electricity supplies cut off. Further resistance is likely to result in the arson or bulldozing of their homes.[29] A million Mexican families will be displaced from their farms as a consequence of the North American Free Trade Agreement. The engine of economic growth has proved far more effective in creating development refugees than in fulfilling its promise to end human deprivation in the world's low-income countries.

If our concern is with sustainable human well-being for all people, then we must penetrate the economic myths embedded in our culture by the prophets of illusion, free ourselves of our obsession with growth, and dramatically restructure economic relationships to focus on two priorities:

1. Balance human uses of the environment with the regenerative capacities of the ecosystem; and
2. Allocate available natural capital in ways that ensure that all people have the opportunity to fulfill their physical needs adequately and to pursue their full social, cultural, intellectual, and spiritual development.

Among the barriers we face to accomplishing this transformation is the powerful coalition of political interests aligned behind an institutional agenda that is taking us in a quite different direction. These are the corporate interests that benefit when societies make the pursuit of economic growth the organizing principle of public policy.

II Contest for Sovereignty

4 Rise of Corporate Power in America

Chartered privileges are a burthen, under which the people of Britain, and other European nations, groan in misery.
—Thomas Earle, pamphleteer, 1823

Today's business corporation is an artificial creation, shielding owners and managers while preserving corporate privilege and existence. Artificial or not, corporations have won more rights under law than people have—rights which government has protected with armed force.
—Richard L. Grossman and Frank T. Adams[1]

The fact that the interests of corporations and people of wealth are closely intertwined tends to obscure the significance of the corporation as an institution in its own right. The corporate charter is a social invention created to aggregate private financial resources in the service of a public purpose. It also allows one or more individuals to leverage massive economic and political resources behind clearly focused private agendas and to protect themselves from legal liability for the public consequences.

Less widely recognized is the tendency of corporations, as they grow in size and power, to develop their own institutional agendas aligned with imperatives inherent in their nature and structure that are not wholly under the control even of the people who own and manage them. These agendas center on increasing their own profits and protecting themselves from the uncertainty of the market. They arise from a combination of market competition, the demands of financial markets, and efforts by individuals within them to advance their careers and increase their earnings. Members of the corporate sector also tend to develop shared political and economic agendas. In the United States, for example, corporations have been engaged for more than 150 years in a process of restructuring the rules and institutions of governance to suit their interests. Some readers may feel uneasy with my anthropomorphizing the corporation, but I do so advisedly.

Corporations have emerged as the dominant governance institutions on the planet, with the largest among them reaching into virtually every country of the world and exceeding most governments in size and power. Increasingly, it is the corporate interest more than the human interest that defines the policy agendas of states and international bodies, although this reality and its implications have gone largely unnoticed and unaddressed.

In this chapter, we examine the long and continuing struggle for sovereignty between people and corporations in America in an effort to provide a historical perspective on what is at stake and why it matters. Although there have been similar struggles in other Western democracies, the U.S. experience assumes special importance because of the dominant role the United States has had in shaping the institutions of the world economy since the end of World War I. This global role became increasingly self-conscious and assertive when the United States emerged from World War II as the world's most powerful nation. Even today as its economic power declines compared with that of Japan and Europe, the United States remains the dominant player in shaping international institutions such as the new World Trade Organization being created under the General Agreement on Tariffs and Trade (GATT), the International Monetary Fund, the World Bank, and the United Nations. As we shall see in following chapters, corporate interests have figured prominently in how the United States has defined its national interest in relation to these and other global institutions. Thus, the history of corporate power in the United States is of more than purely national significance.

The corporate charter is a grant of privilege extended by the state to a group of investors to serve a public purpose. Its history goes back at least to the sixteenth century. At that time, an individual's debts were inherited by his or her descendants and could result in the descendants' imprisonment through no doing of their own. Those who sailed forth from England to trade for spices in the East Indies faced not only the inevitable perils of the dangerous sea voyage but also the prospect that they and their families could be ruined, even into future generations, if their cargo were lost to bad weather or pirates.[2] The corporation represented an important institutional innovation to overcome this barrier to international commerce. Like so many important inventions, the corporate charter opened enormous new opportunities to advance the interests of human societies—so long as civil society held in check the potential abuse that the concentration of power made possible.

Specifically, the corporate charter represented a grant from the crown that limited an investor's liability for losses of the corporation to the amount of his or her investment in it—a right not extended to individual citizens. Each charter set forth the specific rights and obligations conferred on a particular corporation—including the share of profits that would go to the crown in return for the special privilege extended. Such charters were bestowed at the pleasure of the crown and could be withdrawn at any time. Not surprisingly, the history of corporate–government relations since that day has been one of continuing pressure by corporate interests to expand corporate rights and to limit corporate obligations.

Holding Corporations at Bay

America was born of a revolution against the abusive power of the British kings. The corporate charter was an institutional instrument of that abuse. Chartered corporations were used by England to maintain control over colonial economies. In addition to such well-known corporations as the East India Company and the Hudson's Bay Company, many American colonies were themselves chartered as corporations. The corporations of that day were chartered by the king and functioned as extensions of the power of the crown. Generally, these corporations were granted monopoly powers over territories and industries that were considered critical to the interests of the English state.[3]

The English Parliament, which during the seventeenth and eighteenth centuries was made up of wealthy landowners, merchants, and manufacturers, passed many laws intended to protect and extend these monopoly interests. One set of laws, for example, required that all goods imported to the colonies from Europe or Asia first pass through England. Similarly, specified products exported from the colonies also had to be sent first to England. The Navigation Acts required that all goods shipped to or from the colonies be carried on English or colonial ships manned by English or colonial crews. Furthermore, although they had the necessary raw materials, the colonists were forbidden to produce their own caps, hats, and woolen and iron goods. Raw materials were shipped from the colonies to England for manufacture, and the finished products were returned to the colonies.[4]

These practices were strongly condemned by Adam Smith in *The Wealth of Nations*. Smith saw corporations, as much as governments, as instruments for suppressing the competitive forces of the market, and his condemnation of them was uncompromising. He makes specific mention of corporations twelve times in his classic thesis, and not once does he attribute any favorable quality to them. Typical is his observation: "It is to prevent this reduction of price, and consequently of wages and profit, by restraining that free competition which would most certainly occasion it, that all corporations, and the greater part of corporation laws, have been established."[5]

It is noteworthy that the publication of *The Wealth of Nations* and the signing of the U.S. Declaration of Independence both occurred in 1776. Each was, in its way, a revolutionary manifesto challenging the abusive alliance of state and corporate power to establish monopolistic control of markets and thereby capture unearned profits and inhibit local enterprise. Smith and the American colonists shared a deep suspicion of both state and corporate power. The U.S. Constitution instituted the separation of governmental powers to create a system of checks and balances that was carefully crafted to limit opportunities for the abuse of state power. It makes no mention of corporations, which suggests that those who framed it did not foresee or intend that corporations would have a consequential role in the affairs of the new nation.

In the young American republic, there was little sense that corporations were either inevitable or always appropriate. Family farms and businesses were the mainstay of the economy, much in the spirit of Adam Smith's ideal, though neighborhood shops, cooperatives, and worker-owned enterprises were also common. This was consistent with a prevailing belief in the importance of keeping investment and production decisions local and democratic.[6]

The corporations that were chartered were kept under watchful citizen and governmental control. The power to issue corporate charters was retained by the individual states rather than being given to the federal government. The intent was to keep that power as close as possible to citizen control. Many provisions were included in corporate charters and related laws that limited use of the corporate vehicle to amass excessive personal power.[7] The early charters were limited to a fixed number of years and required that the corporation be dissolved if the charter were not renewed. Generally, the corporate charter set limits on the corporation's borrowing, ownership of land, and sometimes even its profits. Members of the corporation were liable in their personal capacities for all debts incurred by the corporation during their period of membership. Large and small investors had equal voting rights, and interlocking directorates were outlawed. Furthermore, a corporation was limited to conducting only those business activities specifically authorized in its charter. Charters often included revocation clauses. State legislators maintained the sovereign right to withdraw the charter of any corporation that in their judgment failed to serve the public interest, and they kept close watch on corporate affairs. By 1800, only some 200 corporate charters had been granted by the states.[8]

The nineteenth century emerged as a time of active and open legal struggle between corporations and civil society regarding the right of the people, through their state governments, to revoke or amend corporate charters. Action by state legislators to amend, revoke, or simply fail to renew corporate charters was fairly common throughout the first half of the century. However, in 1819, the U.S. Supreme Court ruled against the state of New Hampshire in a case in which New Hampshire had attempted to revoke the charter issued to Dartmouth College by King George III before U.S. independence. The Supreme Court overruled the revocation on the ground that the charter contained no reservation or revocation clause.

This decision was seen as an attack on state sovereignty by outraged citizens, who insisted that a distinction be made between a corporation and the property rights of an individual. They argued that corporations were created not by birth but by the pleasure of state legislatures to serve a public good. Corporations were therefore public, not private, bodies, and elected state legislators thereby had an absolute legal right to amend or repeal their charters at will. The public outcry led to a significant strengthening of the legal powers of the states to oversee corporate affairs.[9]

As late as 1855, in *Dodge v. Woolsey*, the Supreme Court affirmed that the Constitution confers no inalienable rights on a corporation, ruling that the people of the states have not

> released their power over the artificial bodies which originate under the legislation of their representatives. . . . Combinations of classes in society . . . united by the bond of a corporate spirit . . . unquestionably desire limitations upon the sovereignty of the people. . . . But the framers of the Constitution were imbued with no desire to call into existence such combinations.[10]

Spoils of the Civil War

The U.S. Civil War (1861–65) marked a turning point for corporate rights. Violent antidraft riots rocked the cities and left the political system in disarray. With huge profits pouring in from military procurement contracts, industrial interests were able to take advantage of the disorder and rampant political corruption to virtually buy legislation that gave them massive grants of money and land to expand the Western railway system. The greater its profits, the more tightly the emergent industrial class was able to solidify its hold on government to obtain further benefits.[11] Seeing what was unfolding, President Abraham Lincoln observed just before his death:

> Corporations have been enthroned. . . . An era of corruption in high places will follow and the money power will endeavor to prolong its reign by working on the prejudices of the people . . . until wealth is aggregated in a few hands . . . and the Republic is destroyed.[12]

The nation was divided by the war against itself; the government was weakened by the assassination of Lincoln and the subsequent election of alcoholic war hero Ulysses S. Grant as president. The nation was in disarray. Millions of Americans were rendered jobless in the subsequent depression, and a tainted presidential election in 1876 was settled through secret negotiations.[13] Corruption and insider deal making ran rampant. President Rutherford B. Hayes, the eventual winner of those corporate-dominated negotiations, subsequently complained, "this is a government of the people, by the people and for the people no longer. It is a government of corporations, by corporations, and for corporations."[14] In his classic *The Robber Barons*, Matthew Josephson wrote that during the 1880s and 1890s, "The halls of legislation were transformed into a mart where the price of votes was haggled over, and laws, made to order, were bought and sold."[15]

These were the days of men such as John D. Rockefeller, J. Pierpont Morgan, Andrew Carnegie, James Mellon, Cornelius Vanderbilt, Philip Armour, and Jay Gould. Wealth begat wealth as corporations took advantage of the disarray to buy tariff, banking, railroad, labor, and public lands legislation that would further enrich them.[16] Citizen groups committed to maintaining corporate accountability continued to battle corporate abuse at state levels, and corporate charters were revoked by both courts and state legislatures.[17]

Gradually, however, corporations gained sufficient control over key state legislative bodies to virtually rewrite the laws governing their own creation. Legislators in New Jersey and Delaware took the lead in watering down citizens' rights to intervene in corporate affairs. They limited the liability of corporate owners and managers and issued charters in perpetuity. Corporations soon had the right to operate in any fashion not explicitly prohibited by law.[18]

A conservative court system that was consistently responsive to the appeals and arguments of corporate lawyers steadily chipped away at the restraints a wary citizenry had carefully placed on corporate powers. Step-by-step, the court system put in place new precedents that made the protection of corporations and corporate property a centerpiece of constitutional law. These precedents eliminated the use of juries to decide fault and assess damages in cases involving corporate-caused harm and took away the right of states to oversee corporate rates of return and prices. Judges sympathetic to corporate interests ruled that workers were responsible for causing their own injuries on the job, limited the liability of corporations for damages they might cause, and declared wage and hours laws unconstitutional. They interpreted the common good to mean maximum production—no matter what was produced or who it harmed.[19] These were important concerns to an industrial sector in which, from 1888 to 1908, industrial accidents killed 700,000 American workers—roughly 100 a day.[20]

In 1886, in a stunning victory for the proponents of corporate sovereignty, the Supreme Court ruled in *Santa Clara County v. Southern Pacific Railroad* that a private corporation is a natural person under the U.S. Constitution—although, as noted above, the Constitution makes no mention of corporations—and is thereby entitled to the protections of the Bill of Rights, including the right to free speech and other constitutional protections extended to individuals.[21]

Thus corporations finally claimed the full rights enjoyed by individual citizens while being exempted from many of the responsibilities and liabilities of citizenship. Furthermore, in being guaranteed the same right to free speech as individual citizens, they achieved, in the words of Paul Hawken, "precisely what the Bill of Rights was intended to prevent: domination of public thought and discourse."[22] The subsequent claim by corporations that they have the same right as any individual to influence the government in their own interest pits the individual citizen against the vast financial and communications resources of the corporation and mocks the constitutional intent that all citizens have an equal voice in the political debates surrounding important issues.

These were days of violence and social instability brought on by the excesses of capitalism that Karl Marx described to powerful political effect. Working conditions were appalling, and wages scarcely covered subsistence. Child labor was widespread. By one estimate, 11 million of the 12.5 million families in America in 1890 subsisted on an average of $380 a year and had to take in boarders to survive.[23] Both organized and wildcat strikes were common, as was industrial sabotage. Employers used every means at their disposal to break strikes, including private security forces and federal and state military troops.

Violence evoked violence, and many died in the industrial wars of this era.

These conditions gave impetus to a growing labor movement. Between 1897 and 1904, union membership rose from 447,000 to 2,073,000.[24] Unions provided fertile ground for the thriving socialist movement that was taking root in America and called for the socialization and democratic control of the means of production, natural resources, and patents. These were times of open class warfare, with zealous new recruits joining the army of the dispossessed in growing numbers—ready to fight and sacrifice for the cause. Socialists who sought to organize labor along class lines vied for primacy with more conventional unionists who preferred to organize along craft or industrial lines.[25]

These movements united ethnic groups. An emergence of black pride and culture began to unify blacks. The women's movement took hold, with women forming their own labor unions, leading strikes, and assuming active roles in populist and socialist movements.[26] In 1920, female suffrage (the right to vote) was guaranteed by a constitutional amendment.

In the end, the conditions of chaos and violence that characterized the period of explosive free-market industrial expansion were not conducive to the interests of either industrialists or labor. Competitive battles between the most powerful industrialists were cutting into profits. There was considerable fear among industrialists of the growing political power of socialist and other popular movements, which threatened to bring fundamental change that might eliminate their privileged position.

These conditions set the stage for consolidation and compromise, which transformed social and institutional relationships. Industrialists merged their individual empires into larger combines that consolidated their power and limited competition among them. Formerly bitter rivals, J. P. Morgan and John D. Rockefeller joined forces in 1901 to amalgamate 112 corporate directorates, combining $22.2 billion in assets under the Northern Securities Corporation of New Jersey. This was a massive sum in its day, equivalent to twice the total assessed value of all property in thirteen states in the southern United States. The result was:

> The heart of the American economy had been put under one roof, from banking and steel to railroads, urban transit, communications, the merchant marine, insurance, electric utilities, rubber, paper, sugar refining, copper, and assorted other mainstays of the industrial infrastructure.[27]

Eventually, major industrialists came to realize that by providing better wages, benefits, and working conditions, they could undercut the appeal of socialism and at the same time win greater worker loyalty and motivation. There was a parallel interest in the regularization of loosely organized craft-based production processes to take greater advantage of the methods of industrial engineering and mass production. This meant organizing around more highly structured rule-driven production processes that demanded worker stability and discipline.

Big business came to see advantages in working with large moderate (nonsocialist) labor unions that negotiated uniform wages and standards throughout an industry and enforced worker discipline according to agreed rules. These arrangements increased stability and predictability within the system without ultimately challenging the power of the industrialists or the market system.[28]

These reforms took place against a backdrop of continuing struggle. A pro-business judicial system that consistently ruled against labor interests helped prompt the labor movement to become increasingly political, resulting in labor's development of a legislative agenda and an alliance with the Democratic Party. Reform legislation at local, state, and national levels began to set new social standards and reshape the context of labor relations. Particularly important to labor was the Clayton Anti-Trust Act, which banned court injunctions against striking workers.[29]

Even so, during the Roaring Twenties, corporate monopolies were allowed to flourish within a loosely regulated national economy. A stock market fueled by borrowed money seemed to be a limitless engine of wealth creation. With faith in the free market and the power of big business at its peak, an ebullient President Herbert Hoover proclaimed, "We shall soon with the help of God be within sight of the day when poverty will be banished from the nation." Irving Fisher, perhaps the leading U.S. economist of the day, announced that the problem of the business cycle had been solved and that the country had settled on a high plateau of endless prosperity.[30]

It was evident that the average American family was better fed, better dressed, and blessed with more of life's amenities than any average family in history.[31] This reality masked the enormous underlying inequality of an America in which just 1 percent of families controlled 59 percent of the wealth.[32] In October 1929, only a few months after Fisher announced the end of business cycles, the highly leveraged financial system came crashing down. Financial fortunes evaporated almost overnight. It took World War II to provide the impetus for a new social contract between government, business, and labor based on Keynesian economic principles that set the global economic system back on the track of prosperity.

Ascendance and Reversal of Pluralism

By the time Franklin D. Roosevelt became president in 1933, business excesses of the 1920s, the depression, and the resulting plight of farmers, laborers, the elderly, blacks, women, and others had produced a wave of political and cultural radicalism throughout the United States. Roosevelt feared that without dramatic action, this radicalism might overwhelm the entire structure of government. He set about to save the system by pushing through an epic agenda of social and regulatory reforms. Congress's passage of his National Industrial Recovery Act (NIRA) was key, as it gave government a mandate to play a more active role in achieving an economic recovery that market forces alone seemed unable to manage.

On May 27, 1935, the Supreme Court voided the NIRA and ruled that states could not set minimum wage standards. This decision continued a century-old pattern of Supreme Court defense of business and corporate interests over civil or human rights. Some observers believe that the Supreme Court's action on NIRA and the minimum wage radicalized a furious Roosevelt, motivating his commitment to a sweeping reform of American institutions. He set about to break up the business trusts, strengthen the regulation of business and financial markets, and push through legislation providing stronger guarantees for worker rights. Programs of public employment were started. A social safety net was put into place.

Roosevelt attacked the Supreme Court with a vengeance and tried to expand its membership with new appointments of his choice. His attempt to "pack" the Court failed, but his charges had a distinct impact on the justices themselves, and the majority became more supportive of progressive initiatives. In the end, Roosevelt's long period in office allowed him to appoint justices to fill seven of the Court's nine seats, setting the Court on a liberal course that lasted until the 1970s, when Republican President Richard Nixon began to re-create the Court in its earlier pro-business image.[33]

World War II brought the government into an even more central and politically accepted role in managing economic affairs. The government placed controls on consumption, coordinated industrial output, and decided how national resources would be allocated in support of the war effort. A combination of a highly progressive tax system put in place to finance the war effort, full employment at good wages, and a strong social safety net brought about a massive shift in wealth distribution in the direction of greater equity. In 1929, there had been 20,000 millionaires in the United States and two billionaires. By 1944, there were only 13,000 millionaires and no billionaires. The share of total wealth held by the top 0.5 percent of U.S. households fell from a high of 32.4 percent in 1929 to 19.3 percent in 1949.[34] It was a great victory for the expanding middle class and for those among the working classes who rose to join its ranks.

Pluralism flourished into the 1960s, a period of cultural rebellion in the United States. A new generation, the flower children, vocally challenged basic assumptions about lifestyles, the military-industrial complex, foreign military intervention, the exploitation of the environment, the rights and roles of women, civil rights, equity, and poverty. The U.S. corporate establishment was badly shaken by the apparent threat to its values and interests. Perhaps most threatening of all was the fact that the young were dropping out of the consumer culture. This generation was rebelling not against poverty and the deprivations of exploitation so much as against the excesses of affluence. This rejection of materialism by a new generation of Americans in some ways presented a more fundamental threat to the system than had earlier generations of angry workers seeking a living wage and safe working conditions.

The names of consumer activist Ralph Nader and environmentalist Rachel Carson became household words. Liberal Democrats had firm control of Congress and were passing important legislation that extended the scope of governmental regulation to strengthen environmental protection and product and worker safety. The government was aggressively pursuing antitrust cases to break up monopolies and keep markets competitive.

Abroad, U.S. corporations were under attack on two fronts. Japan and Asia's newly industrializing countries (NICs)—Taiwan, South Korea, Singapore, and Hong Kong—had become enormously successful in penetrating U.S. markets. At the same time, U.S. corporations were being prevented from fully penetrating Southern economies, including those of the NICs, by Southern governments' aggressive support of domestic industries, protectionism, and foreign investment restrictions. These Southern government policies militated against a "level playing field" for U.S. corporations. With high taxes on corporations and investor incomes and rigorous enforcement of environmental and labor standards at home, U.S. corporations felt doubly handicapped in global competition.[35]

It was a critical historical moment, and the corporate establishment rallied to protect its interests—as will be examined in more detail in Part III. The election of Ronald Reagan as president in 1980 ushered in a concerted and highly successful effort to roll back the clock on the social and economic reforms that had created the broadly based prosperity that made America the envy of the world and to create a global economy that was more responsive to U.S. corporate interests.

In his insightful book *Dark Victory*, Philippine economist Walden Bello provides a Southern perspective on the Reagan agenda:

[A] highly ideological Republican regime in Washington . . . abandoned the grand strategy of "containment liberalism" abroad and the New Deal modus vivendi at home. Aside from defeating communism, Reaganism in practice was guided by three other strategic concerns. The first was the re-subordination of the South within a US-dominated global economy. The second was the rolling back of the challenge to US economic interests from the NICs, or "newly industrializing countries," and from Japan. The third was the dismantling of the New Deal's "social contract" between big capital, big labor, and big government which both Washington and Wall Street saw as the key constraint on corporate Amer-ica's ability to compete against both the NICs and Japan.[36]

The debt crisis of 1982 provided the opportunity to address the threat of prospective new NICs. The U.S.-dominated World Bank and International Monetary Fund moved to restructure the economies of debt-burdened Southern countries to open them to penetration by foreign corporations. The "structural adjustment" imposed by these institutions rolled back government involvement in economic life in support of domestic entrepreneurs, eliminated protectionist barriers to imports from the North, lifted restrictions on foreign investment, and integrated Southern economies more tightly into the Northern-dominated world economy. Trade policy was the weapon of choice for imposing similar "reforms" on the NICs.[37]

The full political resources of corporate America were mobilized to regain corporate control of the political agenda and the court system. High on the political agenda were domestic reforms intended to improve the global competitiveness of the United States by getting government "off the back" of business. Taxes on the rich were radically reduced. Restraints on corporate mergers and acquisitions were removed. And the enforcement of environmental and labor standards was weakened. The government sided with aggressive U.S. corporations seeking to make themselves more globally competitive by breaking the power of unions, reducing wages and benefits, downsizing corporate workforces, and shifting manufacturing operations abroad to benefit from cheap labor and lax regulation.[38]

As these measures took hold in the United States, unemployment became a chronic problem, and labor unions lost members and political clout. Wages began to decline, as did the incomes of the poorest households. A fortunate few profited handsomely. The earnings of big investors, top managers, entertainers, star athletes, and investment brokers skyrocketed. The number of billionaires in the United States increased from one in 1978 to 120 in 1994.[39] Lending abuses by a deregulated savings and loan industry left U.S. taxpayers with a bill for $500 billion to clean up the mess. They were hard times for ordinary citizens. Greed had a field day.

As the Reagan initiatives took hold abroad, backed by similar conservative revivals in other Western nations, there were parallel declines in most of the other Western countries as well as the indebted countries of the South. Inequality increased within and between countries. Unemployment rose to alarming levels, and many social indicators that had shown steady improvement over the previous three decades stagnated or in some instances began to decline. Many of the indebted Southern countries fell even further into international debt. The number of billionaires in the world increased from 145 in 1987 to 358 in 1994.[40]

The Reagan administration had pledged to arrest U.S. decline. However, it made a number of strategic policy blunders that strengthened U.S. military might and economic growth in the short term but seriously weakened the U.S. position in the global economy over the longer term. First, massive deficit spending on the military contributed to making the United States the world's leading international debtor country. The main holder of that debt was Japan, the major competitor of the United States. Second, by denying any government role in economic planning and priority setting, the Reagan administration left the economic future of the United States entirely in the hands of corporations that were being pressed by the capital markets to focus only on short-term profits. Third, by allowing corporations to pursue their antilabor strategy, the United States squandered its key resource in the competitive global marketplace—its human capital.[41] The overall result was a significant weakening of U.S. economic strength compared with that of Japan and Western Europe. The consequences were clearly harmful to ordinary American citizens. In the end, they may have been harmful to U.S. corporations as well.

This was not the result of a conspiracy. Major shifts in national policy do not come about as a consequence of corporate and political elites gathering in a conference room to define a strategy for imposing global adjustment. They are far too independent minded and represent too broad a range of conflicting interests. As Bello observes:

> What usually occurs is a much more complex social process in which *ideology* mediates between interests and policy. An ideology is a belief-system—a set of theories, beliefs, and myths with

some internal coherence—that seeks to universalize the interests of one social sector to the whole community. In market ideology, for instance, freeing market forces from state restraints is said to work to the good not only of business, but also to that of the whole community.

Transmitted through social institutions such as universities, corporations, churches or parties, an ideology is internalized by large numbers of people, but especially by members of the social groups whose interests it principally expresses. An ideology thus informs the actions of many individuals and groups, but it becomes a significant force only when certain conditions coincide. . . . Market ideology became a dominant force only when a political elite which espoused it ascended to state power on the back of an increasingly conservative middle-class social base, at the same time that the corporate establishment was deserting the liberal Keynesian consensus in its favor, because of the changed circumstances of international economic competition.[42]

A Question of Governance

Interwoven into the political discourse about free markets and free trade is a persistent message: the advance of free markets is the advance of democracy. Advocates of the free market would have us believe that free markets are a more efficient and responsive mechanism for political expression than even the ballot, because business is more efficient and more responsive to people's needs than are inefficient and uncaring politicians and bureaucrats. The logic is simple: In the free market, people express their sovereignty directly by how they vote with their consumer dollars. What they are willing to buy with their own money is ultimately a better indicator of what they value than the ballot, and therefore the market is the most effective and democratic way to define the public interest.

Given the growing distrust of government, it is a compelling message, and it embodies an important truth: markets and politics are both about governance, power, and the allocation of society's resources. It is also a misleading message that masks an important political reality. In a political democracy, each person gets one vote. In the market, one dollar is one vote, and you get as many votes as you have dollars. No dollar, no vote. Markets are inherently biased in favor of people of wealth. Even more important in our present world, and less often acknowledged, is that markets have a very strong bias in favor of very large corporations, which command far more massive financial resources than even the wealthiest of individuals. As markets become freer and more global, the power to govern increasingly passes from national governments to global corporations, and the interests of those corporations diverge ever farther from the human interest—assertions documented in detail in Parts III and IV.

People, even the greediest and most ruthless among us, are living beings with needs and values beyond money. We need air to breathe, water to drink, and food to eat. Most of us have families. All but the most truly demented among us find inspiration in things of beauty, including a natural landscape or a newborn baby. Our bodies are of flesh, and real blood runs through our veins.

Behind its carefully crafted public-relations image and the many fine and ethical people it may employ, the body of a corporation is its corporate charter, a legal document, and money is its blood. It is at its core an alien entity with one goal: to reproduce money to nourish and replicate itself. Individuals are dispensable. It owes only one true allegiance: to the financial markets, which are more totally creatures of money than even the corporation itself.

The problem is deeply embedded in the structure and rules by which corporations are compelled to operate. The marvel of the corporation as a social innovation is that it has the ability to bring together thousands of people within a single structure and compel them to act in concert in accordance with a corporate purpose that is not necessarily their own. Those who revolt or fail to comply are expelled and replaced by others who are more compliant.[43]

As Washington journalist William Greider writes in *Who Will Tell the People?*

> [The corporations'] . . . tremendous financial resources, the diversity of their interests, the squads of talented professionals—all these assets and some others are now relentlessly focused on the politics of governing.
>
> This new institutional reality is the centerpiece in the breakdown of contemporary democracy. Corporations exist to pursue their own profit maximization, not the collective aspirations of the society. They are commanded by a hierarchy of managers, not the collective aspirations of the society.[44]

Human societies have long faced the question whether the power to rule will reside with the rich or the poor. We now face a different and even more ominous question, which—to the extent that its implications are fully understood—should unite rich and poor alike in a common cause. Will the power to rule reside with people, no matter what their financial circumstances, or will it reside with the artificial persona of the corporation?

During this critical historical moment, in which one of the most fundamental challenges our species faces is to rediscover the purpose and unity of life, we must decide whether the power to govern will be in the hands of living people or will reside with corporate entities driven by a different agenda. To regain control of our future and bring human societies into balance with the planet, we must reclaim the power we have yielded to the corporation. One important step will be to free ourselves from the illusions of the ideology that legitimates the policies that are freeing the corporation as an institution from human accountability.

5 Assault of the Corporate Libertarians

> *If there were an Economist's Creed, it would surely contain the affirmations, "I believe in the Principle of Comparative Advantage," and "I believe in free trade."*
> —Paul Krugman, MIT economist[1]

> *The difference between a system dominated by General Motors and Exxon and one based upon the individual landholding farmer and small businessperson of an earlier day in American history may very well be greater—in the real life experience of the average person—than the difference between a system based upon large private bureaucracies in the United States and public bureaucracies in socialist nations.*
> —Gar Alperovitz[2]

In the quest for economic growth, free-market ideology has been embraced around the world with the fervor of a fundamentalist religious faith. Money is its sole measure of value, and its practice is advancing policies that are deepening social and environmental disintegration everywhere. The economics profession serves as its priesthood. It champions values that demean the human spirit, it assumes an imaginary world divorced from reality, and it is restructuring our institutions of governance in ways that make our most fundamental problems more difficult to resolve. Yet to question its doctrine has become virtual heresy, invoking risk of professional censure and damage to one's career in most institutions of business, government, and academia. In the words of Australian sociologist Michael

Pusey, it has reduced economics to "an ideological shield against intelligent introspection and civic responsibility,"[3] and infused the study
of economics in most universities with a strong element of ideological indoctrination.

The Sanctification of Greed

The beliefs espoused by free-market ideologues are familiar to anyone who is conversant with the language of contemporary economic
discourse:

- Sustained *economic growth*, as measured by gross national product, is the path to human progress.
- *Free markets*, unrestrained by government, generally result
  in the most efficient and socially optimal allocation of resources.
- *Economic globalization*, achieved by removing barriers to the
  free flow of goods and money anywhere in the world, spurs
  competition, increases economic efficiency, creates jobs,
  lowers consumer prices, increases consumer choice, increases economic growth, and is generally beneficial to almost everyone.
- *Privatization*, which moves functions and assets from governments to the private sector, improves efficiency.
- The primary responsibility of government is to provide the
  infrastructure necessary to advance commerce and enforce the
  rule of law with respect to *property rights and contracts*.

These beliefs are based on a number of explicit underlying assumptions embedded in the theories of neoclassical economics:

- Humans are motivated by self-interest, which is expressed primarily through the quest for financial gain.
- The action that yields the greatest financial return to the
  individual or firm is the one that is most beneficial to society.
- Competitive behavior is more rational for the individual and
  the firm than cooperative behavior; consequently, societies
  should be built around the competitive motive.
- Human progress is best measured by increases in the value of
  what the members of society consume, and ever higher levels of consumer spending advance the well-being of society
  by stimulating greater economic output.

To put it in harsher language, these ideological doctrines assume that:

- People are by nature motivated primarily by greed.
- The drive to acquire is the highest expression of what it means to be human.
- The relentless pursuit of greed and acquisition leads to socially optimal outcomes.
- It is in the best interest of human societies to encourage, honor, and reward the above values.

A number of valid ideas and insights have become twisted into an extremist ideology that raises the baser aspects of human nature to a self-justifying ideal. Although this ideology denigrates the most basic human values and ideals, it has become so deeply embedded within our values, institutions, and popular culture that we accept it almost without question. It exists all around us and plays a critical role in shaping nearly every aspect of public policy. It plays to declining economic fortunes and well-founded public distrust of big government to build a populist political constituency for agendas with decidedly nonpopulist consequences.

Reminiscent of Marxist ideologues now passed from the scene, advocates of this extremist ideology seek to cut off debate by proclaiming the inevitability of the historical forces advancing their cause. They tell us that a globalized free market that leaves resource allocation decisions in the hands of giant corporations is inevitable, and we had best concentrate on learning how to adapt to the new rules of the game. They warn that those who hold back and fail to get on board will be swept aside and excluded from the rewards that will go only to those who acquiesce.

The extremist quality of their position is revealed in the stark choices they pose between a "free" market unencumbered by governmental restraint and a centrally planned, state-controlled economy based on the former Soviet model. Similarly, it is implied that the only alternative to throwing open national borders to the unrestrained flow of goods and money is to build impenetrable walls that cut us off from the rest of the world and deprive us of the benefits of participating in international commerce. As they would have it, if you are not a free trader, then you are a protectionist. There is no middle ground.

In defiance of history and logic, they see no place in the public discourse for those who reject free markets in favor of markets that function within a framework of public accountability. Nor will they countenance the possibility of countries managing exchanges of money and goods among themselves in a fair and balanced way that works to the mutual benefit of their citizens.

In its various guises, this ideology is known by different names—neoclassical, neoliberal, or libertarian economics; neoliberalism, market capitalism, or market liberalism. In Australia and New Zealand, Michael Pusey's book *Economic Rationalism in Canberra* has popularized the term *economic rationalism* and injected it into the public debate.[4] Latin Americans commonly use the term *neoliberalism*. However, in most countries—including the United States—it goes without a generally recognized name. Unnamed, it goes undebated—its underlying assumptions unexamined.

The Corporate Libertarian Alliance

At least three major constituencies—economic rationalists, market liberals, and members of the corporate class—have formed a powerful political alliance committed to advancing a shared ideological agenda with a dogmatic fervor that is normally associated with religious crusades.

Economic Rationalists. The economic rationalists are predominantly professional economists of the neoclassical school of economics. Rationalism, defined by the dictionary as "the doctrine that knowledge comes wholly from pure reason, without aid from the senses,"[5] is the foundational philosophy of contemporary mainstream economics—whose practitioners pledge their faith to rational structures of analysis derived deductively from first principles. This commitment to rationalism has given standing to the claim that economics is the only truly objective, value-free social science. The first principle of the logical structure of neoclassical economics is that individuals are motivated by self-interest and, given maximum freedom from restraint, individual choices based on the pursuit of self-interest lead to socially optimal outcomes. Economic rationalism gives the free-market ideology its intellectual legitimacy, and the coalition formed around the ideology gives economists a powerful political base.

Market Liberals. The market liberals bring to the coalition a moral philosophy grounded in individual rights that has strong appeal for those who harbor a natural distrust of big government. As articulated by Roger Pilon of the Cato Institute, a Washington, D.C., think tank devoted to advancing market liberalism, the market liberal's position begins from "a premise of moral equality defined—by rights, not values." Market liberals believe that individuals have the right to pursue whatever values they wish, as long as they respect the same rights of others. This "implies that we alone are responsible for ourselves, for making as much or as little of our lives as we wish and can." Market liberals believe that "rights and property are inextricably connected.

. . . Broadly understood . . . property is the foundation of all our natural rights. Exercising those rights, consistent with the rights of others, we may pursue happiness in any way we wish." This includes forming voluntary associations with others through the mechanism of the contract.[6] The only responsibilities attached to these rights are to respect the same rights of others, obey the law, and honor contractual agreements. Market liberalism gives the dominant ideology its cast of moral legitimacy. In return, leading proponents of market liberalism, such as the Cato Institute, receive major financial support and political leverage from the major corporations whose interests it advances.

Members of the Corporate Class. This class comprises people such as corporate managers, lawyers, consultants, public-relations specialists, financial brokers, and wealthy investors who stand to gain from advancing the rights and freedom of the corporate persona. Some are driven to corporate libertarianism by self-interest, others by moral conviction, and many simply because they are employed to do so. They are generally strong advocates of both market freedom and property rights as vested in the legal persona of the corporation. Though they are not necessarily interested in the details of academic theories or moral philosophy, they find a natural common cause with an intellectual tradition that legitimates the objective of freeing market institutions from the restraining hand of government and with a philosophy that absolves the corporation of moral responsibility for many of the social and environmental consequences of its actions. They have at their command the enormous resources of the corporation to channel to those who serve the corporate interest.

These three groups form a powerful political alliance that combines an intellectual tradition and a moral philosophy with a political interest. As is often the case in political alliances, however, they make strange bedfellows. Furthermore, contrary to outward appearances, participation in the alliance serves even its own members poorly. For the economic rationalists, the alliance has seriously debased the integrity and social utility of economics by reducing it to a system of ideological indoctrination that violates its own theoretical foundations and is deeply at odds with reality. It has similarly engaged the moral philosophers who advocate individual freedom in a cause that increases the ability of corporations to co-opt the property rights of people and to suppress the individual freedoms of all but society's wealthiest members. The enormous political success of the alliance in restructuring economic institutions in line with the corporate interest is creating a monster that even the members of the corporate class no longer control. It is creating a world that they would scarcely wish to bequeath to their children.

In the name of individual freedom, this alliance advances an ideological doctrine most accurately described as *corporate libertarianism*, because its consequence is to place the rights and freedoms of corporations ahead of the rights and freedoms of individuals. Presented as an economic agenda, it is in truth a governance agenda. Who will have the power to rule, and to what end?

The contemporary corporation increasingly exists as an entity apart—even from the people who compose it. Every member of the corporate class, no matter how powerful his or her position within the corporation, has become expendable—as growing numbers of top executives are learning. As corporations gain in autonomous institutional power and become more detached from people and place, the human interest and the corporate interest increasingly diverge. It is almost as though we were being invaded by alien beings intent on colonizing our planet, reducing us to serfs, and then excluding as many of us as possible.

I do not make these strong assertions lightly. Their documentation is an underlying theme of the remainder of this and subsequent chapters.

The Betrayal of Adam Smith and David Ricardo

The proponents of corporate libertarianism regularly pay homage to Adam Smith as their intellectual patron saint. His writing remains the intellectual foundation on which the whole structure of the deductive reasoning of the economic rationalists has been built. It is a tragic irony that although the economic rationalists now call upon that structure to give intellectual legitimacy to the ideology of corporate libertarianism, Smith's epic work *The Wealth of Nations*, first published in 1776, actually presented a radical condemnation of business monopolies sustained and protected by the state. Adam Smith's ideal was a market composed solely of small buyers and sellers. He showed how the workings of such a market would tend toward a price that provides a fair return to land, labor, and capital; produce a satisfactory outcome for both buyers and sellers; and result in an optimal outcome for society in terms of the allocation of its resources. He made clear that this outcome can result only when no buyer or seller is sufficiently large to influence the market price. Such a market implicitly assumes a significant degree of equality in the distribution of economic power.

Smith was firmly opposed to any kind of monopoly power, which he defined as the power of a seller to maintain a price for an indefinite time above its natural price. Indeed, he asserted that trade secrets confer a monopoly advantage and are contrary to the principles of a free market.[7] He would surely have strongly opposed current efforts by market libertarians to strengthen corporate monopoly control of intellectual property rights through the General Agreement on Tariffs and Trade (GATT). The idea that a major corporation might have exclusive control over a lifesaving drug or device and therefore charge whatever the market will bear would have been anathema to him.

Furthermore, Smith never advocated a moral philosophy in defense of unrestrained greed. He was talking about small farmers and artisans trying to get the best price for their products to provide for themselves and their families. That is self-interest—not greed. Greed is a high-paid corporate executive firing 10,000 employees and then rewarding himself with a multimillion-dollar bonus as a reward for having saved the company so much money. Greed is what the economic system being constructed by the corporate libertarians encourages and rewards.

Smith had a strong dislike for both governments and corporations. He viewed government primarily as an instrument for extracting taxes to subsidize elites and intervening in the market to protect monopoly. In his words, "Civil government, so far as it is instituted for the security of property, is in reality instituted for the defence of the rich against the poor, or of those who have some property against those who have none at all."[8] Smith made no mention of government intervention to set and enforce minimum social, health, worker safety, and environmental standards in the common interest—to protect the poor and nature against the rich. We can imagine that, given the experience of his day, the possibility never occurred to him.

The theory of market economics, in contrast to free-market ideology, specifies a number of basic conditions needed for a market to set prices efficiently in the public interest. The greater the violation of these conditions, the less efficient the market system. Most basic is the condition that markets must be competitive. I recall the professor in my elementary economics course using the example of a market comprising small wheat farmers selling to small grain millers to illustrate the idea of perfect market competition. Today, four companies—Conagra, ADM Milling, Cargill, and Pillsbury—mill nearly 60 percent of all flour produced in the United States, and two of them—Conagra and Cargill—control 50 percent of grain exports.[9]

In the real world of unregulated markets, successful players get larger and, in many instances, use the resulting economic power to drive or buy out weaker players to gain control of even larger shares of the market. In other instances, "competitors" collude through cartels or strategic alliances to increase profits by setting market prices above the level of optimal efficiency. The larger and more collusive market players become, the more difficult it is for newcomers and small independent firms to survive, the more monopolistic and less competitive the market becomes, and the more political power the biggest firms can wield to demand concessions from governments that allow them to externalize even more of their costs to the community.

Given this reality, one might expect the economic rationalists to be outspoken in arguing for the need to restrict mergers and acquisitions and break up monopolistic firms to restore the conditions of a competitive market. More often, they argue exactly the opposite position—that to "compete" in today's global markets, firms must merge into larger combinations. In other words, they espouse a theory that assumes small firms but advocate policies that strengthen monopoly.

Another basic condition of efficient market allocation is that the full costs of production must be borne by the producer and be included in the producer's selling price. Economists call it *cost internalization*. This condition is so basic to market theory that it is rarely disputed even by the most doctrinaire of free-market ideologues. If some portion of the cost of producing a product is borne by third parties who in no way participate in or benefit from the transaction, then economists say that the costs have been externalized, and the price of the product is distorted accordingly. Another way of putting it is that every externalized cost involves privatizing a gain and socializing its associated costs onto the community.

Externalized costs don't go away—they are simply ignored by those who benefit from making the decisions that result in others incurring the costs. For example, when a forest products corporation obtains rights to clear-cut Forest Service land at giveaway prices and leaves behind a devastated habitat, the company reaps the immediate profit and the society bears the long-term cost. When logging companies are contracted by the Mitsubishi Corporation to cut the forests of the Penan tribespeople of Sarawak, the corporation bears no cost for devastating native culture and ways of life.[10]

Similarly, a giant chemical corporation externalizes production costs when it dumps wastes without adequate treatment, thus passing the resulting costs of air, water, and soil pollution onto the community in the form of additional health costs, discomfort, lost working days, a need to buy bottled water, and the cost of cleaning up what has been contaminated. A mega-retailer externalizes costs when it buys from Chinese contractors who pay their workers too little to maintain their basic physical and mental health, or who fail to maintain adequate worker safety standards and then dismiss without compensation those workers who are injured.

When the seller retains the benefit of an externalized cost, this represents an unearned profit—an important source of market inefficiency, because it rewards cost externalizing behaviors. Passing the benefit to the buyer in the form of a lower price creates still another source of inefficiency by encouraging forms of consumption that use finite resources inefficiently. For example, the more the environmental and social costs of producing and driving automobiles are externalized, the more automobiles people buy and the more they drive them. Urban sprawl increases, more productive lands are paved over, more pollutants are released, petroleum reserves are depleted more rapidly, and voters favor highway construction over public transportation, sidewalks, and bicycle paths.

Yet rather than demanding that costs be fully internalized, the corporate libertarians are active advocates of eliminating government regulation, pointing to potential cost savings for consumers and ignoring the social and environmental consequences. Similarly, they advise localities in need of employment opportunities for their residents that they must become more internationally competitive in attracting investors by offering them more favorable conditions, that is, more opportunities to externalize their costs through various subsidies, low-cost labor, lax environmental regulations, and tax breaks.

Market forces create substantial pressure on business to decrease costs and increase profits by increasing efficiency. The corporate rationalists fail to mention that one way firms increase their "efficiency" is to externalize more of their costs. The more powerful the firm, the greater its ability to take this course. As ecological economist Neva Goodwin observed, "power is largely what externalities are about. What's the point of having power, if you can't use it to externalize your costs—to make them fall on someone else?"[11] When corporate libertarians promote practices that allow corporations and wealthy investors to socialize their costs and privatize their gains, they reveal their fidelity to a political interest rather than to economic principles.

A third condition basic to the market theories of Adam Smith and the trade theories of David Ricardo—but rarely noted by corporate libertarians—is that capital must be locally or nationally rooted and its owners directly involved in its management. Adam Smith made quite explicit in *The Wealth of Nations* his assumption that capital would be rooted in place in the locality where its owner lived and that this condition is critical to enabling the invisible hand of the market to translate the pursuit of self-interest into optimal public benefit.

> By preferring the support of domestic to that of foreign industry, he [the entrepreneur] intends only his own security, and by directing that industry in such a manner as its produce may be of the greatest value, he intends only his own gain, and he is in this, as in many other cases, led by an invisible hand to promote an end which was no part of his intention.[12]

The circumstance that Adam Smith believed induced the individual to invest locally was the inability to supervise his or her capital when it was employed far from home. In the current age of instant communication by phone, fax, and computer and twenty-four-hour air travel to anywhere in the world, that circumstance no longer applies. However, local ownership of productive investment remains desirable from the standpoint of the community and the larger society. Local investment provides rooted local employment and is more easily held to local standards.

Smith was also quite explicit that optimal market efficiency depends on the owners of capital being directly involved in its management—the owner-managed enterprise—because he believed that owners exercise greater diligence in ensuring the most efficient use of assets than do managers who have no ownership stake.

> The directors of such companies, however, being the managers rather of other people's money than of their own, it cannot well be expected, that they should watch over it with the same anxious vigilance with which the partners in a private copartnery frequently watch over their own. . . . Negligence and profusion, therefore, must always prevail, more or less in the management of the affairs of such a company.[13]

Thus his vision of an efficient market was one composed of small owner-managed enterprises located in the communities where the owners resided. Such owners would share in the community's values and have a personal stake in its future. It is a market that has little in common with a globalized economy dominated by massive corporations without local or national allegiance, managed by professionals who are removed from real owners by layers of investment institutions and holding companies.

The theory of comparative advantage, which free traders regularly invoke as proof of their argument that free trade advances the public good, was originally articulated by David Ricardo in 1817. Ricardo's theory provides an elegant demonstration that, *under certain conditions*, free trade between two countries works to the benefit of the people of both. Three conditions are fundamental to this outcome: capital must not be allowed to cross national borders from a high-wage to a low-wage country, trade between the participating countries must be balanced, and each country must have full employment.

In Ricardo's time, most trade involved the exchange of finished national goods produced by national enterprises. Today, products are commonly assembled using components and services produced in many different countries. Global corporations, rather than national economies, are likely to be the coordinating units, with the result that roughly a third of the $3.3 trillion in goods and services traded internationally in 1990 consisted of transactions within a single firm.[14] A growing portion of international trade is intraindustry, meaning that countries are exchanging the same product—for example, when the United States and Japan sell automobiles to each other—making it difficult to argue that natural comparative advantage is involved and rendering trade theory irrelevant in assessing the consequent costs and benefits.

Most corporate libertarians do much more than neglect the underlying assumptions of Ricardo's theory; they actively promote (through GATT and other trade agreements) the removal of restrictions on the international movement of capital—thus violating one of the essential conditions of trade theory. In truth, the "trade agreements" advocated by corporate libertarians are not about trade, they are about economic integration. Although the theory of comparative advantage applies to balanced trade between otherwise independent national economies, a very different theory—the theory of downward leveling—applies when national economies are integrated.

When capital is confined within the national borders of trading partners, it must flow to those industries in which its country of origin has a comparative advantage. When the economies are merged, capital can flow to whatever localities offer the maximum opportunity to externalize costs. The basic consequence is to shift income from workers to investors and to shift costs from investors to the community.[15]

Economist Neva Goodwin, who heads the Global Development and Environment Institute at Tufts University, suggests that the very definition of the disciplinary boundaries of neoclassical economics invites distortion and misuse of economic theory. As she points out, the neoclassical school of economics may be roughly characterized as the political economy of Adam Smith minus the political analysis of Karl Marx:

> The classical political economy of Adam Smith was a much broader, more humane subject than the economics that is taught in universities today. . . . For at least a century it has been virtually taboo to talk about economic power in the capitalist context; that was a communist (Marxist) idea. The concept of class was similarly banned from discussion.[16]

Adam Smith was as acutely aware of issues of power and class as he was of the dynamics of competitive markets. However, the neoclassical economists and the neo-Marxist economists bifurcated his holistic perspective on the political economy, one taking those portions of the analysis that favored the owners of property, and the other taking those that favored the sellers of labor. Thus, the neoclassical economists left out Smith's considerations of the destructive role of power and class, and the neo-Marxists left out the beneficial functions of the market. Both advanced social experiments on a massive scale that embodied a partial vision of society, with disastrous consequences.

Economics and Demagoguery

On the evening of December 1, 1994, a lame-duck session of the U.S. Senate approved GATT by a margin of seventy-six to twenty-four. A broad coalition of Republican and Democratic senators supported the measure in the face of widespread and growing opposition among those Americans familiar with the agreement and the threat it posed to jobs, the environment, and democracy. The strong and unequivo-cal backing of the agreement by President Bill Clinton and Vice President Albert Gore Jr. further deepened the chasm between them and their core labor and environmental constituencies.

C-Span, a cable television news channel, held a telephone call-in session following the vote. Doug Harbrecht, the trade editor of *Business Week*, was the guest resource person. As caller after caller phoned in to express outrage at the politicians who voted for the agreement in support of big-money interests and total disregard of the popular will, Harbrecht commented that the pro-GATT position represented impeccable economics but bad politics. As did many of his colleagues, Harbrecht failed to discriminate between good economics and politi-cally correct free-market ideology. The global economic integration being implemented through GATT is advancing conditions that are at odds with the most basic principles of market economics and is putting in place an economic system that is designed to self-destruct—at an enormous cost to human societies. This can scarcely be consid-ered the practice of good economics.

One may wonder how economic rationalists can advocate eco-nomic integration if it advances conditions that are at odds with those required for efficient market function. An important part of the answer is found in their legendary ability to assume away reality. This ability has been immortalized in an apocryphal story about three scientists—a physicist, a chemist, and an economist—marooned on a desert island. They've salvaged a can of beans from the wreck of their ship, but unfortunately, they have no evident means of opening it. They agree that with so much scientific brainpower among them, they can surely complete the simple task. The physicist points to a nearby palm tree and suggests that she will climb the tree and drop the can on a rock below at the proper angle to pop it open. The chemist points out that the beans will be spilled on the ground and suggests that they might use salt water to create a chemical reaction that will rust away the top. Then the economist says, "You are both making this simple task too complicated. First, we will assume a can opener." Like the economist in this popular story, when the real world diverges from the conditions necessary to support their preferred policy options, economic rationalists are prone to solve the conflict by assuming the conditions that support their recommendations.

Take the case of the obvious reality that the human economy is embedded in and dependent on the natural environment. As far back as 1798, Thomas Robert Malthus suggested that environmental limits might make population growth a problem for the future of humanity. Neoclassical economists have dealt with this inconvenience by adopting a model of analysis that assumes that economies consist of isolated, wholly self-contained, circular flows of exchange values (labor, capital, and goods) between firms and households without reference to the environment. In other words, their model assumes away the existence of the environment. Then, in defiance of logic, they use this model to prove that the environment is of little importance to the function of the economy. Those who challenge the possibility of infinite growth on a finite planet are dismissed with the stinging epithet "neo-Malthusianism." A belief in the possibility of unlimited growth is the very foundation of the ideological doctrine of corporate libertarianism, because to accept the reality of physical limits is to accept the need to limit greed and acquisition in favor of economic justice and sufficiency. Growth would have to give way to redistribution and reallocation of environmental resources as the focus of economic policy.

The propensity of the economic rationalists to choose their assumptions to fit their conclusions is revealed with particular clarity in the computer simulations they use to demonstrate the economic benefits of lowering trade barriers. During the public debates on the North American Free Trade Agreement (NAFTA), proponents of the agreement aggressively brandished the results of many computer simulations, known as general equilibrium models, as proof that NAFTA would create large numbers of new jobs for each of the participating NAFTA countries: Canada, the United States, and Mexico.[17] Economist James Stanford examined the models used to generate these projections and produced an inventory of the assumptions built into them. He found that each one incorporated assumptions from classical trade theory that were sharply at odds with the economic reality of the NAFTA countries. To illustrate the contradictions, he related the following hypothetical discussion between an auto worker in the midwestern United States and one of the pro-NAFTA economic modelers. The worker related to the modeler her fears that:

> If NAFTA is approved, Ford will surely move its Taurus plant to Mexico where it can hire workers for a tenth of my pay with no independent union and export cars back to the United States. With the labor market already depressed in this part of the country I don't see any prospect of finding a job at comparable pay.

The economic modeler, looking surprised, assures her that he is an expert on the subject of trade and that her fears are entirely unfounded:

> Don't worry. I've constructed a computer simulation that shows you will actually benefit from the trade agreement because of the new jobs NAFTA will create in America. Here's how it works. In my model I assume *capital is immobile*. Therefore, Ford cannot move its plant to Mexico. Nor would it want to, because I assume *unit labor costs are the same in both countries* and in my model *Americans have a clear preference for U.S.-made products, even if they are more expensive*.
>
> My model also assumes *full employment* and specifies that *anything imported to the U.S. from Mexico must be balanced by American exports*, so new export industries will necessarily spring up here to replace any industries that might be displaced by Mexican imports. Since you earn above-average wages at Ford, you obviously possess valuable skills. With full employment you will certainly find another job very shortly in one of these new export industries, probably with higher pay than your current job. So NAFTA will be great for you.

One can understand that a worker confronted with such an explanation might conclude that the economic modeler had just arrived from an alien planet with little knowledge of affairs on Earth. Although the discussion is hypothetical, the assumptions articulated by the economist (highlighted by italics for ease of identification) are not. Each of them is built into one or more of the economic models that trade experts used to prove that the United States would realize employment gains from NAFTA. In comparing the models and their results, Sanford found a direct relationship between unrealistic assumptions and favorable job projections—the less realistic the assumptions, the more optimistic the projections. The more realistic models predicted either negative or negligible economic consequences for at least one of the partners.[18]

Those who use these models to press their case make no mention of the underlying assumptions. The misrepresentations are so flagrant and persistent that one sometimes suspects an intent to misinform the public. For example, during the NAFTA debates, the unabashedly pro-free trade *New York Times* took the unusual step of presenting a trade economics primer on its front page. The primer provided a text-book explanation of the theory of comparative advantage to bolster its editorial position in support of the NAFTA legislation. No mention was made, however, of the underlying assumptions of the theory, let alone of how those assumptions diverge from reality. Letters submitted by me and others to the editor of the *New York Times* pointing out the omission were not published.

Those who engage in such distortion promote as beneficial to the common good those policies that deeply institutionalize economic rules that advantage the greediest among us and disadvantage the rest.

The Moral Justification of Injustice

The moral philosophers of market liberalism perpetrate similar distortions by neglecting the distinction between the rights of money and the rights of people. Indeed, they have equated the freedom and rights of individuals with market freedom and property rights. The freedom of the market is the freedom of money, and when rights are a function of property rather than personhood, only those with property have rights. Furthermore, by maintaining that the only obligation of the individual is to honor contracts and the property rights of others, the "moral" philosophy of market liberalism effectively releases those who have property from an obligation to those who do not. It ignores the reality that contracts between the weak and the powerful are seldom equal, and that the institution of the contract, like the institution of property, tends to reinforce and even increase inequality in unequal societies. It legitimates and strengthens systems that institutionalize poverty, even while maintaining that poverty is a consequence of indolence and inherent character defects of the poor.

The most basic premise of democracy is that each individual has equal rights before the law and an equal voice in political affairs—one person, one vote. We can rightfully look to the market as a democratic arbiter of rights and preferences—as market liberals advocate—only to the extent that property rights are equally distributed. Although a market can allocate efficiently with less than complete equality, when 358 billionaires enjoy a combined net worth of $760 billion—equal to the net worth of the poorest 2.5 billion of the world's people—it cannot be assumed that the market will function either justly or efficiently, and the market's very legitimacy as an institution is called into question.[19]

Publications such as *Fortune, Business Week, Forbes,* the *Wall Street Journal,* and *The Economist*—all ardent advocates of corporate libertarianism—

rarely if ever praise an economy for its progress toward eliminating the poverty that leaves more than a billion people living in absolute deprivation or making strides toward greater equity. Rather, they regularly evaluate the performance of economies by the number of millionaires and billionaires they produce, the competence of managers by the cool dispassion with which they fire thousands of employees, the success of individuals by how many millions of dollars they acquire in a year, and the success of companies by the global reach of their power and their ability to dominate global markets.

Take, for example, the cover story of the July 5, 1993, issue of *Forbes*, trumpeting the extraordinary accomplishments of the free market under the banner "Meet the World's Newest Billionaires":

> As disillusion with socialism and other forms of statist economics spreads, private, personal initiative is being released to seek its destiny. Wealth, naturally, follows. The two big openings for free enterprise in this decade have come in Latin America and the Far East. Not surprisingly, the biggest clusters of new billionaires on our list have risen from the ferment of these two regions. Eleven new Mexican billionaires in two years, seven more ethnic Chinese. (p. 87)

Taking a slightly more populist view, *Business Week* presented a special report titled "A Millionaire a Minute" in its November 29, 1993, issue. It included this breathless account of what the free market has accomplished in Asia:

> Wealth. To most Asians just one generation ago, it meant moving to the U.S.—or selling natural resources to Japan. But now, East Asia is generating its own wealth on a speed and scale that probably is without historical precedent. The number of non-Japanese Asian multimillionaires is expected to double to 800,000 by 1996. . . . East Asia will surpass Japan in purchasing power within a decade. And with savings increasing $550 billion annually, it is becoming the world's biggest source of liquid capital. "In Asia," says Olarn Chaipravat, chief executive of Siam Commercial Bank, "money is everywhere." . . . There are new markets for everything from Mercedes Benz cars to Motorola mobile phones to Fidelity mutual funds. . . . To find the nearest precedent, you need to rewind U.S. history 100 years to the days before strong unions, securities watchdogs and antitrust laws. (pp. 100–102)

Such stories do not simply glorify the pursuit of greed, they perversely elevate it to the level of a personal religious mission. Never mind that although a few Asians have made vast fortunes and a tiny minority of

Asians have risen to the overconsumer class, the suffering of the 675 million Asians who live in absolute poverty continues unabated. In a special 1994 issue, "21st Century Capitalism," *Business Week* confirmed that market economics is a class issue and that the corporate libertarians are clear as to whose class interests they are advancing:

> The death throes of communism clearly gave birth to the new era, leaving most nations with only one choice—to join ... the market economy. ... Almost 150 years following the publication of the *Communist Manifesto*, and more than half a century after the rise of totalitarianism, the bourgeoisie has won. (pp. 13, 16)

The self-proclaimed "value-free objectivity" of economic rationalism aligns easily with the elitist moral philosophy of market liberalism. Seldom has this been more starkly revealed than in a widely publicized staff memo written by Lawrence Summers in his capacity as chief economist of the World Bank. Summers argued that it is economically most efficient for the rich countries to dispose of their toxic wastes in poor countries, because poor people have both shorter life spans and less earning potential than wealthy people.[20] In a subsequent commentary on the Summers memo, *The Economist* argued that it is a moral duty of the rich countries to export their pollution to poor countries because this provides poor people with economic opportunities of which they would otherwise be deprived.[21]

In another self-justifying twist of moral logic, economic rationalists commonly argue that rich countries best help poor countries by increasing their own consumption to increase demand for the exports of poor countries, thus stimulating their economic growth and lifting their poor up from poverty.[22] Denying or ignoring the existence of environmental limits, they maintain that there is no moral or practical basis for reducing the consumption of the rich to relieve the deprivation of the poor.[23] To the contrary, they argue, it is the moral duty of the rich to consume more to create more growth to provide more opportunities for the poor—a convenient rationalization for tax breaks for investors and the colonization of ever more of the world's resources to support self-indulgent consumption by those who can afford it. It is scarcely surprising that economic rationalism and market liberalism appeal to people of wealth.

If economic rationalists and market liberals had a serious allegiance to market principles and human rights, they would be calling for policies aimed at achieving the conditions in which markets function in a democratic fashion in the public interest. They would be calling for measures to end subsidies and preferential treatment for large corporations, break up corporate monopolies, encourage the distribution of property ownership, internalize social and environmental costs, root capital in place, secure the rights of workers to the just fruits of their labor, and limit opportunities to obtain extravagant individual incomes far greater than productive contributions.

Corporate libertarianism is not about creating the market conditions that market theory argues will result in optimizing the public interest. It is not about the public interest at all. It is about defending and institutionalizing the right of the economically powerful to do whatever best serves their immediate interests without public accountability for the consequences. It places power in institutions that are blind to issues of equity and environmental balance.

Millions of thoughtful, intelligent people who are properly suspicious of big government, believe in honest hard work, have deep religious values, and are committed to family and community are being deceived by the false information and the distorted intellectual and moral logic repeated constantly in the corporate-controlled media. They are being won over to a political agenda that runs counter to both their values and their interests. Those who work within our major corporate, academic, political, governmental, and other institutions find the culture and reward systems so strongly aligned with the corporate libertarian ideology that they dare not speak out in opposition for fear of jeopardizing their jobs and their careers. We must break through the veil of illusion and misrepresentation that is holding us in a self-destructive cultural trance and get on with the work of re-creating our economic systems in service to people and the living earth.

6 Decline of Democratic Pluralism

> *What an astounding thing it is to watch a civilisation destroy itself because it is unable to re-examine the validity under totally new circumstances of an economic ideology.*
>
> *—Sir James Goldsmith[1]*

The champions of corporate libertarianism gleefully greeted the disintegration of the Soviet empire in 1989 as a victory for the free market and a mandate to press forward their cause. Francis Fukuyama proclaimed that the long path of human evolution was reaching its ultimate conclusion—a universal, global consumer society. He called it the end of history.[2]

The governments and corporations of the West quickly reached out to urge Eastern Europe and the countries of the former Soviet Union to embrace the lessons of Western success by opening their borders and freeing their economies. Armies of Western experts were fielded to help these and other "transition states" write laws that would prepare the way for Western corporations to penetrate their economies.

Simultaneously, the industrial West intensified its effort to create a unified global economy through the General Agreement on Tariffs and Trade (GATT), establish a powerful World Trade Organization (WTO), and create regional markets through such initiatives as the North American Free Trade Agreement (NAFTA), Maastricht (the European common market), and the Asia-Pacific Economic Community (APEC). Anxious to please powerful corporate interests and lacking other viable ideas, U.S. President Bill Clinton embraced economic globalization as both his jobs program and his foreign policy.

Marxist socialism has indeed died an ignoble death. However, it is no more accurate to attribute the West's economic and political triumph to the unfettered marketplace than it is to blame the U.S.S.R.'s failure on an activist state. Contrary to the boastful claims of corporate libertarians, the West did not prosper in the post–World War II period by rejecting the state in favor of the market. Rather, it prospered by rejecting extremist ideologies of both Right and Left in favor of democratic pluralism: a system of governance based on a pragmatic, institutional balance among the forces of government, market, and civil society.

Driven by the imperatives of depression and war, America emerged from World War II with government, market, and civil society working together in a healthier, more dynamic, and more creative balance than at any time since the pre–Civil War years. A relatively egalitarian income distribution created an enormous mass market, which in turn drove aggressive industrial expansion. America certainly was far from socialist, but neither was it truly capitalist. We might more accurately call it pluralist. This is the America that readily withstood the challenges posed by the Soviet empire and emerged as the Cold War victor. The America of democratic pluralism and equality defeated communism, not "free" market America.

Although the specifics differed, similar patterns prevailed in most of the Western industrial democracies. Some moved more toward the public ownership and management of nationalized industries than others, but within a pluralistic framework in which both market and government were strong players.

In contrast, the Soviet system embraced an ideological extremism so strongly statist that the market and the private ownership of property were virtually eliminated. The same ideology resulted in the elimination of the governance role of civil society, leaving the state dominant and unaccountable. Lacking the pluralistic balance and civic accountability essential to a healthy society, the Soviet economy was both unresponsive to popular needs and inefficient in the use of resources. The consequent suffering of the Soviet people was not a consequence of an activist state. It was the consequence of an extremist ideology that excluded everything except the state.

The West is now heading down a similar extremist ideological path; the difference is that we are being driven to dependence on detached and unaccountable corporations rather than a detached and unaccountable state. It is ironic that the closer the corporate libertarians move us toward their ideological ideal of free-market capitalism, the greater the failure of the market regimes—for much the same reasons that the Marxist regimes failed:

- Both lead to the concentration of economic power in unaccountable centralized institutions—the state in the case of Marxism, and the transnational corporation in the case of capitalism.
- Both create economic systems that destroy the living systems of the earth in the name of economic progress.
- Both produce a disempowering dependence on mega-institutions that erodes the social capital on which the efficient function of markets, governments, and society depends.
- Both take a narrow economistic view of human needs that undermines the sense of spiritual connection to the earth and to the community of life that is essential to maintaining the moral fabric of society.

An economic system can remain viable only so long as society has mechanisms to counter abuses of either state or market power and the erosion of the natural, social, and moral capital that such abuses commonly exacerbate. Democratic pluralism isn't a perfect answer to the governance problem, but it seems to be the best we have discovered in our imperfect world.

Maintaining Competitive Markets

Although business often complains that government interferes unduly with its affairs, most calls for freeing the market ignore a basic reality: the efficient function of market economies depends on strong governments. This need is well established in contemporary market economic theory and has been demonstrated in practice. In their exhaustive critique of corporate libertarianism titled *For the Common Good*, Herman E. Daly and John Cobb Jr. set forth a list of conditions on which the market depends for its efficient function, yet which the market cannot provide for itself.[3]

Fair Competition. By its nature, competition creates winners and losers. Winners become more powerful as they grow. Losers disappear. The bigger the winners, the more difficult for new entrants to gain a foothold and the more monopolistic the market becomes. Even children who play the family board game Monopoly know how it works.

As the game progresses, Monopoly players acquire property on which they charge one another rent. Those who get property early in the game eventually drive the less fortunate bankrupt. The game officially ends when all players have gone bankrupt save one. Astute players know that anyone who arrives late and joins the game after others have acquired initial properties doesn't stand a chance. Most players drop out after one player gains a substantial advantage as there is no prospect of a clever or lucky player coming back from behind to win a surprise victory.

Real-world monopoly is much the same, except that the larger players have the additional advantage of being able to use their financial power to influence legislators to rewrite the rules of the game to give themselves even more advantage. The result is an inexorable tendency toward monopolization that can be restrained only by a firm government hand. Politicians are rarely willing to exert such a strong hand, however, without crisis and the demands of an active and well-organized civil society.

Moral Capital. Although market theory assumes self-interested individuals and real-world markets often reward greedy, dishonest, and immoral behavior, the day-to-day interactions of an efficient market depend on trust. A market in which participants are driven purely by greed and a desire to obtain momentary competitive advantage by any means—a market without trust, cooperation, compassion, and individual integrity—not only would be an unpleasant place to do business but also would be highly inefficient, requiring inordinate costs for lawyers, security guards, and other defensive measures. Neither a society nor a market economy can function efficiently without a moral foundation.

Public Goods. Many investments and services that are essential to the public good—such as investments in basic scientific research, public security and justice, public education, roads, and national defense—are not supplied by the market because once they have been produced, they are freely available for use by anyone. Even most corporate libertarians recognize a role for government in providing such public goods, especially those shared goods and services that are essential for the profitable function of private business. The actual work may be done by private contractors, but the bills must be paid by governments out of tax revenues.

Full-Cost Pricing. The market produces an optimal allocation of resources only when sellers and buyers bear the full cost of the products they produce, purchase, and consume. Rarely, if ever, will full costs be internalized in an unregulated market, because competitive pressures make it necessary to externalize costs whenever possible. A producer that successfully externalizes social and environmental costs will earn a higher profit and attract more investors and can offer a lower price and capture a greater market share. As its economic power increases, so too does its political influence, which is commonly translated into further subsidies. It is wonderful when a company discovers that there are inherent economic advantages in reducing its waste and paying workers a fair wage, but experience shows that there is nothing inherent in the workings of the market to ensure such behavior without active governmental intervention.

Just Distribution. In a market system, there is a strong tendency, especially during periods of economic expansion, for the owners of capital to increase their wealth and incomes while the incomes of those who sell their labor lag or decline. Yet a market in which economic power is unjustly distributed will allocate resources in an unjust and socially inefficient manner. Market efficiency and institutional legitimacy depend on governmental intervention to constantly restore the equity that the forces of the market inexorably erode.

Ecological Sustainability. As the human economy grows to fill its ecological space, limiting the scale of the economic subsystem to maintain an optimal balance with nature becomes necessary for species survival. Carbon dioxide emissions must be maintained below absorption levels. Fisheries harvests must be held to sustainable levels. Unfortunately, the free market is blind to countless such constraints. Government must set the limits and ensure that appropriate signals are sent to the market. Even proposed "market solutions" to environmental problems, such as pollution permits, depend on government intervention to set the limits, issue permits, and monitor compliance.

The market produces socially optimal outcomes *only* when government and civil society are empowered to act to maintain these six conditions for market efficiency. A market freed from governmental restraint is inherently unsustainable because it erodes its own institutional foundations.

The Corrosive Effects of Globalization

Market mechanisms are essential to modern societies. We must learn to use them in ways that recognize self-interest as an important and enduring human motivation and put it to work with maximum constructive benefit. At a minimum, this requires that business recognize and accept the need for effective action from agencies external to the market—usually government—to provide a context for the market that maintains these and other conditions on which market efficiency depends. It must also be accepted by both business and the public that when government intervenes to this end it may reduce corporate profits, limit the freedom of corporate action, and increase the prices of some consumer goods. The potential payoffs include good jobs that pay a living wage and protect the health and safety of workers and the community, a clean environment, economic stability, job security, and strong and secure families and communities.

There will also be cases of government inefficiency, just as there are cases of corporate inefficiency. It is appropriate to reduce the costs of such inefficiency both to taxpayers and to business. It is also appropriate to ensure that increases in consumer prices do not make it more difficult for people of modest incomes to meet their basic needs. However, we should *not* be concerned when governmental intervention in the public interest makes it more costly to consume things that we may not really need, reduces excessive corporate profits, and gives corporations fewer freedoms than people.

To play its essential role in relation to the market, a government must have jurisdiction over the economy within the borders of its territory. It must be able to set the rules for the domestic economy without having to prove to foreign governments and corporations that such rules are not barriers to international trade and investment. A government must be able to assess taxes and regulate the affairs of corporations that conduct business within its jurisdiction without being subject to corporate threats to withhold critical technologies or transfer jobs to foreign facilities. For such jurisdiction to be maintained, economic boundaries must coincide with political boundaries. If not, government becomes impotent, and democracy becomes a hollow facade. When the economy is global and governments are national, global corporations and financial institutions function largely beyond the reach of public accountability, governments become more vulnerable to inappropriate corporate influence, and citizenship is reduced to making consumer choices among the products corporations find it profitable to offer.

Domestic economies that favor locally owned businesses that serve community interests in ways that foreign producers and footloose investors cannot need not exclude imported goods and outside investors. Where they find benefits in foreign trade and investment, they should surely welcome them. But the people and their government have both the right and the need to be in control of their own economic lives. And they have every moral right to build economic speed bumps on their borders to create an advantage for local investment. Such a strategy worked for the Western nations during the post–World War II economic boom and resulted in the broad domestic sharing of economic benefits. It is a much sounder framework than corporate libertarianism offers.

It is instructive to reflect on what might have happened if we had emerged from World War II as a corporate libertarian (free-market capitalist) society rather than a pluralistic democracy. Rather than building a broad, stabilizing middle class that included a growing proportion of the working classes, the consequence would surely have been to deepen the division between super rich owners of capital and a deprived working class—the kind of division that had fueled earlier socialist movements in the United States and other Western countries.

Fortunately, Western societies did not succumb to ideological extremism of either the socialist or the capitalist stripe—at least not until the 1980s—and they prospered accordingly.

The Case of Sweden

Sweden is known among the Western industrial countries for its success in achieving prosperity and equity through mixing elements of both capitalist and socialist models within a strong framework of democratic pluralism. Sweden's experience offers instructive insights into the dynamics of pluralism and the consequences of globalization.

Few realize that industrialization came a hundred years later to Sweden than to England. And until the years following World War II, Sweden remained an extremely poor country. In the countryside, many people lived on small farms that, given the poor soil and climate, barely provided them a living. Some died in famines or emigrated. Many others, even well into this century, lived in serflike conditions on large estates. Illiteracy was widespread. In the late 1940s, it was still common for a family to live in an apartment consisting of one room plus a kitchen (toilet facilities were shared with other families). Even the Swedish royal house was relatively poor by the standards of most of its European cousins.[4]

Sweden's modern success was a creation of the Swedish Social Democratic Party, which melded and sustained a national consensus that kept it in power for forty-four years, from 1932 to 1976.[5] The Social Democrats built Sweden's elaborate social welfare system. Their wage policies brought working people into the middle class and created a substantial degree of wage equity and greater equity between the wages of women and men than in any other capitalist country.[6] The Social Democrats placed a high priority on maintaining full employment. To encourage Swedish transnational firms such as Volvo, Electrolux, Saab, and Ericsson to concentrate their operations in Sweden, the applicable real effective tax rate was much lower for profits generated in Sweden than for those generated abroad.[7]

An alliance between the major Swedish industrial corporations and organized labor served as the party's political base and supported the centralized and peaceful negotiation of wages and working conditions by national union and employers' organizations. This alignment produced significant benefits for both big labor and big capital. The arrangement had important structural flaws, however, that eventually destabilized it. One was a tax system that subsidized larger firms that were expanding and investing at the expense of small-scale and family firms. This led to increasing concentration and monopolization of ownership of the Swedish economy. Although wage policies stressed equality within the working class, the gap between the working class and those who controlled capital grew substantially. At the time, this was considered the price of maintaining the industrialists' commitment to the coalition. In the end, it brought about the coalition's destruction.[8]

When the first shock of rising oil prices hit in 1973–74, the resulting economic slowdown brought a fiscal crisis and triggered popular resistance to higher taxes. During this same period, Sweden was opening its economic borders and becoming a more active player in the international economy. This loosened the bonds that tied capital to local labor and weakened national labor movements.

In the early stages of globalization, the outward expansion of Swedish firms generated new employment at home, and the objectives of the two sides of the alliance did not significantly conflict. But once Sweden's transnationals began to define their own interests as global rather than national, the alliance between blue-collar workers and the owners of capital began to disintegrate. By this time, Sweden's highly educated white-collar workers outnumbered blue-collar workers, and the younger generation was taking the welfare state for granted—further weakening the political base of Sweden's Social Democrats.[9]

The growing contradiction between government support for the global expansion of Swedish transnationals and the need to create employment and rising real wages at home could no longer be sustained. In 1976, the Social Democrats lost the election to a three-party center-right coalition government.

When the Social Democrats returned to power in 1982, they were a chastened party intent on promoting policies that would allow Sweden's industrialists sufficient profit margins on domestic investment to keep them "believing in Sweden," a phrase coined by P. G. Gyllenhammar, the chairman of Volvo. Maintaining a belief in Sweden meant increasing the share of the national product going to profits compared with wages so that Sweden's industrialists would find it worthwhile to invest at home. This was accepted as the price of maintaining full employment at a time when unemployment elsewhere in Europe was running at 8 to 9 percent or higher.[10]

The resulting policies pushed corporate profits to previously unimaginable levels. With so much more money in their pockets than could be absorbed by productive investments, Swedish investors turned to speculation, driving up the prices of real estate, art, stamps, and other speculative goods. To stop the upward spiral, the government loosened monetary controls so that the excess funds could spill over into Europe. Money flowed out at such a rate that it helped push real estate prices in London and Brussels to record highs. As the speculative bubble fed on itself, the quick profits offered by speculation drained funds away from productive investments within Sweden. When the bubble in Swedish real estate finally burst, the Swedish banking system lost $18 billion. The bill was picked up by the state and passed on to the Swedish taxpayers.[11]

During this period, Sweden's major industrialists played an active role in dismantling the "Swedish model" that had been constructed by the Social Democratic alliance. The Swedish Employers' Federation rejected centralized wage bargaining, which had been one of the model's cornerstones, and allied itself with the Conservative Party. It also bankrolled think tanks espousing a corporate libertarian economic ideology and conducted a major public-relations effort praising individualism and the free market while denouncing the Social Democratic state as oppressive and inept.[12] This led to a weakening of the political apparatus of the state and its ability to define long-term policies.

In 1983, Volvo chairman P. G. Gyllenhammar stepped in to fill the void by forming the Roundtable of European Industrialists, made up of the heads of the leading European transnationals, including Fiat, Nestlé, Philips, Olivetti, Renault, and Siemens. The purpose was to define long-term policies for the state and to serve as an international lobby to press for their implementation.[13]

By the end of 1992, the richest 2 percent of Swedish households owned 62 percent of the value of the shares traded on the Stockholm stock exchange and 23 percent of all wealth in the country. While the average Swedish household grew poorer from 1978 to 1988, the richest 450 households doubled their assets.[14] Unemployment had been below 3 percent when the Social Democrats were first voted out of office.[15] It rose to 5 percent in 1992 and was projected to reach 7 percent, even though another 7 percent of the workforce was already engaged in countercyclical retraining programs and public employment projects.

From the beginning, the Swedish model contained the seeds of its own destruction. It built a powerful financial elite whose interests were far removed from those of the majority middle class. It bred a sense of welfare complacency among the Swedish people. It failed to install in the younger generation an awareness of democracy's need to be continually re-created through constant citizen vigilance and political activism. And its prosperity had been built on the unsustainable exploitation of Sweden's natural resources of timber, iron ore, and hydroelectric power.

As the elites gained more financial power, they were able to pyramid their claims on the resources of society without making a corresponding productive contribution. As the economic borders were opened, the jobs of those who depended on earning wages for doing productive work became hostage to those who controlled capital. The more the government, in its desperation to keep jobs at home, gave in to the demands of the financial elites, the greater the amount of money that passed into their hands, the greater their power to dictate public policy in their own interest, and the greater the stresses on the social fabric. The parallels to the U.S. experience examined in Part III are striking.

The Swedish experience reveals a lesson of fundamental importance: democratic pluralism cannot long survive extreme inequality.

The Need for Creative Balance

In our complex modern world, a society ruled by a single sector is inevitably dysfunctional. The institutions of the civic, governmental, and market sectors each have their necessary roles in serving the needs of a well-functioning society.

Civic Sector. The civic or citizen sector is composed of a vast array of alliances of people acting to demand their rights and to fulfill their responsibilities as citizens. Such alliances include, among others, the many *representational organizations* that serve personal-interest constituencies—such as labor unions that represent workers, medical associations that represent doctors, or groups such as the NAACP that represent African Americans. They also include the countless *voluntary organizations* that organize around shared values to advance a public-interest commitment.

In their political roles, civic organizations supplement political parties as varied and flexible mechanisms through which citizens define and articulate a broad range of interests, meet local needs, and make demands on government. In their educational roles, they provide training grounds for democratic citizenship, develop the political skills of their members, recruit and train new political leaders, stimulate political participation, and educate the broader public on a wide variety of public-interest issues. In their watchdog roles, they serve, along with the press, as checks on what Larry Diamond described as "the relentless tendency of the state to centralize its power and to evade civic accountability and control."[16] The civic sector is the foundation of democratic societies. To a substantial degree, citizen organizations and networks are replacing the increasingly corporate-dominated press in the function of public watchdog.

Although it is civil society that grants the mega-institutions of government and the market their power, the institutions of the civic sector are themselves more limited in their ability to amass concentrations of political and economic power. Unlike the institutions of government and the market, which derive their power from their size and financial resources, the strength of the civic sector is found in the number and diversity of its organizations and the speed and flexibility with which they form complex and shifting alliances around shared values and interests. Through such alliances, civic organizations can achieve powerful scale and leverage.

The cacophony of competing voices within an active civil society can be deafening. However, the ability of civic organizations to form alliances around clearly defined public-interest agendas gives them a distinctive role as catalysts of values-based social innovation—defining, articulating, advocating, and building constituencies for positions that may eventually find their way into the political mainstream.

Governmental Sector. Government is the one sector to which society gives the authority to use coercive power in the public interest. Society cedes to government the power to confiscate assets and to deprive a person of physical liberty and even life. In a democracy, this authority is freely, if reluctantly, granted by the citizens—who have the right to withdraw it at their discretion. It is the legitimate exercise of coercive power that gives government its ability to meet essential needs to maintain public order and national security, collect taxes, and reallocate society's resources to meet public needs—such as the need for sufficient equity to maintain the legitimacy and viability of society's institutions.

Government also has important incapacities. Because of its ability to command resources, it is insulated from market forces and the discipline those forces impose. Thus government is generally less efficient in the production of goods and services than are organizations whose survival depends on their ability to compete in the marketplace. Government's competence is in reallocating wealth—an essential social function—not in creating it.

Governments are political organizations and respond to political power. Even democratic governments serve the public interest only when political power is widely shared within a strong and politically active civil society.

Market Sector. The market sector properly specializes in functions involving economic exchange—producing goods and services for sale in response to market demand. The market has a distinctive competence in creating new wealth through value-added activities and is society's primary source of essential economic entrepreneurship and technological innovation.

However, markets don't tell people with substantial incomes to consume no more than their rightful share of ecosystem resources. They don't tell retailers not to sell guns to children. They don't tell producers that their wastes must be recycled. They don't give priority in the allocation of scarce resources to the basic needs of those with little or no money before providing luxuries for those who have great wealth. Indeed, in each instance, they generally do exactly the opposite.

Markets respond to money and financial values. They do not distinguish between profits earned from the efficient production of goods and unearned profits gained by exercising monopoly power, externalizing social and environmental costs onto the community, privatizing common property resources, or creating artificial demand through marketing campaigns for unnecessary and even harmful products. In other words, markets are blind to many of the needs of healthy human societies and often encourage behaviors exactly contrary to fundamental human interests—and even to the needs of the market itself.

Furthermore, when market power becomes concentrated in very large corporations, these acquire a distinctive form of coercive power that civil society never intended them to have—the power to deprive people of their means of livelihood. This power represents a social dysfunction that only a democratically accountable government can correct.

There is no substitute in a complex modern society for the market as an efficient mechanism for setting most prices, motivating productive activity, and processing routine economic transactions. However, although markets are useful institutions for *implementing* public priorities, they are inappropriate institutions for *setting* them.

Democratic pluralism melds the forces of the market, government, and civil society to maintain a dynamic balance among the often competing societal needs for essential order and equity, the efficient production of goods and services, the accountability of power, the protection of human freedom, and continuing institutional innovation. This balance finds expression in the *regulated* market, not the *free* market, and in trade policies that link national economies to one another within a framework of rules that maintains domestic competition and *favors* domestic enterprises that employ local workers, meet local standards, pay local taxes, and function within a robust system of democratic governance.

The order of precedence among the three primary sectors is fundamental to the healthy and balanced function of society. A civic sector without government and an organized market is anarchy. This is why civil societies create governments and organized markets. Civil society is, however, the first sector. The authority and legitimacy of all other human institutions flow from it. Since government is the body through which citizens establish and maintain the rules within which the market will function in the human interest, government is appropriately viewed as the second sector. The institutions of the market appropriately function as the third sector.

Globalizing national economies and giving free reign to corporate power invert this order. The market becomes the first sector, government becomes subordinated to corporate interests, and the ability of civil society to hold government accountable to the public interest is seriously weakened. When the market reigns, the corporation is king.

Playing by Different Rules

One of the most basic rules of market economics is that participants in market transactions must bear the full costs of their decisions—in addition to reaping the benefits. In practice, market players commonly go to considerable lengths to capture the benefits of success for themselves and pass the costs to others. This creates a tension between what efficient markets require and what self-interested market participants are prone to do.

Market players are attracted to the corporation as a form of business organization specifically because the legal nature and structure of the corporation tend to exempt both the corporation and its decision makers from accountability for many of the costs of their activities. Actual shareholders, the real owners, rarely have any voice in corporate affairs and bear no personal liability beyond the value of their investments. Directors and officers are protected from financial liability for acts of negligence or commission by insurance policies paid for by the corporation. The generous compensation of top mangers bears little relation to performance, and they are rarely prosecuted for the illegal acts of the corporation. Acts that would bring stiff prison sentences or even death for individuals result—at worst—in small fines for corporations that are generally inconsequential in relation to corporate assets.[17] Civil liability suits pose perhaps the greatest threat to corporate malfeasance, but even here, corporations can marshal massive legal resources in their own defense and they aggressively seek legislation further limiting their liability; if they lose, insurance companies may pick up the tab. It is with good reason that William M. Dugger characterizes the corporation as "organized irresponsibility."[18]

Unlike real people, who are all eventually rendered equal by the grave and whose fortunes are subject to confiscation by inheritance taxes, corporations are able to grow and reproduce themselves without limit, "living" and amassing power indefinitely. Eventually, that power evolves beyond the ability of any mere human to control, and the corporation becomes an autonomous entity unto itself, using its power to "create its own culture, using the lens of career to focus corporate culture on profit, size, and power."[19] Those who serve the corporate interest are well rewarded and derive substantial personal power from their positions. But in the end, their power is conferred by the corporation, and they serve the corporation's interest at the corporation's pleasure.

No real person can begin to match the political resources that a large corporation is able to amass in its own behalf. Corporations may lack the right to vote, but that is a minor inconvenience, given their ability to mobilize hundreds of thousands of votes from among their workers, suppliers, dealers, customers, and the public.

The corporate charter remains a useful social innovation that allows us to meet needs that could not be met through other forms of organization. However, like most technologies, it is subject to abuse and has a tendency to take on a life of its own quite apart from the human interest. Left to their own devices, corporations colonize markets and defeat the very mechanisms that theory tells us make the market work in the human interest. We might consider corporations to be *anti*market institutions. Thus it is fully appropriate that citizens view corporations with the same skepticism as the early American settlers did, granting corporate charters judiciously, setting clear rules for their function, and holding them accountable for their actions. Most important of all, we must get corporations out of politics.

The owners and managers of corporations have the full rights of any citizen—in their capacity as citizens—to participate in defining public goals and policies. However, corporations themselves, as nonhuman legal entities created to serve the public interest, have no place using their resources to influence the processes by which citizens define the public interest and set the rules of corporate conduct. Corporations are not people. They are alien to the ways of life and blind to the complex nonmaterial needs of human societies. They should be wholly barred from any form of political participation—a point elaborated in Part VI.

A corporate charter represents a privilege—not a right—that is extended in return for the acceptance of corresponding obligations. It is up to the people, the members of civil society—not the fictitious persona of the corporation—to define these privileges and obligations.

We are learning through harsh experience that the survival of democracy depends on holding firmly to this principle.

It is a profound paradox that extremist ideologies become most attractive during times of uncertainty, when rapid change is making old solutions obsolete. At such times, people have an understandable craving for the security of the simple, self-justifying prescriptions of ideological demagogues. Yet this is also the time when societies can least afford the rigidity, the self-justifying interpretation of failure, and the suppression of debate and experimentation that are the hallmarks of ideological extremism.

Democratic pluralism faces a related paradox. It is during such times of change that societies most need the full creative potential of their citizens that only democratic pluralism can release. Yet it is in such stressful times that, from a psychological standpoint, democratic pluralism seems least adequate and most susceptible to the certainty offered by the simplistic appeals of ideological demagogues. Instead of offering direction, democratic pluralism calls on people to find their own direction with a view to the good of the whole. Instead of certainty, it nurtures variety to the point of apparent chaos. These are its weakness, but also its genius. Democratic pluralism provides a framework within which each citizen contributes what he or she can toward addressing—in the context of family, community, and nation—the countless changing needs faced by complex and dynamic human societies. Gradually, through a diffuse and chaotic social learning process, the lessons from countless innovations are distilled into changes in local, national, and ultimately global institutions and policies.

Democratic pluralism provides the institutional framework within which people can bring to bear their full creative powers toward finding innovative solutions to shared problems and, in the process, recreate societies that are responsive to the challenges of the coming ecological age. We need that creative power now as never before.

7 Illusions of the Cloud Minders

This troubled planet is a place of the most violent con-
trasts. Those that receive the rewards are totally sepa-
rated from those who shoulder the burdens. It is not a
wise leadership.
                    —Spock, *"The Cloud Minders,"* Star Trek[1]

With the information technologies already available,
I can sit on the beach of my Florida home with a laptop
computer and a cellular telephone and monitor the
video images installed throughout my manufacturing
company in Ohio to insure that my people are on the
job and doing their work properly.
                    —*Interview with company owner on*
            U.S. National Public Radio, August 31, 1994

"The Cloud Minders," episode 74 of the popular science fiction television series *Star Trek*, took place
on the planet Ardana. First aired on February 28, 1969,
it depicted a planet whose rulers devoted their lives to
the arts in a beautiful and peaceful city, Stratos, sus-
pended high above the planet's desolate surface. Down
below, the inhabitants of the planet's surface, the Troglytes, worked in misery and violence in the planet's
mines to earn the interplanetary exchange credits used
to import from other planets the luxuries the rulers
enjoyed on Stratos. In this modern allegory, an entire
planet had been colonized by rulers who successfully
detached and isolated themselves from the people and
the localities of the planet's surface on whose toil their
luxuries depended.

The imagery of this *Star Trek* episode has stuck vividly in my mind. How like our own world it is, where

the truly rich and powerful work in beautifully appointed executive suites in tall office towers; travel to meetings by limousine and helicopter; jet between continents high above the clouds, pampered with the finest wines by an attentive crew; and live in protected estates, affluent suburbs, and penthouse suites amid art, beauty, and a protected environment. They are as insulated from the lives of the ordinary people of our planet as those who lived on Stratos were insulated from the lives of the Troglytes. They too are living in a world of illusion, dependent on draining the world of its resources and so isolated from reality that they know not what they do, nor how else to live.

The Magic Market

The isolation of the rich and powerful is exemplified by the annual gathering of the directors of the World Bank and the International Monetary Fund (IMF). The following is an account by journalist Graham Hancock from one such meeting:

> I had come [to Washington, D.C.] simply to attend the joint annual meeting of the Boards of Governors of the World Bank and the International Monetary Fund—two institutions that play a central role in mobilizing and disbursing funds for impoverished developing countries. . . . The total cost of the 700 social events laid on for delegates during that single week was estimated at $10 million. . . . A single formal dinner catered by Ridgewells cost $200 per person. Guests began with crab cakes, caviare and *crème fraîche*, smoked salmon and mini beef Wellingtons. The fish course was lobster with corn rounds followed by citrus sorbet. The *entrée* was duck with lime sauce, served with artichoke bottoms filled with baby carrots. A hearts of palm salad was also offered accompanied by sage cheese soufflés with a port wine dressing. Dessert was a German chocolate turnip sauced with raspberry coulis, ice-cream bonbons and flaming coffee royale. . . . Washington limousine companies were doing a roaring trade.[2]

At the same meeting that favored its delegates with $10 million worth of lavish meals and social events, Barber Conable, the former U.S. congressman and then recently appointed president of the World Bank, presented the following charge to the 10,000 men and women present:

Our institution is mighty in resources and in experience but its labours will count for nothing if it cannot look at our world through the eyes of the most underprivileged, if we cannot share their hopes and their fears. We are here to serve their needs, to help them realise their strength, their potential, their aspirations. . . . Collective action against global poverty is the common purpose that brings us together today. Let us therefore rededicate ourselves to the pursuit of that great good.[3]

If the delegates had indeed made an effort to look at their world through the eyes of the most underprivileged, they might well have lost their appetites. Take, for example, this simple interview with a sharecropper's child in nearby Selma, Alabama, by Raymond Wheeler of CBS TV:

"Do you eat breakfast before school?"
"Sometimes, sir. Sometimes I have peas."
"And when you get to school, do you eat?"
"No, sir."
"Isn't there any food there?"
"Yes, sir."
"Why don't you have it?"
"I don't have the 35 cents."
"What do you do while the other children eat lunch?"
"I just sits there on the side" (his voice breaking).
"How do you feel when you see the other children eating?"
"I feel ashamed" (crying).[4]

Far from encouraging delegates to see the world through the eyes of the poor, the organizers of the World Bank–IMF meetings take great care to shield them from the specter of poverty.

The World Bank and IMF are leading proponents of economic rationalism and free-market, export-led growth strategies. They have for years been lauding South Korea, Taiwan, Singapore, and Hong Kong as examples of success. Thus when the directors met in Bangkok, Thailand, in October 1991, it was natural that the meeting serve as a celebration of the recent "success" story of free-market, export-led growth in Thailand.

No expense or inconvenience was spared by Thailand's government to impress the delegates that Thailand had arrived as a full member of the elite club of newly industrialized nations (NICs). To ensure the desired impression, a shiny new convention complex was rushed to completion in downtown Bangkok to host the conference. Two hundred families were evicted from their homes to widen roads to and from the site.[5] A nearby squatter settlement was leveled so that the delegates would not be troubled by unpleasant views of Bangkok's poverty. Schools and government offices were closed to limit traffic congestion and help clear the air of emissions so that the delegates might rush with the least inconvenience, free of respiratory distress in their air-conditioned cars, between elegant cocktail parties and official dinners along routes chosen—and walled off, where necessary— to avoid disconcerting views of Bangkok's slums. English-speaking engineers, doctors, and lawyers were pressed into service as drivers for the delegates; nurses and teachers waited tables in the conference restaurants to ensure that instructions were understood and that no need of a visiting dignitary would go unmet.

Such cosmetic measures could only partially hide the reality that Bangkok, a once beautiful city, has been ravaged by the consequences of its development "success." Amidst shining shopping malls, high-rise office buildings, and luxury hotels, filth and squalor abound. Three hundred thousand new vehicles are added to Bangkok's monumental traffic jams each year, slowing traffic to an average of less than ten kilometers (about six miles) per hour. On more than 200 days a year, air pollution in Bangkok exceeds maximum World Health Organization safety limits, and emissions are increasing by 14 percent a year.[6]

The World Bank–IMF meeting in Thailand was a fitting metaphor for the illusion within which the world's power holders live. The illusion is maintained in part through the construction of a life of luxury set apart in enclaves, and in part by self-justifying belief systems, such as corporate libertarianism, and by the adulation of wealth and the wealthy by the business press and a plethora of economic researchers and consultants. Most of all, it is maintained by the dysfunctions of an economic system that lavishes rich rewards on power holders for decisions that place terrible burdens on the rest of humanity.

The Great Divide

The gap that separates the world's rich and poor, both within and between countries, is unconscionable and growing. In 1992, the United Nations Development Programme (UNDP) dramatized the inequity by representing the world's income distribution with a graph in the shape of a champagne glass.[7]

As shown in Figure 7.1, the 20 percent of the world's people who live in the world's wealthiest countries receive 82.7 percent of the world's income; only 1.4 percent of the world's income goes to the 20 percent who live in the world's poorest countries. In 1950—about

Figure 7.1 Global Income Distribution

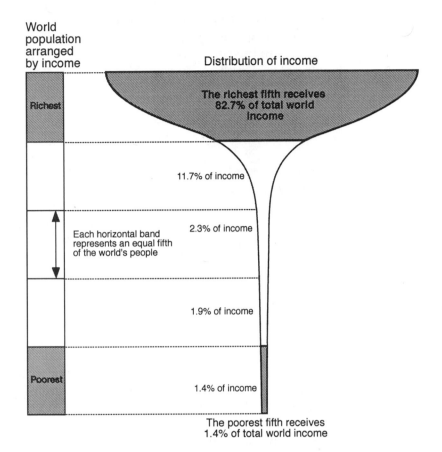

Source: UNDP, *Human Development Report 1992* (New York: Oxford University Press, 1992).

the time the commitment was made to globalize the development process—the average income of the 20 percent of people living in the wealthiest countries was about thirty times that of the 20 percent living in the poorest countries. By 1989, this ratio had doubled to sixty times.

Based on national averages, these figures represent disparities among countries and substantially understate the disparity among people. For example, all Americans are placed in the world's top income category—including the homeless, the rural poor, and the urban slum dwellers. When the UNDP estimated the global distribution based on individual incomes rather than on national averages, the average income of the top 20 percent was 150 times that of the lowest 20 percent.

Even this figure masks the extreme inequity revealed when the incomes of the top 20 percent are desegregated. Although global data are not available, data from the United States illustrate the point. In 1989, the top 20 percent of American households had an average income of $109,424 a year.[8] However, those households in the eightieth to ninetieth percentiles received, on average, a relatively modest $65,900. Those in the top 1 percent averaged $559,795—receiving as a group more total income than the bottom 40 percent of all Americans.[9]

Yet even this is mere pocket change to Wall Street investment brokers such as the infamous Michael Milken, who in one year took home a cool half billion dollars for his labors selling junk bonds on Wall Street, and to the chief executives officers (CEOs) of America's major corporations and the top earning celebrities. In 1992, Thomas F. Frist Jr., CEO of Hospital Corporation of America, led the pack of overpaid American executives with $127 million, nearly 780,000 times the average $163 per capita income of the poorest 20 percent of the world's people! The 1992 average take of the CEOs of the 1,000 largest corporations surveyed by *Business Week* was $3.8 million—up 42 percent from the previous year. Furthermore, the gap between the pay of top executives and the pay of those who work for them is growing rapidly.[10] In 1960, the average CEO of a major company received forty times the compensation of the average worker. In 1992, he (there were only two women among *Business Week*'s top 1,000 CEOs) received 157 times as much.[11]

These well-paid executives are, however, only pretenders to wealth compared with the wealth of those who live by the earnings of their investment portfolios. *Forbes*'s "four hundred richest people in America" enjoyed an increase in their combined net worth of $92 billion between 1982 and 1993, bringing them to a total of $328 billion[12]—more than the combined 1991 gross national products (GNPs) shared by a billion people living in India, Bangladesh, Sri Lanka, and Nepal.[13]

Eager to assure its wealthy readers that their good fortune was not at the expense of others, *Forbes* prefaced its inventory of the wealthiest Americans with the following caveat:

Aha! Then the redistributionists are right. The rich have gotten richer. Yes and no. The truly rich may have gotten richer, but there's no evidence that their proportionate share of the nation's wealth has grown. The price of admission to the Forbes Four Hundred has increased approximately as much as the stock market, as measured by the Dow Jones index. The tremendous increase in the stock market—which has rubbed off nicely on the super rich—rubs off on every pension holder and shareholder in America as well. . . .

Weep not for the rich. But don't get the dumb idea that they have gotten rich off the rest of us.[14]

Surely there were some widows and pensioners of modest means among the beneficiaries of the stock market gains. However, the protestation of *Forbes* (a publication of and for the Stratos dwellers) that equity has been maintained is but one manifestation of the isolation of the Stratos dwellers and their belief that their world is *the* world. The 400 richest Americans may not have increased their share of total stock wealth, but apart from stocks owned by pension funds, 83.1 percent of the stock market wealth owned by American households is owned by the wealthiest 10 percent. Moreover, 37.4 percent of stock wealth is owned by the richest 0.5 percent.[15]

From 1977 to 1989, the average real income of the top 1 percent of U.S. families increased by 78 percent, whereas that of the bottom 20 percent *decreased* by 10.4 percent.[16] Thus the poorest among us became not only relatively poorer but also absolutely poorer. What these figures don't tell us is that these absolute decreases occurred in spite of the fact that those who were employed in 1989 were working longer hours than they had in 1977, and far more families had two people working full time as more women entered the workforce. For many U.S. families among the bottom 60 percent, even longer hours and an extra breadwinner were not enough to make up for the decline in wages.

The simple truth that the *Forbes* editors and other Stratos dwellers are prone to ignore is that each time a major corporation announces a cutback of thousands of jobs, the Stratos families get richer and the incomes of the thousands of workers whose jobs have been eliminated decline. It is part of an ongoing process of shifting wealth and economic power from those who are engaged in the production of real value to those who already have large amounts of money and believe that it is their right to increase those amounts without limit, regardless of their own needs or productive contributions.

Is it possible for those who sip from the lip of the champagne glass to truly appreciate the lot of the vast mass of humanity that shares only the meager dregs that settle into the stem? If they were to acknowledge that their own abundance is the cause of the plight of those so deprived, could any person bear the terrible moral burden? There is substantial incentive to avoid facing such moral contradictions by maintaining the reassuring cultural illusions of Stratos.

A Different World

Forbes prefaced its 1993 listing of the 400 richest people in America
with an article on the struggle of the very rich to make ends meet in
today's economy. In one year's time, the price of a one-kilo tin of be-
luga malossol caviar had increased by 28 percent to $1,408. A Sikorsky
S-780 helicopter with full executive options had increased 8 percent
to $7 million. And a suitable night's hotel lodging in New York was up
15 percent to $750.[17] Theirs is a different world.

When Henry Kissinger, long one of the most influential players in
U.S. foreign policy circles, takes his dog, Amelia, with him on his
morning constitutional, a bodyguard follows behind to handle the
scooper duties. When Henry goes on vacation, Amelia rides by limousine to Mrs. Peepers' kennel in rural Maryland, where she stays as a
houseguest in a private room.[18] Many Americans were amused when
the press caught George Bush gazing in wonder at a grocery checkout
scanner and realized that he was one of the last people in the United
States to encounter this addition to the checkout routine.

When Alexander Trotman assumed the post of chairman, president, and CEO of Ford Motor Company in 1993, he was responsible
for making more than 3 million vehicles a year. Yet he did not own a
car of his own and had never bought one from a dealer. Ford, as is
common practice in the auto industry, provides all its top executives
with new cars—ensuring that they always have cars that are in perfect
working order without ever having the experience of negotiating with
a dealer and hassling with registration, insurance, repairs, and maintenance.[19]

In 1989, Lone Star Industries took a $271 million loss. Its CEO James
E. Stewart ordered layoffs, sold off $400 million of corporate assets,
eliminated the dividend to stockholders, and told his managers to fly
coach. Yet he maintained a $2.9 million expense account for himself
and continued to commute in the corporate jet between his home in
Florida and the company headquarters in Stamford, Connecticut. As
CEO of RJR Nabisco, F. Ross Johnson built a palatial hangar in Atlanta to house the corporation's ten planes and twenty-six corporate
pilots. Next door he built a three-story VIP lounge complete with inlaid
mahogany walls, Italian marble floors, and an atrium with a Japanese
garden.[20] Ivan Boesky, the global financier, was known to order eight
entrées from the menu at the exclusive Café des Artistes, sample each,
and then decide which he would eat.[21]

In June of 1991, I attended the annual conference of the American
Forum for Global Education in Hartford, Connecticut. Ed Pratt, the

chairman and CEO of Pfizer, Inc., a drug and medical products producer with annual worldwide sales of $7 billion, was an opening speaker. He received an award for his contributions to global education and shared his insights on educational needs with several hundred American educators, telling them that the education of young Americans must focus on giving them the greatest competitive edge in the new global economy. In his view, there was no time for unnecessary frills—such as studying foreign languages. He reported that in his travels around Pfizer's world operations, he found that everyone with whom there was any need to talk already spoke English. So he advised that the classroom hours that children in other countries spend learning English be devoted to teaching American students science and economics.

Nike, a major footwear company, refers to itself as a "network firm." This means that it employs 8,000 people in management, design, sales, and promotion and leaves production in the hands of some 75,000 workers hired by independent contractors. Most of the outsourced production takes place in Indonesia, where a pair of Nikes that sells in the United States or Europe for $73 to $135 is produced for about $5.60 by girls and young women paid as little as fifteen cents an hour. The workers are housed in company barracks, there are no unions, overtime is often mandatory, and if there is a strike, the military may be called to break it up. The $20 million that basketball star Michael Jordan reportedly received in 1992 for promoting Nike shoes exceeded the entire annual payroll of the Indonesian factories that made them.[22]

When asked about the conditions at plants where Nikes are produced, John Woodman, Nike's general manager in Indonesia, gave a classic Stratos-dweller response. Although he knew that there had been labor problems in the six Indonesian factories making Nike shoes, he had no idea what they had been about. Furthermore, he said, "I don't know that I need to know. It's not within our scope to investigate."[23]

The Nike case is a striking example of the distortions of an economic system that shifts rewards away from those who produce real value to those whose primary function is to create marketing illusions to convince consumers to buy products they do not need at inflated prices. It is little wonder that many managers, like the Nike manager who avoided contact with Indonesian workers, prefer to avoid talking to too many people outside the elite circles.

It seems fitting that in 1993 the winner in the annual executive compensation package sweepstakes was master illusionist Michael Eisner, chairman of the Walt Disney Company—a corporation dedicated to the creation of fantasy worlds. Eisner's compensation package of $203.1

million equaled 68 percent of the company's total profits of $299.8 million for that year—surely ample to create a few personal illusions of his own.[24]

This is the cloud world in which the architects of the global economic order live. For themselves and their corporations, local markets become too confining. No amount of wealth and power is enough. They must constantly push new frontiers, build new empires, and colonize new markets. There is good reason to conclude that people who are so isolated from the daily reality of those they rule are ill prepared to define the public interest.

Redefining North—South

Great wealth and the embrace of a world of illusion are not found only in "wealthy" countries. The *Forbes* 1993 directory of the world's wealthiest people listed eighty-eight billionaires from low- and middle-income countries, up from sixty-two only a year earlier. Mexico headed the list with twenty-four billionaires in 1993, up from thirteen in 1992.[25]

Consider the Philippines, a poor economic performer by the standards of East and Southeast Asia. Its per capita GNP is $730, and an estimated 60 percent of its people lack adequate incomes to provide even a minimum healthy diet for themselves and their families. *Forbes* listed two Philippine billionaires in 1992 and five in 1993.

From 1988 to 1992, I worked from an office located on the eleventh floor of a high-rise building in Makati, the commercial and financial center of Manila, the capital city of the Philippines. From my window I looked out on three of Manila's five-star hotels and a number of high-rise bank buildings. Almost any time of the day I could see one or more private helicopters ferrying Manila's business elites to and from the tops of these high-rise buildings far above the cars stalled in Manila's legendary traffic jams and the lines of carless commuters waiting amidst thick diesel fumes for public transportation. On the other side of Manila, thousands of less fortunate Filipinos had built their shacks of scavenged materials on top of Smokey Mountain, a steaming garbage dump, and made their livings picking through the stinking mountain of garbage for bottles, bits of plastic, and other salable items.

Hundreds of thousands of Filipinos go abroad each year in a desperate search for work to sustain themselves and their families. Many of the women arrive in Japan to work as "entertainers" or take jobs as household servants in the Middle East. They commonly find themselves working under conditions of virtual slavery and the objects of sexual exploitation. The Philippine government considers its overseas workers to be an essential source of foreign exchange earnings to pay for, among other things, imports to stock the country's luxurious, air-conditioned mega-malls with advanced consumer electronics and designer fashions and to service the country's $32 billion foreign debt.

In an earlier day, when economies were defined by national borders and even by individual localities, rich and poor alike who lived within the borders of a nation or a town generally shared a sense of national and community interest. No matter how great the conflicts among them might be, their destinies intertwined. Industrialists had a stake in the educational system that produced their workers and in the physical infrastructure of transportation and other public facilities on which their productive enterprises depended. No matter how begrudgingly, they accepted the obligation to pay taxes to help support essential social and physical infrastructure.

In recent years, one of the demographic realities of the United States has been an increasing geographical segregation by income. Those in the upper income brackets have been clustering in affluent suburban communities organized as independent political jurisdictions, where they share facilities only with members of their own affluent class. Thus, they are able to finance good schools and other public services without the need for additional taxes to contribute toward providing similar facilities for lower-income families. Low-income families thus become similarly clustered in low-income jurisdictions that have a far greater need for social services than the wealthier clusters but lack the tax base to finance them.[26]

The consequences of this separation by political jurisdiction were exacerbated in the United States during the 1980s when the federal government began shifting greater responsibility to local jurisdictions for funding social services. In 1978, when federal transfers to local governments peaked, almost 27 percent of state and local funding came from federal grants. By 1988, federal funding had fallen to 17 percent. This was all part of a larger effort by the Reagan administration to dismantle the income-redistribution mechanisms that earlier administrations had put into place during America's era of democratic pluralism. Robert Reich refers to it as the secession by the privileged few from the rest of America. The result has been a growing gap in the quality of education and other public services enjoyed by rich and poor; a deepening of the class divide, commonly exacerbated by racial lines; and an increasing isolation of the wealthy in their worlds of illusion.[27]

Of any country I have visited, Pakistan most starkly exemplifies the experience of elites living in enclaves detached from local roots. The country's three modern cities—Karachi, Lahore, and Islamabad—feature enclaves of five-star hotels, modern shopping malls, and posh residential areas within a poor and feudalistic countryside governed by local lords who support private armies with profits from a thriving drug and arms trade and are inclined to kill any central government official who dares to enter. Health and education indicators for Pakistan's rural areas are comparable to those for the most deprived African nations.

On two of my visits to Pakistan, I was the guest of some of the country's most successful businessmen. Widely traveled and graduates of the best British and American universities, they spoke and moved with the confidence, demeanor, and sense of hospitality typical of cosmopolitan aristocrats who are fully at ease with their money and position. My hosts regularly traveled the world to supervise their widespread business interests, moving easily among the global business elites and feeling as much at home in New York or London as in Karachi, Lahore, or Islamabad.

Particularly striking, however, was the extent to which—in contrast to their knowledge of and interest in the rest of the world—they had little knowledge of or interest in what was happening in their own country beyond the borders of their enclave cities. It was as though the rest of Pakistan were an inconsequential foreign country unworthy of notice or mention. They were almost completely detached from any sense of national interest. What I failed to realize at the time was that this phenomenon was not an aberration of underdevelopment so much as the cutting edge of a global social and political trend—a melding of the world's financial elites into a stateless community in the clouds, detached from the world in which the vast majority of ordinary mortals live.

We have long thought of the world as divided into rich and poor countries. As economic globalization progresses, we find growing islands of great wealth in poor countries and growing seas of poverty in rich countries. The North and South distinction is now most meaningfully used to acknowledge the reality of a world divided by class lines more than by geography.

A Self-Destructing System

The global economic system is rewarding corporations and their executives with generous profits and benefits packages for contracting out their production to sweatshops paying substandard wages, for clear-cutting primal forests, for introducing labor-saving technologies that displace tens of thousands of employees, for dumping toxic wastes, and for shaping political agendas to advance corporate interests over human interests. The system shields those who take such actions from the costs of their decisions, which are borne by the system's weaker members—the displaced workers who no longer have jobs, the replacement workers who are paid too little to feed their families, the forest dwellers whose homes have been destroyed, the poor who live next to the toxic dumps, and the unorganized taxpayers who pick up the bills. The consequence of delinking benefits from their costs is that the system is telling the world's most powerful decision makers that their decisions are creating new benefits, when in fact they are simply shifting more of the earth's available wealth to themselves at the expense of people and the planet.

Systems theorists, who concern themselves with understanding the dynamics of complex, self-regulating systems, would say that the economic system is providing these decision makers with positive feedback—rewarding them for decisions that upset the system's dynamic equilibrium and cause the system to oscillate out of control, risking eventual collapse. Stable systems depend on negative feedback signals that provide incentives to correct errant behavior and move the system back toward equilibrium.

The genius of Adam Smith's conception of a market economy is that, although he never used the cybernetic terminology of the systems theorists, he was one of the first to recognize the basic principles of a complex, self-regulating human system. Implicitly, he applied those principles to create an idealized model of a self-regulating economic system that would efficiently allocate society's resources to produce those things that people most want without the intervention of a powerful central ruler. It was a brilliant intellectual achievement and had enormous appeal to intellectuals who were attracted to elegant theories, to populists who had a deep distrust of powerful rulers—and to propertied elites who found in it a moral justi-fication for greed.

Unfortunately, the economic rationalists who are Smith's intellectual descendants took a narrower and more mechanistic view of economic systems and embraced market freedom as an ideology—without Smith's focus on the conditions required to maintain the market's self-regulating balance. Ideologues make poor system designers because they are oriented to simplistic prescriptions rather than to the creation of balanced, self-regulating systems.

As resulting social tensions mount and the system's failures become more evident, established political alignments are becoming increasingly strained. Capitalizing on a growing sense of public uncertainty and fear, political demagogues and opportunists are now having a field day. In the United States, they are attacking big government and environmentalists while calling for tax cuts, government down-sizing, the restoration of family values and individual responsibility, the elimination of restrictions on natural resource exploitation, increased defense expenditures, a tougher stand on crime, market deregulation and free trade. Posing as conservatives committed to protecting ordinary people from the abuses of big government, they play simultaneously to the self-reliant, who are distrustful of government; to the economically burdened, who seek tax relief; to workers in resource-based industries, who fear environmental restrictions; and to corporate interests, which are eager for greater freedom to increase profits by externalizing costs. The proposals offered to attract these varied constituencies are rife with contradictions. Few of the proposals will contribute to restoring the values of family, community, and self-reliance. To the contrary, they allow the world's largest corporations the freedom to colonize still more of the world's markets and resources to the benefit of the already rich, further shift tax burdens from those best able to pay to those least able to pay, and enlarge the police powers of the state to stem the resulting social unrest.

The opportunists and demagogues of corporate libertarianism have linked corporate money and power with populist interests to advance an agenda that results in placing corporate interests above human interests. This contradiction remains unexposed so long as the corporate libertarians are allowed to define the issues as a struggle between tax-and-spend big-government liberals and family-values conservatives fighting for individual freedom and responsibility. In this guise, they have enjoyed great success in attacking social programs for the poor, providing tax breaks for the rich, and giving greater freedom to corporations. The consequence is to shift still more power and wealth to the big and central—the corporate world of the cloud minders—at the expense of the small and local. Ironically, the cause that many conservative voters believe themselves to be serving is that of reclaiming power for the small and local.

The terms of the political debate must be redefined to focus clearly on the real issue: the contest for power between the big and central and the small and local—between corporations and ordinary people. The time is ripe for a realignment of political alliances, which is likely to come into full flower only when the true populists realize that their enemy is not only big central government but also the giant corporations that owe no allegiance to place, people, or human interest.

Economic globalization is the foundation on which the empires of the new corporate colonialism are being built. The corporate libertarians tell us that the process of economic globalization is advancing in response to immutable historical forces and that we have no choice but to adapt and learn to compete with our neighbors. It is a disingenuous claim that belies the well-organized, generously funded, and purposeful efforts by the cloud minders to dismantle national economies and build the institutions of a global market. In Part III we examine their vision and how they have gone about realizing it.

III Corporate Colonialism

8 Dreaming of Global Empires

The world economy has become more integrated. But to travel is not the same as to arrive. Full integration will be reached only when there is free movement of goods, services, capital and labour and when governments treat firms equally, regardless of their nationality.

—The Economist[1]

The men who run the global corporations are the first in history with the organization, technology, money, and ideology to make a credible try at managing the world as an integrated economic unit. . . . What they are demanding in essence is the right to transcend the nation-state, and in the process, transform it.

—Richard J. Barnet and Ronald E. Muller[2]

T he past two decades have seen the most rapid and sweeping institutional transformation in human history. It is a conscious and intentional transformation in search of a new world economic order in which business has no nationality and knows no borders. It is driven by global dreams of vast corporate empires, compliant governments, a globalized consumer monoculture, and a universal ideological commitment to corporate libertarianism. To counter the economic, social, and environmental devastation being wrought nearly everywhere by the realization of this corporate colonial vision, we must learn to recognize its message and the methods of its propagation.

The Vision

One of the most respected and articulate visionaries of the new economic order is Akio Morita, the founder and chairman of Sony Corporation. The June 1993 *Atlantic Monthly* carried an open letter from
Morita to the heads of state who were then preparing for the 1993
G-7 Summit in Tokyo. He called on them to find:

> the means of lowering *all* economic barriers between North
> America, Europe, and Japan—trade, investment, legal, and so
> forth—in order to begin creating the nucleus of a new world eco-
> nomic order that would include a harmonized world business
> system with agreed rules and procedures that transcend national
> boundaries.[3]

Morita went on to make clear that, in his view, it is time for all local
interests, including local cultures and other symbols of local identity,
to give way to the larger good that the free-market system makes possible. In his ideal world:

> Japanese rice farmers would not be able to keep their market
> closed, nor would Japanese *keiretsu* be allowed to exclude foreign
> suppliers from their production systems or imported goods from
> retail shelves. But neither would Americans be able to deal with
> perceived unfairness through methods such as unilateral tariffs.
> And Europeans would not be able to sit in unilateral judgment
> on what is or isn't a "European" car.
>   Over time we should seek to create an environment in which
> the movement of goods, services, capital, technology, and people
> throughout North America, Europe, and Japan is truly free and
> unfettered.[4]

Within such a world order, complaints about restrictions on foreign
access to markets would be quickly investigated and resolved by supranational arbitration panels that would "propose specific remedies to
facilitate foreign entry in areas found to be unfair or insufficiently
open."[5] Governmental efforts to maintain competition through antitrust regulations would be tempered by acceptance of the needs of
companies that are "sharing research and development, carrying out
joint manufacturing, or forming various kinds of beneficial partnerships and alliances." Governments would coordinate exchange rates
to reduce arbitrary risks from currency fluctuations incurred by global corporations as they move goods and capital freely around the
world to wherever offers the greatest return.[6]

The underlying message is clear. Local people, acting through their governments, should no longer have the right to govern their own economies in the local interest. Government should respond instead to the needs of the global corporation. Morita's words echo those of George Ball, America's undersecretary of state for economic affairs, who in 1967 said to the British National Committee of the International Chamber of Commerce:

> [T]he political boundaries of nation-states are too narrow and constricted to define the scope and activities of modern business. . . . By and large, those companies that have achieved a global vision of their operations tend to opt for a world in which not only goods but all the factors of production can shift with maximum freedom.[7]

In the July 15, 1991, issue of its official newsletter, the International Monetary Fund drew on a study by DeAnne Julius, the chief economist of Shell International Petroleum Company, to stress the importance of trade agreements that would assure capital the same freedom of movement as goods. It proposed three principles:

- Foreign companies should have complete freedom of choice as to whether they participate in a local market by importing goods or by establishing a local production facility.
- Foreign firms should be governed by the same laws and be accorded the same rights in a country as domestic firms.
- Foreign firms should be allowed to undertake any activity in a country that is legally permissible for domestic firms to undertake.

Carla Hills, U.S. trade representative under the Bush administration, expressed her commitment to this goal: "We want corporations to be able to make investments overseas without being required to take a local partner, or export a given percentage of their output, to use local parts, or to meet any of a dozen other restrictions."[8] It is a view widely shared in corporate circles. An international survey of business executives conducted by the *Harvard Business Review* in 1990 found that some 12,000 respondents from twenty-five countries agreed by a substantial margin that there should be free trade between nations and the least possible protection for domestic enterprise. By a similar margin, they rejected the idea that businesses should be committed to their home country or face barriers to moving facilities to another part of the world.[9]

The corporate empire builders are rapidly making their dream a reality. From 1965 to 1992, the percentage of world economic output traded between countries rose from just under 9 percent to just under 19 percent.[10] Overall, trade has been expanding at roughly twice the rate of growth in economic output. From 1983 to 1990, worldwide foreign investment grew four times faster than world output and three times faster than world trade, leading *The Economist* to conclude that foreign investment is the area "where the most rapid progress has been made since 1980."[11] Given that as much as 70 percent of world trade is controlled by just 500 corporations,[12] and a mere 1 percent of all multinationals own half the total stock of foreign direct investment,[13] it seems that *The Economist* measures progress by the rate at which a few transnational corporations are consolidating their hold on the global economy.

Corporations beyond National Interests

It has become a matter of pride and principle for corporate executives to proclaim that their firms have grown beyond any national interest. Typical is the statement of Charles Exley, CEO of National Cash Register, who proudly told the *New York Times*, "National Cash Register is not a U.S. corporation. It is a world corporation that happens to be headquartered in the United States."[14] According to C. Michael Armstrong, senior vice president in charge at IBM World Trade Corporation, "IBM, to some degree, has successfully lost its American identity."[15]

Such statements are not mere posturing. IBM Japan employs 18,000 Japanese workers and is one of Japan's major computer exporters, including to the United States.[16] In 1993, General Motors Corporation of the United States announced an agreement with Toyota Motor Corporation of Japan under which General Motors would produce up to 20,000 cars a year in the United States for sale in Japan under the Toyota brand name.[17]

In truth, the question of national origin of the content of a product has become so complex that it is nearly impossible to determine with certainty. It is not evident that even the companies in question know, or particularly care, the percentage distribution of the national origin of the content of their products. In a 1990 cover story, *Business Week* noted:

> Though few companies are totally untethered from their home countries, the trend toward a form of "stateless" corporation is unmistakable. The European, American, and Japanese giants heading in this direction are learning how to juggle multiple identities and multiple loyalties. . . . These world corporations are

developing chameleon-like abilities to resemble insiders no matter where they operate. At the same time, they move factories and labs "around the world without particular reference to national borders," says Unisys Corp. Chairman W. Michael Blumenthal.[18]

In other words, in their day-to-day operations, the allegiance of the world's largest corporations is purely to their own bottom lines. However, for the purposes of seeking tax breaks, research subsidies, or governmental representation in negotiations that bear on their global marketing and investment interests, they wrap themselves in national flags and call for support from their "home" governments in the name of advancing "national" global competitiveness.

There is a continuing tension between the *multinational* and the *transnational* view of the global corporation. A multinational corporation takes on many national identities, maintaining relatively autonomous production and sales facilities in individual countries, establishing local roots and presenting itself in each locality as a good local citizen. Its globalized operations are linked to one another but are deeply integrated into the individual local economies in which they operate, and they do function to some extent as local citizens.

The trend, however, is toward transnationalism, which involves the integration of a firm's global operations around vertically integrated supplier networks. For example, when Otis Elevator set about to create an advanced elevator system, it contracted out the design of the motor drives to Japan, the door systems to France, the electronics to Germany, and small geared components to Spain. System integration was handled from the United States.[19] Although a transnational corporation may choose to claim local citizenship when that posture suits its purpose, local commitments are temporary, and it actively attempts to eliminate considerations of nationality in its effort to maximize the economies that centralized global procurement makes possible.[20]

The Economist has suggested that the appropriate strategy for those who own the rights to products or processes in a fully globalized economy is not to produce anything. Instead, they should simply license rights to the products and processes for an amount sufficient to yield the same profits they would have made if they had produced the products locally or for export.[21] In other words, those who hold monopoly control of patented technologies should not be expected to produce anything—simply collect the profits. It is a far cry from Adam Smith's ideal of a competitive market economy in which the returns go to small producers.

The more protected individual markets are, the more a global firm is forced to function in a multinational mode—producing locally in each setting to achieve access to that market and integrating itself into the local economy. As local settings are opened to the global economy, it becomes possible, and highly profitable, for a firm to take advantage of the differences between localities with regard to wages, market potential, employment standards, taxes, environmental regulations, local facilities, and human resources. This means arranging its global operations to produce products where costs are lowest, sell them where markets are more lucrative, and shift the resulting profits to where tax rates are least burdensome. The ability to shift production from one country to another weakens the bargaining power of any given locality and shifts the balance of power from the local human interest to the global corporate interest.

The more readily a firm is able to move capital, goods, technology, and personnel freely among localities in search of such advantage, the greater the competitive pressure on localities to subsidize investors by absorbing their social, environmental, and other production costs. The larger and more open the markets, the greater the profit opportunity they present to firms that are sufficiently large and nimble to capitalize on the differences—and the greater their competitive advantage over smaller local firms that remain rooted in a particular community and play by its rules.

A recent study of multinational enterprises (MNEs) by the Office of Technology Assessment of the U.S. Congress observed:

> [B]ecause they span national borders, many MNEs are less concerned with advancing national goals than with pursuing objectives internal to the firm—principally growth, profits, proprietary technology, strategic alliances, return on investment, and market power. . . . The U.S. economy (or any other, for that matter) cannot remain competitive unless MNEs that sell and conduct business in America also contribute to its research and technology base, employment, manufacturing capabilities, and capital resources. . . .
>
> The interests of all nations ought to be fairly straightforward— quality jobs, a rising standard of living, technological and industrial development, ensured rights of workers and consumers, and a high-quality environment at home and globally. . . . As compared to nations, the interests of MNEs are far more situation-oriented and linked to opportunity.[22]

In general, Japanese firms have been more oriented toward a Japanese national interest than have American firms, which have taken the lead in rejecting national interests in favor of a more narrowly defined corporate interest. European firms tend to fall somewhere in between. The clear trend, however, is toward corporate transnationalism.

Governments in the Service of Consumerism

Kenichi Ohmae, managing director of McKinsey & Company Japan, is another widely respected guru of the new economic order. In his widely read book *The Borderless World*, Ohmae tells national governments that clinging to their traditional roles as economic managers of national economies is futile, because national economies no longer exist. For example, when governments attempt to use traditional interest rate and money supply instruments to stimulate a nonexistent national economy, the jobs that result may well be created in other countries that experience a resulting increase in demand for their exports. If a government raises interest rates to control inflation, foreign funds will gush in from abroad and render the policy meaningless.[23]

Globalization has rendered many of the political roles of government obsolete as well. Companies with globalized operations routinely and effortlessly sidestep governmental restrictions based on old assumptions about national economies and foreign policy. For example, Honda circumvents restrictions on the importation of Japanese cars into Taiwan, South Korea, and Israel by shipping Honda vehicles to these countries from its U.S. plant in Ohio. When Japan opened bidding on new telecommunications facilities to U.S. manufacturers, Canada's Northern Telecom Ltd. moved many of its production facilities to the United States so that it could win Japanese contracts as a U.S. company. When U.S. President Ronald Reagan ordered economic sanctions against Libya in January 1986, Brown & Root, Inc., a Houston engineering concern, simply shifted a $100 million contract for work on Libya's Great Man-Made River Project to its British subsidiary.[24]

The appropriate response for the bureaucrats, in Ohmae's view, is to yield to the inevitable—accept the reality that government is obsolete, get out of the way, and let goods and money flow freely in response to market forces:

> [M]ultinational companies are truly the servants of demanding consumers around the world. . . . When governments are slow to grasp the fact that their role has changed from protecting their people and their natural resource base from outside economic threats to ensuring that their people have the widest range of choice among the best and the cheapest goods and services from around the world—when, that is, governments still think and act like the saber-rattling mercantilist ruling powers of centuries past—they discourage investment and impoverish their people. Worse, they commit their people to isolation from an emerging

world economy, which, in turn effectively dooms them to a downward spiral of frustrated hopes and industrial stagnation. . . . [As] recent events in Eastern Europe have shown, the people—as consumers and as citizens—will no longer tolerate this antiquated role of government.[25]

Ohmae counsels governments to actively join global corporations in assuring consumers that they should not be concerned about where a product is produced. He supports his argument by pointing out that production costs are typically only about 25 percent of the end-user price; the major contribution to a product's price comes increasingly from marketing and support functions. "Such functions as distribution, warehousing, financing, retail marketing, systems integration, and services are all legitimate parts of the business system and can create as many, and often more jobs than simply manufacturing operations."[26] In effect, Ohmae is arguing that a country can meet its employment needs by concentrating on marketing and consuming goods that are produced elsewhere.

The United States has already largely embraced Ohmae's vision as the organizing principle of its economy. Foreign producers now supply 30 percent of the goods, other than oil, sold in the U.S. domestic market, up from 15 percent at the beginning of the 1980s.[27] Meanwhile, the United States has become the world's major international debtor nation, while suffering rising unemployment and falling wages.

If people were indeed only consumers, there might be merit to Ohmae's argument. But people have other roles and values that lead to real and legitimate concerns about such matters as where a good is produced and what rules will govern local economic affairs. The human interest and the corporate interest differ.

Community versus Corporate Interests

The global economy has created a dynamic in which competition among localities has become as real as competition among firms. Moore County, South Carolina, won a competitiveness bid in the 1960s and 1970s when it lured a number of large manufacturers from the unionized industrial regions of the northeastern United States with promises of tax breaks, lax environmental regulations, and compliant labor. Proctor Silex was one of the companies attracted. Later, when Proctor Silex expanded its local plant, Moore County floated a $5.5 million municipal bond to finance necessary sewer and water hookups—even though nearby residents were living without running water and other basic public services. Then in 1990, the company decided that Mexico offered more competitive terms and moved again. It left behind 800 unemployed Moore Country workers, drums of buried toxic waste, and the public debts the county had incurred to finance public facilities in the company's behalf.[28]

Americans need go no farther than the Mexican border to get an idea of what it now takes to be globally competitive. The *maquiladoras* are assembly plants in the free-trade zone on the Mexican side of the border with the United States. The zone has become a powerful magnet, attracting many U.S. companies—including General Electric, Ford, General Motors, GTE Sylvania, RCA, Westinghouse, and Honeywell—that are seeking low-cost locations in which to produce for the U.S. market.[29] Growth has been explosive, from 620 *maquiladora* plants employing 119,550 workers in 1980 to 2,200 factories employing more than 500,000 Mexican workers in 1992. Many feature the most modern high-productivity equipment and technology. Although the productivity of Mexican workers who work in modern plants is comparable to that of U.S. workers, average hourly wages in *maquiladora* factories are just $1.64, compared with an average manufacturing wage of $16.17 in the United States.

To maintain the kind of conditions transnational corporations prefer, the Mexican government has denied workers the right to form independent labor unions and has held wage increases far below productivity increases. In the summer of 1992, more than 14,000 Mexican workers at a Volkswagen plant turned down a contract negotiated by their government-dominated labor union. The company fired them all, and a Mexican court upheld the company's action. In 1987, in the midst of a bitter two-month strike in Mexico, Ford Motor Company tore up its union contract, fired 3,400 workers, and cut wages by 45 percent. When the workers rallied around dissident labor leaders, gunmen hired by the official government-dominated union shot workers at random in the factory.

Loose enforcement of environmental regulations is another attraction. An investigative team from the U.S. General Accounting Office reported to Congress that all six newly opened U.S. plants it inspected in Mexico were operating without the required environmental licenses. Other studies have found evidence of massive toxic dumping in the *maquiladora* zones, polluting rivers, groundwater and soils and causing severe health problems among workers and deformities among babies born to young women working in the zone.

Since investors are exempted from property taxes on their factories, public infrastructure—roads, water, housing, and sewage lines—is grossly inadequate. The workers live in shantytowns that stretch for miles. The dwellings are constructed of scrap materials and have no sewer systems; most have no running water. Worker families commonly store water in discarded barrels with markings showing that they once contained toxic chemicals.

According to Professor Valdes-Villalva of the Colegio de la Frontera Norte in Juarez:

> We have begun to see more fourteen-year-olds in the plants. Because of the intensive work it entails, there is a constant burnout. If they've been here three or four years, workers lose efficiency. They begin to have problems with eyesight. They begin to have allergies and kidney problems. They are less productive.[30]

Mexican workers, including children, are heroes of the new economic order in the eyes of corporate libertarians—sacrificing their health, lives, and futures on the altar of global competition.

Not all global corporations locate in Mexico. In 1993, South Carolina was again being praised by business publications for its aggressive efforts to win the favor of international investors. Its major coup was a successful bid for a new BMW auto plant. BMW had spent three years assessing offers from 250 localities in ten countries before deciding to place its $400 million facility in South Carolina. According to *Business Week*, company officials were attracted by the temperate climate, year-round golf, and the availability of a number of mansions at affordable prices. They also liked the region's cheap labor, low taxes, and limited union activity. When BMW indicated that it favored a 1,000-acre tract on which a large number of middle-class homes were already located, the state spent $36.6 million to buy the 140 properties and leased the site back to the company at $1 a year. The state also picked up the costs of recruiting, screening, and training workers for the new plant and raised an additional $2.8 million from private sources to send newly hired engineers for training in Germany. The total cost to the South Carolina taxpayers for these and other subsidies to attract BMW will be $130 million over thirty years.[31]

This is an all-too-typical example of how taxpayers are subsidizing the production costs of major global companies. In 1957, corporations in the United States provided 45 percent of local property tax revenues. By 1987, their share had dropped to about 16 percent.[32] A 1994 study by the Progressive Policy Institute of the Democratic Leadership Conference identified what it considered to be unjustified subsidies and tax benefits extended to corporations in the United States amounting to $111 billion over five years.[33] The trend is clear. The largest corporations are paying less taxes and receiving more subsidies.

This is the globally competitive market at work, forcing localities to absorb private costs to increase private profits. The game of global competition is rigged. It pits companies against people in a contest that the people almost always lose.

A serious reading of the financial press and the treatises of the architects of globalization suggests that the ideal world of the global dreamers can be characterized as one in which:

- The world's money, technology, and markets are controlled and managed by gigantic global corporations;
- A common consumer culture unifies all people in a shared quest for material gratification;
- There is perfect global competition among workers and localities to offer their services to investors at the most advantageous terms;
- Corporations are free to act solely on the basis of profitability without regard to national or local consequences;
- Relationships, both individual and corporate, are defined entirely by the market; and
- There are no loyalties to place and community.

Embellished by promises of limitless and effortless affluence, the vision of a global economy has an entrancing appeal. Beneath its beguiling surface, however, we find a modern form of enchantment, a siren song created by the skilled image makers of Madison Avenue, enticing societies to weaken community to free the market, eliminate livelihoods to create wealth, and destroy life to increase unneeded and often unsatisfying consumption. Contrary to what the corporate libertarians would have us believe, the seductive melodies that beckon us are not produced by inexorable historical forces beyond human influence. They come from the well-rehearsed human voices of Stratos dwellers calling out to us from their city in the clouds across a great gap that most of humanity can never cross.

9 Building Elite Consensus

The foreign policies of nation-states, particularly economic and monetary policies, have always been a highly elitist matter. Policy options are proposed, reviewed, and executed within the context of a broad bipartisan consensus that is painstakingly managed by very small circles of public and private elites. . . . Where necessary, a consensus is engineered on issues which must get congressional/parliamentary approval, but wherever possible executive agreements between governments are used to avoid the democratic process altogether.

—Peter Thompson[1]

Strong growth in the poorer parts of the world will be needed to sustain enough growth in the West to maintain adequate levels of employment and to enable Western governments to deal with their pressing social problems.

—Felix Rohatyn[2]

It is helpful to understand how economic globalization has been crafted and carried forward as a policy agenda largely outside the public discourse. It is not a matter of a small elite group meeting in secret to craft a master plan for taking over the world. It works much more like any networking or shared culture building process out of which alliances among individuals and groups emerge and evolve. There is no conspiracy, though in practical terms, the consequences are much as if there were.

In this chapter, we take a brief look at each of three major forums that have served the consensus-building process in support of economic globalization: the

Council on Foreign Relations, the Bilderberg, and the Trilateral Commission. They are not the only organizations important to this process, but they are distinctive in their effectiveness in bringing together key individuals from government, business, the media, and academia to create a consensus that aligns our most powerful institutions with the economic globalization agenda.

Visions of American Hegemony

The roots of the current drive toward economic globalization go back to the trauma of the depression that preceded World War II. America's policy elites were deeply concerned about ensuring that nothing similar would ever recur. There were two prevailing ideas as to how this might be accomplished. One would have required major reforms of the U.S. economy, including strong governmental intervention in the market. The other depended on ensuring the domestic American economy sufficient access to foreign markets and raw materials to sustain the continuous expansion required to maintain full employment without market reforms. The latter was by far the more popular alternative among those in power, including a small elite group of foreign policy planners associated with the Council on Foreign Relations.

A meeting ground for powerful members of the U.S. corporate and foreign policy establishments, the Council on Foreign Relations styles itself as a forum for the airing of opposing views—an incubator of leaders and ideas. Its activities are organized around dinner meetings and study programs for its members—often involving influential world figures or foreign policy thinkers—in settings that are conducive to candid off-the-record discussion. It similarly styles its influential *Foreign Affairs* journal as a forum for the open debate of significant foreign policy issues.[3]

The portion of the Council's history that is of particular interest to our present inquiry began on September 12, 1939, less than two weeks after the outbreak of World War II. On that day, Walter Mallory, executive director of the Council, and Hamilton Armstrong, the editor of *Foreign Affairs*, met in Washington with George Messersmith, assistant secretary of state and a member of the Council. They outlined a long-range planning project to be carried out by the Council in close collaboration with the State Department on long-term problems of the war and plans for the peace. Several war and peace studies groups composed of foreign policy experts would produce confidential expert recommendations for President Franklin D. Roosevelt,[4] who, during his tenure as governor of New York, had lived in a town house next door to the Council's headquarters. Relations between Roosevelt and the Council continued to be close. At that point in history, the State Department lacked the funds and personnel to undertake such studies, so its leadership accepted the Council's proposal. By the end of the war, the partnership had produced 682 confidential memoranda for the government, with funding provided in part from the Rockefeller Foundation.[5]

The planners anticipated that the defeat of Germany and Japan and the wartime devastation of Europe would leave the United States in an undisputed position to dominate the postwar economy. They believed the more open that economy was to trade and foreign investment, the more readily the United States would be able to dominate it. Working from that logic, the plans produced by the State Department–Council planning groups placed a substantial emphasis on creating an institutional framework that would create an open global economy.[6]

In April 1941, a confidential memo from the Economic and Financial Group of the Council provided the government with the following suggestion on how to frame the public presentation of U.S. objectives for propaganda purposes during the war:

> If war aims are stated which seem to be concerned solely with Anglo-American imperialism, they will offer little to people in the rest of the world, and will be vulnerable to Nazi counter promises. Such aims would also strengthen the most reactionary elements in the United States and the British Empire. The interests of other peoples should be stressed, not only those of Europe, but also of Asia, Africa, and Latin America. This would have a better propaganda effect.[7]

Memorandum E-B34, issued by the Council to the president and the State Department on July 24, 1941, outlined the concept of a "Grand Area." This was the area of the world that the United States would need to dominate economically and militarily to ensure materials for its industries with the "fewest possible stresses."[8] The minimum necessary Grand Area would consist of most of the non-German world. Its preferred scope would consist of the Western Hemisphere, the United Kingdom, the remainder of the British Commonwealth and Empire, the Dutch East Indies, China, and Japan. The concept outlined in the memo involved working for economic integration within the largest available core area and then expanding outward to weave other areas into the core, as circumstances allowed.

This same memorandum called for the creation of worldwide financial institutions for stabilizing currencies and facilitating programs of capital investment in the development of backward and underdeveloped regions.[9] This recommendation aligned with similar proposals being put forward by Harry White at the U.S. Department of Treasury that led to establishment of the International Monetary Fund (IMF) to be responsible for keeping currencies stable and liquid to facilitate trade and the International Bank for Reconstruction and Development (IBRD), commonly known as the World Bank, to facilitate capital investments in "backward and underdeveloped" regions and open them for development.[10]

The subsequent U.S. initiative on behalf of economic globalization worked from two basic premises. First, in order to maintain the existing capitalist economic system, the United States must have access to the resources and markets of much of the world so that it could create a sufficient export surplus to maintain full employment at home. Second, by spreading the U.S. economic model throughout the world within a globalized economy, the world would become united in peace and prosperity. Apparently, little note was taken of the evident contradiction that if maintaining the prosperity of a U.S.-style economy required access to most of the world's resources and markets, it would be impossible for other countries to replicate its experience. Nor is it evident that much thought was given to the contradiction of financing industrial exports to low-income countries with international development loans that could be repaid by these countries only if they developed export surpluses with the countries that had initially extended the loans.

If such questions were raised, they were quickly pushed into the background by the urgency of the war effort and the powerful interests the vision served. Furthermore, much as the U.S. foreign policy planners anticipated, the United States was in the driver's seat immediately following World War II. America's foreign policy elites were gripped by a sense of America's newfound power and responsibility in the world. A bit of hubris was perhaps inevitable.

The North Atlantic Alliance

Europe's emergence from the ashes of war, the decision to form a European political and economic union, and the West's confrontation with the communist empire of the Soviet Union created an imperative to expand the earlier hegemonic U.S. vision to embrace the idea of a North Atlantic community that would provide the leadership in a Western-dominated global system. This created an obvious need for mechanisms through which the policies of the North Atlantic countries might be coordinated. The formal mechanisms, such as the North Atlantic Treaty Organization (NATO) formed in 1949 and the

Organization for Economic Cooperation and Development (OECD) established in 1961, are well known to the public.

Less known is a powerful but unofficial group with no acknowledged membership known simply as the Bilderberg, named for the Hotel de Bilderberg of Oosterbeek, Holland, at which a group of North American and European leaders first met in May 1954. Subsequent Bilderberg meetings and the relationships they nurtured played a significant role in advancing the European union and shaping a consensus among leaders of the Atlantic nations.[11] Participants include heads of state, other leading politicians, key industrialists and financiers, and an assortment of intellectuals, trade unionists, diplomats, and influential representatives of the press with demonstrated sympathy for establishment views. One Bilderberg insider observed that "today there are very few figures among governments on both sides of the Atlantic who have not attended at least one of these meetings."[12]

U.S. President Eisenhower regularly sent Gabriel Hauge, his White House domestic policy chief and former director and treasurer of the Council on Foreign Relations, as his personal representative to Bilderberg meetings. President Kennedy appointed Bilderberg alumni to virtually every senior position in his State Department—Secretary of State Dean Rusk, Undersecretary of State George W. Ball, George McGhee, Walter Rostow, McGeorge Bundy, and Arthur Dean.[13]

Joseph Retinger, a founder and permanent secretary of Bilderberg until his death in 1960 and a leading proponent of European unification, explained that the Bilderberg meetings provided a freedom in discussing difficult issues that more official forums could not provide:

> Even if a participant is a member of a government, a leader of a political party, an official of an international organization or of a commercial concern, he does not commit his government, his party or his organization by anything he may say. . . . Bilderberg does not make policy. Its aim is to reduce differences of opinion and resolve conflicting trends and to further understanding, if not agreement, by hearing and considering various points of view and trying to find a common approach to major problems. Direct action has therefore never been contemplated, the object being to draw the attention of people in responsible positions to Bilderberg's findings.[14]

Trilateralism

The subsequent emergence of Japan as a third economic force within the orbit of the West led to the idea of a *trilateral* alliance that would merge the economic interests of three regional partners: North America (the United States and Canada), Western Europe, and Japan. This idea became a frequent topic of discussion at Bilderberg meetings. It was decided to create a new forum that included the Japanese and had a more formal structure than Bilderberg.

In 1973, the Trilateral Commission was formed by David Rockefeller, chairman of Chase Manhattan Bank, and Zbigniew Brzezinski, who served as the Commission's director and coordinator until 1977, when he became national security advisor to U.S. President Jimmy Carter.[15] The Trilateral Commission describes itself as follows:

> The Commission's members are about 325 distinguished citizens, with a variety of leadership responsibilities from these three regions. When the first triennium of the Trilateral Commission was launched in 1973, the most immediate purpose was to draw together—at a time of considerable friction among governments—the highest level unofficial group possible to look together at the common problems facing our three areas. At a deeper level, there was a sense that the United States was no longer in such a singular leadership position as it had been in earlier post–World War II years, and that a more shared form of leadership—including Europe and Japan in particular—would be needed for the international system to navigate successfully the major challenges of the coming years. These purposes continue to inform the Commission's work.[16]

In contrast to Bilderberg, which is known for its secrecy, the Trilateral Commission is a more transparent organization that readily distributes its membership and publication lists to anyone who calls its publicly listed phone number, and its publications are available for sale to the public. Whereas Bilderberg includes many heads of state, other top government officials, and royalty, members of the Trilateral Commission who assume highly administrative positions in government resign from the Commission for the period of their tenure.[17]

The collective power of the Commission's members is impressive. They include the heads of four of the world's five largest nonbanking transnational corporations (ITOCHU, Sumitomo, Mitsubishi, and Mitsui & Co.); top officials of five of the world's six largest international banks (Sumitomo Bank, Fuji Bank, Sakura Bank, Sanwa Bank, and Mitsubishi Bank); and heads of major media organizations (Japan Times, Ltd.; Le Poit; Times Mirror Co.; the Washington Post Co.; Cable News Network [CNN]; and Time Warner).

U.S. Presidents Jimmy Carter, George Bush, and Bill Clinton were all members of the Trilateral Commission, as was Thomas Foley, former

Speaker of the U.S. House of Representatives. Many key members of the Carter administration were both Bilderbergers and Trilateral Commission members, including Vice President Mondale, Secretary of State Vance, National Security Advisor Brzezinski, and Treasury Secretary Blumenthal.[18] Former members of the Trilateral Commission who went on to hold key positions under the Clinton administration include Warren Christopher, secretary of state; Bruce Babbitt, secretary of the interior; Henry Cisneros, secretary of housing and urban development; Alan Greenspan, chairman of the U.S. Federal Reserve System; Joseph Nye Jr., chairman of the National Intelligence Council, Central Intelligence Agency; Donna E. Shalala, secretary of health and human services; Clifton Wharton Jr., deputy secretary of state; and Peter Tarnoff, undersecretary of state for political affairs.[19]

Although the Commission publishes its own position papers, its views are conveyed through many outlets not necessarily associated with it. The trilateralist vision of Sony chairman Akio Morita that was published in *Atlantic Monthly* and discussed in the previous chapter is an example. At the time, Morita was the Japanese chairman of the Trilateral Commission.

It is important to note that the Council on Foreign Relations, the Bilderberg, and the Trilateral Commission bring together heads of competing corporations and leaders of competing national political parties for closed-door discussions and consensus-building processes that the public never sees. Although the participants may believe that they represent a broad spectrum of intersectoral and even international perspectives, in truth, it is a closed and exclusive process limited to elite Stratos dwellers. Participants are predominantly male, wealthy, from Northern industrial countries, and, except for the Japanese on the Trilateral Commission, Caucasian. Other voices are excluded.

The resulting narrowness of perspective is evident in the publications of the Trilateral Commission. They are written by seasoned and thoughtful professionals, and a diversity of views is presented. Yet they all accept without question the ideological premises of corporate libertarianism. The benefits of economic integration and a harmonization of the tax, regulatory, and other policies of the trilateral countries—and ultimately of all countries—are assumed as an article of faith. The debate centers on how, not whether.

No note is taken of the fact that harmonizing standards—which necessarily means setting standards—can be accomplished only through international negotiations, which by their nature must be carried out in secret by the administrative branches of governments. Thus, in the

absence of an elected international parliament, a call to harmonize standards is a call to take decisions regarding the standards by which businesses will operate out of the hands of democratically elected national legislative bodies and pass them to the unelected bureaucrats who represent governments in international negotiations. Such a situation lends itself especially well to cozy insider deal making—especially when these bureaucrats come from the same elite circles as members of the Trilateral Commission. For example, Carla Hills, who as U.S. trade representative under President George Bush played a key role in negotiating the General Agreement on Tariffs and Trade (GATT) that established the new World Trade Organization, was a member of the Trilateral Commission.

The fact that George Bush and Bill Clinton were both members of the Trilateral Commission makes it easy to understand why there was such a seamless transition from the Republican Bush administration to the Democratic Clinton administration with regard to the U.S. commitment to pass the North American Free Trade Agreement (NAFTA) and GATT. Clinton's leadership in advancing what many progressives thought to be a Bush agenda on these agreements won him high marks from his colleagues on the Trilateral Commission but seriously alienated major elements of his core constituency, who had looked to him to provide a less corporatist view of the trade agenda. On this most fundamental of issues, the electoral system gave the voters only the illusion of choice.

The policy actions being advanced by the elite consensus constitute an increasingly effective attack on the institutions of democracy—the very purpose of which is to prevent a small inside elite from capturing control of the instruments of governance. Their dominance of the policy debate largely precludes raising alternatives to prevailing assumptions.

Economic globalization is neither in the human interest nor inevitable. It is axiomatic that political power aligns with economic power. The larger the economic unit, the larger its dominant players, and the more political power becomes concentrated in the largest corporations. The greater the political power of corporations and those aligned with them, the less the political power of the people, and the less meaningful democracy becomes. There is an alternative: to localize economies, disperse economic power, and bring democracy closer to the people. However, networks and alliances made up exclusively of Stratos dwellers are unlikely to articulate and pursue such an alternative. To the contrary, as we shall see in the next chapter, the Stratos dwellers are mobilizing the full resources of the world's largest corporations behind an effort to consolidate global corporate rule.

10 Buying Out Democracy

> *Funds generated by business (by which I mean profits, funds in business foundations and contributions from individual businessmen) must rush by multimillions to the aid of liberty ... to funnel desperately needed funds to scholars, social scientists, writers, and journalists who understand the relationship between political and economic liberty.*
>
> —William Simon, former secretary of the U.S. Treasury Department[1]

> *Before NAFTA we thought corporations could only buy Southern governments. Now we see they also buy Northern governments.*
>
> —Ignacio Peon Escalante, Mexican Action Network on Free Trade

U.S. corporations entered the 1970s besieged by a rebellious anticonsumerist youth culture, a mushrooming environmental and product safety movement, and a serious economic challenge from Asia. Not only was their dream of global hegemony in tatters, they even risked losing control of their own home turf. In response, they mobilized their collective political resources to regain control of the political and cultural agenda. Their methods included a combination of sophisticated marketing techniques, old-fashioned vote buying, funding for ideologically aligned intellectuals, legal action, and many of the same grassroots mobilization techniques that environmental and consumer activists had used against the corporations during the 1960s and 1970s. Their campaigns were well funded, involved sophisticated strategies, and were professionally organized. The major goals were deregulation, economic globalization, and the limitation of corporate liability—in short, to enlarge corporate rights and reduce corporate responsibilities. And their campaign continues in full force.

Mobilizing Corporate Political Resources

In 1971, the U.S. Chamber of Commerce sought the advice of Virginia attorney and future Supreme Court Justice Lewis Powell about the problems facing the business community. Powell produced a memorandum entitled "Attack on American Free Enterprise System" that warned of an assault by environmentalists, consumer activists, and others who "propagandize against the system, seeking insidiously and constantly to sabotage it." He argued that it was time "for the wisdom, ingenuity and resources of American business to be marshaled against those who would destroy it."[2] This set the stage for an organized effort by a powerful coalition of business groups and ideologically compatible foundations to align the U.S. political and legal system with their ideological vision.

Among Powell's recommendations was a proposal that the business community create a business-organized and -funded legal center to promote the general interests of business in the nation's courts. This led to the formation of the Pacific Legal Foundation (PLF) in 1973. Housed in the Sacramento Chamber of Commerce building, it was the first of a number of corporate-sponsored "public-interest" law firms dedicated to promoting the interests of their sponsoring corporations.[3] It specialized in defending business interests against "clean air and water legislation, the closing of federal wilderness areas to oil and gas exploration, workers' rights, and corporate taxation." Some 80 percent of its income was from corporations or corporate foundations.[4]

In a 1980 speech, PLF's managing attorney Raymond Momboisse turned reality on its head by attacking environmentalists for their "selfish, self-centered motivation . . . ; their ability to conceal their true aims in lofty sounding motives of public interest; their indifference to the injury they inflict on the masses of mankind; their ability to manipulate the law and the media; and, most of all, their power to inflict monumental harm on society."[5]

Business interests funded the establishment of law and economics programs in leading law schools to support scholarly research advancing the premise that the unregulated marketplace produces the most efficient—and thereby the most just—society. Business funded all-expense-paid seminars at prestigious universities such as George

Mason and Yale to introduce sitting judges to these economic principles and their application to jurisprudence.[6]

Before the 1970s, business interests were represented by old-fashioned corporate lobbying organizations with straightforward names: Beer Institute, National Coal Association, Chamber of Commerce, or American Petroleum Institute. As aggressive public-interest groups succeeded in mobilizing broad-based citizen pressures on Congress, business decided that another approach was needed.

Corporations began to create their own "citizen" organizations with names and images that were carefully constructed to mask their corporate sponsorship and their true purpose. The National Wetlands Coalition, which features a logo of a duck flying blissfully over a swamp, was sponsored by oil and gas companies and real estate developers to fight for the easing of restrictions on the conversion of wetlands into drilling sites and shopping malls. Corporate-sponsored Consumer Alert fights government regulations on product safety. Keep America Beautiful attempts to give its sponsors, the bottling industry, a green image by funding antilitter campaigns, while those same sponsors actively fight mandatory recycling legislation. The strategy is to convince the public that litter is the responsibility of consumers—not the packaging industry.[7]

The views of these and similar industry-sponsored groups—thirty-six of them are documented in *Masks of Deception: Corporate Front Groups in America*—are regularly reported in the press as the views of citizen advocates. The sole reason for their existence is to convince the public that the corporate interest *is* the public interest. The top funders of such groups include Dow Chemical, Exxon, Chevron USA, Mobil, DuPont, Ford, Philip Morris, Pfizer, Anheuser-Busch, Monsanto, Procter & Gamble, Phillips Petroleum, AT&T, and Arco.[8]

Business interests funded the formation of new conservative policy think tanks such as the Heritage Foundation and revived lethargic pro-establishment think tanks such as the American Enterprise Institute, which experienced a tenfold increase in its budget.[9] In 1978, the Institute for Educational Affairs was formed to match corporate funders with sympathetic scholars producing research studies supportive of corporate views on economic freedom.[10]

In 1970, only a handful of the Fortune 500 companies had public-affairs offices in Washington, but by 1980, more than 80 percent did. In 1974, labor unions accounted for half of all political action committee (PAC) money used to provide special-interest campaign support for politicians. By 1980, the unions accounted for less than a fourth of this funding.[11] With the inauguration of U.S. President Ronald Reagan in 1981, the ideological alliance of corporate libertarians consolidated its control over the instruments of power.

Although many of those involved in these campaigns truly believe that they are acting in the public interest, what we are seeing is a frontal assault on democratic pluralism to advance the ideological agenda of corporate libertarianism. Though advanced in the name of freedom and democracy, this massive abuse of corporate power mocks them both.

Building Business Lobbies

Business roundtables are national associations of the chief executive officers (CEOs) of the largest transnational corporations. Whereas more inclusive business organizations such as national chambers of commerce and national associations of manufacturers include both large and small firms representing many different interests and perspectives, the members of business roundtables are all large transnational corporations aligned with the economic globalization agenda.

The first Business Roundtable was formed in the United States in 1972. Its 200 members include the heads of forty-two of the fifty largest Fortune 500 U.S. industrial corporations, seven of the eight largest U.S. commercial banks, seven of the ten largest U.S. insurance companies, five of the seven largest U.S. retailers, seven of the eight largest U.S. transportation companies, and nine of the eleven largest U.S. utilities. In this forum, the CEO of DuPont chemical company sits with the CEOs of his three major rivals: Dow, Occidental Petroleum, and Monsanto. The head of General Motors sits with the heads of Ford and Chrysler—and so on with each major industry. In this forum, the heads of the world's largest U.S.-based corporations put aside their competitive differences to reach a consensus on issues of social and economic policy for America. The U.S. Business Roundtable describes itself as:

> an association of chief executive officers who examine public issues that affect the economy and develop positions which seek to reflect sound economic and social principles. Established in 1972, the Roundtable was founded in the belief that business executives should take an increased role in the continuing debates about public policy.
>
> The Roundtable believes that the basic interests of business closely parallel the interests of the American people, who are directly involved as consumers, employees, investors and suppliers.

. . . Member selection reflects the goal of having representation varied by category of business and by geographic location. Thus, the members, some 200 chief executive officers of companies in all fields, can present a cross section of thinking on national issues.[12]

The Roundtable, surely one of America's most exclusive and least diverse membership organizations, has an unusually narrow notion of what constitutes a "cross section" of thinking on national issues. With few, if any, exceptions, its membership is limited to white males over fifty years of age whose annual compensation averages more than 170 times the U.S. per capita gross national product.[13] Its members head corporations that disavow a commitment to national interests and stand to gain substantially from economic globalization. Once positions are defined, the Roundtable organizes aggressive campaigns to gain their political acceptance, including personal visits by its member CEOs to individual senators and representatives.

The Roundtable took an especially active role in campaigning for the North American Free Trade Agreement (NAFTA). Recognizing that the public might see free trade as a special-interest issue if touted by an exclusive club of the country's 200 largest transnationals, the Roundtable created a front organization, USA*NAFTA, that enrolled some 2,300 U.S. corporations and associations as members. Although USA*NAFTA claimed to represent a broader constituency, every one of its state captains was a corporate member of the Business Roundtable. All but four Roundtable members enjoyed privileged access to the NAFTA negotiation process through representation on advisory committees to the U.S. trade representative. Using the full range of communication resources available, Roundtable members bombarded Americans with assurances through editorials, op-ed pieces, news releases, and radio and television commentaries that NAFTA would provide them with high-paying jobs, stop immigration from Mexico, and raise environmental standards.

Nine of the USA*NAFTA state captains (Allied Signal, AT&T, General Electric, General Motors, Phelps Dodge, United Technologies, IBM, ITT, and TRW) were among the U.S. corporations that, according to the Inter-Hemispheric Resource Center, had already shipped up to 180,000 jobs to Mexico during the twelve years prior to the passage of NAFTA. Some among the NAFTA captains were corporations that had been cited for violating worker rights in Mexico and for failing to comply with worker safety standards. Many were leading polluters in the United States and had exported to or produced in Mexico products that were banned in the United States.[14]

Democracy for Hire

Washington's major growth industry consists of the for-profit public-relations firms and business-sponsored policy institutes engaged in producing facts, opinion pieces, expert analyses, opinion polls, and direct-mail and telephone solicitation to create "citizen" advocacy and public-image-building campaigns on demand for corporate clients. William Greider calls it "democracy for hire."[15] Burson Marsteller—the world's largest public-relations firm, with net 1992 billings of $204 million—worked for Exxon during the *Exxon Valdez* oil spill and for Union Carbide during the Bhopal disaster. The top fifty public-relations firms billed over $1.7 billion in 1991.[16]

In the United States, the 170,000 public-relations employees engaged in manipulating news, public opinion, and public policy to serve the interests of paying clients now outnumber actual news reporters by about 40,000—and the gap is growing. These firms will organize citizen letter-writing campaigns, provide paid operatives posing as "housewives" to present corporate views in public meetings, and place favorable news items and op-ed pieces in the press. A 1990 study found that almost 40 percent of the news content in a typical U.S. newspaper originates from public-relations press releases, story memos, and suggestions. According to the *Columbia Journalism Review*, more than half of the *Wall Street Journal*'s news stories are based solely on press releases.[17] The distinction between advertising space and news space grows less distinct with each passing day.

While the Republicans have long been known as the party of money, the Democratic Party was historically the party of the people, with strong representation of working-class and minority interests. The Democrats once depended heavily on their strong grassroots political organization—on people more than money—to deliver the votes on election day. These structures in turn forced politicians to maintain some contact with the grassroots and ensured a degree of local accountability. Ties to the party were strong. With the growing role of television in American life and the decline in the U.S. labor movement, costly television-based media campaigns have become increasingly central in deciding election outcomes. As a consequence, the grassroots organization that was once the foundation of the Democratic Party structure has disintegrated, causing it to lose its populist moorings and leaving those who once constituted its political base feeling unrepresented.

With the breakdown of this structure, those who run for office under the Democratic Party banner have become increasingly dependent on developing their own fund-raising organizations. This has left them more vulnerable to the influence of monied interests and greatly strengthened the hand of big business in setting the policy agendas of both parties. William Greider maintains that the policy directions of the Democratic Party are now largely set by six Washington law firms that specialize in selling political influence to monied clients and in raising money for Democratic politicians. Working closely with Republicans as well, these firms are in the business of brokering power to whomever will pay their fees.[18] This is the sorry state of American democracy.

The Republican Party has responded most handily to the new circumstances, expertly adapting sophisticated techniques of mass marketing to the task of winning elections. With these techniques, it has accomplished the improbable task of exploiting the alienation of powerless citizens to build a populist political base in support of an elitist agenda.

> As men of commerce, Republicans naturally understood marketing better than Democrats, and they applied what they knew about selling products to politics with none of the awkward hesitation that inhibited old-style politicians. As a result, voters are now viewed as a passive assembly of "consumers," a mass audience of potential buyers. Research discovers through scientific sampling what it is these consumers know or think and, more important, what they feel, even when they do not know their own "feelings." A campaign strategy is then designed to connect the candidate with these consumer attitudes. Advertising images are created that will elicit positive responses and make the sale.[19]

American democracy isn't for sale only to America's transnational corporations. The Mexican government spent upwards of $25 million and hired many of the leading Washington lobbyists to support its campaign for NAFTA. In the late 1980s, Japanese corporations were spending an estimated $100 million a year on political lobbying in the United States and another $300 million building a nationwide grassroots political network to influence public opinion. Together, the Japanese government and Japanese companies employed ninety-two Washington law, public-relations, and lobbying firms on their behalf. This compared with fifty-five for Canada, forty-two for Britain, and seven for the Netherlands. The purpose is to rewrite U.S. laws in favor of foreign corporations—and it often works.[20]

Corporate libertarianism—an ideology whose claims and promises are as false and self-serving as the claims of cigarette companies that nicotine is nonaddictive and cigarette smoke poses no health hazard—has become the dominant philosophy of our political culture and of our most powerful institutions. This is the accomplishment of a persistent campaign that uses the most sophisticated techniques yet developed by the masters of mass marketing and media manipulation. It is one element of a larger campaign to globalize their markets and to embed corporate libertarianism and consumerism in a homogenized global culture.

11 Marketing
the World

*Whoever has the power to project a vision of the good
life and make it prevail has the most decisive power of
all. . . . American business, after 1890, acquired such
power and . . . in league with key institutions, began the
transformation of American society into a society preoc-
cupied with consumption, with comfort and bodily well-
being, with luxury, spending, and acquisition, with more
goods this year than last, more next year than this.*
—William Leach[1]

*Corporate executives dream of a global market made
up of people with homogenized tastes and needs. . . .
Logos on bottles, boxes, and labels are global banners,
instantly recognizable by millions who could not tell
you the color of the U.N. flag.*
—Richard J. Barnet and John Cavanagh[2]

In modern societies, television has arguably become
our most important institution of cultural reproduction. Our schools are probably the second most important. Television has already been wholly colonized by
corporate interests, which are now laying claim to our
schools. The goal is not simply to sell products and
strengthen the consumer culture. It is also to create a
political culture that equates the corporate interest with
the human interest in the public mind. In the words of
Paul Hawken, "Our minds are being addressed by ad-
dictive media serving corporate sponsors whose purpose is to rearrange reality so that viewers forget the
world around them."[3]

The rearrangement of reality begins with the claim
that in a market economy, the consumer decides and

the market responds. In a world of small buyers and sellers, this may have been true. No individual seller could expect to create a new culture conducive to buying his or her product. This is not our current reality. Present-day corporations have no reservations about reshaping the values of whole societies to create a homogenized culture of indulgence conducive to spurring consumption expenditures and advancing corporate political interests. As corporate demand has grown for supporting services in advertising, graphics, media, creative production, consumer research, marketing education, and countless others, whole industries have emerged to help corporations create insatiable desires for the things they sell and cultivate political values aligned with the corporate interest.

First America, Then the World

There was a day when the prevailing American culture was the mass marketer's worst nightmare. Frugality and thrift were central to the famed "Puritan ethic" that the early Puritan settlers brought with them to America. The Puritans believed in hard work, participation in community, temperate living, and devotion to a spiritual life. Their basic rule of living was that one should not desire more material things than could be used effectively. They taught their children, "Use it up, wear it out, make do, or do without."[4]

The Quakers also had a strong influence on early America and, although more tolerant and egalitarian, shared with the Puritans the values of hard work and frugality as important to one's spiritual development. Ralph Waldo Emerson and Henry David Thoreau, both important early American writers, viewed simplicity as a path to experiencing the divine.[5]

The consumer culture emerged largely as a consequence of concerted efforts by the retailing giants of the late nineteenth and early twentieth centuries to create an ever-growing demand for the goods they offered for sale. American historian William Leach has documented in *Land of Desire: Merchants, Power, and the Rise of a New American Culture* how they successfully turned a spiritually oriented culture of frugality and thrift into a material culture of self-indulgence. Leach finds the claim that the market simply responds to consumer desires to be nothing more than a self-serving fabrication of those who make their living manipulating reality to convince consumers to buy what corporations find it profitable to sell:

Indeed, the culture of consumer capitalism may have been among the most nonconsensual public cultures ever created, and it was nonconsensual for two reasons. First, it was not produced by "the people" but by commercial groups in cooperation with other elites comfortable with and committed to making profits and to accumulating capital on an ever-ascending scale. Second, it was nonconsensual because, in its mere day-to-day conduct (but not in any conspiratorial way), it raised to the fore only one vision of the good life and pushed out all others. In this way, it diminished American public life, denying the American people access to insight into other ways of organizing and conceiving life, insight that might have endowed their consent to the dominant culture (if such consent were to be given at all) with real democracy.[6]

The populist cultures that grew out of the hearts and aspirations of ordinary people in America stressed the democratization of property and the virtues of a republic based on independent families owning their own land and tools, producing for themselves much of what they consumed, and participating in communities of sharing. Theirs was the model of a strong social economy, supplemented by involvement in the money economy at the margin of their lives.

The shift from a social economy of household and community production to a primarily monetized economy took place in America in the mid-1800s, during the period in which the large corporations came into ascendance. As late as 1870, however, the average number of workers in a given firm was still fewer than ten. Markets remained predominantly local or regional, and most businesses were individually owned and managed—a world still close to the ideal of Adam Smith.

Large corporations became increasingly skillful in creating desire for their products. Eventually, marketing was born as a management specialty, and the early business schools began offering courses to meet the demand. As more people became dependent on wage employment in the factories, governments gained a stake in promoting consumerism as a way of maintaining employment.

Business became skilled in using colors, glass, and light to create exciting images of a this-world paradise conveyed by elegant models and fashion shows. Museums offered displays depicting the excitement of the new culture. Gradually, the individual was surrounded by messages reinforcing the culture of desire. Advertisements, department store show windows, electric signs, fashion shows, the sumptuous environments of the leading hotels, and billboards all conveyed artfully crafted images of the good life. Credit programs made it seem effortless to buy that life. According to Leach:

The United States was the first country in the world to have an economy devoted to mass production and it was the first to create the mass consumer institutions and the mass consumer enticements that rose up in tandem to market and sell the mass-produced goods. More effectively and pervasively than any other nation, America . . . forged a unique bond among different institutions that served to realize business aims.[7]

Today, television is the primary medium through which corporations shape the culture and behavior of Americans. The statistics are chilling.[8] The average American child between the ages of two and five watches three and a half hours of television a day; the average adult, nearly five hours. Only work and sleep occupy more of the average adult's life—with television effectively replacing community and family life, cultural pursuits, and reading. At this rate, the average American adult is seeing approximately 21,000 commercials a year, most of which carry an identical message: "Buy something—do it now!" The 100 largest corporations in America pay for roughly 75 percent of commercial television time and 50 percent of public television time. With a half minute of prime-time network advertising selling for between $200,000 and $300,000, only the largest corporations can afford it. Although there may be no overt control over program content, television producers are hired to produce television programming that advertisers will buy and necessarily have these corporations and their views of proper programming content constantly in mind.

Jerry Mander explains why television is a nearly ideal communications medium for serving the corporate purpose:

By its ability to implant identical images into the minds of millions of people, TV can homogenize perspectives, knowledge, tastes, and desires, to make them resemble the tastes and interests of the people who transmit the imagery. In our world, the transmitters of the images are corporations whose ideal of life is technologically oriented, commodity oriented, materialistic, and hostile to nature. And satellite communications is the mechanism by which television is delivered into parts of the planet that have, until recently, been spared this assault.[9]

As global corporations reach out to the four corners of the earth, they bring with them not only established products and brand names but also their favored media and the sophisticated marketing methods by which they colonize every culture they touch.

The Economist reported that in 1989, global corporate spending for advertising totaled more than $240 billion. Another $380 billion was spent on packaging, design, and other point-of-sale promotions. Together, these expenditures amounted to $120 for every single person in the world.[10] Although the bulk of this corporate expenditure is directed toward creating demand for specific products, it also contributes to creating a generalized global consumer culture and to making a connection in the public mind between corporate interests—in particular the interests of large corporations—and the public interest.

Overall, corporations are spending well over half as much per capita to create corporation-friendly consumers as the $207 per capita ($33 for Southern countries) the world spends on public education.[11] Furthermore, growth in advertising expenditures far outpaces increases in education spending. Advertising expenditures have multiplied nearly sevenfold since 1950—one-third faster than the world economy.[12]

The One World of MTV Knows —"Coke Is Best"

In his *Atlantic Monthly* article in praise of economic integration, Akio Morita identified distinctive local cultures as a trade barrier.[13] The need to respect local tastes and cultural differences as a condition of gaining consumer acceptance greatly complicates global marketing campaigns. The dream of corporate marketers is a globalized consumer culture united around brand-name loyalties that will allow a company to sell its products with the same advertising copy in Bangkok as in Paris or New York. It is happening. In the words of Robert C. Goizueta, chairman of Coca-Cola Company, "people around the world are today connected by brand name consumer products as much as by anything else."[14] Coca-Cola's success in making itself a global symbol has served as an inspiration for corporate executives everywhere.

Few media provide greater potential for realizing this advertisers' dream than MTV, the rock music television channel. Its near universal appeal to teenagers and preteens around the world makes it an ideal instrument for the globalization of the consumer culture. By 1993, MTV's popular rock-and-roll programming, with its kaleidoscope of brief, disconnected images, was available on a daily basis to 210 million households in seventy-one countries. According to Richard J. Barnet and John Cavanagh, the MTV entertainment network, which specializes in pop videos and serves as a continuous commercial for a wide array of commercial products, "may be the most influential educator of young people on five continents." They continue:

> The performances and the ads merge to create a mood of longing—for someone to love, for something exciting to happen, for an end to loneliness, and for things to buy—a record, a ticket to a rock concert, a T-shirt, a Thunderbird. The advertising is all the more effective because it is not acknowledged as such. . . . All across

the planet, people are using the same electronic devices to watch or to listen to the same commercially produced songs and stories.[15]

Sarah Ferguson believes that the commercialization of youth culture, especially the music that was once a primary instrument of expressive rebellion for adolescents, keeps youth from owning even their own rebellion and actively inhibits the development of a counterculture. She writes, "The loop taken by a new musical style from the underground to the mainstream is now so compressed that there's no moment of freedom and chaos when a counterculture can take root."[16]

Among the most aggressive efforts to universalize the consumer culture is that of the Avon beauty products company. On August 2, 1994, the show *TV Nation* documented the campaign by Avon to win new customers among dirt-poor campesinas in the Amazon basin of Brazil, where 70,000 Avon saleswomen take the Avon message to every rural doorstep. Ademar Serodio, president of Avon Brazil, explained, "Instead of asking people to buy more from us, we start discovering people who never bought from us before." As revealed in footage of Avon saleswomen making door-to-door house calls in the remote village of Santarem, many of these new customers are thin, aging, wrinkled women living with their barefoot children in shacks with dirt floors. Most people in Santarem don't read or write, and the average household income is $3 per day.

Hundreds of Avon saleswomen were fielded in Santarem to follow up on TV advertising showing romantic scenes of sensuous, young, light-skinned women with dashingly handsome young men. They tell the aged women, broken by years of childbearing and toil in the sun, that they can be beautiful if they use Avon products. A major promotion centers on a skin-renewal product called Renew—costing $40 a jar—which works by burning off the top layer of the user's skin. A TV ad uses special effects to create the image of a woman peeling away years of aging from her face to appear magically younger. According to Rosa Alegria, communications director for Avon Brazil, "Women do everything to buy it. They stop buying other things like clothes, like shoes. If they feel good with their skin they prefer to stop buying clothes and buy something that is on the television. People think it is a real miracle."[17]

Corporations in the Classroom

Corporations are now moving aggressively to colonize the second major institution of cultural reproduction, the schools. According to

Consumers Union, 20 million U.S. schoolchildren used some form of corporate-sponsored teaching materials in their classrooms in 1990. Some of these are straightforward promotions of junk food, clothing, and personal-care items. For example, the National Potato Board joined forces with Lifetime Learning Systems to present "Count Your Chips," a math-oriented program celebrating the potato chip for National Potato Lovers' Month. NutraSweet, a sugar substitute, sponsored a "total health" program.[18]

Corporations have also been aggressive in getting their junk foods into school vending machines and school lunch programs. Trade shows and journals aimed at school food-service workers are full of appeals such as: "Bring Taco Bell products to your school!" "Pizza Hut makes school lunch fun." Coca-Cola launched a lobbying attack on proposed legislation to ban the sale of soft drinks and other items of "minimal nutritional value" in public schools. Randal W. Donaldson, a spokesman for Coca-Cola in Atlanta, said: "Our strategy is ubiquity. We want to put soft drinks within arm's reach of desire. We strive to make soft drinks widely available, and schools are one channel we want to make them available in."[19]

Other messages seek to indoctrinate young minds in the beliefs and values of corporate liberalism. Thus Mobil Corporation, which is well known for buying op-ed space in the *New York Times* to promote its view of the public interest, offered a curriculum module produced by the Learning Enrichment Corporation for classroom use that claimed to help students evaluate the North American Free Trade Agreement (NAFTA), mainly by touting its benefits.

Faced with the inevitability of an environmentally aware public, corporations have responded by painting themselves green and seeking to define the problem and its solutions in ways that support corporate objectives. Another Mobil contribution to public education is a video prepared for classroom use that touts plastic as the best waste to put in landfills. An Exxon module titled "Energy Cube" omits discussion of fuel efficiency, alternatives to fossil fuels, and global warming. Indeed, it attempts to equate gasoline with solar energy in students' minds by explaining that its "energy value comes from solar energy stored in its organic chemical bonds."

Mobil and other corporations actively support the National Council on Economic Education, whose mission is to promote the teaching of economics in elementary and high schools. A paid Mobil op-ed piece in the *New York Times* lamented the fact that high school seniors were able to give correct answers to only 35 percent of questions on a national economic literacy survey. Obviously, Mobil has its own idea of what a correct answer is. The op-ed piece notes:

When it comes to domestic issues, it helps to understand the impact that raising or cutting taxes will have on job security and your standard of living. And when it comes to environmental policy and regulations, it's necessary to comprehend basic economic principles such as supply and demand, cost versus benefit and a company's need for profits.[20]

General Motors mailed a video entitled "I Need the Earth and the Earth Needs Me" to every public, private, and parochial elementary school in the country. Against a backdrop of happy children swimming in sparkling waters and running in picturesque landscapes, the GM video promotes such activities as planting trees and recycling. There is no mention of mass transit or the need to redesign cities to reduce transportation needs. GM recommends forming car pools and recycling used motor oil. All the statements made in the video and the accompanying teacher's guide are accurate. Yet the overall picture is misleading because it omits mention of critical facts and ideas.

Channel One, an advertiser-sponsored school television program, beams its news and ads for candy bars, fast food, and sneakers directly into the classroom for twelve minutes a day in more than 12,000 schools. In exchange for a satellite dish and video equipment for each classroom, the school must agree that Channel One will be shown on at least 90 percent of school days to 90 percent of the children. *Teachers are not allowed to interrupt the show or turn it off.* A survey found that most students thought that since Channel One was shown in school, the products advertised on it must be good for them.[21]

Mark Evans, a senior vice president of Scholastic, Inc., presented the following challenge to business in an essay in *Advertising Age*:

> More and more companies see educational marketing as the most compelling, memorable and cost-effective way to build share of mind and market into the 21st century. . . . [A Gillette program introducing teenagers to its safety razors is] . . . building brand and product loyalties through classroom-centered, peer-powered lifestyle patterning. . . . Can you devise promotions that take students from the aisles in school rooms to the aisles in supermarkets?[22]

If not, presumably Scholastic, Inc., one of the leading U.S. producers of school curriculum materials, stands ready to help.

Other corporations are proposing to operate the public schools on a for-profit basis. The possibilities for profiting by turning classrooms into new mass media outlets for corporate marketing, image building, and ideological molding pitched to young and malleable minds are staggering—and frightening.

The World of *1984*

Corporations spend money on advertising, lobbying, advocacy, and public relations, whether in schools or the mass media, to encourage individual and public actions that support and advance corporate interests using whatever methods will elicit the desired consumer response. As Paul Hawken describes their methods:

> Soft-focus shots of deer in virgin forests are used as totemic proof of a paper company's commitment to the future even as they continue to clear-cut and fight congressional renewal of the Endangered Species Act. Native Americans look approvingly over a littered wild flower meadow being cleaned up by children using plastic bags advertised as biodegradable which in fact are not. (Mobil Oil was sued and chastised by attorney generals in several states for this ad.) Simpson Paper introduces a line of "recycled" paper with fractional amounts of post-consumer waste under the names of Thoreau, Whitman, and Leopold. British nuclear power companies announce that nuclear energy is green energy since it does not pollute the air.[23]

Tobacco companies spend millions to convince the public that there is no scientific basis for claims that smoking is harmful to their health; auto manufacturers fight emissions standards; gun manufacturers fight gun controls; chemical companies illegally dump their toxic wastes; and drug companies engage in monopoly pricing. It happens every day. For all the corporate claims to the contrary, *Business Week* itself said it well: "Modern multinationals are not social institutions. They will play governments off one another, shift pricing to minimize taxes, seek to sway opinion, export jobs, or withhold technology to maintain a competitive edge."[24]

Corporate efforts to shape our culture and our politics through control of television bring to mind George Orwell's *1984* and his images of an authoritarian society ruled by ever-present television monitors that manipulate citizens' perceptions of the world. Our reality is more subtle and the techniques more sophisticated than Orwell anticipated. And the strings are pulled by corporations rather than governments. We are ruled by an oppressive market, not an oppressive state.

The techniques have an elegant simplicity. They center on manipulating the cultural symbols in which our individual identities and values are anchored. Before mass media, these symbols were collective creations of people relating to one another and expressing their inner feelings through artistic media. They represented our collective sense of who we are. The more time we spend immersed in the corporate-controlled and -packaged world of television, the less time we have for the direct human exchanges through which cultural identity and values were traditionally expressed, reinforced, and updated. Increasingly, those who control mass media control the core culture.

The architects of the corporate global vision seek a world in which universalized symbols created and owned by the world's most powerful corporations replace the distinctive cultural symbols that link people to particular places, values, and human communities. Our cultural symbols provide an important source of identity and meaning; they affirm our worth, our place in society. They arouse our loyalty to and sense of responsibility for the health and well-being of our community and its distinctive ecosystem. When control of our cultural symbols passes to corporations, we are essentially yielding to them the power to define who we are. Instead of being Americans, Norwegians, Egyptians, Filipinos, or Mexicans, we become simply members of the "Pepsi generation," detached from place and any meaning other than those a corporation finds it profitable to confer on us. Market tyranny may be more subtle than state tyranny, but it is no less effective in enslaving the many to the interests of the few.

12 Adjusting the Poor

They no longer use bullets and ropes. They use the World Bank and the IMF.

—Jesse Jackson[1]

To attract companies like yours . . . we have felled mountains, razed jungles, filled swamps, moved rivers, relocated towns . . . all to make it easier for you and your business to do business here.

—Philippine government ad in Fortune[2]

In the flurry of global institution building that followed World War II, the spotlight of public attention was focused on the United Nations (UN), which was to be inclusive of all countries, each with an equal voice—at least in its General Assembly. Delegates to the UN are public figures, and debates are open to public view and often heated. Yet the General Assembly has little real power. The real ability to act is vested in the Security Council, in which each of the major powers maintains the right of veto. Judging from its governance structures, it must be concluded that the UN was created primarily to function as a forum for debate.

In contrast, three other multilateral institutions were created with relatively little fanfare to operate outside the public eye—the International Bank for Reconstruction and Development (commonly known as the World Bank), the International Monetary Fund (IMF), and the General Agreement on Tariffs and Trade (GATT). These three agencies are commonly referred to as the

Bretton Woods institutions, in tribute to a meeting of representatives of forty-four nations who gathered in Bretton Woods, New Hampshire, July 1–22, 1944, to reach agreement on an institutional framework for the post–World War II global economy. The public purpose of what became known as the Bretton Woods system was to unite the world in a web of economic prosperity and interdependence that would preclude nations' taking up arms. Another purpose in the eyes of its architects was to create an open world economy unified under U.S. leadership that would ensure unchallenged U.S. access to the world's markets and raw materials.[3] Two of the Bretton Woods institutions—the IMF and the World Bank—were actually created at the Bretton Woods meeting. The GATT was created at a subsequent international meeting.

Although formally designated as "special agencies" of the UN, the Bretton Woods institutions function nearly autonomously from it. Their governance and administrative processes are secret—carefully shielded from public scrutiny and democratic debate. Indeed, the internal operating processes of the World Bank are so secretive that access to many of its most important documents relating to country plans, strategies, and priorities is denied to even its own governing executive directors. In the World Bank and the IMF, the big national powers have both veto power over certain decisions and voting shares in proportion to their shares of the subscribed capital—ensuring their ability to set and control the agenda.[4]

In this chapter, we examine how, in playing out their roles, the World Bank and the IMF have worked in concert to deepen the dependence of low-income countries on the global system and then to open their economies to corporate colonization. In the following chapter, we look at how the GATT and its successor, the World Trade Organization (WTO), are being used by the world's largest corporations to consolidate their power and place themselves beyond public accountability.

Creating a Demand for Debt

The primary original purpose of the World Bank was to finance European reconstruction. However, there was very little demand from the European countries for World Bank loans. What Europe needed was rapidly dispersing grants or concessional loans for balance-of-payment support and imports to temporarily meet basic needs while its own economies were being rebuilt. The U.S. Marshall Plan provided this type of assistance; the World Bank did not. By 1953—nine years after its establishment—total Bank lending was only $1.75 billion, of which only $497 million was for European reconstruction. That amount paled in comparison to the $41.3 billion transferred to Europe under the Marshall Plan.[5]

The Bank's annual report for 1947–48 acknowledged that lack of demand for its loans was not limited to Europe. As the Bank began to look to the low-income countries for customers, it ran into a similar problem. Countries simply were not presenting the Bank with acceptable projects. Two problems were identified. The first was the borrowers' lack of technical and planning skills to prepare loan proposals.[6] The second problem, meticulously documented by Robin Broad in her study of the World Bank and the IMF in the Philippines, was more basic: the business elites who regularly rotated in and out of key government positions were split between economic nationalists and transnationalists.

The economic nationalist group comprised those businesspeople who were engaged primarily in serving the local market. They naturally favored avoiding international economic entanglements and sought to protect national markets and resources from the uncertainties of the international economy.[7] Most were wary of international lenders and spurned the Bank's overtures. In the Bank's early days, control over economic policy in most low-income countries was firmly in the hands of economic nationalists.

Transnationalists were more closely aligned with the Bank's ideology and were inclined to be more receptive to moves that drew the national economy into the global orbit. They were the Bank's natural allies.[8] Transnationalists were found among two groups. The first was made up of businesspeople who had links with transnational banks and corporations through joint ventures, licensing agreements, marketing arrangements, and other connections that aligned their interests with policies that allow the free international flow of goods and capital. The second group comprised the highly educated technical bureaucrats who had studied economics, often abroad, and interacted on a regular basis with foreign or multilateral institutions.[9]

The development debates of the day centered on a key question: where would newly industrializing countries find the market demand to drive the growth of their economies, particularly their industrial sectors? The leading protagonists in the debate recognized only two possibilities—either concentrating industrialization on providing locally produced substitutes for those goods that the country currently imported (import-substitution strategies) or building domestic industry primarily to serve foreign export markets (export-led strategies). The former strategy, advocated by Argentine economist Raul Prebisch and the UN Economic Commission for Latin America (ECLA), was oriented toward self-reliance and ran directly counter to the mandates of the Bank and the IMF to open domestic economies to the expansion of foreign trade and investment.[10] Import substitution reduced the requirement for imports and thus the need for foreign exchange. The strategy was anathema to a bank that existed primarily to make foreign currency loans to increase the purchase of goods and services from the Northern industrial countries. Economic nationalists were inclined to favor an import-substitution strategy, whereas transnationalists were more likely to favor an export-led strategy.

In the 1950s, the Bank pursued a strategy designed to address both barriers. It gave priority to "institution-building" projects aimed at creating autonomous governmental agencies that would be regular World Bank borrowers. Generally, Bank staff sought to ensure that these agencies were relatively autonomous from their governments and would be staffed primarily by transnational technocrats with strong professional, as well as financial, ties to the Bank. In 1956, the Bank created the Economic Development Institute. It initially offered seminars to senior government officials from borrowing countries to imbue them with the Bank's point of view on the theory and practice of development. It also provided technical training for personnel from the newly created agencies in the Bank's procedures and methods for loan preparation and implementation.[11]

The Bank's claim that it simply responds to the needs and requests of borrowing countries is as false as the claim by corporate libertarians that the market simply responds to consumer demand. The Bank did what the big retail outlets did in the 1800s when faced with a frugal culture that failed to produce sufficient customers. It set about to reshape values and institutions in ways that would create customers for its product. And much like the corporations that chose this course, the Bank gave scant attention to the larger consequences of actions taken primarily to meet its own needs.

Once its demand-creation strategy was in place, the Bank set about to further increase its leverage over the policies of its more important client countries by establishing donor coordination groups under its direction on a country-by-country basis. For example, the Bank had flooded India with loans in the 1950s in an unsuccessful effort to build enough leverage to win India away from a policy of import substitution and active government intervention in the economy. Still, its advice went unheeded by India's powerful nationalist finance minister. The Bank changed its tactics, formed a donor group, and promised substantial increases in aid if India moved toward more free-market, export-oriented policies. By 1971, the Bank chaired sixteen such donor groups.[12] This opened a new era of cooperation among donors under the leadership of the World Bank and increased the Bank's policy leverage.[13]

When the Bill Collector Calls

In 1943, Wilbert Ward, a vice president of National City Bank of New York, raised a prophetic question about the proposal to establish the World Bank:

> If you are going to set up a bank you should set up an organization to finance transactions that will in the end liquidate themselves. Otherwise it is not a bank. . . . Where can we loan thirty to fifty billion around the world with any prospects of its being repaid?[14]

To this day, this question has never been satisfactorily answered. The standard response of World Bank economists is that World Bank loans will be repaid out of returns from the economic growth they stimulate. The reality is that most borrowing countries have been able to service existing international debts only by increasing their international borrowing. The more they borrow, the more they become dependent on international borrowing and the more their attention is focused not on their own development but on obtaining more loans. It becomes like a drug addiction.

In the 1970s, price increases imposed by the Organization of Petroleum Exporting Countries (OPEC) placed oil-importing low-income countries in a critical foreign exchange position. At the same time, commercial banks were awash in petrodollars deposited by the OPEC countries and were looking for places to loan them profitably. There seemed to be an ideal fit between the needs of the banks and the needs of low-income countries. By this time, the World Bank's client countries had become accustomed to supplementing their export-based foreign exchange earnings with borrowing, and the line between foreign borrowing for self-liquidating investments and borrowing for current consumption had become badly blurred. Given the low real interest rates prevailing at the time the OPEC money was being recycled through the system, the offers being made by the commercial banks seemed like a potential bonanza, and countries borrowed with abandon. Few on either side of the lending–borrowing frenzy seemed to notice that the whole scheme was a house of cards, dependent on borrowing ever more to cover debt service on former loans while still yielding net inflows.

Lending from the World Bank and its sister regional banks had been a fairly orderly process until the late 1970s, when the rise in oil prices effected by the OPEC countries caused the foreign debts of Southern countries to skyrocket. From 1970 to 1980, the long-term external debt of low-income countries increased from $21 billion to $110 billion. That of middle-income countries rose from $40 billion to $317 billion.[15] As real interest rates soared, it became evident that the borrowing countries were so seriously overextended that default was imminent—leading potentially to a collapse of the whole global financial system. The World Bank and the IMF, acting as overseers of the global financial system, stepped in—much as court-appointed receivers in bankruptcy cases—to set the terms of financial settlements between virtually bankrupt countries and the international financial system.

In their capacity as international receivers, the World Bank and the IMF imposed packages of policy prescriptions on indebted nations under the rubric of *structural adjustment*. Each structural adjustment package called for sweeping economic policy reforms intended to channel more of the adjusted country's resources and productive activity toward debt repayment and to further open national economies to the global economy. Restrictions and tariffs on both imports and exports were reduced, and incentives were provided to attract foreign investors.

Some of the reforms, such as a reduction of subsidies to the rich, were long overdue. However, others provided new subsidies for exporters and foreign investors. Government spending on social services for the poor was reduced in order to free more funds for loan repayment. In adjusted countries in Africa and Latin America, aggregate governmental spending per person was reduced between 1980 and 1987. The share of the total budget devoted to interest payments increased, as the share of all other budget categories—including defense—decreased. In Latin America, the portion of government budgets allocated to interest payments increased from 9 percent to 19.3 percent. In Africa, it rose from 7.7 percent to 12.5 percent.[16]

There were two underlying purposes for these reforms. The first was to ensure that loans from both the commercial and the multilateral banks were repaid. There was a strong emphasis on policies to strengthen exports and attract foreign investment in order to generate foreign exchange for this purpose. The second purpose was to advance the integration of domestic economies into the global economy. Import barriers were reduced or removed, based on the argument that this was necessary to improve access to materials used by export-oriented industries and to create competitive pressures to increase the efficiency of domestic firms so that they might, in turn, compete successfully in global markets.

The World Bank and the IMF proclaimed their structural adjustment programs to be a resounding success and declared the debt crisis resolved. They pointed to the fact that many of the adjusted countries subsequently experienced higher growth rates, expanded their export sectors, increased the total value of their exports, attracted new foreign investment, and became current on their debt repayments. They could not, however, argue that international debts or trade deficits had been reduced or that social conditions had improved.

To attract foreign investors, governments have suppressed union organizing to hold down wages, benefits, and labor standards. They have given special tax breaks and subsidies to foreign corporations and cut corners on environmental regulations. The fact that dozens of countries have sought to increase foreign exchange earnings by increasing the export of natural resources and agricultural commodities has driven down the prices of their export goods in international markets— creating pressures to extract and export even more to maintain foreign exchange earnings. Falling prices for export commodities, profit repatriation by foreign investors, and increased demand for manufactured imports stimulated by the reduction of tariff barriers have resulted in continuing trade deficits for most countries. From 1980, the beginning of the World Bank–IMF decade of structural adjustment, to 1992, low-income countries' excess of imports over exports increased from $6.5 billion to $34.7 billion. The Bank and IMF have responded with more loans as a reward for carrying out structural adjustment. As a result, the international indebtedness of low-income countries increased from $134 billion in 1980 to $473 billion in 1992. Interest payments on this debt increased from $6.4 billion to $18.3 billion.[17] Rather than increasing their self-reliance, the world's low-income countries, under the guidance of the World Bank and the IMF, continue to mortgage more of their futures to the international system each year.

Calling it guidance may be too polite. In their roles as international debt collectors, the World Bank and the IMF have become increasingly intrusive in dictating the public policies of indebted countries and undermining progress toward democratic governance and public accountability. As Jonathan Cahn argues in the *Harvard Human Rights Journal*:

> The World Bank must be regarded as a governance institution, exercising power through its financial leverage to legislate entire legal regimens and even to alter the constitutional structure of borrowing nations. Bank-approved consultants often rewrite a country's trade policy, fiscal policies, civil service requirements, labor laws, health care arrangements, environmental regulations, energy policy, resettlement requirements, procurement rules, and budgetary policy.[18]

In its governance role, the World Bank—a global bureaucracy—is making decisions for people to whom it is not accountable that would normally be the responsibility of elected legislative bodies. The very process of the borrowing that created the indebtedness that gave the World Bank and the IMF the power to dictate the policies of borrowing countries represented an egregious assault on the principles of democratic accountability. Loan agreements, whether with the World Bank, the IMF, other official lending institutions, or commercial banks, are routinely negotiated in secret between banking officials and a handful of government officials—who in many instances are themselves unelected and unaccountable to the people on whose behalf they are obligating the national treasury to foreign lenders. Even in democracies, the borrowing procedures generally bypass the normal appropriation processes of democratically elected legislative bodies. Thus, government agencies are able to increase their own budgets without legislative approval, even though the legislative body will have to come up with the revenues to cover repayment. Foreign loans also enable governments to increase current expenditures without the need to raise current taxes—a feature that is especially popular with wealthy decision makers. The same officials who approve the loans often benefit directly through participation in contracts and "commissions" from grateful contractors. The system creates a powerful incentive to over-borrow.

In effect, those officials who sign foreign loan agreements are obligating the people of the country to future financial obligations completely outside of any process of public review and consent. This becomes especially egregious when, as has happened to millions of people in Bank client countries, the loan-funded projects displace the poor from homes and lands, pollute their waters, cut down their forests, and destroy their fisheries. Then, adding insult to injury, when the bills come due, the poor are told that their social services and wages must be cut to repay the country's loan obligations.

The Corporate Connection

Although it seeks to create an image of serving the poor and their borrowing governments, the World Bank is primarily a creature of the transnational financial system. The Bank's direct financial links to the transnational corporate sector on both the borrowing and the lending ends of its operation have received far too little attention. Technically, the Bank is owned by its member governments, which contribute its paid-in capital; this was only $10.53 billion, as of 1993. In addition, member governments have pledged $155 billion that can be called by the Bank if needed to meet its financial obligations. The paid-in capital and the pledges are not actually loaned out. They secure the Bank's extensive borrowing operations in the international financial markets, where it raises the funds that are then re-lent to governments at more favorable rates than they could obtain by borrowing directly.

Although the Bank lends to governments, its projects normally involve large procurement contracts with transnational construction firms, large consulting firms, and procurement contractors. These firms are one of the Bank's most powerful political constituencies. The area of Bank operations that is watched most closely by the Bank's executive directors—representatives of its shareholder governments—is the procurement process. Each director wants to ensure that the countries he or she represents are getting at least their fair share of procurement contracts. The U.S. Treasury Department is quite up front in its appeals to the corporate interest in supporting funding replenishments for the Bank. Treasury officials point out that for every $1 the U.S. government contributes to the World Bank, more than $2 comes back to U.S. exporters in procurement contracts. As Treasury Secretary Lloyd Bentsen assured Congress in 1994, "The dollars we have sent abroad through the development banks come back home in increased U.S. exports and more U.S. jobs."[19]

The sole function of one arm of the World Bank, the International Finance Corporation, is to make government-guaranteed loans on favorable terms to private investors whose projects are too risky to qualify for commercial bank financing. It accounts for 10 to 12 percent of total World Bank lending.[20] The potentials for abuse are even greater than with the Bank's core lending programs. To date, the Bank has kept the International Finance Corporation so far out of the public eye that it is seldom mentioned, even by Bank critics. However, given its own ideological belief in free-market forces, it seems difficult for the Bank to justify a major operation devoted to using publicly guaranteed funds to finance large private ventures that are so risky that commercial banks will not fund them.

If the Poor Mattered

When the formation of the World Bank was proposed, Republican Senator Robert Taft emerged as a formidable opponent. His argument, made in 1945, reveals a significant insight into why foreign aid based on large financial flows is a deeply flawed idea:

> I think we overestimate the value of American money and American aid to other nations. No people can make over another

people. Every nation must solve its own problems, and whatever
we do can only be of slight assistance to help it over its most severe problems. . . . A nation that comes to rely on gifts and loans
from others is too likely to postpone the essential, tough measures
necessary for its own salvation.[21]

Taft maintained that the major beneficiaries would be Wall Street investment bankers: "it is almost a subsidy to the business of investment
bankers, and will also undoubtedly increase the business to be done
by the larger banks."[22] Subsequent events have substantially affirmed
Taft's argument.

Properly understood, development is a process by which people
increase their human, institutional, and technical capacities to produce
the goods and services needed to achieve sustainable improvements
in their quality of life using the resources available to them. Many of
us call such a process people-centered development—not only because
it benefits people but also because it is centered in people. It is especially important to involve the poor and excluded, thus allowing them
to meet their own needs through their own productive efforts.[23] A small
amount of help from abroad can be very useful in a people-centered
development process, but too much foreign funding can prevent real
development and even break down the existing capabilities of a people
to sustain themselves.

Debates about import-substitution versus export-led development
rarely acknowledge the people-centered alternative. Both start from
the top, focusing on the production of more of the things that people
who are already well-off want to buy. Poor people seldom buy imported
goods. Their needs are met by simple locally produced goods. When
a country seeks to replace imports with domestic production, it usually means producing at home more of the goods that those who are
relatively well-off buy from abroad. When a country seeks to increase
its exports, it generally means gearing domestic productive capability
to producing things for relatively well-off foreigners. In theory, either
strategy will produce more jobs for poor people so that they can participate in the money economy. But usually the jobs these strategies
provide are too few and too poorly compensated to eliminate poverty.
Either strategy can, and in all too many instances does, displace local
production of the things that poor people use in order to produce more
of the things that wealthier people want—even depriving the poor of
their basic means of livelihood, such as when the lands of small farmers are taken over by estates producing for export.

Let's reduce the problem to its basics. Poverty—generally defined
as a lack of adequate money—is not the issue. It is the deprivation associated with a lack of money that is the problem—the lack of access

to adequate food, clothing, shelter, and other essentials of a decent life. This simple fact suggests a people-centered alternative to both the import-substitution and export-led development models: pursuing policies that create opportunities for people who are experiencing deprivation to produce the things that they need to have a better life.

This is, in many respects, what Japan, Korea, and Taiwan did. Each made significant investments to achieve a high level of adult literacy and basic education, carried out radical land reform to create a thriving rural economy based on small farm production, and supported the development of rural industries that produced things needed by small farm families. These became the foundation of larger industries. The development of these countries was equity-led, not export-led— contrary to the historical revisionism of corporate libertarians. Only after these countries had developed broad-based domestic economies did they become major exporters in the international economy.

From the standpoint of transnational corporate capital and the World Bank, a people-centered development strategy presents a major problem. Since it creates very little demand for imports, it also creates little demand for foreign loans. Furthermore, it favors local ownership of assets and thus provides few profit opportunities for transnational corporations.

During my first visit to South Africa in January 1992, I used a hypothetical example to illustrate this point. By the time of my visit, the era of apartheid had come to an end, and the country was preparing for a transition to black rule. I was struck by the strict demarcation of living space that isolated the black population in remote townships. Although this was not a surprise, the lack of evidence of economic activity in the townships was. There were neither modern commercial centers nor the myriad shops, stalls, and street vendors that are ubiquitous in poor neighborhoods in most of the world. It was then that I realized the full extent to which the economy had been designed to ensure that blacks remained wholly dependent on the white urban economy. Developing black entrepreneurship seemed an obvious and necessary goal toward the creation of a fully integrated society.

The World Bank was especially aggressive among the foreign aid donors pouring into the country with offers of assistance. One of the few blessings of apartheid was that because of the resulting international sanctions, South Africa had accumulated very little foreign debt. With its abundant resources, it was, from an international banker's perspective, an "underborrowed" country. The World Bank was thus drawn to South Africa like a bear to honey. Among other projects, the Bank was proposing a large loan for housing in the black townships. Everyone agreed that housing was a critical need. The question was how that need might best be met. Consider three hypothetical options:

Option 1. The World Bank provides a major foreign exchange loan for housing. The proceeds are used to import foreign building materials and construction equipment and to hire foreign contractors to build completed housing tracts. South African blacks will have new houses within a fairly brief time. Apart from temporary employment, few if any new local capacities will be developed, and there will be little impact on the local economy, until it comes time to generate the foreign exchange to repay the loan. Then the country will need to boost its exports, a task that will justify measures favoring the white firms that are in a position to reach out to export markets. Others will face austerity, particularly the poor blacks whose public services will be cut back.

Option 2. The World Bank provides a major loan for housing. The foreign exchange proceeds from the loan are exchanged for South African rand at South Africa's Central Bank, and the rand are used to contract large white-owned corporations to build the housing, using local labor and domestically produced building materials. The black communities get their housing and some temporary employment, the white economy gets a major boost, and the country gets a one-time temporary injection of foreign exchange that may be used to import luxury goods or arms for the military or to transfer assets of white South Africans to foreign accounts. The dependence of the black economy on the white economy remains intact. The international economic dependence of South Africa increases. The loan must be repaid in foreign exchange, with consequences the same as those in option 1.

Option 3. South Africa graciously thanks the Bank staffers for their visit, declines their offer, and puts them on the next plane back to Washington. Local funds are mobilized from the existing excess liquidity of the domestic banking system to finance black housing. Programs are put in place to provide training for black South Africans in a variety of entrepreneurial and technical skills. Incentives and support are provided to encourage the formation of small black firms to produce door frames, bricks, and basic plumbing and electrical fixtures and to provide construction contracting services. The technologies and materials involved in low-income housing are quite basic and are readily available in South Africa. There is virtually nothing for which foreign exchange is needed, so there is no legitimate reason to incur foreign debt. With this option, the black population gets its housing plus new skills, new economic power, new sources of livelihood, and a start toward a thriving black-controlled economy. A system is in place to build and maintain housing as required. The white economy would also benefit, as it would necessarily be the source of some of the materials and services. There would be no new foreign debt to repay.

Of the three options, only the third creates new black capabilities and economic power and strengthens economic self-reliance. It is the only option that can be considered truly developmental. The greater the involvement of foreign aid agencies, especially the World Bank or a regional development bank, the less likely it becomes that option 3 will be chosen, because it gives the foreign donor little, if any, role.

Of course, South Africa is something of a special case in the extent of its domestic resources and technical capabilities. There is, however, scarcely any country in the world that does not have the resources and technology needed to provide its people with their basic needs for food, clothing, shelter, education, and health care—if these are priorities.

Foreign aid, even grant aid, becomes actively antidevelopmental when the proceeds are used to build dependence on imported technology and experts, encourage import-dependent consumer lifestyles, fund waste and corruption, displace domestically produced products with imports, and drive millions of people from the lands and waters on which they depend for their livelihoods—all of which are common outcomes of World Bank projects and structural adjustment programs.

On top of this, there is evidence that the majority of Bank projects are failures, even by the Bank's own narrowly defined economic criteria. In 1992, an internal Bank study team headed by Willi Wapenhans published a report titled "Effective Implementation: Key to Development Impact," which concluded that 37.5 percent of Bank-funded projects completed in 1991 were failures at the time of completion.[24] An earlier study by the Bank's Operations Evaluation Department conducted four- to ten-year follow-up evaluations on projects that the Bank had rated as successful at the time of completion. It found that twelve of twenty-five projects that had been rated successful when completed eventually turned out to be failures.[25] If only half of the projects rated successful at completion in 1991 actually achieve their projected returns (as is likely to be the case), then less than a third of Bank projects will have provided sufficient economic return to justify the original investment. Yet failures or not, the loan must be repaid in scarce foreign exchange. The Bank bears no liability for its own errors.

If measured by contributions to improving the lives of people or strengthening the institutions of democratic governance, the World Bank and the IMF have been disastrous failures—imposing an enormous burden on the world's poor and seriously impeding their development. In terms of fulfilling the mandates set for them by their original architects—advancing economic globalization under the domination of the economically powerful—they both have been a resounding success. In addition, the IMF was highly successful in averting, at least temporarily, a global financial crisis on terms favorable to the Northern commercial banks. Together, the Bank and the IMF have helped build powerful political constituencies aligned with corporate libertarianism, weakened the democratic accountability of Southern governments, usurped the functions of democratically elected officials, and removed most consequential legal and institutional barriers to the recolonization of Southern economies by transnational capital. They have arguably done more harm to more people than any other pair of nonmilitary institutions in human history.

We now turn to the third institution in the Bretton Woods triumvirate—the GATT–WTO—to examine its role in creating and enforcing a transnational corporate bill of rights.

13 Guaranteeing Corporate Rights

*Cosmopolitan globalism weakens national boundaries
and the power of national and subnational communities, while strengthening the relative power of transnational corporations.*

—*Herman E. Daly*[1]

*In the corporate economies of the contemporary West,
the market is a passive institution. The active institution is the corporation . . . an inherently narrow and
short-sighted organization. . . . The corporation has
evolved to serve the interests of whoever controls it, at
the expense of whomever does not.*

—*William M. Dugger*[2]

The framework for a post–World War II economy,
which had been worked out largely between the
United States and Britain, called for the creation of
three multilateral institutions: the World Bank, the International Monetary Fund (IMF), and an international
trade organization. The latter organization was still-
born because of concerns in the U.S. Congress that its
powers would infringe on U.S. sovereignty. The General Agreement on Tariffs and Trade (GATT) served
in its stead, with a somewhat ambiguous status, as the
body through which multilateral trade agreements were
fashioned and enforced.

It was not until January 1, 1995, that the triumvirate
was finally completed. A new global organization, the
World Trade Organization (WTO), was quietly born
during the Uruguay round of GATT. It was a landmark
triumph for corporate libertarianism. A trade body with
an independent legal identity and staff similar to that

of the World Bank and the IMF is now in place, with a mandate to press forward and eliminate barriers to the free movement of goods and capital. The needs of the world's largest corporations are now represented by a global body with legislative and judicial powers that is committed to ensuring their rights against the intrusions of democratic governments and the people to whom those governments are accountable. What the World Bank and the IMF had accomplished in institutionalizing the doctrines of corporate libertarianism in low-income countries, the WTO now has a mandate and enforcement powers to carry forward in the industrial countries.

The World's Highest Judicial and Legislative Body

A key provision in the some 2,000 pages of the GATT agreement creating the WTO is buried in paragraph 4 of Article XVI: "Each member shall ensure the conformity of its laws, regulations and administrative procedures with its obligations as provided in the annexed Agreements." The "annexed Agreements" include all the substantive multilateral agreements relating to trade in goods and services and intellectual property rights. Once these agreements are ratified by the world's legislative bodies, any member country can challenge, through the WTO, any law of another member country that it believes deprives it of benefits it expected to receive from the new trade rules. This includes virtually any law that requires imported goods to meet local or national health, safety, labor, or environmental standards that exceed WTO accepted international standards. Unless the government against which the complaint is lodged can prove to the satisfaction of the WTO panel that a number of narrowly restrictive provisions have been satisfied, it must bring its own laws into line with the lower international standard or be subject to perpetual fines or trade sanctions. The WTO's goal is the "harmonization" of international standards. Regulations requiring that imported products meet local standards on such matters as recycling laws, use of carcinogenic food additives, auto safety requirements, bans on toxic substances, labeling, and meat inspection could all be subject to challenge. The offending country must prove that a purely scientific justification exists for its action. The fact that its citizens simply do not want to be exposed to the higher level of risk accepted by lower WTO standards isn't acceptable to the WTO as a valid justification.

Conservation measures that restrict the export of a country's own resources—such as forestry products, minerals, and fish products— could be ruled unfair trade practices, as could requirements that locally harvested timber or other resources be processed locally to provide local employment. Cases may also be brought against countries that attempt to give preferential treatment to local over foreign investors or that fail to protect the intellectual property rights (patents and copyrights) of foreign companies. Local interests are no longer a valid basis for local laws under the new WTO regime. The interests of international trade, which are primarily the interests of transnational corporations, take precedence.

Challenges may also be brought against the laws of state and local governments located within the jurisdiction of a member country, even though these governments are not signatories to the new agreement. The national government under whose jurisdiction they fall becomes obligated to take all reasonable measures to ensure the compliance of these state or local administrations. Such "reasonable measures" include preemptive legislation, litigation, and withdrawal of financial support.

The fact that local laws are subject to challenge under the WTO does not necessarily mean that they will be. However, there are numerous cases in which these same types of laws were successfully challenged under the previous, less stringent, GATT rules. Even before the GATT–WTO was ratified, the United States, Canada, the European Community, and Japan had each compiled extensive lists of one another's laws that they intended to target for challenge once the agreement was in place.

Although the GATT–WTO is an agreement among countries, and challenges are brought by one country against another, the impetus for a challenge normally comes from a transnational corporation that believes itself to be disadvantaged by a particular law. That corporation looks for a government that can be encouraged to bring a challenge. It need not be the government of its country of incorporation; a challenge can be brought by the government of any country that can make a reasonable case that its economic interest is being harmed. For example, a U.S. company growing fruit in Mexico uses a pesticide that leaves a toxic residue on the fruit that complies with the international standard but is greater than the standard of the state of California. The corporation might convince the Mexican government to bring a case against the California standard under WTO. California would have no right to appeal an unfavorable WTO decision in either California or U.S. courts.

Elsewhere in the world, tobacco companies have repeatedly used trade agreements to fight health reforms intended to reduce harm from cigarette smoking. When Taiwan was working on a law that would ban cigarette sales in vending machines, restrict public smoking areas, prohibit all forms of tobacco advertising and promotion, and fund a public education campaign to encourage people to give up smoking, the U.S. trade representative responded to complaints from transnational tobacco companies by threatening to call for trade sanctions against Taiwan—even though these laws would affect domestic Taiwanese tobacco companies and U.S. imports equally. After bans on foreign tobacco companies were repealed in Korea as a result of similar pressure, the percentage of male teenage smokers rose from 1.6 percent to 8.7 percent of the male teen population.[3]

When a challenge to a national or local law is brought before the WTO, the contending parties present their case in a secret hearing before a panel of three trade experts—generally lawyers who have made careers of representing corporate clients on trade issues. There is no provision for the presentation of alternative perspectives, such as amicus briefs from nongovernmental organizations, unless a given panel chooses to solicit them. Documents presented to the panels are secret, except that a government may choose to release its own documents. The identification of the panelists who supported a position or conclusion is explicitly forbidden. The burden of proof is on the defendant to prove that the law in question is not a restriction of trade as defined by the GATT.

When a panel decides that a domestic law is in violation of WTO rules, it may recommend that the offending country change its law. Countries that fail to make the recommended change within a prescribed period face financial penalties, trade sanctions, or both.

Under the proposed rules, the recommendations of the review panel are automatically adopted by the WTO sixty days after presentation unless there is a *unanimous* vote of WTO members to reject them. This means that over 100 countries, including the country that won the decision, must vote against a panel decision to overturn it—rendering the appeals process virtually meaningless.

As was GATT, the WTO is a trade organization, and its mandate is to eliminate barriers to international trade and investment. The national representatives who vote in its councils are specialized trade representatives whose primary mandate is to open other markets to exports from their own countries. Responsibilities for maintaining foreign exchange balances; full employment; health, safety, and environmental standards; and protecting the democratic rights of citizens fall under the jurisdictions of other bureaucracies. It may reasonably be anticipated that the WTO will follow the pattern of GATT in giving trade goals precedence over all other public policy concerns.

The WTO has legislative as well as judicial powers. GATT allows the WTO to change certain trade rules by a two-thirds vote of WTO member representatives. The new rules become binding on all members. The WTO is, in effect, a global parliament composed of unelected bureaucrats with the power to amend its own charter without referral to national legislative bodies.

Because economic activities have assumed such a large role in modern societies, control of economic rules is one of the most important powers in the world today. Under the WTO, a group of unelected trade representatives will become the world's highest court and most powerful legislative body, to which the judgments and authority of all other courts and legislatures will be subordinated.

Governance in the Corporate Interest

The world's major transnational corporations have had a highly influential insider role in GATT negotiations and will be similarly active in the WTO. They are especially well represented in the U.S. delegations, which have had a pivotal role in shaping the GATT agreements. The key to this corporate access is the U.S. Trade Act of 1974, which provides for a system of trade advisory committees to bring a public perspective to U.S. trade negotiations.[4] The trade committees must conform to the Federal Advisory Committee Act of 1972, which sets guidelines for the membership of all such federal advisory committees. The public representation must be "fairly balanced in terms of points of view represented and the functions to be performed by the advisory committee." Advisory committee processes are also required to be open to public scrutiny.

The U.S. trade representative's office has chosen to define this requirement to mean only that the advisory committee membership must be representative of the business community with regard to "balance among sectors, product lines, between small and large firms, among geographical areas, and among demographic groups."[5] A study by Public Citizen's Congress Watch released in December 1991 found that of 111 members of the three main trade advisory committees, only two represented labor unions. An approved seat for an environmental advocacy organization had not been filled, and there were no consumer representatives. The trade panels rarely announced their meetings to the public and never allowed the public to attend.

The corporate interest, in contrast to the public interest, was well represented. The study found that ninety-two members of the three committees represented individual companies, and sixteen represented trade industry associations—ten of them from the chemical industry. Members of the Advisory Committee for Trade Policy and Negotiations, the most important of the panels, included such corporate giants as IBM, AT&T, Bethlehem Steel, Time Warner, 3M, Corning, BankAmerica, American Express, Scott Paper, Dow Chemical, Boeing, Eastman Kodak, Mobil, Amoco, Pfizer, Hewlett Packard, Weyerhaeuser, and General Motors—all of which were also members of the U.S. Business Roundtable. Of the corporate members, all but General Motors were represented by either the chairman of the board or the president—in most instances, whichever of these officers functioned as chief executive officer (CEO). According to Public Citizen's Congress Watch:

> Advisory committees are so intertwined with governmental trade negotiators that panel members require security clearances. One of the perks of membership is a special reading room filled with classified documents available for perusal by nongovernmental advisors. To enable trade advisors' opinions regarding the current GATT talks to reach negotiators more quickly, a database has been established that instantly puts an advisory committee member's words at the negotiators' fingertips. Government sponsors of the trade advisory system take enormous trouble to keep trade advisors fully informed of every twist and turn in the negotiating process. Despite their enormous influence, the corporate trade counselors work in near total obscurity.[6]

A 1989 Department of Commerce document described the involvement of advisory committee members in the 1979 Tokyo round of GATT:

> The advisory members spent long hours in Washington consulting directly with negotiators on key issues and reviewing the actual texts of proposed agreements. For the most part, government negotiators followed the advice of the advisory committee. . . . Whenever advice was not followed, the government informed the committees of the reasons it was not possible to utilize their recommendations.[7]

Of the ninety-two corporations represented on the three trade advisory panels, twenty-seven companies or their affiliates had been assessed fines by the U.S. Environmental Protection Agency (EPA) totaling more than $12.1 million between 1980 and 1990 for failure to comply with existing environmental regulations. Five—DuPont, Monsanto, 3M, General Motors, and Eastman Kodak—made the EPA's top ten list of hazardous waste dischargers. Twenty-nine of the member companies or their affiliates had collectively contributed more than $800,000 in a failed attempt to defeat California's Safe Drinking

Water and Toxics Enforcement Act, a statewide initiative to require accurate labeling on potentially cancer-causing products and to limit toxic discharges into drinking water. Twenty-nine had put up over $2.1 million in a successful bid to defeat another California initiative called Big Green, which, among other provisions, would have set tighter standards for the discharge of toxic chemicals.[8]

Clayton Yeutter, in his capacity as U.S. secretary of agriculture under George Bush, stated publicly that one of his main goals was to use GATT to overturn strict local and state food safety regulations. He rationalized, "If the rest of the world can agree on what the standard ought to be on a given product, maybe the US or EC will have to admit that they are wrong when their standards differ."[9]

The WTO's global health and safety standards relating to food are set by a group known as the Codex Alimentarius Commission, or Codex. It is an intergovernmental body established in 1963 and run jointly by the UN Food and Agriculture Organization (FAO) and the World Health Organization (WHO) to establish international standards on things such as pesticide residues, additives, veterinary drug residues, and labeling. Critics of Codex observe that it is heavily influenced by industry and has tended to harmonize standards downward. For example, a Greenpeace USA study found that Codex safety levels for at least eight widely used pesticides were lower than current U.S. standards by as much as a factor of twenty-five.[10] The Codex standards allow DDT residues up to fifty times those permitted under U.S. law.[11]

Governmental delegations to Codex routinely include nongovernmental representatives, but they are chosen almost exclusively from industry. One hundred forty of the world's largest multinational food and agrochemical companies participated in Codex meetings held between 1989 and 1991. Of a total of 2,587 individual participants, only twenty-six came from public-interest groups.[12] Nestle, the world's largest food company, had thirty-eight representatives. A Nestle spokesperson explained, "It seems to me that governments are more likely to find qualified people in companies than among the self-appointed ayatollahs of the food sector."[13]

Protecting Information Monopolies

Many of the GATT–WTO provisions have been put forward as necessary to ensure the efficient functioning of competitive markets. Yet the GATT–WTO does nothing to limit the ability of transnational corporations to use their economic power to drive competitors out of the market by unfair means; absorb competitors through mergers and acquisitions; or form strategic alliances with competitors to share technology, production facilities, and markets. Indeed, one area in which GATT calls for strengthening government regulation and standards is its agreement on intellectual property rights—patents, copyrights, and trademarks. Here the call is for strong government intervention to protect corporate monopoly rights over information and technology.

Particularly ominous is the extension through the GATT–WTO of international patent right protection of genetic materials, including seeds and natural medicinals. U.S. companies have aggressively pursued patent protection for seeds and genetic materials in the United States, convincing the U.S. government to extend patent protection to all genetically engineered organisms, from microorganisms to plants and animals—excluding only genetically engineered humans. By patenting the processes by which genes are inserted into a species of seeds, a few companies have effectively obtained monopoly rights over genetic research on an entire species and on any useful products of that research. These companies have been pressing hard to turn such patents into worldwide monopolies under the GATT–WTO. In 1992, Agracetus, Inc., a subsidiary of W. R. Grace, was granted a U.S. patent on all genetically engineered or "transgenic" cotton varieties and has applications pending for similar patents in other countries accounting for 60 percent of the world's cotton crop, including India, China, and Brazil, and in Europe. In March 1994, it received a European patent on all transgenic soybeans and has a similar patent pending in the United States.

Through the ages, farmers have saved seed from one harvest to plant their next crop. Under existing U.S. patent law, a farmer who saves and replants the offspring of a patented seed is in violation of patent law.[14] The move to globalize the protection of seed and other life-form patents has been the subject of massive demonstrations by farmers in India, who realized that under the GATT–WTO agreements, they could be prohibited from growing their own seed stocks without paying a royalty to a transnational corporation.[15]

The industry view of what is right and proper with regard to people's rights to their means of subsistence has been clearly expressed by Hans Leenders, secretary general of the industry association of corporate seed houses and breeders:

> Even though it has been a tradition in most countries that a farmer can save seed from his own crop, it is under the changing circumstances not equitable that a farmer can use this seed and grow a commercial crop out of it without payment of a royalty. . . . The seed industry will have to fight hard for a better kind of protection.[16]

Measures extending patent protection over genetic materials are promoted on the ground that they will speed the advance of agricultural research and improve global food security. Critics argue that such patents stifle research by preventing the use of genetic materials and techniques by any researcher not working under specific license granted by the patent holder. Vandana Shiva, a leader of the Southern opposition to the patenting of life-forms, says, "This is just another way of stating that global monopoly over agriculture and food systems should be handed over as a right to multinational corporations."[17] What we are seeing is a blatant effort by a few corporations to establish monopoly control over the common biological heritage of the planet.[18]

A review of the accomplishments of the three Bretton Woods institutions brings their actual functions into sharp focus. The World Bank has served as an export-financing facility for large Northern-based corporations. The IMF has served as the debt collector for Northern-based financial institutions. GATT has served to create and enforce a corporate bill of rights protecting the rights of the world's largest corporations against the intrusion of people, communities, and democratically elected governments.

The Bank and the IMF celebrated their fiftieth anniversary in 1994. Citizen organizations from around the world marked the event by organizing a global campaign around the theme "Fifty Years Is Enough." Fifty years of Bretton Woods has indeed been far more than enough. The world's people and environment can scarcely afford more.

World War II did not end the global domination of the weak by strong states. It simply cloaked colonialism in a less obvious, more beguiling form. The new corporate colonialism is no more a consequence of immutable historical forces than was the old state colonialism. It is a consequence of conscious choices based on the pursuit of elite interest. This elite interest has been closely aligned with the corporate interest in advancing deregulation and economic globalization. As a consequence, the largest transnational corporations and the global financial system have assumed ever greater power over the conduct of human affairs in the pursuit of interests that are increasingly at odds with the human interest. It is impossible to have healthy, equitable, and democratic societies when political and economic power is concentrated in a few gigantic corporations. We have created a system that is now beyond the control even of those who created it and whom it richly rewards for serving its ends. Indeed, the system is now turning against them as well. In Part IV, we examine the nature and dynamics of this system.

IV A Rogue Financial System

14 The Money Game

In this new market . . . billions can flow in or out of an economy in seconds. So powerful has this force of money become that some observers now see the hot-money set becoming a sort of shadow world government—one that is irretrievably eroding the concept of the sovereign powers of a nation state.

—Business Week[1]

E ach day, half a million to a million people arise as dawn reaches their part of the world, turn on their computers, and leave the real world of people, things, and nature to immerse themselves in playing the world's most lucrative computer game: the money game.[2] As their computers come on-line, they enter a world of cyberspace constructed of numbers that represent money and complex rules by which the money can be converted into a seemingly infinite variety of forms, each with its own distinctive risks and reproductive qualities. Through their interactions, the players engage in competitive transactions aimed at acquiring for their own accounts the money that other players hold. Players can also pyramid the amount of money in play by borrowing from one another and bidding up prices. They can also purchase a great variety of exotic financial instruments that allow them to leverage their own funds without actually borrowing. It is played like a game. But the consequences are real.

The story of economic globalization is only partly a tale of the fantasy world of Stratos dwellers and the dreams of global empire builders. There is another story of impersonal forces at play, deeply embedded in our institutional systems—a tale of money and how its evolution as an institution is transforming human societies in ways that no one intended toward ends that are inimical to the human interest. It is a tale of the pernicious side of the market's invisible hand, of the tendency of an unrestrained market to reorient itself away from the efficient *production* of wealth to the *extraction* and *concentration* of wealth. It is a tragic tale of how good and thoughtful people have become trapped in serving, even creating, a system devoted to the unrestrained pursuit of greed, producing outcomes they neither seek nor condone.

Although the consequences are global, our primary focus here, as in previous chapters, is predominantly on the United States—because, since World War II, the United States has had the dominant role in shaping the global economy and its institutions. Thus there has been a tendency for the strengths and dysfunctions of the global system to first become revealed in the United States and then spread throughout the larger system.

Delinking Money from Value

To understand what has happened to the global financial system, we must begin with an understanding of the nature of money. Money is one of humanity's most important inventions, created to meet an important need.

The earliest market transactions were based on the direct exchange of things of equal value, which meant that a transaction could occur only when two individuals met who each possessed an item they were willing to trade for an item possessed by the other. The useful expansion of commerce was greatly constrained. This constraint was partially relieved when people began to use certain obects that had their own intrinsic value as a medium of exchange—decorative shells, blocks of salt, bits of precious metals or precious stones. Eventually, metal coins provided more standardized units of exchange based on the amount of precious metal, generally silver or gold, they contained. Later, the idea emerged that it was more convenient to keep the precious metal in a vault and issue paper money that could be exchanged for the metal on demand. In a sense, the paper bill was the equivalent of a receipt showing that the bearer owned an amount of precious metal, but the paper was more convenient and transportable.

Each of these innovations was, however, a step toward delinking money from things of real value. An additional step was taken at the historic 1944 Bretton Woods conference that created the World Bank and the International Monetary Fund. The countries represented at this meeting agreed to create a new global financial system in which each participating government guaranteed to exchange its own currency on demand for U.S. dollars at a fixed rate. The U.S. government, in turn, guaranteed to exchange dollars on demand for gold at a rate of $35 per ounce. This effectively placed all the world's currencies on the gold standard, backed by the U.S. gold stored at Fort Knox. Many governments thus came to accept the U.S. dollar as gold deposit certificates and chose to hold their international foreign exchange reserves in dollars rather than gold.

This system worked reasonably well for more than twenty years, until it became widely evident that the United States was creating far more dollars to finance its massive military and commercial expansion around the world than it could back with its gold. If all the countries that were holding dollars decided to redeem them for gold, the available supply would be quickly exhausted, and those who had placed their faith in the integrity of the dollar would be left holding nothing but worthless pieces of paper.

To preclude this eventuality, on August 15, 1971, President Richard Nixon declared that the United States would no longer redeem dollars on demand for gold. The dollar was no longer anything other than a piece of high-grade paper with a number and some intricate artwork issued by the U.S. government. The world's currencies were no longer linked to anything of value except the shared expectation that others would accept them in exchange for real goods and services.

Once computers came into widespread use, the next step was relatively obvious—eliminate the paper and simply store the numbers in computers. Although coins and paper money continue to circulate, more and more of the world's monetary transactions involve direct electronic transfers between computers. Money has become almost a pure abstraction. And the creation of money has been delinked from the creation of value.

Four developments are basic to this transformation of the financial system:

1. The United States financed its global expansion with dollars, many of which now show up on the balance sheets of foreign banks and foreign branches of U.S. banks. These dollars are not subject to the regulations and reserve requirements of the U.S. Federal Reserve system.
2. Computerization and globalization melded the world's financial markets into a single global system in which an individual

at a computer terminal can maintain constant contact with price movements in all major markets and execute trades almost instantaneously in any or all of them. A computer can be programmed to do the same without human intervention, automatically executing transactions involving billions of dollars in fractions of a second.

3. Investment decisions that were once made by many individuals are now concentrated in the hands of a relatively small number of professional investment managers. The pool of investment funds controlled by mutual funds doubled in three years to total $2 trillion at the end of June 1994, as individual investors placed their savings in professionally managed investment pools rather than buying and holding individual stocks.[3] Meanwhile, there has been a massive consolidation of the banking industry—more than 500 U.S. banks merged or closed between September 1992 and September 1993 alone[4]— concentrating control of huge pools of funds within the major international "money center" banks. Pension funds, now estimated to total $4 trillion in assets, are managed mostly by trust departments of these giant banks, adding enormously to their financial power. The pension funds alone account for the holdings of about a third of all corporate equities and about 40 percent of corporate bonds.[5]

4. Investment horizons have shortened dramatically. The managers of these investment pools compete for investors' funds based on the returns they are able to generate. Mutual fund results are published on a daily basis in the world's leading newspapers, and countless services compare fund performance on a monthly and yearly basis. Individual investors have the ability to switch money among mutual funds with the push of a button on a Touch-Tone phone or with their personal computers on the basis of these results. For the mutual fund manager, the short term is a day or less and the long term is perhaps a month. Pension fund managers have a slightly longer evaluation cycle.

Individual savings have become consolidated in vast investment pools managed by professionals under enormous competitive pressures to yield nearly instant financial gains. The time frames involved are far too short for a productive investment to mature, the amount of money to be "invested" far exceeds the number of productive investment opportunities available, and the returns the market has come to expect exceed what most productive investments are able to yield even over a period of years. Consequently, the financial markets have largely abandoned productive investment in favor of extractive investment and are operating on autopilot without regard to human consequences.

The financial system increasingly functions as a world apart at a scale that dwarfs by orders of magnitude the productive sector of the global economy, which itself functions increasingly at the mercy of the massive waves of money that the money game players move around the world with split-second abandon.

Joel Kurtzman, formerly business editor of the *New York Times* and currently editor of the *Harvard Business Review*, estimates that for every $1 circulating in the productive world economy, $20 to $50 circulates in the economy of pure finance—though no one knows the ratios for sure. In the international currency markets alone, some $800 billion to $1 trillion changes hands each day,[6] far in excess of the $20 billion to $25 billion required to cover daily trade in goods and services. According to Kurtzman:

> Most of the $800 billion in currency that is traded . . . goes for very short-term speculative investments—from a few hours to a few days to a maximum of a few weeks. . . . That money is mostly involved in nothing more than making money. . . . It is money enough to purchase outright the nine biggest corporations in Japan—overvalued though they are—including Nippon Telegraph & Telephone, Japan's seven largest banks, and Toyota Motors. . . . It goes for options trading, stock speculation, and trade in interest rates. It also goes for short-term financial arbitrage transactions where an investor buys a product such as bonds or currencies on one exchange in the hopes of selling it at a profit on another exchange, sometimes simultaneously by using electronics.[7]

This money is unassociated with any real value. Yet the money managers who carry out the millions of high-speed, short-term transactions stake their reputations and careers on making that money grow at a rate greater than the prevailing rate of interest. This growth depends on the ability of the system to endlessly increase the amount of money circulating in the financial economy, independent of any increase in the output of real goods and services. As this growth occurs, the financial or buying power of those who control the newly created money expands, compared with other members of society who are creating value but whose real and relative compensation is declining.[8]

The Great Money Machine

There are two common ways to create money without creating value. One is by creating debt. Another is by bidding up asset values. The global financial system is adept at using both of these devices to create money delinked from the creation of value.

Debt

The way in which the banking system creates money by pyramiding debt is familiar to anyone who has taken an elementary economics course. Say Person A, a wheat farmer, sells $1,000 worth of wheat and deposits the money in Bank M. Retaining 10 percent of the deposit as a reserve, Bank M is able to loan $900 to Person B, which Person B deposits in her account in Bank N. Now Person A has a cash asset of $1,000 in Bank M and Person B has a cash asset of $900 in Bank N. Keeping a 10 percent reserve, Bank N is able to make a loan of $810 to Person C, who deposits it in Bank O, which then loans $729 to Person D, and so on. The deposit of the original $1,000 earned from producing a real product for consumption by real people ultimately allows the banking system to generate $9,000 in additional new deposits by generating a corresponding $9,000 in new debt—new money created without a single thing of value having necessarily been produced.

The banks involved in this series of transactions now have $9,000 in new outstanding loans and $10,000 in new deposits on the loans on the basis of the original deposit of $1,000 from the sale of wheat. They expect to receive the going rate of interest, let us say 6 percent. This means that the banking system expects to obtain a minimum annual return of $540 on money that the system has basically created out of nothing. This is part of what makes banking such a powerful and profitable business.

In this instance, we have used the classic textbook example of how banks create money, taking into account the 10 percent reserve (the actual average is a bit less) that under present law must be deposited with the U.S. Federal Reserve system.[9] Without such a reserve requirement, the banking system could, in theory, pyramid a single loan without limit.

As the United States has spent beyond its means, a growing portion of the total supply of dollars circulating in the world has accumulated in the accounts of foreign banks or foreign branches of U.S. banks. Known as Eurodollars, they are not subject to the reserve requirement of the U.S. Federal Reserve. In instances where the governments under whose jurisdiction the banks holding these accounts fall do not impose a reserve requirement, these banks can loan out the full amount of these deposits, should they choose to do so, giving the global banking system the capacity to expand the supply of dollars without limit.

As the global financial system has expanded, many kinds of financial institutions other than banks have become involved in large-scale lending operations, Each contributes to the money creation process in ways identical to the banking system, but often with less stringent controls and reserve requirements than those placed on banks located within the United States.

Asset Values

The price of a stock or of a tangible asset such as land or a piece of art is determined by the market's demand for it. In an economy awash with money and investors looking for quick returns, that demand is substantially influenced by speculators' expectation that other speculators will continue to push up the price. Nicholas F. Brady, who served as U.S. treasury secretary under President George Bush, observed, "If the assets were gold or oil, this phenomenon would be called inflation. In stocks, it is called wealth creation."[10] The process tends to feed on itself. As the price of an asset rises, more speculators are drawn to the action and the price continues to increase, attracting still more speculators—until the bubble bursts as when the crash of the overinflated Mexican stock market caused the 1995 peso crisis.

Vast changes in the buying power of people who own such assets can occur within a very short time, with no change whatever in the underlying value the asset represents or in the ability of society to produce real goods and services. We are so conditioned to the idea that changes in buying power are related to changes in real wealth that even those who know the difference well often forget it. Consider the following excerpt from Joel Kurtzman's book *The Death of Money*—a book specifically about how money creation has been delinked from the creation of value. Kurtzman is describing what happened on October 19, 1987, when the New York Stock Exchange's Dow Jones Industrial Average fell by 22.6 percent in one day:

> If measured from the height of the full market in August 1987, investors lost a little over $1 trillion on the New York Stock Exchange in a little more than two months. That loss was equal to an eighth of the value of everything that is manmade in the United States, including all homes, factories, office buildings, roads, and improved real estate. It is a loss of such enormous magnitude that

it boggles the mind. One trillion dollars could feed the entire world for two years, raise the Third World from abject poverty to the middle class. It could purchase one thousand nuclear aircraft carriers.[11]

Those who were invested in the stock market did indeed lose individual buying power. Yet the homes, factories, office buildings, roads, and improved real estate to which Kurtzman refers did not change in any way. In fact, this $1 trillion could not have fed the world for even five minutes for the simple reason that people can't eat money. They eat food, and the collapse of stock market values did not in itself increase or decrease the world's actual supply of food by so much as a single grain of rice. Only the prices at which shares in particular companies could be bought and sold changed. There was no change in the productive capacity of any of those companies or even in the cash available in their own bank accounts.

Furthermore, although stock values represent potential purchasing power for individual investors, they do not accurately reflect the aggregate buying power of all investors in the market for the simple reason that you can't buy much with a stock certificate. You cannot, for example, give one to the checkout clerk at your local grocery store as payment for your purchase. You first have to convert the stock to cash by selling it. Now, although any one individual can sell a stock certificate at the prevailing price and spend the money to buy groceries, if everyone with money in the stock market decided to convert their stocks into money to buy groceries, much the same thing would happen as happened on October 19, 1987. The aggregate value of their stock holdings would deflate like a pricked balloon. The "money"— the buying power—would instantly evaporate. What we are dealing with is a situation in which market speculation creates an illusion of wealth. It conveys real powers on those who hold it—but only as long as the balloon remains inflated.

The whole nature of trading these vast sums in the world's financial markets is changing dramatically. The trend is toward replacing financial analysts and traders with theoretical mathematicians, "quants," who deal in sophisticated probability analysis and chaos theory to structure portfolios on the basis of mathematical equations. Since humans cannot make the calculations and decisions with the optimal speed required by the new portfolio management strategies, trading in the world's financial markets is being done directly by computers, based on abstractions that have nothing to do with the business itself. According to Kurtzman:

These computer programs are not trading stocks, at least in the old sense, because they have no regard for the company that issues the equity. And they are not trading bonds per se because the programs couldn't care less if they are lending money to Washington, London, or Paris. They are not trading currencies, either, since the currencies the programs buy and sell are simply monies to be turned over in order to gain a certain rate of return. And they are not trading futures products. The futures markets are only convenient places to shop. The computers are simply . . . trading mathematically precise descriptions of financial products (stocks, currencies, bonds, options, futures). Which exact product fits the descriptions hardly matters as long as all the parameters are in line with the description contained in the computer program. For stocks, any one will do if its volatility, price, exchange rules, yield, and beta [risk coefficient] fit the computer's description. The computer hardly cares if the stock is IBM or Disney or MCI. The computer does not care whether the company makes nuclear bombs, reactors, or medicine. It does not care whether it has plants in North Carolina or South Africa.[12]

The decisions of the financial system are increasingly being made by computers on the basis of esoteric mathematical formulas with the sole objective of replicating money as a pure abstraction. It is a long way from the invisible hand of the market Adam Smith had in mind when *The Wealth of Nations* was published in 1776. It is the reality of a world ruled by "free-market" forces in the 1990s. The global financial system has become a parasitic predator that lives off the flesh of its host—the productive economy.

15 Predatory Finance

You can't make any money like this. The dollar is moving sideways, the movement is too narrow. . . . Anyone speculating or trading in the dollar or any other currency can't make money or lose money. You can't do anything. It's been a horror.
—Carmine Rotondo, foreign exchange trader at Security Pacific Bank[1]

One of the ideological premises of corporate libertarianism is that investment is by nature *productive* in the sense that it increases the size of the economic pie, adds to the net well-being of society, and therefore is of potential benefit to everyone. In a healthy economy, most investment is productive. The global economy is not, however, a healthy economy. In all too many instances, it rewards *extractive* investors who do not create wealth but simply extract and concentrate existing wealth. The extractive investor's gain is at the expense of other individuals or the society at large.

In the worst case, an extractive investment actually decreases the overall wealth of the society, even though it may yield a handsome return to an individual. This occurs when an investor acquires control of a productive asset or resource—such as land, timber, or even a corporation—from a group that is maintaining the asset's productive potential and liquidates it for immediate profit. The investor is extracting value, not creating it.

In some instances, such as an ancient forest, the asset may be irreplaceable. When an investment simply creates money or buying power—such as through the inflation of land or stock values—without creating anything of corresponding value, this is also a form of extractive investment. The investor creates nothing, yet his or her share of a society's buying power is increased.

Speculation is another form of extractive investment. The financial speculator is engaged in little more than a sophisticated form of gambling—betting on the rise and fall of selected prices. When the speculator wins, he or she is simply capturing wealth. When the speculator loses, the survival of major financial institutions may be placed at risk—resulting in demands for a public bailout to protect the integrity of the financial system. In either instance, the public loses. Rarely does the speculator's activity contribute consequentially to the creation of new wealth.

Although in some instances there is merit to speculators' claims that their activities increase market liquidity and stability, they have a hollow ring in increasingly volatile globalized financial markets in which speculative financial movements are a major source of instability and economic disruption. Furthermore, whatever contribution speculators may make to increasing the efficiency of financial markets, it comes at a substantial cost in terms of the profits and fees they extract. The additional risks and economic distortions created by a sophisticated class of financial instruments known as derivatives are an especially important source of concern.

The derivatives contracts that are currently a hot topic in the financial press involve bets on movements of stock prices, currency prices, interest rates, and even entire stock market indices. Futures contracts on interest rates didn't exist until the late 1970s. Now outstanding contracts on interest rates total more than half the gross national product of the United States.[2] The total value of outstanding derivatives contracts was estimated to be about $12 trillion in mid-1994—with growth projected to $18 trillion by 1999.[3] In 1993, *The Economist* estimated the value of the world's total stock of productive fixed capital to be around $20 trillion.[4]

What makes derivatives particularly risky is the fact that they are commonly purchased on margin, meaning that the buyer initially puts up only a small deposit against the potential financial exposure. The largest players may not be required to put up any money at all—even though their potential financial exposure may run into hundreds of millions of dollars.[5]

The more sophisticated derivatives are highly complex and are often not well understood, even by those who deal in them. In the words of *Fortune*:

When they are employed wisely, derivatives make the world simpler, because they give their buyers an ability to manage and transfer risk. But in the hands of speculators, bumblers, and unscrupulous peddlers, they are a powerful leveraged mechanism for *creating* risk.[6]

Creating Uncertainty and Risk

Corporations engaged in producing real goods and services prefer a stable and predictable financial system that provides reliable sources of investment funds at stable exchange and interest rates. For them, fluctuations in the financial markets are sources of risk that may disrupt their operations and balance sheets with little warning. For global firms, the sometimes considerable swings in the exchange relationships among different currencies can be a serious problem, possibly playing a larger role in determining profit or loss than productive efficiency or market share. Those who manage productive investments see this volatility as a major problem, a source of unwanted risk. The situation is exactly the opposite for speculators, who are looking for quick extractive returns. Speculators thrive on volatility—it is their source of opportunity.

Although the specifics of their strategies may be extremely complicated, those who specialize in financial extraction profit from volatility through three activities:

1. *Arbitraging* temporary price differences for the same or similar commodities or financial instruments in two markets. The arbitrager makes a simultaneous purchase in the market where the price is lower and a corresponding sale in the market where the price is higher. The margins are narrow, but the action is essentially riskless, and when large sums of money are involved, the strategy can be quite profitable. The key is to act before anyone else notices the same opportunity. Speed is so important that one firm recently spent $35 million to buy a supercomputer simply to gain a two-second advantage in arbitraging stock futures in Tokyo.[7]
2. *Speculating* on price changes in commodities, currency exchange rates, interest rates, and financial instruments such as stocks, bonds, and various derivative products. Speculation involves betting on short-term price fluctuations. These bets can involve significant risks, especially if they are leveraged with borrowed money or by use of margin accounts.
3. *Insuring* others against the risks of future price changes. Those who sell derivatives contracts promote them as a form of risk

insurance. The more sophisticated derivative packages that have become popular may involve complex combinations of speculating, insuring, and arbitraging.

None of these sources of profit would exist in a perfectly stable financial market. In each instance, the extractive investor is taking advantage of price fluctuations to claim a portion of the value created by productive investors and by people doing real work. The speculator's take represents a kind of tax on the financial system to no useful end. It is difficult to see, for example, how arbitraging electronically linked markets to reduce two-second differentials in price adjustments serves any public purpose. The greater the volatility of financial markets, the greater the opportunity for these forms of extraction.

The riskier and more destabilizing forms of extractive investment have received a major boost from the formation of a new breed of mutual funds—called hedge funds—that specialize in high-risk, short-term speculation and require a minimum initial investment of $1 million. The biggest of these, Quantum Fund headed by George Soros, controls more than $11 billion of investor money. Since aggressive hedge funds may leverage investor money to borrow as much as $10 for every investor dollar, this gives the Quantum Fund potential control over as much as $110 billion. Many of the largest hedge funds produced a return of more than 50 percent for their shareholders in 1993. The downside risks are also substantial, however. One small hedge fund lost $600 million in two months in the mortgage markets and went out of business.[8]

The fact that hedge funds are generally highly leveraged greatly increases both the potential gains and the risks. It also ties up the funds of the banking system in activities that are of questionable benefit to society when the credit needs of home buyers, farmers, and productive businesses go unmet.

The claim that speculators increase price stability by moving markets more quickly toward their equilibrium was recently debunked by George Soros himself in testimony before the Banking Committee of the U.S. House of Representatives. Soros told the committee that when a speculator bets that a price will rise and it falls instead, he is forced to protect himself by selling, which accelerates the price drop and increases market volatility. Soros, however, told the committee that price volatility is not a problem unless everyone rushes to sell at the same time and a "discontinuity" is created, meaning that there are no buyers. In such an instance, those with positions in the market are unable to bail out and may suffer "catastrophic losses."[9] His testimony clearly revealed the perspective of the professional speculator, for whom volatility is a source of profits. If he were involved in productive forms of investment, he would surely have had a different view.

Soros speaks from experience when he claims that speculators can shape the directions of market prices and create instability. He has developed such a legendary reputation as a shaper of financial markets that a *New York Times* article titled "When Soros Speaks, World Markets Listen" credited him with being able to increase the price of his investments simply by revealing that he has made them. After placing bets against the German mark, he published a letter in the *Times* (London) saying, "I expect the mark to fall against all major currencies." According to the *New York Times*, it immediately did just that "as traders in the United States and Europe agreed that it was a Soros market."[10] On November 5, 1993, the *New York Times* business pages included a story titled "Rumors of Buying by Soros Send Gold Prices Surging."

In September 1992, Soros sold $10 billion worth of British pounds in a bet against the success of British Prime Minister John Major's effort to maintain the pound's value.[11] In so doing, he was credited with a major role in forcing a devaluation of the pound that contributed to breaking up the system of fixed exchange rates that governments were trying to put into place in the European union. Fixed exchange rates are anathema for speculators because they eliminate the volatility on which speculators depend. For his role in protecting the opportunity for speculative profits, Soros extracted an estimated $1 billion from the financial system for his investment funds.[12] The resulting gyrations in the money markets caused the British pound to fall 41 percent against the Japanese yen over a period of eleven months. These are the kinds of volatility that speculators considered a source of opportunity.[13]

There is a substantial and growing basis for the conclusion of Felix Rohatyn, a senior partner with Lazard Frères & Co, that:

> In many cases hedge funds, and speculative activity in general, may now be more responsible for foreign exchange and interest-rate movements than interventions by the central banks.
>
> ... Derivatives ... create a chain of risks linking financial institutions and corporations throughout the world; any weakness or break in that chain (such as the failure of a large institution heavily invested in derivatives) could create a problem of serious proportions for the international financial system.[14]

The fact that many major corporations, banks, and even local governments have become active players in the derivatives markets as a means of boosting their profits began to attract the attention of the business press in 1994. The risks can be substantial, yet the institutions that have been major players generally do not disclose their financial exposure in derivatives in their public financial statements, preferring to treat them as "off-balance-sheet" transactions. This makes it impossible for investors and the public to properly assess the real risks involved.

The truth becomes known only as major losses are reported, as when Procter & Gamble announced a $102 million derivatives loss when interest rates rose more sharply than anticipated,[15] or when bad real estate loans required a federal bailout of the Bank of New England. The bank's balance sheet showed about $33 billion in total assets. Regulators, however, found that it had off-balance-sheet commitments of $36 billion in various derivatives instruments.[16] The Paine Webber Group announced in July 1994 that it would spend $268 million to bail out one of its money market funds, which had been marketed as a safe and secure investment, when it came up short on a derivatives speculation. In 1994, BankAmerica and PiperJaffray Companies took similar actions.[17]

The most publicized derivatives shock of 1994 came in December, when California's Orange County announced that its investment fund of $7.4 billion in public monies from 187 school districts, transportation authorities, and cities faced losses of $1.5 billion. It had borrowed $14 billion to invest in interest-sensitive derivatives and lost its bet when interest rates turned up. News then began to break regarding the extent of derivatives holdings and losses of other local governments, and on December 7, prices in the usually stable $1.2 trillion municipal bond market dropped more than a point. Questions were raised whether the investment houses that had loaned Orange County the $14 billion to finance its speculation had informed their own shareholders where their money was going. Orange County faced a severe cutback in public services, including its schools, and the possibility of sharp tax increases.[18]

Other major shocks followed, including the announcement on February 25, 1995, that a twenty-eight-year-old trader in the Singapore office of Barings Bank had, over roughly a four-week period, bet $29 billion of the firm's money on derivatives tied to Japanese Nikkei stock-index futures and Japanese interest rates—and ran up losses of $1.3 billion. The loss wiped out the venerable 233-year-old bank's $900 million in capital and forced it into bankruptcy.[19] In the first four hours of trading following the announcement, the Tokyo Nikkei index fell by 4.6 percent.[20] That the actions of a single trader of no particular personal wealth or reputation could produce such a consequence is one of a growing number of indicators of the instability of a globalized financial system in which hundreds of billions of dollars may move instantly in response to the latest news break.

Profiting from Volatility

The financial resources that private financial institutions can bring into play in the world's money markets now dwarf even those of the most powerful governments. That power mocks governmental efforts to manage interest and exchange rates to maintain economic stability and growth. Allen Metzler, one of the world's leading authorities on central banks and monetary policy, estimates that if the world's central bankers agreed among themselves on a coordinated commitment to protect a currency from a speculative attack, they might at best be able to muster $14 billion a day, a mere drop in the bucket compared with the more than $800 billion that currency speculators trade on a daily basis.[21]

The U.S. dollar fell by approximately 10 percent against both the Japanese yen and the German mark during the first half of 1994. On June 24, 1994, the U.S. Federal Reserve and sixteen other central banks mobilized a coordinated intervention and bought an estimated 3 to 5 billion U.S. dollars to slow the fall. The market scarcely noticed.

We have reached a point at which such interventions do little to decrease volatility. They simply transfer taxpayer dollars into the hands of speculators.

The onset of the Mexican peso crisis in December 1994 gave new insight into how costly the dysfunctions of the financial system have become. Although little discussed by the financial press, the backdrop to Mexico's financial crisis was very different from the picture of an economic miracle that had been presented to the public by big business and the Clinton administration during their campaign to sell the North American Free Trade Agreement (NAFTA).

For years, Mexico increased its foreign borrowing—and thereby its foreign debt—to cover consumer imports, capital flight, and debt service payments. This borrowing took many forms, including selling high-risk, high-interest bonds to foreigners; selling public corporations to private foreign interests; and attracting foreign money with the speculative binge that sent Mexico's stock market skyrocketing. As little as 10 percent of the some $70 billion in foreign "investment" funds that flowed into Mexico over the previous five years actually went to the creation of capital goods to expand productive capacity and thereby create a capacity for repayment. Prices of many of the assets transferred to foreign ownership were based on fictitiously inflated balance sheets. Projected debt service payments alone came to exceed the country's projected export revenues. Mexico's "economic miracle" was little more than a giant Ponzi scheme.[22]

Who benefited from these inflows? A few Mexicans built huge fortunes during this period. *Forbes* identified fourteen Mexican billionaires in its 1993 survey of the world's billionaires. It identified twenty-four in its 1994 survey.[23]

The bubble burst in December 1994. The Mexican stock market lost more than 30 percent of its money value in peso terms as speculators rushed to pull their money out. Downward pressure on the overvalued peso due to the flight of money out of Mexico pushed the Mexican government into a deep financial crisis and forced it to devalue a highly overvalued peso. This resulted in a dramatic shift in the terms of trade between the United States and Mexico and priced most U.S. imports out of reach of the Mexican market. When it appeared that the Mexican government might be forced to default on its foreign obligations, the Wall Street investors who held Mexican bonds ran to the U.S. government with cries that the sky would fall unless U.S. taxpayers financed a bailout. President Clinton responded by circumventing a reluctant Congress to put together a bailout plan totaling more than $50 billion in taxpayer money to ensure that the Wall Street banks and investment houses would recover their money. Critics of the bailout noted that not a penny of this money would go to the millions of poor and middle-class Mexicans who are bearing the major burden of the crisis.[24]

Neither the bailout nor interest rates as high as 92 percent on Mexican government securities had stemmed the continuing decline of the peso by mid-March 1995.[25] Austerity measures imposed by the Mexican government were expected to put 750,000 Mexicans out of work during the first four months of 1995, and interest rates of 90 percent or more on mortgages, credit cards, and car loans would push many families into insolvency.[26] Estimates of the number of U.S. jobs that would be lost due to the related drop in exports to Mexico ran as high as 500,000.[27]

Shock waves from the Mexican crisis reverberated throughout the world's interlinked financial markets as speculators scurried to move their money to safer havens. When the Mexican stock market bubble burst, speculators with holdings in other Latin American countries got nervous and quickly pulled out their money, resulting in a fall of more than 30 percent in one month in the per share value of the leading Latin American stock funds.[28] When the U.S. bailout linked the dollar to the falling peso, wary currency speculators sold dollars to buy German marks and Japanese yen—further weakening the dollar in international currency markets.[29]

How did this look to the Stratos dwellers from high above the clouds? I happened to be flying from New York to San Francisco in the midst of the Mexican peso debacle. The March 1995 issue of the United Airlines magazine *Hemispheres*, placed in every seat pocket, featured an article praising the success of NAFTA and calling for its extension to the rest of the Western Hemisphere.[30]

The global system of speculative flight money did not create the Mexican crisis. It did, however, help make it possible and greatly exacerbated and spread the consequences when the bubble burst.

The ability to move massive amounts of money instantly between markets has given speculators a weapon by which to hold public policy hostage to their interests, and they are increasingly open about calling attention to it. Economist Paul Craig Roberts of the Cato Institute, a Washington, D.C., think tank devoted to the propagation of corporate libertarianism, lectured President Clinton in a *Business Week* op-ed piece:

> The dollar is also under pressure because investors have realized that Clinton favors big government "solutions," while other parts of the world, especially Asia and Latin America, are curtailing the scope of government and growing rapidly as a result. Equity investors have developed a global perspective, and they prefer markets where government is downsizing and the prospects for economic growth are good. . . . It would also help if Congress were to repeal hundreds of ill-considered laws that benefit special interests at the expense of the overall performance of the economy, and if thousands of counterproductive rules in the Code of Federal Regulations were removed.[31]

The process is simple. If the speculators who are shuffling hundreds of billions of dollars around the world decide that the policies of a government give preference to "special interests"—by which they mean groups such as environmentalists, working people, or the poor—over the interests of financial speculators, they take their money elsewhere, creating economic havoc in the process. In their minds, the resulting economic disruption only confirms their thesis that the policies of the offending government were unsound. Typical is the view expressed to the *Washington Post* by a New York foreign exchange analyst: "A lot of central banks love to blame it on the speculators. I think it's more a question of their gross incompetence in managing their monetary policy than a speculative attack."[32]

The fact that most of these financial movements occur in a globalized cyberspace makes oversight or regulation by any individual government extremely difficult, and those who profit handsomely from the resulting lack of public accountability are quick to assure lawmakers and the public that the system is working in the public interest. They maintain that the only threat to the public good is from regulation itself. Typical is the position articulated by Thomas A. Russo, managing director and chief legal officer of Lehman Brothers, Inc., a major investment house, in a *New York Times* op-ed piece.

> Derivatives play a key role in the formation of capital and the management of risk by helping governments, manufacturers, hospitals, utilities and fast-food chains deliver the best products and services at the lowest cost. . . . The evolution of financial products has not been followed by a regulatory evolution, and the mismatch has created problems. . . . The system's artificial distinctions create legal uncertainty, hamper, and distort the development of new products and encourage self-interested tinkering with product definitions. In the fast-moving field of derivatives, these failings inflict great harm, including chasing the American derivatives business offshore.
>
> To add more rules to a system that was never designed for derivatives can only enlarge these problems. On the other hand, a complete overhaul of the system is politically unrealistic. The only remaining remedy: derivatives dealers and regulators should jointly formulate principles of good business practice for the industry.
>
> . . . new derivatives should be evaluated for risk not only by the people who develop and trade them, but also by an independent group within the company. Another principle might advise that traders—the first line of defense in managing risk—be urged to admit mistakes quickly and be fired for hiding them.[33]

Russo's observation that the financial system has acquired such political power as to virtually preclude its reform is, of course, accurate. Regulation is made all the more difficult by the fact that, in the words of James Grant, editor of *Grant's Interest Rate Observer*, "The markets are global and sleepless and will flow to the area of least regulation."[34] As for Russo's argument that derivatives and other speculative financial tools strengthen the productive economy and that the system is capable of self-regulation, the most polite thing that can be said is that it demonstrates the extent to which Stratos dwellers have become detached from reality.

Almost coincidentally with the publication of Russo's op-ed piece touting the adequacy of self-regulation, Kidder, Peabody & Company—an investment house that prides itself on integrity and tight controls—announced that one of its senior traders had, over a more than two-year period, single-handedly recorded trades totaling $1.76 *trillion*—nearly 10 percent of total annual global economic output—and reported profits on those trades of $349.7 million. Yet no one in the firm had noticed that only $79 billion of these trades had ever actually been made or that these trades had cost the firm $85.4 million in losses. Accepting the trader's report, management had given him $11 million in bonuses, a promotion, and a chairman's award and reported his false profits as real profits to General Electric, the firm's parent company. It took more than two years for either his supervisors or the firm's accounting and internal audit systems to pick up the discrepancies.

Edward A. Cerullo, the $20-million-a-year head of the Kidder, Peabody division in which the fraud had occurred, gave the following explanation of his failure to detect the problem earlier: "Somehow, to single out one supervisor as singularly responsible for a department with 700 or 800 people, $100 billion in assets and $20 billion in daily transactions and earnings of $1 billion is totally unrealistic."[35] With a system so out of control that its best and soundest institutions cannot protect themselves from flagrant fraud and abuse by their own staff, it takes an enormous leap of faith to assume that these institutions are capable of self-regulation in the public interest.[36]

It is worth a passing note that while this was going on, senior officers of Kidder, Peabody were engaged in pitting Connecticut, New Jersey, and New York City against one another in a bidding war for the company's headquarters. According to Michael A. Carpenter, Kidder, Peabody's chairman, New York City's offer of subsidized electricity, sales tax breaks on equipment and services, and property tax reductions worth a total of $31 million would "enable Kidder, Peabody to continue to operate in Manhattan on a cost-competitive basis."[37]

The financial press continues to describe what is happening in terms of global investors and international capital flows—as though we were still living in a world in which those who have savings seek to commit them to productive uses beneficial to society in the expectation of steady long-term returns. When the system falters, the blame is placed on a lack of management controls and the failure of governments to submit to the beneficial discipline of the market to maintain investor confidence.

The reality that the Stratos dwellers are loath to acknowledge is that as corporations have delinked from the human interest, the institutions of finance have delinked from both the human and the corporate interest. Financial institutions that were once dedicated to mobilizing funds for productive investment have transmogrified into a predatory, risk-creating, speculation-driven global financial system engaged in the unproductive extraction of wealth from taxpayers and the productive economy.

This system is inherently unstable and is spiraling out of control—spreading economic, social, and environmental devastation and endangering the well-being of every person on the planet. Among its more specific sins, the transmogrified financial system is cannibalizing the corporations that once functioned as good local citizens, making socially responsible management virtually impossible and forcing the productive economy to discard people at every hand as costly impediments to economic efficiency.

16 Corporate Cannibalism

Mergers, acquisitions, and leveraged buyouts completed in 1988 cost a staggering $266 billion. . . . None of this . . . paid for as much as a single connecting bolt in a new machine . . . for an ounce of new fertilizer nor a single seed for a new crop. . . . A corporation that takes the long view of its profits and the broad view of its social responsibilities is in great danger of being acquired by an investor group that can gain financially by taking over the corporation and turning it to the pursuit of more immediate profit.

—William M. Dugger[1]

Finding ways to create new value in a sophisticated modern economy is seldom easy. Finding ways to create new value that will produce returns in the amount and with the speed demanded by a predatory financial system many times larger than the productive economy is virtually impossible.[2] The quickest way to make the kind of profit the system demands is to capture and cannibalize existing values from a weaker market player. In a free market, the "weaker" player is often the firm that is committed to investing in the future; providing employees with secure, well-paying jobs; paying a fair share of local taxes; paying into a fully funded retirement trust fund; managing environmental resources responsibly; and otherwise managing for the long-term human interest. Such companies are a valuable community asset, and in a healthy economy, they pay their shareholders solid and reliable—but not extravagant—dividends over the long term. They do not, however, yield the instant shareholder gains that computerized trading portfolios demand.

As Joel Kurtzman points out, by current market logic it is the duty of such firms to sell their assets and pay out the proceeds to shareholders:

> Companies dismembering themselves look good on the computerized maps in the investors' nose cones. They pay rich rewards, their stock prices remain high, and they have virtually no investment in the future in research and development. This sort of company would be all payoff, and the computers would fight one another to buy it.[3]

When responsible managers are disinclined to cannibalize their own companies, the financial system stands eager to fund those who will buy them out. In consequence, a predatory financial system teams up with a predatory market to declare responsible managers "inefficient" and purge them from the system. It makes the socially responsible corporation an endangered species.

Raiding the "Inefficient" Corporation

A special breed of extractive investor, the corporate raider, specializes in preying on established corporations. The basic process is elegantly simple and profitable, though the details are complex and the power struggles often nasty. The raider identifies a company traded on a public stock exchange that has a "breakup" value in excess of the current market price of its shares. Sometimes they are troubled companies. More often, they are well-managed, fiscally sound companies that are being good citizens and looking to the long term. They may have substantial cash reserves to cushion against an economic downturn and may have natural resources holdings that they are managing on a sustainable yield basis. Often the raider is looking specifically for companies that have reserves and long-term assets that can be sold off and that have costs that can be externalized onto the community.

Once such a company is identified, the prospective raider may form a new corporation as a receptacle for the acquired company. Often the receptacle corporation is financed almost entirely with debt and has little or no equity. The borrowed funds are used to quietly buy shares of the target company on the public stock exchanges at the prevailing market price up to the maximum allowed by law. An offer is then tendered to the company's board of directors to buy the outstanding shares of the company's stock at a price above the going market price, but below its breakup value. If the takeover bid is successful, the acquiring company consolidates the purchased company into itself—thus passing to the acquired company the debt that was used to buy it. Through a bit of financial sleight of hand, the acquired company has been purchased by using its own assets to secure the loans used to buy it.

Those who organize the deal ensure virtually risk-free gains for themselves by collecting large fees for their "services" in putting the deal together. Since the deals are financed mostly with money from banks or investment funds, the risks are borne largely by others, including the public that insures the bank deposits and gives up tax revenues to subsidize interest payments on the loan financing, and the small investors and pensioners whose money is at stake.

The "new" company now has considerable additional debt. To pay off that debt, the new management may draw down its cash reserves and pension funds, sell off profitable units for quick cash returns, bargain down wages, move production facilities abroad, strip natural resources holdings, and cut back maintenance and research expenditures to increase short-term gain—generally at the expense of long-term viability. Nearly 2,000 cases have been identified in which the new owners have virtually stolen a total of $21 billion of what they often declare to be "excess" funding from company pension accounts to apply to debt repayment.[4]

Once the debt is paid down and the company is reporting rapid growth in annual profits from the disposal of its assets and the shifting of money from interest payments to profits, the firm may be sold back to the public through a stock offering at a significant premium. The raider congratulates himself or herself for "increasing economic efficiency" and "adding value" to the economy and seeks out another target. These are the essentials of the leveraged buyout, a form of corporate cannibalism.

The key to the leveraged buyout is the ability to assemble the financing package. One might think that responsible bankers and investment brokers would shun such deals, which involve making huge unsecured loans to newly formed companies with no assets. To the contrary, since the deal makers offer unusually high interest rates to offset the lack of collateral, banks and investment houses often compete with one another for the opportunity to participate. During the 1980s, some large banks, awash in the same petrodollars that they were lavishing on indebted Southern countries in the 1970s, sought out the deal makers with offers of financing at the first rumor that a new takeover strike might be in the offing. Normally, the final financing package involves a combination of bank loans and funds realized from the sale of high-interest bonds—commonly called "junk bonds" because they are issued by shell corporations with no assets.

It is all played out with a chilling sense of moral detachment. In the words of Dennis Levine, a Wall Street high-flyer who was imprisoned for insider trading:

> We had a phenomenal enterprise going on Wall Street, and it was easy to forget that the billions of dollars we threw around had any material impact upon the jobs and, thus, the daily lives of millions of Americans. All too often the Street seemed to be a giant Monopoly board, and this game-like attitude was clearly evident in our terminology. When a company was identified as an acquisition target, we declared that it was "in play." We designated the playing pieces and strategies in whimsical terms: white knight, target, shark repellent, the Pac-Man defense, poison pill, greenmail, the golden parachute. Keeping a scorecard was easy—the winner was the one who finalized the most deals and took home the most money.[5]

What happens all too often after the buyout is complete is exemplified by the acquisition of the Pacific Lumber Company and its holdings of ancient redwoods on the California coast by corporate raider Charles Hurwitz. Before Hurwitz acquired it in a hostile takeover, the family-run Pacific Lumber Company was known as one of the most economically and environmentally sound timber companies in the United States. It was exemplary in its pioneering development and use of sustainable logging practices on its substantial holdings of ancient redwood timber stands, was generous in the benefits it provided to its employees, overfunded its pension fund to ensure that it could meet its commitments, and maintained a no-layoffs policy even during downturns in the timber market.[6] These practices made it a prime takeover target.

After establishing control of the company, Hurwitz immediately doubled the cutting rate of the company's thousand-year-old trees. According to *Time*, "In 1990 the company reamed a broad, mile-and-a-half corridor into the middle of the Headwaters forest and called it, with a wink and a snicker, 'our wildlife-biologist study trail.'"[7] On a visit to Pacific's mills at Scotia, Hurwitz told the employees, "There's a story about the golden rule. He who has the gold rules." With that pronouncement, he drained $55 million from the company's $93 million pension fund.[8] The remaining $38 million was invested in annuities of the Executive Life Insurance Company, which had financed the junk bonds used to make the purchase—and which subsequently failed.[9]

The hypocrisy of some corporate raiders is even more outrageous than their actions. To justify his role in the mass firings and wage cuts that followed the takeover of the Safeway supermarket chain, investor George Roberts told the *Wall Street Journal* that the supermarket chain's employees "are now being held accountable. . . . They have to produce up to plan, if they are going to be competitive with the rest of the world. It's high time we did that."[10]

Roberts and his principal partner, each of whom is worth more than $450 million, had taken over Safeway along with three other partners. Together, the group put up roughly $2 million of their personal money to complete the deal. *Forbes* magazine heralded it in a headline as "The Buyout That Saved Safeway" by freeing the company "from the albatross of uncompetitive stores and surly unions."[11] The pay of Safeway workers in Denver was cut by 15 percent, and truck drivers complained of being forced to work sixteen-hour shifts. Some $500 million was shifted from taxes to interest payments, and evaporated the hundreds of millions in taxes that tens of thousands of former Safeway employees no longer pay. For their contribution to making America more competitive by stemming the greedy impulses of Safeway's stock clerks, the five partners reaped a profit of more than $200 million.[12]

The fact that interest payments are tax deductible helps make all this possible. Since operating profits that would have been taxable are turned into deductible interest payments, the public is subsidizing the cannibalization of the nation's productive corporate assets. The effect on the U.S. taxpayer is far from trivial. During the 1950s, American corporations paid out $4 in taxes for every $1 in interest. During the 1980s, the increase in debt financing reversed the ratio, with corporations paying out $3 in interest for every $1 in taxes. One study concluded that $92 billion a year was thus shifted from taxes to interest payments. Whereas corporations paid 39 percent of all taxes collected in the United States in the 1950s, they paid only 17 percent in the 1980s. The share paid by individuals rose from 61 percent to 83 percent. Many corporations even collected refunds on taxes paid in the years before a takeover![13]

Corporate raiding and other forms of predatory extractive investment have become a source of handsome rewards for those with the stomach for it. In 1982, it required assets of $100 million to make the *Forbes* magazine list of the 400 wealthiest Americans. Only nineteen of those who made the list had made their fortunes in finance. Just five years later, in 1987, the smallest fortune that qualified was $225 million, and sixty-nine of the 400 who qualified were from finance—most of them having cashed in on the wave of corporate takeovers.[14]

The corporate raiders boldly assert that they are performing an important service to the American economy by eliminating inefficiency and restoring American competitiveness in the global economy. A compliant press dutifully reports their claims with minimal challenge. "The twisted logic of the robber barons of the Reagan era," writes Jonathan Greenberg, a financial journalist, "is that the living wage of middle America has decimated our economy." As Greenberg concludes, "The truth of the era of corporate takeovers has little to do with economic competitiveness. It's this simple: we've been robbed."[15]

Weeding Out Social Responsibility

We hear repeatedly from defenders of corporate libertarianism that the greening of management within a globalized free market will provide the answer to the world's social and environmental problems. With financial markets demanding maximum short-term gains and corporate raiders standing by to trash any company that isn't externalizing every possible cost, efforts to fix the problem by raising the social consciousness of managers misdefine the problem. There are plenty of socially conscious managers. The problem is a predatory system that makes it difficult for them to survive. This creates a terrible dilemma for managers with a true social vision of the corporation's role in society. They must either compromise their vision or run a great risk of being expelled by the system.

The Stride Rite Corporation, a shoe company, provides an example.[16] In addition to its generous contributions to charitable causes, it became known for its policy of locating plants and distribution facilities in some of America's most depressed inner cities and rural communities to revitalize them and provide secure, well-paying jobs for minorities. The policy was a strong personal commitment of Arnold Hiatt, Stride Rite's chief executive officer (CEO), who believed that business could and should contribute more to community life than simply profits to its stockholders. As CEO, Hiatt was able to hold his board of directors in line behind this policy until 1984.

In that year, a 68 percent drop in income, the first drop in thirteen years, convinced the company's directors that the survival of the firm depended on moving production abroad. They were concerned, among other things, that if they did not make that move, the company would become a takeover target. Hiatt fought the board of directors on this policy for as long as he could and ultimately resigned. According to Myles Slosberg, a director and former executive vice president of Stride Rite, the pursuit of low-cost labor bargains has since become something of a "Holy Grail" for the company. The systemic forces bearing on Stride Rite were enormous. Its U.S. workers averaged $1,200 to $1,400 a month for wages alone, plus fringe benefits. The skilled workers in China who are hired by contractors to produce Stride Rite's shoes earn $100 to $150 a month, working fifty to sixty hours a week. In addition to moving its plants abroad, Stride Rite moved its national distribution center for the United States from Massachusetts to Louisville, Kentucky, to take advantage of lower-cost U.S. labor there and an offer of tax abatements from the state valued at $24 million over ten years.

Stride Rite sales have doubled since 1986, and the price of its stock has increased sixfold, making it a favorite on the New York Stock Exchange—including among socially conscious investors who continue to be impressed by its record of corporate giving. According to Ervin Shames, Stride Rite's current chairman, "Putting jobs into places where it doesn't make economic sense is a dilution of corporate and community wealth."[17]

The Stride Rite experience presents a chilling example of the inexorable workings of a predatory global economy. Through a combination of the bidding down of Stride Rite's share of the public tax burden and the shifting of jobs from well-paid to poorly paid workers, Stride Rite's management participated in a massive exercise in wealth redistribution from poor communities and people of modest incomes to its shareholders—from those who produce value through their skills and physical exertion to those who are contributing only the use of surplus money. Yet Stride Rite's management cannot be blamed for this move.

If Hiatt, as Stride Rite's CEO, had carried the day, stuck to his convictions, and refused to move production abroad, it is almost certain that a hovering group of investment bankers would have noted this "breech of fiduciary responsibility" to the firm's shareholders. They would have acquired the company through a hostile takeover, fired Stride Rite's socially concerned management, and moved the production abroad far more abruptly and with even worse consequences for the workers and the community.

Some investment funds specialize in buying and selling companies in labor-intensive industries that have resisted moving to low-wage countries. The AmeriMex Maquiladora Fund, a group of U.S. and Mexican investors initially backed by Nafinsa, Mexico's largest national development bank, was formed specifically to target U.S. companies that have resisted the move abroad. According to its prospectus:

> The Fund will purchase established domestic United States companies suitable for maquiladora acquisitions, wherein a part or all of the manufacturing operations will be relocated to Mexico to take advantage of the cost of labor. The Fund will seek to acquire companies where labor is a significant component of a

company's cost of goods sold. It is anticipated that within six to 18 months after a company has been acquired by the Fund, the designated portion of the company's manufacturing operations will be relocated to Mexico to take advantage of reduced labor costs.

We anticipate that manufacturing companies that experience fully loaded, gross labor costs in the $7–$10 per hour range in the U.S. may be able to utilize labor in a Mexico maquiladora at fully loaded, gross labor cost of $1.15–$1.50 per hour. Though each situation may vary, it is estimated that this could translate into annual savings of $10,000–$17,000 per employee involved in the relocated manufacturing operations. It is anticipated that most investments will be retained for three to eight years.[18]

The potential profits from reselling such relocated companies are substantial. At a saving of $17,000 per employee, shifting 1,000 jobs from the United States to Mexico creates a potential increase of $17 million in annual profits. Assuming that the company's stock normally sells for ten times the company's annual earnings, this translates into an increase of $170 million in the market value of the company's stock.[19] Clearly those who invest in such schemes are not doing so out of concern for providing secure and well-paying jobs to needy Mexican workers.

A rogue financial system is actively cannibalizing the productive corporate sector. In the name of economic efficiency, it is rendering responsible management ever more difficult. Those who call on corporate managers to exercise greater social responsibility miss this basic point. Corporate managers live and work in a system that is virtually feeding on the socially responsible. That system is transforming itself into a two-tiered structure, creating a world that is becoming more deeply divided between the privileged and the dispossessed, between those who have the power to place themselves beyond the prevailing market forces and those who have become sacrificial offerings on the altar of global competition.

17 Managed Competition

The business system is increasingly taking the form of lean and mean core firms, connected . . . to networks of other large and small organizations, including firms, governments, and communities. . . . [These] networked forms of industrial organization . . . exhibit a tendency to reinforce, and perhaps to worsen, the historic stratification of jobs and earnings.

—*Bennett Harrison*[1]

On September 14, 1993, E. I. Du Pont de Nemours & Company announced that it would dismiss 4,500 employees in its U.S.-based chemical business by mid-1994 to cut costs. While 4,500 families struggled to adjust to the fact that the economy had labeled their breadwinners redundant burdens, the money markets cheered. It was part of a larger cutback of 9,000 people from Du Pont's total worldwide workforce of 133,000—all part of a plan intended to cut the company's costs by $3 billion a year.[2] The price of a share of Du Pont stock jumped $1.75 on the day of the announcement. Such announcements have become daily fare in the financial press. It is clear that important changes are occurring in the structure of industry. According to *The Economist*:

> The biggest change coming over the world of business is that firms are getting smaller. The trend of a century is being reversed. . . . Now it is the big

firms that are shrinking and small ones that are on the rise. The trend is unmistakable—and businessmen and policy makers will ignore it at their peril.[3]

It is a widespread perception that the massive corporate giants have become too large and bureaucratic to compete against the more nimble and innovative smaller firms that we are told are rapidly gaining the advantage in highly competitive global markets. Proponents of this view point to the fact that large firms are shedding employees by the hundreds of thousands and cite statistics showing that the new employment and technological innovations are being generated primarily by more competitive small and medium-sized firms. It makes for a reassuring thesis. However, it is only one more illusion crafted by corporate libertarians that obscures our vision of what is really happening.

Shedding Jobs and Concentrating Power

Although there are regional variations, the world's most successful transnational corporations—whether Japanese, European, or American—are engaged in a process of transforming themselves and the structures of global capitalism to further consolidate their power through complex networking forms of organization. Bennett Harrison, author of *Lean and Mean: The Changing Landscape of Corporate Power in the Age of Flexibility*, calls it, "concentration without centralization." Four elements of that transformation are of particular relevance to our analysis.[4]

Downsizing. Drastic cuts in personnel are the most visible aspect of downsizing, but they are in most instances only one part of a larger organizational strategy. The larger scheme is to trim the firm's in-house operations down to its "core competencies"—generally the finance, marketing, and proprietary technology functions that represent the firm's primary sources of economic power. The staffing of these functions is reduced to the bare minimum and consolidated within the corporate headquarters.

Peripheral functions, including much of the manufacturing activity, is farmed out to networks of relatively small outside contractors—often in low-wage countries. This process involves shifting employment from the corporate core to peripheral contractor organizations that form part of a production network of firms that are dependent on the markets and technology controlled by the corporate core. Peripheral activities that are not contracted out and cannot be automated may be located far away from corporate headquarters. These are, for example, the "back offices" of the big insurance companies and banks, which are generally staffed with poorly paid female clerical workers.

Computerization and Automation. The core corporation brings the full capabilities of computerization and automation to bear in whatever manufacturing functions it retains and in the management information systems by which it flexibly coordinates the product network's far-flung activities. Automation has two key purposes. One is to pare down the number of workers to an absolute minimum, such as in AT&T's plans to replace thousands of telephone operators with computerized voice-recognition systems.[5] The second is to minimize inventories by linking dispersed suppliers with marketing outlets using "just-in-time" delivery of parts and supplies.

Mergers, Acquisitions, and Strategic Alliances. The corporations that stand at the cores of major networks pursue a variety of strategies to manage the potentially destructive competition among themselves. One is to meld through mergers and acquisitions. Another is to construct strategic alliances through which they share technology, production facilities, and markets and engage in joint research.

Headquarters Teamwork and Morale. Substantial attention is given to maintaining conditions that are conducive to high morale and effective teamwork among core personnel.

This restructuring creates a two-tiered or dualistic employment system. Those employees engaged in the core corporate headquarters functions are well compensated, with full benefits and attractive working conditions. The peripheral functions—farmed out either to subordinate units within the corporation or to outside suppliers dependent on the firm's business—are performed by low-paid, often temporary or part-time "contingent" employees who receive few or no benefits and to whom the corporation has no commitment.

The two tiers also differ significantly with regard to competitive pressures. There is considerable, if uneasy, cooperation among the corporations that control the cores of major networks to maintain their collective monopoly control over markets and technology. The peripheral units, even those that remain within the firm, function as independent small contractors pitted in intense competition with one another for the firm's continuing business. They are thus forced to cut their own costs to the bone. This dualistic structure is an important part of the explanation for the growing income gap found in the United States and many other countries.

According to Harrison, "It is the strategic downsizing of the big firms that is responsible for driving down the average size of business organizations in the current era, *not* some spectacular growth of the small firms sector, per se."[6] The largest 1,000 companies in America account for over 60 percent of the gross national product (GNP), leaving the balance to 11 million small businesses.[7] The contracting-out process does create new opportunities for smaller firms, but the power remains right where it has been all along—with the corporate giants. Lacking independent access to the market, the smaller firms that orbit core corporations function more as dependent appendages than as independent businesses.

The power relationships between companies of the core and the periphery are remarkably similar to those that prevailed between core and peripheral countries in the days of colonial empires. The dominant players in both systems capture the resources and surpluses of the players at the periphery to maintain the core in relative affluence. Core players may reach out and absorb peripheral players, such as when core corporations buy out smaller firms that control promising technologies or lucrative markets. Colonial states also crafted alliances of convenience with one another to manage the often destructive competition among themselves—much like present-day strategic alliances among core corporations. The tyranny of state colonialism worked very well for a rather small percentage of the world's population. It was disastrous for the rest. Modern corporate colonialism is little different.

Thus we witness the paradox that when the world's largest corporations unceremoniously shed well-educated, loyal, and hardworking employees, they are increasing their economic power. From 1980 to 1993, the Fortune 500 industrial firms shed nearly 4.4 million jobs, more than one out of four that they previously provided. During that same period, their sales increased by 1.4 times and assets by 2.3 times. The average annual chief executive officer (CEO) compensation at the largest corporations increased by 6.1 times to $3.8 million.[8]

Although downsizing has been an unavoidable response to weak markets and lax management for some companies, others have downsized from a position of considerable strength. GTE announced plans on January 13, 1994, to lay off more than 17,000 employees in the face of a strong market and a steady growth in operating income. Other companies enjoying growth in markets and profits announced significant layoffs at the end of 1993 or the beginning of 1994: Gillette (2,000 employees), Arco (1,300), Pacific Telesis (10,000), and Xerox (10,000). Some cut real fat from the payrolls. Other cuts were part of the shift to outsourcing. Many were made possible by new technologies. Major job cuts often accompany mergers and acquisitions, which are usually aimed at strengthening and consolidating market share while reducing employment costs. After Chevron merged with Gulf in 1984, it reduced the combined workforce by nearly half, to about 50,000 people. It cut another 6,500 people in 1992–93.[9]

General Electric (GE) shed 100,000 employees over eleven years to bring total employment down to 268,000 in 1992. During that same period, its sales went up from $27 billion to $62 billion, and net income from $1.5 billion to $4.7 billion.[10] GE became smaller only in terms of the number of employees who shared the benefits of its growth in profits and market share. It had shed mainly its commitment to provide productive and well-remunerated employment for 100,000 people and their families. It did not shed its technical, financial, or market power.

Within this restructuring drama, we see a secondary drama being played out in a major contest between the manufacturing giants and the retailing giants for control of the core network positions. The growing success of the retailing giants is revealed in the growing rate of bankruptcy among retailers in the United States. Since 1991, retail firms have been going bankrupt at a rate of more than 17,000 a year, up from approximately 11,000 in 1989. Many of them have been driven out of business by the mega-retailers.[11] According to *Business Week*:

> A vast consolidation in U.S. retailing has produced giant "power retailers" that use sophisticated inventory management, finely tuned selections, and above all, competitive pricing to crowd out weaker players and attract more of the shopper's dollar. . . . They're telling even the mightiest of manufacturers what goods to make, in what colors and sizes, how much to ship and when. . . . Leading the pack, of course, is Wal-Mart Stores. The nation's No. 1 retailer is expected to grow 25% this year, to some $55 billion in sales, at a time when retailers as a whole will be lucky to grow 4%.[12]

When Wal-Mart grows at a rate of 25 percent in an industry that is growing at no more than 4 percent, its growth is clearly at the expense of rivals that lack comparable clout. The smaller retailers that used to be the commercial core of and major employers in most towns and cities have been hit particularly hard. It has been predicted that retailers accounting for half of all sales in the United States in 1992 will have disappeared by the year 2000. Systems analyst and syndicated columnist Donella Meadows describes what happens when a Wal-Mart comes to town:

> In Iowa the average Wal-Mart grosses $13 million a year and increases total area sales by $4 million, which means it takes $9 million worth of business from existing stores. Within three or four years of a Wal-Mart's arrival, retail sales within a 20-mile

radius go down by 25 percent; 20 to 50 miles away, sales go down 10 percent.

A Massachusetts study says a typical Wal-Mart adds 140 jobs and destroys 230 higher-paying jobs. . . . Despite public investments in restoring downtown business districts, vacancies increase. Rents drop, and the remaining enterprises pay lower wages and taxes. Competing chain stores in existing malls leave and are not replaced.[13]

The mass retailing superpowers—Wal-Mart, Kmart, Toys 'R' Us, Home Depot, Circuit City Stores, Dillard Department Stores, Target Stores, and Costco, among others—are increasingly becoming the core firms in vast consumer goods networks. The mega-retailers are notorious for playing off suppliers against one another and for abruptly shifting their sourcing from domestic firms to low-labor-cost countries such as China or Bangladesh. Many small manufacturers have suddenly found themselves in bankruptcy when the major part of their market evaporated. Even the manufacturing giants, such as Procter & Gamble, that lack their own retail outlets are under intense pressure from the retailing giants to cut their prices and profit margins.

As the big retailers grow, they tend to favor larger suppliers that have the resources and sophistication to meet their demands for customized products and packages, computer linkups, and special delivery schedules. This contributes to further consolidation on the manufacturing side. Only a decade ago, no single toy maker controlled more than 5 percent of the market.[14] Now, in a toy industry dominated by Toys 'R' Us and general discounting giants such as Wal-Mart, Kmart, and Target Stores, the manufacturing side is dominated by just six companies.

While basically applauding this as a move toward greater efficiency, even *Business Week* sounds a cautionary note: "what if the growing clout of power retailers stifles too many small companies and forces too many large ones to dodge risks? The close ties between retailers and their surviving suppliers could ultimately end up raising consumer prices and reducing innovation."[15]

The Growth of Centrally Managed Economies

The scale of the concentration of economic power that is occurring is revealed in the statistics: of the world's hundred largest economies, fifty are corporations,[16] and the aggregate sales of the world's ten largest corporations in 1991 exceeded the aggregate GNP of the world's hundred smallest countries.[17] General Motors' 1992 sales revenues

($133 billion) roughly equaled the combined GNP of Tanzania, Ethiopia, Nepal, Bangladesh, Zaire, Uganda, Nigeria, Kenya, and Pakistan. Five hundred fifty million people inhabit these countries, a tenth of the world's population.

The world's 500 largest industrial corporations, which employ only 0.05 of 1 percent of the world's population, control 25 percent of the world's economic output.[18] The top 300 transnationals, excluding financial institutions, own some 25 percent of the world's productive assets.[19] The combined assets of the world's fifty largest commercial banks and diversified financial companies amount to nearly 60 percent of *The Economist*'s estimate of a $20 trillion global stock of productive capital.[20] The global trend is clearly toward greater concentration of the control of markets and productive assets in the hands of a few firms that make a minuscule contribution to total global employment. The giants are shedding people but not control over money, markets, or technology.

This concentration of economic power in relatively few corporations raises an interesting contradiction. Corporate libertarians regularly proclaim that central economic planning does not work and is contrary to the broader public interest. Yet successful corporations maintain more control over the economies defined by their product networks than the central planners in Moscow ever achieved over the Soviet economy. Central management buys, sells, dismantles, or closes component units as it chooses, moves production units around the world at will, decides what revenues will be given up by subordinate units to the parent corporation, appoints and fires managers of subsidiaries, sets transfer prices and other terms governing transactions among the firm's component organizations, and decides whether individual units can make purchases and sales on the open market or must do business only with other units of the firm. Unless top management chooses to invite dissenting views, its decisions on such matters are seldom open to question or review by any subordinate person or unit.

Although no global corporation yet manages a planned economy on the scale of the former Soviet economy, they are coming closer. The 1991 sales of the world's five largest diversified service companies (all of which happen to be Japanese) were roughly equivalent to the entire 1988 gross domestic product (GDP) of the former Soviet Union. Cuba, with a GDP of $26.1 billion, now ranks seventy-second among the world's centrally managed economies; the first seventy-one are all global corporations. Tiny North Korea wouldn't even make the list of the world's 500 largest centrally managed economies.

It is far from an incidental consideration that in its internal governance structures, the corporation is among the most authoritarian of organizations and can be as repressive as any totalitarian state. Those who work for corporations spend the better portion of their waking hours living under a form of authoritarian rule that dictates their dress, their speech, their values, their behavior, and their levels of income—with limited opportunity for appeal. With few exceptions, their subject employees can be dismissed without recourse on almost momentary notice. The current "lean and mean" transformation of the corporation is about extending this authoritarian rule beyond the boundaries of the corporation itself over far larger networks of organizations in ways that allow the core to consolidate its control while reducing its responsibility for the well-being of any member of the network.

When equating the market system with freedom, the question of whether freedom is consistent with hired labor in a world in which giant corporations control most jobs is seldom asked. Most social reformers have accepted a corporate-dominated wage system and chosen to pursue social policies that provide job security, tolerable working conditions, equitable wages, and the right to organize labor unions within the context of that system.[21] If we are serious about human freedom and democracy, we must reopen the question of whether such adjustments are adequate or even possible within the existing system of business.

Cooperation at the Core

For all their praise of free-market competition, most corporations seek to suppress it at every opportunity. As Adam Smith observed in 1776, "People of the same trade seldom meet together, even for merriment and diversion, but the conversation ends in a conspiracy against the public, or in some contrivance to raise prices."[22] Such cooperation need not be born of evil motives. Competition creates turbulence. Turbulence is embraced as opportunity by speculators, but for those who manage productive enterprises, the resulting uncertainty makes investment planning inherently difficult, disrupts the orderly function of the firm, and can result in serious economic inefficiency. The desire to increase control and predictability by reducing competition might be considered one of the natural laws of the market.

Firms try to reduce competition in the global economy by the same means they have always used, by increasing their control over capital, markets, and technology. The new element is found in the combination of a globalized economy and modern information technologies that make it possible to consolidate that control on a scale never before possible. The competitive tactics are also familiar. Weaker competitors are crushed, colonized, or absorbed. Accommodation is sought with stronger competitors through strategic alliances, mergers, acquisitions, and interlocking boards of directors.

A favorite corporate libertarian argument for globalization is that the opening of national markets introduces greater competition and leads to increased efficiency. Although it is an interesting theoretical argument, it neglects a simple reality. When markets are global, the forces of monopoly transcend national borders to consolidate at a global level. First comes the call to open borders to increase competitive forces. Then comes the call to allow mergers into ever more powerful combinations in order to be "competitive" in the global marketplace. When a Philip Morris acquires a Kraft and a General Foods, as it did in the 1980s to create the United States' largest food company, it does not make U.S. markets more competitive; it creates a strengthened platform from which to create and project monopoly power on a global scale.

As a rule of thumb, economists consider a domestic market to be monopolistic when the four top firms account for 40 percent or more of sales. Through a series of mergers and consolidations, the top four major appliance corporations in the United States (Whirlpool, General Electric, Electrolux/WCI, and Maytag) controlled 92 percent of the U.S. appliance market as of 1990, and four airlines (United, American, Delta, and Northwest) accounted for 66 percent of U.S. revenue passenger miles. Four computer software companies (Microsoft, Lotus, Novell/Digital, and WordPerfect) controlled 55 percent of the U.S. software market in 1990, and two of them (Novell and WordPerfect) merged on June 27, 1994.[23]

When five firms control more than half of a global market, that market is considered to be *highly* monopolistic. *The Economist* recently reported five-firm concentration ratios for twelve global industries. The greatest concentration was found in consumer durables, where the top five firms control nearly 70 percent of the entire world market in their industry. In the automotive, airline, aerospace, electronic components, electrical and electronics, and steel industries, the top five firms control more than 50 percent of the global market, clearly placing them in the monopolistic category. In the oil, personal computer, and media industries, the top five firms control more than 40 percent of sales, which shows strong monopolistic tendencies.[24]

The argument that globalization increases competition is simply false. To the contrary, it strengthens tendencies toward global-scale monopolization.

Agriculture has been a major subject in trade negotiations, with U.S. trade negotiators making a strong appeal for a reduction of barriers to free trade in agricultural commodities and the elimination of protection for small farmers in Europe and Japan. The story of U.S.

agriculture reveals why U.S. agribusiness companies are so enthusiastically calling for the "freeing" of agricultural markets. It is part of the process of restructuring global agriculture into a two-tiered system controlled by the agribusiness giants.

From 1935 to 1989, the number of small farms in the United States declined from 6.8 million to under 2.1 million; during the same period, U.S. population roughly doubled. As farmers have gone out of business, so too have the local suppliers, implement dealers, and other small businesses that once supported them. Entire rural communities have disappeared. Meanwhile, the major U.S. agribusiness corporations have grown and consolidated their power. The top ten "farms" in the United States are now international agribusiness corporations with names like Tyson Foods, ConAgra, Gold Kist, Continental Grain, Perdue Farms, Pilgrims Pride, and Cargill—each with annual farm products sales ranging from $310 million to $1.7 billion.

Two grain companies—Cargill and ConAgra—control 50 percent of U.S. grain exports. Three companies—Iowa Beef Processors (IBP), Cargill, and ConAgra—slaughter nearly 80 percent of U.S. beef. One company—Campbell's—controls nearly 70 percent of the U.S. soup market. Four companies—Kellogg, General Mills, Philip Morris, and Quaker Oats—control nearly 85 percent of the U.S. cold cereal market. Four companies—ConAgra, ADM Milling, Cargill, and Pillsbury—mill nearly 60 percent of U.S. flour. This concentration is in part the consequence of 4,100 food industry mergers and leveraged buyouts in the United States between 1982 and 1990—and the consolidation process continues.[25]

Often these core firms find that it is most profitable and least risky to contract out the actual production to smaller producers. These smaller producers hold the major capital investment and bear the risks inherent in agriculture. The large firms control the market and maintain control over the terms under which the producers operate. It is common for the core firm to force farmers to purchase required inputs—such as fertilizer and feed—from itself, prescribe the production methods, and purchase the crops or animals produced on whatever terms it chooses. The only choice left to farmers is to accept the terms, go out of business, or find another crop whose market is not yet controlled by a core corporation. This restructuring of agriculture has contributed to decreasing the farmers' share of consumers' food dollars from 41 percent in 1910 to 9 percent in 1990.[26]

Figures compiled in 1980 by the U.S. Department of Agriculture revealed that production and marketing contracts covered the production of 98 percent of sugar beets, 95 percent of fluid-grade milk, 89 percent of chicken broilers, 85 percent of processed vegetables, and 80 percent of all seed crops. When a contractor firm controls the market, producers are at its mercy. When Del Monte decided, for example, to transfer the bulk of its peach procurement from northern California to Italy and South Africa, most of its contract farmers saw their market vanish for reasons that had nothing to do with the local appetite for peaches.[27]

Such conditions mock Adam Smith's notion of a competitive market comprising small buyers and sellers. The farmer receives a lower price and the consumer pays a higher price than either would have obtained under conditions of true competition.[28] This is the system that the dominant agribusiness companies hope to extend to the world.

In a globalizing market, the widespread image is one of the corporate titans of Japan, North America, and Europe battling it out toe-to-toe in international markets. This image is increasingly a fiction that obscures the extent to which a few core corporations are strengthening their collective monopoly market power through joint ventures and strategic alliances with their major rivals. Through these arrangements, firms share access to special expertise, technology, production facilities, and markets; spread the costs and risks of research and new product development; and manage the competitive relationships with their major potential rivals.

For example, American computer giants IBM, Apple Computer, and Motorola have formed an interfirm alliance to develop the operating system and microprocessor for the next generation of computer.[29] In 1991, Apple Computer turned to Sony Corporation to manufacture the cheapest version of its PowerBook notebook computer.[30]

GM now owns 37.5 percent of the Japanese auto manufacturer Isuzu, which produces automobiles for sale under the GM and Opel brand labels. Chrysler has had an ownership stake in Mitsubishi, Maserati, and Fiat.[31] Ford Motor Company has a 25 percent stake in Mazda and names three outside directors to the Mazda board. Ford and Mazda jointly own a dealer network in Japan, cooperate in new product design, and share production techniques.[32] *The Economist* recently suggested the following exercise:

> Take a really big international industry such as cars, in which the products are complicated and fairly expensive. Write down all the manufacturers' names (there are more than 20 large ones for cars) along the four sides of a square. Now draw lines connecting manufacturers that have joint ventures or alliances with one another, whether in design, research, components, full assembly, distribution or marketing, for one product or for several, anywhere in

the world. Pretty soon, the drawing becomes an incomprehensible tangle, just about everyone seems to be allied with everyone else. And the car industry is not an exception. It is a similar story in computer hardware, computer software, aerospace, drugs, telecommunications, defence and many others.[33]

Cyrus Friedheim, vice-chairman of Booz, Allen & Hamilton, a management consulting firm, foresees an economic future dominated by what he calls "the relationship-enterprise," a network of strategic alliances among firms spanning different industries and countries that act almost as a single firm. He points to the discussions among Boeing, members of the Airbus consortium, McDonnell Douglas, Mitsubishi, Kawasaki, and Fuji about cooperating on the joint development of a new super-jumbo jet and the group formed by the world's major telecommunications firms to provide a worldwide network of fiber-optic underwater cables. According to Friedheim, these corporate juggernauts will dwarf existing global corporate giants, with individual relationship enterprises reaching total combined revenues approaching $1 trillion by early next century, making them larger than all but the six largest national economies.[34]

The world's corporate giants are creating a system of managed competition by which they actively limit competition among themselves while encouraging intensive competition among the smaller firms and localities that constitute their periphery. It is all part of the process of forcing the periphery to absorb more of the costs of the "value added" process so that the core can produce greater profits for its own insatiable master, the global financial system.

The underlying patterns of the institutional transformation being wrought by economic globalization are persistently in the direction of moving power away from people and communities and concentrating it in giant global institutions that have become detached from the human interest. We have become captives of the tyranny of a rogue system that is functioning beyond human direction. Driven by its own imperatives, that system has gained control over many of the most important aspects of our lives to demand that we give ourselves over to its purpose—the making of money. We now face an even more ominous prospect. Having found its own direction and gained control of the institutions that once served our needs, the system that now holds us captive is finding that it has little need for people.

V No Place for People

18 Race to
the Bottom

> *[F]reer markets and freer trade in the new global eco-
> nomic system are what will ultimately put an end to
> slow growth and high unemployment in the industrial
> world . . . that's what the new economic order is all
> about.*
>
> —Business Week[1]

> *The recent quantum leap in the ability of transnational
> corporations to relocate their facilities around the world
> in effect makes all workers, communities and countries
> competitors for these corporations' favor. The conse-
> quence is a "race to the bottom" in which wages and
> social conditions tend to fall to the level of the most
> desperate.*
>
> —Jeremy Brecher[2]

While competition is being weakened at the core,
it is intensifying among smaller businesses, workers, and localities at the periphery as they become pitted against one another in a desperate struggle for
survival. What the corporate libertarians call "becoming more globally competitive" is more accurately described as a race to the bottom. With each passing day
it becomes more difficult to obtain contracts from one
of the mega-retailers without hiring child labor, cheat-
ing workers on overtime pay, imposing merciless quo-
tas, and operating unsafe facilities. If one contractor
does not do it, his or her prices will be higher than those
of another who does. With hundreds of millions of
people desperate for any kind of job the global economy
may offer, there will always be willing competitors.
Faced with its own imperatives, the core corporations

can do little more than close their eyes to the infractions and insist that they have no responsibility for the conditions of their contractors.

Modern Slavery

Descriptions of the working conditions of millions of workers, even in the "modern and affluent" North, sound like a throwback to the days of the early industrial revolution. Consider this description of conditions at contract clothing shops in modern affluent San Francisco:

> Many of them are dark, cramped and windowless. . . . Twelve-hour days with no days off and a break only for lunch are not uncommon. And in this wealthy, cosmopolitan city, many shops enforce draconian rules reminiscent of the nineteenth century. "The workers were not allowed to talk to each other and they didn't allow us to go to the bathroom," says one Asian garment worker. . . . Aware of manufacturers' zeal for bargain-basement prices, the nearly 600 sewing contractors in the Bay Area engage in cutthroat competition—often a kind of Darwinian drive to the bottom. . . . Manufacturers have another powerful chip to keep bids down. Katie Quan, a manager of the International Ladies Garment Workers Union in San Francisco, explains, "They say, 'If you don't take it, we'll just ship it overseas, and you won't get work and your workers will go hungry.'"
>
> In 1992 a [Department of Labor] investigation of garment shops on the U.S. protectorate of Saipan found conditions akin to indentured servitude: Chinese workers whose passports had been confiscated, putting in eighty-four-hour weeks at subminimum wages.[3]

The line between conditions in the South and the North as defined by geography becomes ever more blurred. Dorka Diaz, a twenty-year-old textile worker who formerly produced clothing in Honduras for Leslie Fay, a U.S.-based transnational, testified before the Subcommittee on Labor-Management Relations of the U.S. House of Representatives that she worked for Leslie Fay in Honduras alongside twelve- and thirteen-year-old girls locked inside a factory where the temperature often hit 100 degrees and there was no clean drinking water. For a fifty-four-hour week, she was paid a little over $20. She and her three-year-old son lived at the edge of starvation. In April 1994, she was fired for trying to organize a union.[4]

When the black women who toiled over knitting machines in a Taiwanese-owned sweater factory in South Africa for fifty cents an hour made it known that with the election of Nelson Mandela they expected "a union shop, better wages and a little respect," the Taiwanese owners responded by abruptly closing their seven South African factories and eliminating 1,000 jobs. Low as the wages were, the cost of labor in South Africa is twice that of labor in Brazil or Mexico and several times that in Thailand or China.[5] Noting that prospective foreign investors have turned wary of South Africa, the *New York Times* suggests, "There are doubts about the Government's long-term commitment to capitalism, about whether Mr. Mandela can contain the expectations of the impoverished majority."[6] In the world of big money and multimillion-dollar compensation packages, greed is a worker who wants a living wage.

In many Southern countries, to say that conditions verge on slavery is scarcely an exaggeration. China has become a favorite of foreign investors and corporations seeking cheap labor and outsourcing for offshore procurement at rock-bottom prices. *Business Week* described the prevailing conditions of Chinese factory workers:

> In foreign-funded factories, which employ about 6 million Chinese in the coastal provinces, accidents abound. In some factories, workers are chastised, beaten, strip-searched, and even forbidden to use the bathroom during work hours. At a foreign-owned company in the Fujian province city of Ziamen, 40 workers—or one-tenth of the work force—have had their fingers crushed by obsolete machines. According to official reports, there were 45,000 industrial accidents in Guangdong last year, claiming more than 8,700 lives. . . . Last month . . . 76 workers died in a Guangdong factory accident.[7]

Although the Chinese government reportedly is trying to tighten up on standards, it has faced enormous problems of unemployment since its decision to free up market forces. Tens of millions of rural workers are streaming to the cities. Urban unemployment stood at 5 million in mid-1994, a 25 percent increase in a year. Two million workers lost their jobs in Heilongjiang province in 1993 alone. Millions more urban workers face pay cuts, and half of the government-owned enterprises that employ approximately half of the urban workforce are losing money, creating prospects of massive layoffs and plant closings.[8] Government efforts to tighten up on standards in this "free-market miracle" are also hampered by skyrocketing rates of crime and corruption.[9]

In Bangladesh, an estimated 80,000 children under age fourteen, most of them female, work at least sixty hours a week in garment factories. For miscounting or other errors, male supervisors strike them or force them to kneel on the floor or stand on their heads for ten to thirty minutes.[10]

It isn't only in the garment industry. In India, an estimated 55 million children work in various conditions of servitude, many as bonded laborers—virtual slaves—under the most appalling conditions. Each child has his or her own story. A few months after his rescue from forced labor, Devanandan told a reporter that he had been coaxed to leave home by a promise of wages up to $100 a month for working at a loom two hours a day while going to school. When he agreed, he found himself locked up in a room where he ate, slept, and was forced to work knotting carpets from four in the morning till late evening for pennies in pay.[11]

Former Indian Chief Justice P. M. Bhagwati has publicly testified to observing examples of boys working fourteen to twenty hours a day: "They are beaten up, branded [with red-hot iron rods] and even hung from trees upside down." The carpet industry in India exports $300 million worth of carpets a year, mainly to the United States and Germany. The carpets are produced by more than 300,000 child laborers working fourteen to sixteen hours a day, seven days a week, fifty-two weeks a year. Many are bonded laborers, paying off the debts of their parents; they have been sold into bondage or kidnaped from low-caste parents. The fortunate ones earn a pittance wage. The unfortunate ones are paid nothing at all. The carpet manufacturers argue that the industry must have child laborers to be able to survive in competition with the carpet industries of Pakistan, Nepal, Morocco, and elsewhere that also use child laborers.[12]

As we rush to enter the race to the bottom in a globally competitive world, it is sobering to keep in mind just how deep the bottom is toward which we are racing.

The Limits of Social Responsibility

Within the apparel industry, a few socially concerned firms such as Levi Strauss, Esprit, and The Gap are attempting to live by their values. They are proving that a responsible, well-managed company need not tolerate the worst of the conditions described above, but they face the same competitive pressures as others in their industry. Almost inevitably, such firms find themselves developing split personalities. In the end, they finance their public good works and the good pay and conditions of their headquarters staffs by procuring most of the goods they sell through contractors that offer low wages and substandard working conditions.

Consider specifically the case of Levi Strauss, a company widely acclaimed as a leader in the realm of corporate responsibility. In April 1994, the Council on Economic Priorities gave Levi Strauss an award for its "unprecedented commitment to nonexploitative work practices in developing countries."[13] In 1984, the company was named one of the hundred best companies to work for in America. In June 1992, *Money* magazine ranked it first among all U.S. companies for employee benefits.[14] Bob Haas, chief executive officer (CEO) of Levi Strauss, was featured in the August 1, 1994, cover story of *Business Week* titled "Managing by Values," which emphasized his belief that social responsibility and ethical practice are good business.

In 1985, Bob Haas, as CEO and a member of the Levi Strauss family, led a $1.6 billion leveraged buyout of the company, taking it private specifically to prevent a takeover by outside speculators. The fact that 94 percent of the stock is in Haas family hands has given the company more flexibility in maintaining its social commitment than a publicly held company might have in an era of hostile takeovers.

Under Haas's leadership, Levi Strauss has set strict standards with regard to the work environment. As evidence that they mean it, the Levi Strauss board of directors voted unanimously to close out $40 million a year in production contracts in China in protest of human rights violations. When the company found that its contractor in Dhaka, Bangladesh, was hiring girls as young as eleven as full-time seamstresses, it worked out an agreement by which Levi Strauss would continue to pay the wages of these girls while sending them to school and paying for their uniforms, books, and tuition. When they reach age fourteen, the minimum employment age set by International Labor Organization standards, they will return to work.[15] By the standards of the industry, Levi Strauss is a candidate for sainthood. But it is sobering to see how constrained even a Levi Strauss can be.

Although Haas asserts that Levi Strauss has made every effort to keep as many of its production jobs in the United States as possible, during the 1980s, it closed fifty-eight U.S. plants and laid off 10,400 workers. According to Haas, if the company had made its decisions on purely economic grounds, its remaining thirty-four production and finishing plants would all have been closed in favor of overseas production.

Even at its plants in the United States, the core-periphery phenomenon is evident. When the authors of *The 100 Best Companies to Work for in America* visited the Levi Strauss plant in El Paso, Texas, they found that *Money* magazine had ranked the company number one on the basis of the benefits enjoyed by its headquarters staff, not by staff at its plants. The benefits received by the El Paso production workers were little different from the marginal conditions at other local textile factories. The authors decided not to include the company among the 100 best in the book's revised edition.[16]

A Spreading Cancer

We have focused here on U.S.-based multinationals, because their dysfunctions seem to be spreading through the world like a cancer. By May of 1994, a binge of corporate restructuring in Europe, similar to that in the United States, had pushed Europe's unemployment rate to 10.9 percent.[17] Even these rates, high as they are, may mask a much deeper dysfunction. In Belgium, unemployment was 8.5 percent in 1992, but 25 percent of the workforce was living on public assistance.[18] Persistent joblessness is resulting in growing social unrest, exacerbating racial tensions, and sparking a vicious backlash against immigrants. Joblessness is especially acute among youth, whose unemployment rate is twice that of the general population and still rising. On March 25, 1994, 50,000 students marched down a Paris boulevard, "taunting police and chanting slogans demanding jobs." A survey of 3,000 European teenagers found them "confused, vulnerable, obsessed with their economic futures."[19]

Pointing out that the unemployment rate in Europe has averaged about 3 percentage points higher than in the United States, *The Economist* cautioned "no trade barrier will keep out the technological changes that are revolutionising work in the rich world; and a trade war is sure to destroy more jobs than it saves."[20] It counseled Europe to respond by emulating the United States to reduce the social safety net benefits that "give the unemployed little incentive to seek work," minimum wages that "cost young workers their jobs," employer social security contributions that reduce demand for labor, and "strict employment-protection rules" that discourage firms from hiring by making "it hard, if not impossible, to lay off workers once they are on the payroll." To those who point out that the quality of jobs in America has deteriorated as a consequence of such policies, *The Economist* has a ready answer:

> Too many [of the jobs being created in America], say the merchants of gloom, are part-time, temporary and badly paid. The real wages of low-skilled workers have fallen over the past decade. Yet in comparison with Europe, this should be seen as a sign of success, an example—of a well-functioning labour market—not a failure. As manufacturing has declined, America and Europe have both faced shrinking demand for low-skilled labour. In America, the relative pay of these workers was allowed to fall, so fewer jobs were lost. European workers, by contrast, have resisted the inevitable and so priced themselves out of work.[21]

In short, Europe's unemployment problem is a result of overpaying the poor, taxing the rich, and imposing regulations on European firms that limit their ability to get on with serious downsizing. *The Economist* editorial pointed to moves by various European countries to reduce minimum wages, cut payroll taxes, and loosen employment-protection laws as signs of hope for Europe.[22] *Business Week* offered similar counsel:

> To ensure it remains competitive once the down-cycle wanes, Europe must be willing to see more of its low-value-added manu-facturing jobs move to Eastern Europe and elsewhere. . . . And it must reduce farm subsidies while continuing to hammer away at high wages and corporate taxes, short working hours, labor im-mobility, and luxurious social programs. If Europeans don't fol-low these prescriptions, this recession may be doomed to be more than just a cyclical one. . . . Putting up trade barriers will only insulate Europeans from the discipline they need to maintain.[23]

Although they are running a bit behind the United States, the evi-dence suggests that European companies and governments are increas-ingly heeding this advice, which means that the unemployment, racial tension, and social unrest currently plaguing Europe are almost cer-tain to spiral upward. We may presume that *The Economist* will then praise Europe for its success.

Although Japan, with unemployment below 3 percent, continues to be the full-employment champion of the industrial world, there is evidence that the commitment there to lifetime employment has begun to break down and that a growing number of Japanese are experiencing the pinch of joblessness.[24] A series of economic shocks has led Japanese manag-ers to look to the United States for lessons on increasing efficiency. According to Michael Armacost, former U.S. ambassador to Japan:

> Japanese business leaders—who just a few years ago thought they had nothing further to learn from us—are examining American business practices with renewed interest and emulating some with interesting results. . . . Daiei, one of the country's largest chain stores, says it will seek to reduce retail prices by 50 percent over three years. . . . Wal-Mart Stores recently established links with two of Japan's supermarket chains. . . . Japanese executives are now studying America's experience with corporate downsizing, merit-pay packages and investment practices.[25]

Armacost goes on to urge American trade negotiators to focus on pushing for regulatory reforms to accelerate these processes.

With or without U.S. tutelage, it is already happening. Domy Co., a discounter, is importing Safeway cola for sale in Japan at forty-seven cents a can, undercutting the price of local beverages by 55 percent. It sees great potential for imports of Safeway lemon-lime soda, cookies, and bottled water. The Japanese government has relaxed size limits on new retail outlets as well as limits on store hours and business days—with the consequence that retailers are seeking the wide-open spaces of the suburbs, and strip malls are springing up throughout the countryside. Retailers are turning to cheap imports, with China as a preferred source. The burgeoning discount retailers have become the darlings of the Japanese stock market. Faced with price cutting based on low-cost imports, Japanese companies have been restructuring to increase their efficiency.[26]

In January 1995, an accord was announced between the United States and Japan under which U.S. investment houses would have the right to participate in the management of Japanese pension funds.[27] Wall Street investment managers may soon be positioned to give the Japanese lessons in their home territory on the money game, predatory finance, corporate cannibalism, and managed competition.

The trend toward concentration in the retail sector is spreading rapidly to other countries, partly as a consequence of changes in trade rules that open domestic markets to the large retail chains. On January 14, 1994, only two weeks after the North American Free Trade Agreement (NAFTA) went into effect, Wal-Mart announced its move into Canada, which began with the purchase of 120 Woolco discount department stores from Woolworth Canada. *Business Week* called it "a full-scale invasion of the Canadian market." Investors rushed to sell holdings of Canada's major retail chains, which were believed to be ill-equipped to meet Wal-Mart's price competition.[28] Canadian retailing consultant John Winter predicted that by the late 1990s, "half of the Canadian retailers you see up here now may not be in business."[29]

With the signing of NAFTA, U.S. retailing giants were poised to quickly "conquer retailing" in Mexico as well, but according to *Business Week*, "Mexico's army of bureaucrats, steeped in protectionist habits, is plaguing them with mountains of paperwork, ever changing regulations, customs delays, and tariffs of up to 300 percent on low-priced Chinese imports favored by the discounters."[30] Mexico thought that it had a free-trade agreement with the United States to become the major low-wage supplier of the U.S. market. It seems to have balked when confronted with the reality that U.S. retailers intended to use NAFTA to open Mexico to goods produced by even lower paid Chinese workers.

The complaints of the U.S. retailing giants aside, we might conclude that the Mexican government showed better sense in putting up a few roadblocks to slow the assault of the mega-retailers than it did in spending millions to promote NAFTA in the first place.

The dream of the corporate empire builders is being realized. The global system is harmonizing standards across country after country—down toward the lowest common denominator. Although a few socially responsible businesses are standing against the tide with some limited success, theirs is not an easy struggle. We must not kid ourselves. Social responsibility is inefficient in a global free market, and the market will not long abide those who do not avail of the opportunities to shed the inefficient. And we must be clear as to the meaning of efficiency. To the global economy, people are not only increasingly unnecessary, but they and their demands for a living wage are a major source of economic inefficiency. Global corporations are acting to purge themselves of this unwanted burden. We are creating a system that has fewer places for people.

19 The End of Inefficiency

We are entering a new phase in human history—one in which fewer and fewer workers will be needed to produce the goods and services for the global population.

—Jeremy Rifkin[1]

Throughout the previous chapters, we have seen a pattern repeated at all levels of society and in every corner of the world—hundreds of millions of peo-ple are being discarded by a global economy that has no need for them. In Mexico, small farmers are displaced to make way for mechanized agriculture. In India, they are forced off their lands by massive new dams needed to produce electricity so that factory workers can be replaced by more efficient machines. On Wall Street, the human traders who key decisions into computer terminals to execute trades in global money markets are replaced by more efficient computer programs. Small-town merchants are driven out by superstores run by mega-retailers, who in turn may be threatened by home shopping networks on cable TV. Voice-recognition devices and automated answering devices replace telephone operators. Multimedia education replaces teachers. Corporate downsizing is eliminating redundant workers and middle managers.

Corporate mergers and consolidation eliminate middle, and even top, managers. There is no end in sight.

First the Muscle, Now the Brain

We are crossing the threshold of the second industrial revolution. The first industrial revolution exploited a newfound human mastery of energy to give machines enormous muscle power and greatly reduced the demand for physical human labor. Machines, however, could not calculate, reason, discriminate visual patterns, or recognize and interpret human speech. Thus, every machine required a human operator to provide it with a brain and a human intermediary to serve as its eyes and ears. The greater the number of the machines, the greater the number of people needed to tend them. The more sophisticated the machines, the greater the skills required of their operators and the higher the wages the skilled operators could command.

The second industrial revolution is exploiting major advances in information technology that use computers and electronic sensors to give machines eyes, ears, and brains to see and hear, interpret and act. These technologies are still in their infancy, and we do not know how far they may go.

Economists with secure tenured positions at leading universities assure us that we have no need to worry. The increases in productivity will spur economic growth, and growth will mean more jobs, they tell us, just as happened in the first industrial revolution. They fail to note that when the British textile industry was mechanized during the first industrial revolution, Britain shifted much of the resulting unemployment to India. It placed prohibitive tariffs on textiles imported from India to Britain, while British colonial administrators in India virtually eliminated the tariff on British textiles imported to India and levied taxes on Indian cloth produced domestically for domestic sale and on household spinning wheels.[2] The colonies also absorbed many migrants who were surplus to the European economy. Exported to the colonies, they commandeered the best lands to grow export crops, such as cotton, to feed the mother-country industries.

The second industrial revolution is based on a process of colonization defined more by class than by geography and is forcing ever more of the world's population into the ranks of the colonized.

Efficiency is about producing a greater output with less input. When we increase productive output per hour of human labor, we speak of increasing productivity. In the simplified examples of the sort favored by economics texts, it seems quite a good thing.

A farmer who buys a small tractor can cultivate more acres to provide more food and income for her family or devote fewer hours to toiling in the fields. Either way the farmer gains, no one loses, and the society is enriched in a variety of ways.

Unfortunately, the real world isn't like such simplified textbook examples. Note that in our example, the manager, the owner, and the laborer are one and the same person—she makes the decision, pays the costs, and decides whether the productivity gain will go toward increasing production or reducing work time. In the real world, the decision is likely to be made by an agribusiness corporation solely on the basis of profitability. A few favored workers will be required to increase their output; the remainder will lose their jobs, with few alternative prospects.

It seems that the only certain beneficiaries of productivity increases in a nonunionized, labor-surplus world are the owners of capital. Yet, as management analyst William Dugger suggests, we may be on the way to displacing them as well:

> The corporation is a true Frankenstein's monster—an artificial person run amok, responsible only to its own soulless self. Some fascinating possibilities present themselves. Corporations have already begun to buy up their own stock, holding it in their treasury. Taken to the logical conclusion, when 100 percent of the stock is treasury stock the corporation will own itself. It will have dispensed entirely with shareholders from the species Homo sapiens. To whom or to what would it then be responsible? Take these speculations about organized irresponsibility a bit further. . . . Could a corporation entirely dispense with not only human ownership but also human workers and managers? . . . What would it be then? . . . It would exist physically as a network of machines that buy, process, and sell commodities, monitored by a network of computers. Its purposes would be to grow ever larger through acquiring more machines and to become ever more powerful through acquiring more computers to monitor the new machines. It would be responsible to no one but itself in its mechanical drive for power and profit. It would represent capitalism at its very purest, completely unconcerned with anything save profit and power.[3]

Perhaps one day, if allowed sufficient freedom to follow its own unrestrained tendencies, a global corporation will achieve the ultimate in productive efficiency, an entity made up solely of computers and machines busily engaged in the replication of money. We might call it the perfectly efficient corporation. Although this is surely not what anyone intends, we are acting as though this is the world we seek to create.

Pain at the Top

Behind their bold public defense of an economic system in an advanced stage of self-destruction, there are growing reports of unease and concern even among the most elite of the Stratos dwellers. In 1980–82, 79 percent of managers reported that their job security was "good" or "very good." By 1992–94, that figure had fallen to 55 percent.[4] It is not simply that their own positions are increasingly at risk. It is a sense that something simply isn't right, that they are leaving their children a deeply troubled world. Many face growing conflicts between their personal values and what their corporate positions demand of them.

When justifying outrageous executive salaries, the press commonly notes the importance of such rewards in motivating the heads of corporations to exert their best efforts. When William A. Anders, the chairman of General Dynamics Corporation, was granted a $1.6 million bonus for having kept his company's stock price above $45 for ten days, a company spokesperson told the *Washington Post* that the bonus plan was needed to give top executives the incentive to change the company's business strategy and focus on maximizing returns to shareholders.[5] It is an extraordinary claim that the most privileged and well-paid professionals in the world require million-dollar bonuses to motivate them to do their jobs.

Derek Bok, the former president of Harvard University, offers a telling explanation. He suggests that top corporate executives must be paid such outrageous sums to ensure that they place the short-term interests of shareholders above all other interests that they might otherwise be tempted to consider—such as those of employees, the community, and even the corporation's own long-term viability.[6] In short, top executives have to be paid outrageous salaries to motivate them to not yield to their instincts toward social responsibility. Viewed from this perspective, these salaries are an indicator of how distasteful the job of top corporate managers has become in the era of corporate downsizing.

With no end to the bloodletting in sight, a growing number are losing their enthusiasm for their jobs, as *Fortune* reported in its July 25, 1994, cover story, "Burned-Out Bosses":

> [M]anagers who were trained to build are now being paid to tear down. They don't hire; they fire. They don't like the new mandate, but most have come to understand that it's not going to

change. That realization makes the daily routine different: Work no longer energizes; it drains.

Under the circumstances it seems almost immoral to take much joy in work. So they become morose and cautious, worrying that they will be washed away in the next wave of discharges. Meanwhile, they work harder and longer to make up for the toil of those who have left. Fatigue and resentment begin to build.[7]

Unlike the financial speculators who move billions of dollars around the world from computer terminals detached from human reality, the managers of companies that produce real things deal on a daily basis with flesh-and-blood humans. It is they who must respond to the demands of the money managers for greater "efficiency" by imposing on their former friends and colleagues an experience almost as devastating as the loss of a loved one. As one CEO related to *Fortune*, "You get through firing people the first time around, accepting it as part of business. The second time I began wondering, 'How many miscarriages is this causing? How many divorces, how many suicides?' I worked harder so that I wouldn't have to think about it."[8]

An executive recruiter reported visiting a manager who had just gone through several rounds of firing immediate subordinates. Previously a strong take-charge executive, he was now smoking, had lost weight, was unable to look the recruiter in the eye, and seemed extremely nervous. For another executive who had previously eliminated thousands of jobs, the need to put several thousand more former colleagues out on the street resulted in a loss of appetite and difficulty sleeping. He began breaking out in spontaneous fits of crying and one day couldn't get out of bed.

Those who achieve the pinnacles of financial and professional success in America seldom lack for physical comforts. They are learning, however, that no amount of money can buy peace of mind, a strong and loving family, caring friends, and a feeling that one is doing meaningful and important work.

The world is changing even for managers who were once at the pinnacle of power and prestige within their industries. Richard E. Snyder, one of the best known and most powerful figures in the publishing business, had a key role during his thirty-three-year career in building Simon and Schuster into a major U.S. communications firm with an annual gross income of $2 billion. On June 14, 1994, he was abruptly and summarily sacked as chairman and CEO during a five-minute meeting with the CEO of Viacom, Inc., which had recently taken over

Simon and Schuster's parent company Paramount Communications. The reason given was simply "a difference in styles."[9]

Under the leadership of its chairman Kay R. Whitmore, Eastman Kodak reported 1992 profits of $1.14 billion—a margin of roughly 5 percent on sales. On August 6, 1993, he was fired by the company's outside directors on the grounds that he was moving too slowly on cost reduction. He had announced 1992 layoffs of only 3,000 of Kodak's 132,000 employees. Institutional shareholders were clamoring for cuts of at least 20,000. Financial analysts heralded his firing as clear evidence that the outside directors were committed to placing the interests of investors ahead of those of management and employees. Kodak stock closed up $3.25 at the end of the day. Investment manager A. G. Monks proclaimed, "This is a great day for the American shareholder."[10]

No one is immune. There is no longer security at any level of the pyramid. *The Economist* recently noted:

> Being the boss of a big American firm has been one of the safest and most richly rewarded jobs in the world. Until recently, that is. Last week the bosses of IBM, Westinghouse and American Express lost their jobs. A few months earlier Robert Stempel was unceremoniously removed as chairman of General Motors. . . . Now those at the top of big companies are wondering who will be next.[11]

The Economist attributes the phenomenon to a shift of shareholder power from the individual investor to performance-oriented investment funds that are flexing their muscles to kick out top managers of corporations that they consider to be "underperforming." There is no need for takeover battles as fund managers realize that they can directly demand that the existing management of the companies whose shares they hold plunder them for the instant returns expected by an extractive financial system.

Limiting Commitment

Corporate restructuring is not simply about the drastic elimination of jobs, it is also about downgrading those that remain. The white-collar labor market is becoming more like the labor exchanges where jobless day laborers gather, hoping to hire out for the day. The "just-in-time" inventory concepts now apply to people too.

The number of workers employed by temporary agencies has increased 240 percent in ten years. Manpower, the largest of 7,000 U.S.

temp agencies, with 600,000 temporary workers on its rolls, is now America's largest private employer. Although some workers are part-time or temporary by choice, in 1993, nearly a third of the 21 million part-time workers in the United States said that they would prefer full-time jobs. Many displaced workers become self-employed, contracting out for temporary work on an individual basis. Most of these have suffered sharp declines in income. Although much of the evidence is anecdotal, Census Bureau statistics reveal that from 1989 to 1992, the real median income of Americans who worked for themselves fell 12.6 percent to $18,544. A good many of the newly self-employed workers are earning well below $18,000 a year—a level that makes supporting a family in the present American economy difficult, if not impossible.[12]

Young professionals are now actively counseled to plan career paths independently of their companies, to build their resumés and their outside contacts so that they are ready to move when a new opportunity arises or when their companies abandon them. The advice to young people starting their careers: treat every job as though you are self-employed.[13]

Not so long ago, the firm for which a person worked was almost like family. It was a primary support system in an otherwise often impersonal and transient world. A good job was far more than an income. It was a source of identity and of valued and enduring relationships. Those days are no more, placing ever more stress on the family itself. In the present job market, the distinction between white-collar and blue-collar workers is less significant than that between those who have permanent jobs and those who don't. The system nurtures an attitude of get what you can from the system while you can. Look out for yourself, because no one else will.

Adjusting to Diminished Prospects

Those forced out of their existing jobs seldom find new ones with comparable pay. Starting pay is dropping rapidly. Six hundred new United Airlines reservation agents hired in July 1994 faced a permanent pay ceiling of $18,000, whereas an agent doing the same job but hired only six months earlier had prospects of earning up to $34,000 after ten years on the job.[14] Those workers who manage to hang on to their jobs often face a choice between giving up salary and benefits or seeing their jobs disappear entirely. In the United States, average hourly wages for production and nonsupervisory workers fell from $11.37 in 1973 to $10.34 in 1991 (in constant 1991 dollars), whereas average annual hours worked increased from 1,683 hours in 1973 to 1,781 hours in 1990.[15]

A declining percentage of full-time jobs pay a living wage. The U.S. Census Bureau reported that in 1992 the wages received by 18 percent of full-time workers in the United States were not adequate to maintain a family of four above the official poverty line of $13,091—compared with 12 percent of full-time workers in 1979. Among full-time workers in the age group eighteen to twenty-four, the report found that 47 percent earned less than a poverty-level wage, up from only 23 percent in 1979. The usually understated Census Bureau referred to this rapid and dramatic shift as "astounding."[16] Some experts say that the census figures seriously understate the number of America's working poor, because an income of at least $20,000 is now required to provide necessities for a family of four.[17]

Even the fortunes of upper-middle-class professionals took a turn for the worse in the 1990s. According to *Business Week*, "Just as the last decade was defined by yuppies and their flamboyant material excesses, the 1990s may come to be the age of 'dumpies'—downwardly mobile professionals."[18] The U.S. Labor Department reports that 20 percent of graduates from U.S. universities in the 1984–90 period took jobs in which they were "underutilized" and predicts that 30 percent of those graduating between 1994 and 2005 will join the ranks of the unemployed or underemployed.[19] The phenomenon of the hotel bellboy with a bachelor's degree has become commonplace. *Time* recently noted one bright spot on the horizon—growing opportunities for prison guards.[20]

Even households with two wage earners in what used to be considered good middle-class white-collar jobs are struggling to make ends meet. Take the case of Paul and Jane Lambert, both of whom have full-time jobs. She is an office manager and he is a Sears phone order taker. Their combined income doesn't allow them to buy new clothes, health insurance, or dental care, let alone go to a movie, fix the car, or eat out. They are able to provide their family with regular meals only because Jane's parents give them money.[21]

Craig Miller was once a unionized sheet-metal worker for TWA. His $15.65-an-hour job gave his family an income of over $36,000 a year. With two cars in the garage and a swing set in the yard, they were a solid middle-class family living the American dream. Miller was laid off in the summer of 1992. He now hustles hamburger orders at McDonald's, drives a school bus, and has started a small business changing furnace filters. He gets home from his school bus duties at 5 P.M. After a hurried dinner, his wife leaves for her six-to-midnight job at Toys 'R' Us, restocking the shelves while her husband watches the children at home. She also works at the same McDonald's as her husband one day a week. Their total income from these jobs comes to about $18,000. They look to a bleak future.

One of Miller's buddies who was also laid off from TWA was unable to find a job paying more than $6 an hour and, at age thirty-nine, moved back in with his parents, abandoning hope for marriage and children. Another former colleague works as a janitor. Marriages have collapsed. Alcoholism has taken its toll. Union officials say that of the several hundred workers TWA dismissed, perhaps a dozen have committed suicide.[22] The tales read like ones from the Great Depression. However, they are tales from what conventional indicators suggest has been a robust economy.

In an economy that measures performance in terms of the creation of money, people become a major source of inefficiency—and the economy is shedding them with a vengeance. When the institutions of money rule the world, it is perhaps inevitable that the interests of money will take precedence over the interests of people. What we are experiencing might best be described as a case of money colonizing life. To accept this absurd distortion of human institutions and purpose should be considered nothing less than an act of collective, suicidal insanity. It is not an entirely new phenomenon, however. We may gain insights into its nature and consequences from more traditional experiences with colonization.

20 People with No Place

We must find new lands from which we can easily obtain raw materials and at the same time exploit the cheap slave labour that is available from the natives of the colonies. The colonies would also provide a dumping ground for the surplus goods produced in our factories.

—Cecil Rhodes, "founder" of Rhodesia[1]

Those of us who have grown up in societies in which survival depends on money easily accept this dependence as a natural part of the human condition. To fully appreciate the extent to which this dependence is a largely artificial condition, we must revisit earlier societies in which relationships were defined by enduring family and community ties. Although we now tend to associate premonetized societies with primitive cultures and harsh living conditions, some such societies had highly advanced cultures and provided their members with socially and spiritually secure and meaningful lives.

Although people in these societies at times endured serious hardships, they seldom experienced the sense of deprivation, insecurity, and isolation that is the daily lot of those who find themselves without money in a monetized society. Indeed, it is likely that in today's monetized world, from 2 to 3 billion people live less secure and less prosperous lives than did their ancestors whose livelihoods were predominantly nonmonetized.

In the Name of Development

Most of the world has now been drawn so far into the globalized money economy that few among us have had the opportunity to experience any other way of living. Anthropologist Helena Norberg-Hodge is an exception. She had the privilege of coming to know life in the traditional villages of Ladakh, a trans-Himalayan region of Kashmir in India, when the area was first opened to outsiders some twenty years ago. Her moving accounts of what she found speak of human possibilities now largely forgotten:

> In traditional Ladakh to link happiness to income or possessions would have been unthinkable. A deep-rooted respect for each other's fundamental human needs and an acceptance of the natural limitations of the environment kept the Ladakhi people free from misplacing values of worth. Happiness was simply *experienced*. Though not an easy lifestyle by western standards, people met their basic physical, social, spiritual and creative needs within the security of a caring, sharing community and an abundant agrarian subsistence economy—and experienced evident joy.

Norberg-Hodge has made regular visits to the region, observing and documenting the subsequent changes as the intrusion of Western-style development has "created a void in people's lives, an inferiority in their self-perceptions and a greed for material wealth." The contemporary colonization of Ladakh has been advanced by a combination of Western tourists, media, educational models, and technology.

> A western tourist can spend more in one day than what a Ladakhi family might in one year. Seeing this, Ladakhis suddenly feel poor. The new comparison creates a gap that never existed before because in traditional Ladakh, people didn't need money in order to lead rich, fulfilling lives. Ladakhi society was based on mutual aid and cooperation; no one needed money for labor, food, clothing or shelter. . . .
>
> In the traditional economy, Ladakhis knew that they had to depend on other people, and that others in turn depend on them. In the new economic system, local interdependence disintegrates along with traditional levels of tolerance. In place of cooperative systems of meeting needs, competition and scarcity become determinants for survival. Passivity also develops, as reliance upon distant government bureaucracies increases. The more government becomes involved in village activities for the sake of "development," the less villagers feel inclined to help themselves.

The Indian government's effort to industrialize the Ladakh region has meant that men leave their families in rural areas to become wage earners in the city. Since the modern world recognizes only wage earners as "productive" members of society—housewives, traditional farmers and the elderly suddenly become identified as "unproductive"—in complete contrast to their roles in traditional Ladakh. The weakening of family and community ties increases individual insecurity, which in turn contributes to a hunger for material status symbols.[2]

We can learn a great deal about the range of human possibilities from memories of highly culturally evolved premonetized societies such as Ladakh without presuming that the answer to our current crisis lies in returning to a premodern past. Studies of their subsequent transformation provide useful—if disturbing—insights into the nature and meaning of modernization.

After more than thirty years as a dedicated development worker, I've only recently come to see the extent to which the Western development enterprise has been about separating people from their traditional means of livelihood and breaking down the bonds of security provided by family and community to create dependence on the jobs and products that modern corporations produce. It is an extension of a process that began with the enclosure, or privatization, of common lands in England to concentrate the benefits of their production in the hands of the few rather than the many.[3] The colonial era extended the process to the people of nonindustrial lands. Post–World War II development assistance and investment continued the same basic process—under a more subtle and friendly guise—monetizing the production and service functions of the social economy, replacing locally controlled systems of agriculture, governance, health care, education, and mutual self-help with systems that were more amenable to central control.

It is also instructive to characterize the era of modern development as expanding opportunities for workers whose functions are exclusive to the money economy—such as corporate executives, marketing people, lawyers, investors, bankers, accountants, investment brokers, and others. These "money workers" produce nothing of intrinsic worth yet receive handsome financial compensation for performing functions that did not exist in premonetized societies. They arguably have been the major beneficiaries of development, the colonizing elites of corporate colonialism.

Noted earlier was the estimate of globalization guru Kenichi Ohmae that in the modern global economy, production accounts for only about 25 percent of the selling price of a typical product. Another way to put it is that 75 percent of the value created by those who produce real goods and services is now being captured by those who do only money work.

One of the major challenges faced by colonial administrators was to force those who obtained their livelihoods from their own lands and common areas to give up their lands and labor to plantation development, that is, to make them dependent on a money economy so that their resources, labor, and consumption might yield profits to the colonizers. A first step was usually to declare all "uncultivated" lands—generally common lands—to be the property of the colonial administration. "At one stroke, local communities were denied legal title to lands they had traditionally set aside as fallow and to the forests, grazing lands and streams they relied upon for hunting, gathering, fishing and herding."[4] Then vast tracts of forestland were declared "reserve forests." Traditional rights of access were curtailed as the lands were sold to European settlers or leased to commercial concerns for plantations, mining, and logging. The Boer settlers in South Africa justified their expulsion of subsistence farmers from their tribal lands with the claim that they were not engaged in any systematic forms of agriculture and therefore were little more than squatters.[5] Forced labor was piously justified as developmentally beneficial to the enslaved. As the French minister of commerce stated in 1901:

> The black does not like work and is totally unaccustomed to the idea of saving; he does not realise that idleness keeps him in a state of absolute economic inferiority. It is therefore necessary to use . . . slavery to improve his circumstances and afterwards lead him into an apprenticeship of freedom.[6]

In many colonized countries, the imposition of taxes payable only in cash was used to force people into the cash economy. By requiring the village elders to collect the tax, the credibility and legitimacy of traditional local governance structures were undermined. Taxes were placed on whatever villagers would find it most difficult to do without. In Vietnam, the French imposed taxes on salt, opium, and alcohol. The British in Sudan taxed crops, animals, houses, and households. In their West African colonies, the French punished tax evasion by holding wives and children hostage, whipping men, burning huts, and leaving people tied up without food for several days.[7] Development was a hard sell in those early days.

Traditional colonialism came to an end after World War II, and the new corporate colonialism—advanced through foreign aid, investment, and trade—stepped into the breach. In the battle for the souls of the colonized, economic conversion replaced religious conversion. Economic growth became imbued with a mystical significance, the elixir of liberation. It was more subtle, more sophisticated, and more appealing than the old colonialism, but the consequence was much the same—ever greater dependence on the money economy and thus on institutions of money that could be controlled by the few. Development economists, the prophets of growth, preached a familiar gospel message. To become modern, the people must be forced off their farms to join the urban labor pool, working in large factories financed with foreign borrowing so that their lands could be consolidated into plantations to produce for foreign markets. Their agriculture must be converted to the use of seeds, fertilizers, and insecticides produced and sold by gigantic corporations. They must hire foreign advisors at exorbitant salaries and luxurious benefits to fill key positions, and they must import foreign technologies and commodities.

Multilateral banks and aid agencies dictated the economic policies of the "developing" countries. Military assistance missions and clandestine political operatives shaped their politics, and multinational corporations exploited their resources and penetrated their markets.[8] Money was the enticement—grant money, loan money, trade money, investment money. To every need and crisis, money was the answer—more specifically, foreign money that bought foreign goods from foreign companies.

At each step of the way, the social fabric was weakened and dependence on the money economy, especially the *foreign* money economy, was strengthened. Governments were encouraged and supported in creating vast public bureaucracies that displaced traditional education, health care, and welfare services. Then came structural adjustment, and the poor who had become dependent on these services were told that the services had become too expensive and a drain on the economy's ability to meet its needs for foreign exchange, especially to pay its obligations to foreign banks. People would have to do without this extravagance. Moreover, they must transfer still more of their agricultural lands to export crops, import more of their own food needs, and attract foreign investors with offers of tax holidays, cheap access to timber, prime agricultural lands, mineral and petroleum reserves, and cheap labor. They must also offer subsidized electricity and physical infrastructure paid for with still more foreign borrowing.

From colonialism to development to structural adjustment, the people of Southern countries have been integrated into the global economy, step by wrenching step. A fortunate few among the Southern elites have availed themselves of the colonization process to amass vast fortunes. Enough have arrived in the middle class for some

Southern countries to develop thriving enclaves of affluent consumerism. The majority of Southern people, however, have been deprived of the support once provided by their now disrupted social economies and denied either place or opportunity in the money economy.

Free Markets, Open Borders

The fate of societies in which the exclusionary processes of colonialism, both old and new, have progressed to their ultimate conclusion is vividly documented in Robert Kaplan's *Atlantic Monthly* article "The Coming Anarchy." The place is West Africa, and Kaplan sees its experience as a premonition of a human future—a place of "disease, overpopulation, unprovoked crime, scarcity of resources, refugee migrations, the increasing erosion of nation-states and international borders, and the empowerment of private armies, security firms, and international drug cartels."[9] In short, it is a borderless free-market economy.

In Kaplan's account, the government of Sierra Leone, run by a seventeen-year-old army captain, is a divided ragtag group that controls the capital city and parts of the rural interior by day. Its presence is made visible mainly by the members of its national army, who threaten travelers to extract tribute at checkpoints. At night, an opposing army of rebels moves in when the national army moves out. Renegade government military commanders align themselves with disaffected village chiefs. Two separate units from the war in Liberia maintain bases within Sierra Leone's borders.

> As a consequence, roughly 400,000 Sierra Leonians are internally displaced, 280,000 more have fled to neighboring Guinea, and another 100,000 have fled to Liberia, even as 400,000 Liberians have fled to Sierra Leone. The third largest city in Sierra Leone, Gondama, is a displaced-persons camp. With an additional 600,000 Liberians in Guinea and 250,000 in the Ivory Coast, the borders dividing these four countries have become largely meaningless. Even in quiet zones, none of the governments except the Ivory Coast's maintains the schools, bridges, roads, and police forces in a manner necessary for functional sovereignty.[10]

Deforestation is progressing at a devastating rate, with consequent soil erosion, flooding, and mosquitoes. Malaria is almost universal. Violence, volatility, and disease are isolating the rural areas from the cities. The Ivory Coast's once thriving cocoa economy makes it a magnet for migrant workers from other countries of West Africa. As much as half of the country's population is now non-Ivorian, with estimates of the foreign population of Abidjan running as high as 75 percent of the total. Shantytowns occupy ever more of the city amidst the skyscrapers that maintain the façade of prosperity in the "Paris of West Africa." The inhabitants of these shantytowns live in shelters made of scrap materials; they defecate in streams filled with garbage and pigs as women do the wash in the same water amongst swarms of malarial mosquitoes. The young men drink beer, palm wine, and gin while gambling by day and rob houses in more prosperous neighborhoods by night.

The people of traditional Ladakh may have endured their own hardships, and few of us living in modern Western societies would wish to trade our lives for theirs. Yet life within the cohesive communities of Ladakh was a paradise compared with life in places like West Africa, where social structures have been torn asunder by successive waves of colonial intrusion.

Kaplan observes that the West African experience is a spreading phenomenon. He cites Martin van Creveld, a military historian at the Hebrew University, who paints the following scenario of an emergent world of extreme inequality, scarcity, and weak states that have lost their capacity to maintain civil order:

> Once the legal monopoly of armed force, long claimed by the state, is wrested out of its hands, existing distinctions between war and crime will break down much as is already the case today in . . . Lebanon, Sri Lanka, El Salvador, Peru, or Colombia. [Urban crime may] develop into low-intensity conflict by coalescing along racial, religious, social, and political lines.[11]

It is an apt description of the violence that has turned many American ghettos into virtual war zones. Kaplan's apocalyptic vision is an alarmingly credible projection of current trends and the dynamics that underlie them. For growing numbers of people around the world, especially youth, minorities, and women, there is no longer a dream of a more prosperous and secure future, only the bleak prospect of exclusion, despair, deprivation, shame, and brutalizing violence.

United Nations (UN) refugee statistics offer one of the most frightening indicators of the accelerating rate of global social disintegration and exclusion. In 1960, the UN classified 1.4 million people as international refugees. By 1970, the number had risen to 2.5 million, by 1980 to 8.2 million, and by 1992 to 18.2 million. The substantial majority subsist in refugee camps in Asia and Africa, with an average of nearly 10,000 people joining their ranks each day.[12] In 1994, in one forty-eight-hour period, more than a million Rwandans fled the bloody battles in their devastated country into neighboring Zaire, bringing the total number of Rwandan refugees to an estimated 2.1 million.[13]

The UN estimates that more than 24 million additional people are currently displaced within the borders of their own countries. This means that roughly one of every 130 people on the planet lives involuntarily separated from the place they consider home. The words of Sadako Ogata, the UN high commissioner for refugees, echo those of Kaplan:

> [F]light is more than ever before the product of vicious internal conflicts. Nationalistic, ethnic or communal tensions have become the predominant factor in refugee movements around the world, be it in the Horn of Africa and the Sudan, the former Soviet Union and the Balkans or in the Middle East and parts of the Asian subcontinent. . . . The loosening grip of authoritarian regimes and the destructive effects of civil war are straining fragile state structures. This has led, in cases such as Somalia and Bosnia and Herzegovina, to the disintegration of states into territories controlled by competing factions.[14]

Millions are also forced from their homes because natural or man-made disasters have made the land on which they live uninhabitable or reduced its ability to sustain the number of people who depend on it. Environmental stresses may in turn contribute to internal armed conflicts, which are commonly associated with a combination of declining economic circumstances, a lack of strong representative political institutions, and the disruption of traditional processes of mediation. Under such circumstances, political conflict readily degenerates into anarchy, leaving the state in the position of being simply one of many contenders for the dwindling spoils and leaving the population without any form of national security. The conflict disrupts food production and distribution, which accounts for the fact that in conflict situations, it is common for far more deaths to result from starvation and disease than from the actual conflict itself. It is scarcely a fit world for either people or corporations—yet it is the world toward which the forces of corporate colonization inexorably move us.

Alternatives for the Excluded

The excluded, for whom a globalized money economy has little to offer, have three basic choices: (1) give in to the inevitable and live on scraps scavenged from relief agencies or refuse piles, slowly starve, or commit suicide; (2) seek the comradeship of violence and live from the spoils of crime and pillage; or (3) join with others in the re-creation of human communities delinked from the global economy. The first of these options needs no elaboration. The latter two define competing visions of the human future: one of doom and one of hope.

Kaplan points to a terrible and disturbing truth. For people whose lives are a collage of brutality and deprivation, organized violence brings a sense of relief:

> A large number of people on this planet, to whom the comfort and stability of a middle-class life is utterly unknown, find war and a barracks existence a step up rather than a step down. . . . Where there has always been mass poverty, people find liberation in violence.[15]

We are learning that much the same can be said for membership in ghetto gangs. They fill a need for companionship and provide a sense of belonging that is otherwise denied. Organized violence fills a void by creating an opportunity to be part of a larger human whole, to find companions who provide social support and legitimacy for the venting of one's rage at an otherwise uncaring world. Violence can be for some an almost religious experience, heightening a sense of consciousness and being by focusing the senses on the here and now and freeing the mind of the distractions of deprivation. So long as forced physical, social, and spiritual deprivation exists among us, violence will be an almost inevitable consequence.

Fortunately, there is a third path for the excluded, the re-creation of communities delinked from a corporate-dominated global economy. As a counterpoint to his descriptions of terrifying anarchy in the slums of West Africa, Robert Kaplan describes the social strength of a shantytown in the Turkish capital of Ankara. Financially poor and materially deprived, its residents maintain a strong cultural identity, values, and social fabric. Crime against persons and alcoholism are rare. The insides of makeshift shelters are spotless, and the children are in school.

It should now be clear that the cure for the deprivations of poverty will not, cannot, be found in the economic growth of a globalized free market that weakens and destroys the bonds of culture and community to the benefit of global corporations. The necessary cure lies instead in restoring and strengthening these bonds. Our collective survival—not only of the poor and excluded but also of the relatively affluent and not yet excluded—depends on creating an institutional and values framework that advances this restoration.

VI Reclaiming Our Power

21 The Ecological Revolution

By deliberately changing the internal image of reality, people can change the world.
                                        —*Willis Harman*[1]

I believe that the world has moved closer to oneness and more people see each other as one with the other. . . . It is possible to have new thoughts and new common values for humans and all other forms of life.
                    —*Wangari Maathai, coordinator,*
                        Kenya Green Belt Movement[2]

No sane person seeks a world divided between billions of excluded people living in absolute deprivation and a tiny elite guarding their wealth and luxury behind fortress walls. No one rejoices at the prospect of life in a world of collapsing social and ecological systems. Yet we continue to place human civilization and even the survival of our species at risk mainly to allow a million or so people to accumulate money beyond any conceivable need. We continue to go boldly where no one wants to go.

We are now coming to see that economic globalization has come at a heavy price. In the name of modernity we are creating dysfunctional societies that are breeding pathological behavior—violence, extreme competitiveness, suicide, drug abuse, greed, and environmental degradation—at every hand. Such behavior is an inevitable consequence when a society fails to meet the needs of its members for social bonding, trust, affection, and a shared sacred meaning.[3] The threefold crisis of deepening poverty, environmental destruction, and social disintegration is a manifestation of this dysfunction.

There is nothing inevitable about the collective madness of pursuing policies that deepen the dysfunction. The idea that we are caught in the grip of irresistible historical forces and inherent human imperfections to which we have no choice but to adapt is pure fabrication. Economic globalization is being advanced by conscious choices made by those who see the world through the lens of the corporate interest. There are human alternatives, and those who view the world through the lens of the human interest have both the right and the power to choose them.

Healthy societies depend on healthy, empowered local communities that build caring relationships among people and help us connect to a particular piece of the living earth with which our lives are intertwined. Such societies must be built through local-level action, household by household and community by community. Yet we have created an institutional and cultural context that disempowers the local and makes such action difficult, if not impossible.

To correct the deep dysfunction, we must shed the illusions of our collective cultural trance, reclaim the power we have yielded to failing institutions, take back responsibility for our lives, and reweave the basic fabric of caring families and communities to create places for people and other living things. It is within our means, but it will require transforming the dominant belief systems, values, and institutions of our societies—an Ecological Revolution comparable to the Copernican Revolution that ushered in the scientific-industrial era. The parallels are instructive.

Competing Visions of Reality

The Copernican Revolution centered around a basic change in the prevailing perception of the nature of reality. The issues involved bear examination, because they go to the root of our present crisis and help define the challenge of the Ecological Revolution.[4]

Transcendental monism (the view that conciousness or spirit gives rise to matter) has formed the philosophical foundation of many Eastern cultures—at least until the recent onslaught of Western science, industrialization, global competition, and consumerism. Adherents of this tradition believe that consciousness is the primary reality and that matter is a creation of consciousness or spiritual energy. Based on the belief that all consciousness, as well as the material manifestations of consciousness, originates from the same underlying unity, transcendental monism considers inner wisdom, accessed through our spiritual connection with the infinite, to be the primary source of valid knowing. This tradition has commonly been associated with a denial of things material, a fatalistic acceptance of one's material condition, a strong sense of community, and a deep reverence for nature.

In the West, the Judeo-Christian tradition took a quite different course, personifying God as a being who lives in a distant and separate realm and whose attention is centered on earth and its human inhabitants. In this tradition, God's will and wisdom were revealed through prophets, such as Moses, or through his incarnation as Jesus. The earth was believed to be the center of the universe, with the sun, stars, and planets revolving around it. These beliefs remained the foundation of scientific thought and moral and political authority in Europe until as recently as 500 years ago.

Then in 1543, Nicholas Copernicus published *Revolution of the Celestial Spheres*, setting forth the thesis that the earth is only one among the planets that revolve around the sun—itself one of countless such stars of the cosmos. This led to a historic confrontation between science and the church as to whether scientific observation or divine revelation is the more valid source of human knowledge. Material monism (the view that matter gives rise to consciousness or spirit) became the image of reality embraced by science and unleashed what historians refer to as the Copernican Revolution. Adherents to this tradition believe that matter is the primary reality, physical measurement is the one valid source of knowledge, and the experience of consciousness is only a manifestation of the material complexity of the physical brain. This makes it inconceivable that any form of consciousness exists independently of a physical presence. Materialistic monism has been the foundation of Western scientific training and culture throughout most of the scientific-industrial era. It has commonly been associated with a denial of the spiritual and an emphasis on materialism, individualism, and the exploitation of nature.

According to historian Edward McNall Burns, the significance of the Copernican Revolution is found in the fact that "No longer need the philosopher pay homage to revelation as a source of truth; reason was now held to be the solitary fount of knowledge, while the whole idea of spiritual meaning in the universe was cast aside like a worn-out garment."[5] The intellectual and moral authority of the church was greatly weakened.

The idea that only those things that can be measured are suitable subjects for scientific study and acceptable as causal explanations has helped science distinguish "scientific explanations from such prescientific interpretations as the whims of the gods or the intervention of divine grace."[6] However, it also meant that consciousness, values, aesthetics, and other aspects of human experience were excluded from consideration in scientific inquiry. By rejecting free will and moral choice as acceptable explanations for behavior, science effectively exempted itself from moral responsibility for the applications of scientific knowledge.

Seventeenth-century philosopher Thomas Hobbes took materialistic monism to its ultimate extreme. He maintained that absolutely nothing exists except matter. If there is a God, he must have a physical body. In his view, good is merely that which gives us pleasure, evil that which brings pain, and the only meaningful purpose in life is to pursue pleasure[7]—a value system that became the implicit moral premise of economic rationalism.

The institutions of religion and science—each with its own view of reality—henceforth competed for the soul of Western societies. Dualism (the view that matter and spirit are two distinct and independent aspects of reality) provided a philosophical validation of this split. While the church ministered to a constricted spiritual life, secular society came to embrace the material world as the primary reality, materialism as the dominant value, and ultimately economic growth as the primary human purpose.

As a philosophy of science, materialistic monism made possible the scientific and technological accomplishments of the scientific-industrial era. As a philosophy of life deeply embedded in modern culture, it has led us to the brink of self-destruction, because it leads naturally to the embrace of Hobbesian values. This makes it difficult to identify with any higher meaning or purpose beyond the indulgence of our physical appetites. Having embraced indulgence as our purpose, an appeal to limit indulgence in the interest of economic justice or concern for future generations becomes a call to sacrifice the one thing that gives life meaning. It follows, as corporate libertarians sometimes maintain, that it is most rational for those who have the financial means to continue to enjoy the party until it ends. If we sacrifice these pleasures and the environmentalists are ultimately proved wrong, we will have sacrificed our reason for living to no end. If the environmentalists are proved right and the party ends in our self-destruction, then at least we enjoyed it while we could.

Materialistic monism also prepared the way for an economics that, intent on achieving the status of a true science, embraced market prices, which can be observed and measured, as the sole arbiter of human values. It is virtually impossible to understand or explain more than purely habitual human behavior without addressing the values, loyalties, aspirations, love, psychological conflicts, altruism, spirituality, conscience, and even metaphysical beliefs that inform them—which are very difficult to observe and measure. Thus, as science defines itself, the term *social science* is a contradiction.

The social scientist must either redefine the assumptions of science or redefine the human being to accord with those assumptions. Economists chose the latter, postulating a hypothetical, mechanistic economic man who seeks only his own pleasure—which it subsequently defined in purely financial terms. Whenever a model requires a human decision maker—irrespective of gender—the economist substitutes the imaginary, decidedly nonhuman, economic man, who evaluates every choice on the basis of its economic return.

Having eliminated the human, economists then eliminated the be-havior. Finding the interactions among people too hopelessly complex and difficult to measure, economists chose to observe the behavior of markets rather than the behavior of people. Market behavior involves prices and flows of money, which are easily observed and measured.

Since a science must be objective and value-free, economics chose to reduce all values to market values as revealed in market prices. Thus air, water, and other essentials of life provided freely by nature are treated as valueless—until scarcity and privatization render them marketable. By contrast, gold and diamonds, which have almost no use in sustaining life, are valued highly. The value of a human life is arrived at by calculating a person's lifetime earning potential or "economic contribution." As a cynic once accurately noted, "Economists know the price of everything and the value of nothing."

The partial and materialistic view of our nature that is embodied in materialistic monism helps explain the basic paradox that modern societies have come to define success in terms of making money—a simple number on a piece of paper, on a coin, or in a computer. Why? It is one of the most baffling puzzles of modern society. Contemporary philosopher Jacob Needleman says it well in *Money and the Meaning of Life*:

> In other times and places, not everyone has wanted *money* above all else; people have desired salvation, beauty, power, strength, pleasure, propriety, explanations, food, adventure, conquest, comfort. But now and here, money—not necessarily even the things money can buy, but *money*—is what everyone wants. The outward expenditure of mankind's energy now takes place in and through money. . . . Therefore, if one wishes to understand life, one *must* understand money in this present phase of history and civilization.[8]

From what source does money—a mere number—derive energy? The key is Needleman's statement, "The outward expenditure of mankind's energy now takes place in and through money." Money derives its energy from us. Its energy is our energy.

In their *New York Times* best-seller *Your Money or Your Life*, Joe Dominguez and Vicki Robin tell us that "money . . . is something we all too often don't have, which we struggle to get, and on which we pin our hopes of power, happiness, security, acceptance, success, fulfillment, achievement and personal worth."[9] Beyond meeting our survival needs, we have come to look to money to provide all these intangibles of good living—forgetting the simple reality that only forgeries of the real thing are up for sale. The real thing must be earned by investing ourselves in loving relationships, being good friends and neighbors, living by ethical principles, and developing and engaging our abilities in ways that contribute to the life of the community.

But marketing experts surround us with a different cultural message. They don't sell laundry soap, they sell acceptance, achievement, and personal worth. They don't sell automobiles, they sell power, freedom, and success—the opportunity to feel alive, connected, and free— that which we really want. To buy what the marketers offer, we need money. As Dominguez and Robin explain:

> Money is something we choose to trade our life energy for. . . .
> Our allotment of time here on earth, the hours of precious life
> available to us. When we go to our jobs, we are trading our life
> energy for money. This truth, while simple, is profound.[10]

Money is not an ordinary number after all. It is our ticket to the same things that people have wanted in other times and places. It is a measure of the life energies expended in its acquisition. It has become our answer to the question What am I worth? and the measure of our collective worth and accomplishment as a nation. Professional charities have even made money the measure of our compassion: "Make a difference. Send us your check today." Defining ourselves in terms of money, we become entrapped in a downward spiral of increasing alienation from living, from our own spiritual nature (see Figure 21.1).

Rather than teaching us that the path to fulfillment is to experience living to the fullest through our relationships with family, community, nature, and the living cosmos, the corporate-dominated media continuously repeat a false promise—whatever our longings, the market is the path to their instant gratification. Our purpose is to consume—we are born to shop. Entranced by the siren song of the market, we consistently undervalue the life energy that we put into obtaining money and overvalue the expected life energy gains from spending it. The more we give our life energies over to money, the more power we yield to the institutions that control our access both

Figure 21.1 Downward Spiral of Deepening Alienation

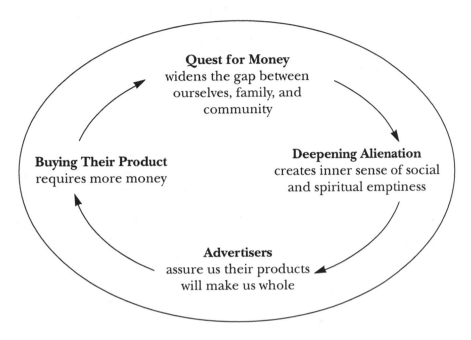

to it and to those things that it will buy. Yielding such power serves the corporate interest well, because corporations are creatures of money. It serves our human interest poorly, because we are creatures of nature and spirit.

Forced to reexamine who we are by the limits of the planet's ability to accommodate our greed, we find ourselves confronted with a beautiful truth. Whereas our pursuit of material abundance has created material scarcity, our pursuit of life may bring a new sense of social, spiritual, and even material abundance.

People who experience an abundance of love in their lives rarely seek solace in compulsive, exclusionary personal acquisition. For the emotionally deprived, no extreme of materialistic indulgence can ever be enough, and our material world becomes insufficient. A world starved of love becomes one of material scarcity. In contrast, a world of love is also one of material abundance. When we are spiritually whole and experience the caring support of community, thrift is a natural part of a full and disciplined life. That which is sufficient to one's needs brings a fulfilling sense of nature's abundance.

The implications are profound. Our seemingly insatiable quest for money and material consumption is in fact a quest to fill a void in our lives created by a lack of love. It is a consequence of dysfunctional societies in which money has displaced our sense of spiritual connection as the foundation of our cultural values and relationships. The result is a world of material scarcity, massive inequality, overtaxed environmental systems, and social disintegration. So long as we embrace the making of money as our collective purpose and structure our institutions to give this goal precedence over all others, the void in our lives will grow and the human crisis will deepen. There is an obvious solution: create societies that give a higher value to nurturing love than to making money.

Idealistic as this may sound, it is entirely within our means. The key is a shift in consciousness that is already being created through an emerging synthesis of scientific and religious knowledge that embraces the integral connection between reality's material and spiritual dimensions.[11] Just as the Copernican Revolution ushered in the scientific-industrial era by freeing us from misperceptions about ourselves and the nature of our reality, an Ecological Revolution, based on a more holistic integration of the spiritual and material, may usher in an ecological era that will open as yet unimagined opportunities for our social and spiritual development. However, to realize this goal, we must reclaim the power that we have yielded to money and a corporate-dominated global economy.

Localizing Economies, Globalizing Consciousness

Our species is distinctive in its ability to anticipate the future and to act with self-awareness to change our behavior in accord with our perception of limits and opportunities. We also have the capacity to discern repeating patterns in evolutionary processes and to distill from those patterns insights into how best to maximize our own evolutionary potentials. One such pattern that is regularly repeated in the self-organizing growth and evolution of crystals, biological organisms, social organizations, and consciousness is a persistent advance toward higher orders of complexity.[12] Those systems that have the highest evolutionary potential in this regard are those that are able to nurture a rich diversity within a coherent unifying structure. The greater the diversity, the greater the evolutionary potential—so long as the unifying structure is maintained.

Arnold Toynbee found this pattern in his epic study of the growth and decline of the world's great civilizations. Civilizations in decline were consistently characterized by a "tendency toward standardization and uniformity." This pattern contrasted sharply with "the tendency toward differentiation and diversity" during the growth stage of civilizations.[13] It appears to be a near universal truth that diversity is the foundation of developmental progress in complex systems and uniformity is the foundation of stagnation and decay.

Standardization and uniformity seem to be almost inevitable outcomes of a globalized economy dominated by massive globe-spanning corporations geared to mass production and marketing in a culturally homogenized world. It is difficult to imagine a civilization moving more totally toward standardization and uniformity than one unified by Coca-Cola and MTV. The processes of economic globalization are not only spreading mass poverty, environmental devastation, and social disintegration, they are also weakening our capacity for constructive social and cultural innovation at a time when such innovation is needed as never before. As a consequence, we are rapidly approaching an evolutionary dead end.

By contrast, economic systems composed of locally rooted, self-reliant economies create in each locality the political, economic, and cultural spaces within which people are able to find their own paths to the future that are consistent with their distinctive aspirations, history, culture, and ecosystems. A global system composed of localized economies can accomplish what a single globalized economy cannot—encourage the rich and flourishing diversity of robust local cultures and generate the variety of experience and learning that is essential to the enrichment of the whole.

Economic globalization deepens the dependence of localities on detached global institutions that concentrate power, colonize local resources, and share little stake in local success or failure. The greater the dependence, the less the ability of a locality to find within its own borders satisfactory solutions to its own problems. Although advocates of economic globalization commonly argue that globalization creates interdependence and shared interests, it is a misrepresentation. What is actually happening is a growing dependence of people and localities on global corporations and financial markets. The consequence of this dependence is to pit people and localities against one another in a self-destructive competition for economic survival—yielding ever more power to the center (see Figure 21.2).

The power of the center stems from a number of interrelated sources: its power to create money, its ownership of the productive assets on which each locality depends, and its control of the institutional mechanisms that mediate relationships among localities. This power increasingly is lodged in global financial markets and corporations, which have established themselves as the de facto governance institutions of the planet. The more globalized the economy, the greater the dependence of the local and the greater the power of central institutions.

A globalized economic system has an inherent bias in favor of the large, the global, the competitive, the resource-extractive, and the short-term. Our challenge is to create a global system that is biased toward the small, the local, the cooperative, the resource-conserving, and the long-term—one that empowers people to create a good living in balance with nature. The goal is not to wall each community off from the world but rather to create zones of local accountability and responsibility within which people can reclaim the power that is rightly theirs to manage their economies in the common interest. It is a fundamental paradox of our time that in the name of market competition we have created a system that unifies corporations while dividing people and forcing them into a global competition for corporate favor. The human purpose is better served by a system that divides corporations and forces them to compete for the favor of people—in the true spirit of a competitive market. Let corporations compete to earn their profits. Let people and communities cooperate to create a good living for all.

People in the modern world are unified not by a global economy but by a global consciousness that we share the same planet and a common destiny. This consciousness is already emerging and has three elements that are unique in human history. First, the formative ideas are the intellectual creations of popular movements involving millions of ordinary people who live and work outside the corridors of elite power. Second, the participation is truly global, bringing together people from virtually every nation, culture, and linguistic group. Third, the new consciousness is rapidly evolving, adapting, and taking on increasing definition as local groups meld into global alliances, ideas are shared, and consensus positions are forged in meetings and via fax, phone, and computer communications.

This process is creating a growing web of understanding, shared interests, and mutual compassion that is the proper foundation of a global community of people. The strength and vitality of this web arise out of the fact that its members, unlike the Stratos dwellers who live in splendid isolation in a world of wealth, are rooted in real-world communities of place. They experience directly the consequences of the spreading crisis. Their experience is real, and they are naturally inclined to the human rather than the corporate interest.

By participating in the social movements that are the driving force of the Ecological Revolution, growing numbers of citizens are committing themselves to rebuilding their local communities and reaching out to others engaged in similar efforts. They are creating an active recognition of the need to act cooperatively in the global human interest through voluntary processes that generate enormous social energies without creating the concentrations of power that are so easily abused.

Figure 21.2 Disempowering the Local

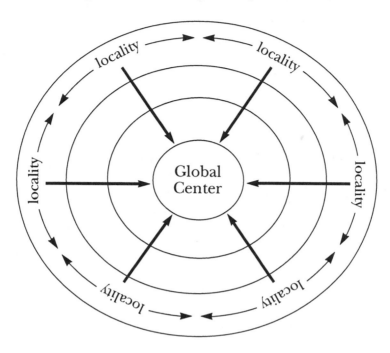

These efforts are building the foundations of new human societies for the ecological age. As they elevate the popular slogan "Think Globally. Act Locally." to the level of a policy agenda, the rallying cry of the Ecological Revolution becomes "Globalize consciousness! Localize economies!"

Guiding Principles

The formative ideas of the Copernican Revolution were products of the scientific observation of physical bodies and can be traced to a handful of prominent scholars from the physical sciences. In contrast, the formative ideas of the Ecological Revolution are products of the collective human experience and the study of both living and nonliving systems. They are articulated in countless consensus documents and declarations of citizen movements and they find theoretical grounding in the intellectual treatises of scholars from a diverse variety of academic disciplines—including history, sociology, ecology, economics, biology, physics, general systems theory, and ecological economics. These ideas may be distilled into a number of guiding principles for the creation of healthy twenty-first century societies.

The Principle of Environmental Sustainability. Healthy societies are environmentally sustainable, which means their economies must satisfy three conditions.[14]

1. Rates of use of renewable resources do not exceed the rates at which the ecosystem is able to regenerate them.
2. Rates of consumption or irretrievable disposal of nonrenewable resources do not exceed the rates at which renewable substitutes are developed and phased into use.
3. Rates of pollution emission into the environment do not exceed the rates of the ecosystem's natural assimilative capacity.

Any use of environmental resources or sink capacities greater than these rates is by definition unsustainable and compromises the opportunities available to future generations. This principle defines a collective property right of future generations that takes natural precedence over individual property rights.

The Principle of Economic Justice. Healthy societies provide all their members—present and future—with those things that are essential to a healthy, secure, productive, and fulfilling life. There is nothing wrong with additional rewards for those who contribute more—but only so long as everyone's basic needs are met, the options of future generations are not impaired, and the distribution of economic power does not become destabilizing.

The Principle of Biological and Cultural Diversity. Healthy societies nurture the biological and cultural diversity of the planet. Diversity is the foundation of evolutionary potential. Nurturing biological and cultural diversity is fundamental to our constructive participation in the evolutionary process.

The Principle of People's Sovereignty (also known as the Principle of Subsidiarity). In healthy societies, sovereignty resides in civil society. The purpose of the human economy is to meet the needs of people—not of money, nor of corporations, nor of governments. The sovereign right of the people to decide what uses of the earth best serve to nourish their bodies and their spirit within the limits of the first three principles is inalienable. People are best able to exercise this right when:

*   The owners of productive assets are patient and the control of assets is locally rooted, thus ensuring that important decisions are made by those who will live with the consequences.
*   Governance authority and responsibility are located in the smallest and most local system unit possible to maximize opportunity for direct, participatory democracy.

- More remote system levels define their roles as serving and supporting the local in achieving self-defined goals.

The Principle of Intrinsic Responsibility. Healthy societies allocate the full costs of resource allocation decisions to those who participate in making them—an essential requirement for efficiency in a self-regulating economic system. This principle applies to individual persons, enterprises, and political jurisdictions. No entity has the right to externalize the costs of its consumption to another. The goal is to structure economic relationships so as to encourage each locality to live within its sustainable environmental means. Much as a *globalized* economic system offers maximum scope in privatizing economic gains while externalizing the costs, a more *localized* economic system of self-reliant local economies encourages the *internalization* of costs, because both the consequences of cost externalization and the power to require that these costs be internalized are local.

The Principle of Common Heritage. Healthy societies recognize that the environmental resources of the planet and the accumulated knowledge of the species are common heritage resources, and it is the right of every person—present and future—to share in their beneficial use. Neither may be rightfully monopolized or used in ways contrary to the broader interest of present and future generations. Indeed, it is the rightful responsibility of those who own environmental resources to serve as trustees in the interest of future generations and of those who possess special knowledge to share it with all who might benefit.

Healthy social function depends on giving the rights and responsibilities defined by these principles' precedence over all other rights—including the property rights of individuals, corporations, and governments. Being people and life centered rather than corporate centered, these principles offer a clear alternative to corporate libertarianism's prescription for social dysfunction.

Healthy societies seek balance in all things. They recognize a role for both government and locally accountable businesses, while resisting domination by powerful distant governments and corporations. Similarly, they seek local self-reliance while freely sharing information and technology, avoiding both external dependence and local isolation.

The appropriate organizational form for the ecological era is likely to be a multilevel system of nested economies with the household as the basic economic unit, up through successive geographical aggregations to localities, districts, nations, and regions (see Figure 21.3).[15] Embodying the principle of intrinsic responsibility, each level would seek to function, to the extent that it is reasonably able, as an integrated self-reliant, self-managing political, economic, and ecological community. Starting from the base unit, each system level would seek to achieve the optimal feasible ecological self-reliance, especially in meeting basic needs.

To compensate for imbalances in environmental service endowments, units at each level would engage in selective exchanges with other units within their cluster—keeping those exchanges as balanced as possible. Households would engage in exchanges with households in their locality, localities with other localities in their district, and so on. The smaller the system unit, the greater the need for exchange. Thus, a substantial amount of the economic activity of households would necessarily involve external exchange. Although many households might grow some of their own food, it would be rare for a household to be self-sufficient. Community eco-economies would be somewhat more self-reliant, and so on, with regions being nearly wholly self-reliant.

Organizing to meet economic needs as close to the local level as feasible would enable the application of the principle of subsidiarity— which maintains that governance authority and responsibility should be vested in the smallest, most local unit possible. This would make it possible to maintain a market system in which market power is balanced with political power at each level. Local firms would enjoy a natural advantage, and there would be less long-haul movement of people and goods.

Less trade and greater local self-reliance may mean less consumer choice. In the Northern climates, we would eat winter or preserved vegetables and would put apples rather than bananas on our cereal. People in forested areas would construct their houses of wood, and those in hot, dry climates would build houses of earthen materials. Some prices might be higher. Overall, the sacrifices would be small compared with the prospects of greater economic security, caring communities in which people can walk the streets at night without fear, improved environmental quality, the survival of our species, and the creation of new evolutionary potentials.

As we reorganize ourselves into a multilevel system, it is likely that we will continue the present process of redrawing national boundaries. Larger countries that have grown too large and complex to be manageable may break up into smaller countries, as happened with the U.S.S.R. and as is being debated in Canada. The present political movement in the United States toward greater local authority and autonomy is in part a response to the fact that the United States has reached an unmanageable size and complexity—even without the North American Free Trade Agreement (NAFTA), the Asia Pacific Economic Community (APEC), and the General Agreement on Tariffs and Trade (GATT). It makes good sense to devolve to the individual states more

Figure 21.3 Nested Economies

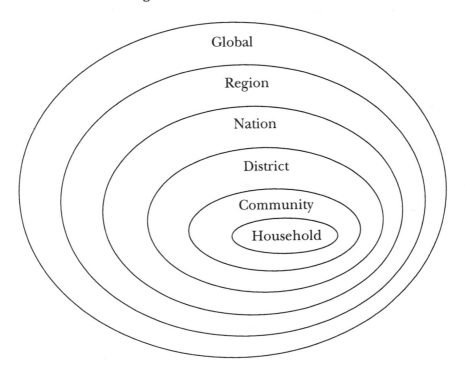

of the powers once lodged at the national level, including the power to regulate commerce and trade. Conversely, many smaller countries may find that they are too small to be viable and decide to undertake some form of merger. In the not too distant future, we may look back on the present, almost frantic press to form ever larger economic blocks through regional trade agreements and GATT as the last desperate gasp of a dying era.

The principles of the Ecological Revolution lead toward a global system of local economies that distributes both power and responsibility, creates places for people, encourages the nurturing of life in all its diversity, and limits the opportunity for one group to externalize the social and environmental costs of its consumption onto others. Instead of forcing localities into international competition as a condition of their survival, a localized global system encourages self-reliance in meeting local needs. Instead of monopolizing knowledge for private gain, it encourages the sharing of knowledge and information. Instead of promoting a homogeneous globalized consumer culture, it nurtures cultural diversity. Instead of measuring success in terms of how much money we make, it encourages measuring success in terms of healthy social function.

In the Human Interest

Although issues of class and political power figure prominently in its agenda, the Ecological Revolution is less a class struggle than a struggle of people against an economic system running out of control. It is in the larger interest of all people, including the Stratos dwellers, that this system be transformed. As we organize ourselves to this end, four points should be kept in mind:

1. *Sovereignty resides only with people—all* people, *real* people who need fresh air to breathe, clean water to drink, uncontaminated food to eat, and livelihoods that allow them to earn their keep. Neither governments nor corporations can usurp that sovereignty unless we chose to yield it.
2. *Corporations have no natural or inalienable rights.* The corporation is a public body created by a public act through the issuance of a public charter to serve a public purpose. We, the sovereign people, have the inalienable right to determine whether the intended public purpose is being served and to establish legal processes to amend or withdraw a corporate charter at any time we so choose. We need only decide.
3. *The problem is the system.* Incremental changes within individual corporations or political institutions cannot provide an adequate solution. The whole system of institutional power must be transformed.
4. *The Ecological Revolution is a revolution of ideas, not guns.* The Ecological Revolution is inclusive and invites the participation of all who seek to create healthy societies in which life may flourish. The human interest is not the corporate interest, but it is the interest of all people.

22 Good Living

*Our village was prosperous. . . . The real foundation
of our prosperity . . . was the deep and enduring sense
of community that enabled us to make the best use of
these resources. . . . We had all the things we needed—
well-crafted, beautiful things that lasted a long time—
but we did not do much "consuming."*
—Eknath Easwaran[1]

By organizing societies around the pursuit of material gratification, we have made a virtue of social
dysfunction and reduced the quality of our living. Humans are complex creatures. We have a demonstrated
capacity for hatred, violence, competition, and greed.
We have as well a demonstrated capacity for love, ten-
derness, cooperation, and compassion. Healthy societies nurture the latter and in so doing create an
abundance of those things that are most important to
the quality of our living. Dysfunctional societies nurture the former and in so doing create scarcity and
deprivation. A healthy society makes it easy to live in
balance with the environment, whereas a dysfunctional
society makes it nearly impossible.

Whether we organize our societies for social and
environmental health or for dysfunction is a choice that
is ours to make. To a considerable degree, it is a choice
between organizing for the human interest and organizing for the corporate interest. What we are coming

to realize is that if we focus on creating societies that enhance the *quality of our living* rather than the *quantity of our consumption,* we can move simultaneously toward sustainability *and* a better life for nearly everyone. In this chapter we explore the possibilities.

Caring Families and Communities

Although a competitive instinct forms an important part of our nature, there is substantial evidence that it is a subtheme to the more dominant theme of bonding, caring, and cooperation. As with all species that depend on social bonding for their survival, humans evolved to *belong* and *cooperate* as well as to *compete.* According to cultural anthropologist Mary Clark:

> The early human species could not have survived without the expanded social bonding beyond parent and offspring needed to protect helpless human infants—a job that mothers alone could not accomplish. Social bonding to one's group was a biological necessity—for adults as well as infants.[2]

Things haven't really changed so much. It is a fundamental, though often neglected, fact that social bonding is as essential to the healthy functioning of a modern society as it was to more traditional or tribal societies. Harvard University political scientist Robert Putnam refers to the bonding that characterizes a strong civil society as "social capital" and has shown its importance in a study of local government effectiveness in Italy.

Beginning in 1970, Italy created twenty regional governments. Their formal structures were identical. There were dramatic differences, however, in the social, economic, political, and cultural context within which these structures were implanted. The localities ranged "from the pre-industrial to the post-industrial, from the devoutly Catholic to the ardently Communist, from the inertly feudal to the frenetically modern." In some localities, the new government structures were "inefficient, lethargic, and corrupt." In others, they were dynamic and effective, "creating innovative day care programs and job training centers, promoting investment and economic development, pioneering environmental standards and family clinics."[3]

Putnam found only one set of indicators that consistently differentiated those localities in which the government worked from those in which it didn't. These were indicators of a strong and active civil society, as measured by "voter turnout, newspaper readership, membership in choral societies and literary clubs, Lions Clubs and soccer clubs." Localities high on these indicators had what Putnam called a highly developed "social capital." Rich networks of nonmarket relationships built a generalized sense of trust and reciprocity that increased the efficiency of human relationships.[4]

We have given too little attention to the importance of social capital to the healthy functioning of societies and rarely consider the impact of economic structures and policies on its formation or depletion. The following questions reveal the nature of this relationship: Do people prefer to shop in small local shops run by merchants they know by name, or in mega–shopping malls and large retail chain outlets? Do they favor the farmers' market or the supermarket? Are farms small, individually owned, and family operated, or are they controlled by huge corporate enterprises and worked mainly by itinerant landless laborers? Do people devote their free time to Little League baseball, community gardens, local theater, community choirs, community centers, and school boards, or to watching commercial TV? Are there credit cooperatives and local banks committed to supporting local enterprise, or only branches of large urban banks attentive primarily to international money markets? Do residents consider the area their permanent home, or are working and professional people largely itinerant? Are productive assets owned locally or by distant corporations? Are forests harvested selectively and sustainably by local firms to provide materials for local industry, or are local forests stripped bare every forty to sixty years by huge global corporations and the raw timber exported directly to distant lands?

The answers to such questions are powerful predictors of the sense of dignity, freedom, responsibility, prosperity, and security of local people and the extent to which relationships are characterized by trust, sharing, and cooperation.

Undeveloping the Sustainers

It is often noted that some 80 percent of environmental damage is caused by the world's 1.1 billion overconsumers. As Alan Durning points out in *How Much Is Enough*, these are the roughly 20 percent of the world's people who organize their lives around cars, meat-based diets, and the use of prepackaged and disposable products.[5] Meanwhile, another 20 percent of the world's people live in absolute deprivation. Durning makes another important point, however, that is generally neglected: roughly 60 percent of the world's people are presently meeting most of their basic needs in relatively sustainable ways (see Table 22.1). As members of the world's sustainer class, they travel by bicycle and public surface transport; eat healthy diets of grains, vegetables, and some meat; buy few prepackaged goods; and recycle most of their wastes. Although their lifestyles do not correspond to our vision of consumer affluence, neither is it a vision of hardship, and in a properly organized society, these can be characteristics of a high and satisfying quality of living.

A society organized around walking, bicycling, and public transportation may offer a higher quality of living than one in which public spaces are dominated by automobiles and freeways. A low-meat, low-fat diet based on natural foods may result in better health and increased mental and physical vitality than a diet high in animal fats. A life freed from chasing fashion fads, impulse buying of junk foods and useless gadgets, and the long hours of work required to buy them is a life freed from much of what alienates us from the life of family, community, and nature.

Herein is revealed the tragedy of nearly fifty years of economic growth and national development. Rather than building societies that create a good life for sustainers and bring the deprived into the sustainer class, we have followed the path of encouraging overconsumers to consume more, converting sustainers into overconsumers, and pushing many of those in the sustainer class into the excluded class. In the process, we have often made life more difficult for those who remain in the sustainer class by displacing the production systems that once met their needs and giving priority to public facilities—such as highways and shopping malls—that serve overconsumers rather than those that serve sustainers—such as public transit and public markets.

From Overconsumption to Sustainable Community

We commonly think about overconsumption in terms of exercising individual discipline to give up many of the things that make our lives comfortable and satisfying. There is another, more attractive, possibility: organize our living spaces and production systems so that we improve the quality of our living while simultaneously eliminating the excessive burdens we now place on the environment. The move that Fran (my spouse) and I made to New York City in 1992 has helped me see the possibilities.

Although New York is deeply afflicted with crime, poverty, and other manifestations of the inequities of modern economic life, we did not experience the cold, impersonal city we had expected. Instead, we

Table 22.1 Earth's Three Socioecological Classes

Overconsumers 1.1 billion > US\$7,500 per capita (Cars, Meat, Disposables)	Sustainers 3.3 billion US\$700–7,500 per capita (Living Lightly)	Excluded 1.1 billion < US\$700 per capita (Absolute Deprivation)
Travel by car and air	Travel by bicycle and public surface transport	Travel by foot or donkey
Eat high-fat, high-calorie, meat-based diets	Eat healthy diets of grains, vegetables, and some meat	Eat nutritionally inadequate diets
Drink bottled water and soft drinks	Drink clean water plus some tea and coffee	Drink contaminated water
Use throwaway products and discard substantial wastes	Use unpackaged goods and recycle wastes	Use local biomass and produce negligible wastes
Live in spacious, climate-controlled, single-family homes	Live in modest, naturally ventilated homes, with extended or multiple families	Live in rudimentary shelters or in the open; usually lack secure tenure
Maintain image-conscious wardrobes	Wear functional clothing	Wear secondhand clothing or scraps

Based on data in Alan Durning, "Asking How Much Is Enough," in Lester R. Brown et al., *The State of the World* 1991 (New York: W. W. Norton, 1991), pp. 153–69.

found a city of ethnically diverse local neighborhoods and small family shops that throbs with a human energy and vitality we have rarely experienced elsewhere. New York is far from a model of sustainability and has much that detracts from the quality of life, but living in New York has helped us appreciate neglected possibilities.

With a high residential population density—an average of 5,000 people per square block, housed in multifamily dwellings—a functioning subway system, and shopping facilities within walking distance of most residences, New York's per capita energy consumption is half the average for the United States as a whole. For the first time in forty years, Fran and I do not have a car. My office is in our apartment, and Fran commutes to work on the subway. More than 90 percent of our shopping needs are met within a three-block radius of our apartment door: pharmacy, hardware, electronics, books, groceries, clothing, housewares—all in abundant selection. For my office needs, there is an ecologically conscious printing shop directly across the street, a software store around the corner, and two office supply stores within a five-minute walk.

Similarly, we have a vast array of restaurants of every conceivable ethnicity and price range, jazz clubs, theater, opera, dance, art galleries, museums, free public concerts, and health clubs—easily accessible by walking or subway. An extraordinary system of parks and botanical gardens even makes nature accessible within the city boundaries. When we feel a need to get out of the city, we take the train or rent a car from a neighborhood agency. Rather than feeling deprived by our lack of a car, we feel liberated—no commutes in heavy traffic, parking problems, insurance hassles, or auto repair ripoffs. The thousands of dollars we save each year help make it possible for me to devote my life to the things I want to do, like write this book.

We especially enjoy the Union Square farmers' market—just half a block from our front door. Here, four days a week, people who operate neighboring small farms, dairies, cottage wineries, and kitchen bakeries sell their wares—eggs and poultry from free-range chickens, milk from cows that are not subjected to bovine growth hormone injections, organically grown fruits and vegetables, fresh meat and fish all free of additives and artificial hormones. Most of the year, I prepare our meals mainly from what is available at the market. Eating nutritious, flavorful, unprocessed, chemical-free foods, we feel healthier and more vital, sleep better, and think more clearly. We enjoy getting to know the farmers and take comfort in the knowledge that our food is being produced in environmentally responsible ways.

Carrying home fresh unpackaged foods from the market in our own shopping bag means that we have little packaging waste. The city recycles cans, glass, plastic, and newspapers. At the Saturday and Wednesday markets, a local voluntary organization collects organic wastes for composting. We now send very little garbage to the landfill.

On the whole, we are leading healthier, happier, and more environmentally responsible lives than we ever have before—not because we are being heroically virtuous, but because the place where we live just happens, for a variety of reasons, to be organized in a way that makes it relatively easy and natural to do so. This experience has helped us see the importance of how we organize ourselves in determining the quality of our social and environmental relationships—and thereby of our living. There are a great many things that could be done to make New York City more livable and sustainable—starting with banning personal automobiles from Manhattan—but what we do have demonstrates some important possibilities.

Consider the implications of the fact that a major part of the burden we overconsumers place on the planet comes from our use of automobiles and airplanes, our consumption of unhealthy foods produced by methods that destroy the earth and leave what we eat poisoned with toxic residues, and our use of throwaway products that come in unnecessary packaging. Would it really be a burden to give up long commutes on crowded freeways, constant noise, job insecurity, gadgets we never use, clothes we seldom wear, unhealthy fatty diets, chemically contaminated fruits and vegetables, products that don't last, useless packaging, tiring business trips, and energy-inefficient homes and buildings? Or what about the military activities that account for approximately 30 percent of all global environmental degradation?[6] Would it be a hardship if we were to resolve our disputes by nonmilitary means?

Our need is to organize societies for sustainable good living. An important point, often neglected, is that many of the actions we need to take to bring our lives into balance with the earth are collective, rather than individual, choices. If we do it properly, the improvements in the quality of our living can more than compensate for the sacrifices involved. Let me illustrate by suggesting some of the things that we need to do to make three major systems—urban space and transportation, food and agriculture, and materials—sustainable. In each instance, it seems that the evolution of our existing systems has been shaped more by the corporate than by the human interest. The changes we must make to create healthy societies may result in hardships for our largest corporations, but they will greatly improve the quality of human living.

Urban Space and Transport

In *Reclaiming Our Cities and Towns*, David Engwicht reminds us that people invented cities as places devoted to human interaction. The purpose of cities is to "facilitate exchange of information, friendship, material goods, culture, knowledge, insight, [and] skills" with little need for travel.[7] Cities once consisted primarily of exchange spaces for people—places such as shops, schools, residences, and public buildings. The pathways that connected exchange spaces were also places to meet and reaffirm relationships with neighbors.

The automobile has changed our cities in fundamental ways, colonizing ever more of the spaces that were once devoted to human exchange and transforming them into systems of parking lots connected by highways. Thus, many of the spaces that once brought us together have been converted into noisy, congested, polluting places that isolate us from one another and destroy the quality of city life. The more densely and faster the traffic flows through our neighborhood, the less we feel at home there and the less likely we are to relate to and befriend our neighbors.[8]

The automobile is not only one of our least energy efficient modes of transportation, it is also one of our least space efficient. When we take into account the multiple parking spaces that each car must have at home, office, shopping center, church, recreational facilities, and school, plus the amount of road space required for its movement, the total space required by each family car is typically three times greater than the space occupied by the average family home.[9]

One reason people flee to the suburbs is to escape the environmental and social consequences of giving cities over to automobiles. Once productive agricultural lands are paved over, we become separated from nature and one another by even greater distances, our dependence on automobiles increases, and per capita energy consumption skyrockets—both for transportation and to heat and cool the detached, single-family dwellings in which suburbanites live. There is sound foundation for the conclusion of urban ecologists William Rees and Mark Roseland that "sprawling suburbs are arguably the most economically, environmentally, and socially costly pattern of residential development humans have ever devised."[10]

Automobile companies sell their products as tickets to freedom, defined in many auto ads as the escape by automobile to the unspoiled countryside. It is ironic, because the automobile has been perhaps the single greatest contributor to making our urban areas unlivable, turning our countryside into sprawling suburbs and strip malls, and making us ever more dependent on cars to survive the consequences of this affliction.

In 1950, the average American drove some 3,800 kilometers (2,356 miles). That figure had risen to 9,700 kilometers (6,014 miles) by 1990. Greater freedom? Roughly half of the miles Americans drive involve commuting to work on congested roadways. Between 1969 and 1990, the number of miles traveled to work by the average American household increased 16 percent. The second major use of cars is shopping. The average distance traveled for shopping increased by 88 percent. A third use is for matters such as business travel, delivering children to and from school, doctor visits, and church attendance—up 135 percent. Social and recreational travel actually declined by 1 percent, perhaps because we had less time left for it. It is estimated that in the largest U.S. urban areas, 1 billion to 2 billion hours a year are wasted due to traffic congestion. In Bangkok, the average worker loses the equivalent of forty-four working days a year sitting in traffic.[11]

It is not difficult to figure out who benefits from this damage to the quality of our living. In terms of sales, the three largest companies in America are General Motors Corporation (cars), Exxon Corporation (oil), and Ford Motor Company (cars). Mobil Corporation (oil) is number seven.

In 1992, Groiningen, a Dutch city of 170,000 people, dug up its city-center highways and took a variety of steps to make the bicycle the main form of transportation. As a consequence, business has improved, rents have increased, and the flow of people out of the city has been reversed. Local businesses that once fought any restraint on the automobile are now clamoring for more restraint.[12]

It is a step that many more cities should take. Few measures would do more to improve the quality of our living and the health of our environment than organizing living spaces to reduce our dependence on the automobile. Other actions to help accomplish this include planning and controlling the use of urban space to increase urban density and the proximity of work, home, and recreation; restricting parking facilities; increasing taxes on gasoline; and investing in public transit and facilities for pedestrians and cyclists.

"Hold on," says the corporate libertarian. "What about the impact on the economy? One job in six in the United States is linked to the auto industry. In Australia, it is one in ten.[13] Unemployment would skyrocket and stock prices would plummet if we were to reorganize space to do away with the automobile. It would be an economic disaster."

It is an important point that is best answered with another question. Is it rational to structure an economy so that investors profit from socially harmful investments and the only employment people can find is doing things that reduce our quality of life? An intelligent species can surely find a better way to provide people with a means of livelihood. We will return to this issue in a moment.

Food and Agriculture

Our food and agriculture system is similarly designed to generate profits for giant chemical and agribusiness corporations with little regard for the health of people and the ecosystem. This system features chemical-intensive mechanized production, long-distance shipping, captive contract producers, migrant laborers paid bare subsistence wages, and large government subsidies paid to giant corporations. The system is well suited to the profitable mass production of standardized food products. It comes at the cost of depleting soils and aquifers, contaminating water with chemical runoff, and driving out the small family farms that were long the backbone of strong rural communities. Much of what this system delivers to the consumer consists of highly processed, wastefully packaged foods of dubious nutritional value contaminated with chemical residues. Although the system keeps supermarkets filled to abundance, it features misleading nutritional claims; strongly resists any effort to inform consumers regarding the additives, synthetic hormones, and toxic residues they may be ingesting; and gives consumers little option of choosing organically grown, unprocessed foods produced by local farmers. Our food choices have largely been reduced to whatever big corporations find it profitable to offer.

Even as adults intent on exercising healthful and responsible choice, we seldom have any way of knowing whether the piece of fish we are about to buy was caught by a massive foreign trawler sweeping the ocean bare with fine mesh drift nets or harvested by a local fisherman using environmentally responsible gear. We have no way of knowing whether a piece of meat is from an animal raised on properly managed natural rangelands or from one raised on unstable lands from which tropical forests were recently cleared and fattened in feedlots on grain that might otherwise have fed hungry people. There is no way to tell whether the cows that supply our milk have been injected with artificial hormones, because under pressure from the Monsanto corporation, the government prohibits the labeling that would tell us.

If our goal is to provide a good living for people, we need to transform our food and agriculture system much as we must transform our habitats and transportation systems. Our goal must be to optimize the use of land and water resources to meet the needs of an expanding population for a nutritionally adequate diet, fiber, and livelihoods. And we must do it in an environmentally sustainable way.

An appropriate system would most likely include a much larger proportion of intensively managed small family farms producing a diverse range of food, fiber, livestock, and energy products for local markets. Farming practices would use biodynamic methods to maintain soil fertility, retain water, and control pests. The food system would be designed to limit, contain, and recycle contaminants—including the recycling of human wastes—and would depend primarily on renewable solar-generated energy sources—including animal power and biogas— for preparation, production, processing, storage, and transport.[14] Steps toward such a system would include carrying out agrarian reform to break up large agricultural holdings, providing adequate credit facilities for small farmers, creating farmer-based research and extension systems oriented to biodynamic methods, requiring full and accurate labeling of food products, eliminating financial and environmental subsidies for agricultural chemicals, increasing the costs of food transport by eliminating energy and other transportation subsidies, and creating locally accountable watershed management authorities to coordinate measures for soil and water protection.

Although moving toward more localized food and agriculture systems and healthier, less fatty diets would require adjustments in our eating habits, this is not a vision of sacrifice and deprivation. Rather, it is a vision of a fertile earth and of vibrant and secure human communities populated by people with healthy bodies and minds nourished by wholesome, uncontaminated foods. The elements of this vision are technically and socially feasible. They simply require restructuring the relevant systems in line with the human rather than the corporate interest.

Materials

To achieve true sustainability, we must reduce our "garbage index"—that which we permanently throw away into the environment that will not be naturally recycled for reuse—to near zero. Productive activities must be organized as closed systems. Minerals and other nonbiodegradable resources, once taken from the ground, must become a part of society's permanent capital stock and be recycled in perpetuity. Organic materials may be disposed into the natural ecosystems, but only in ways that assure that they are absorbed back into the natural production system.

Individual consumers are regularly urged to sort and recycle discards—an important but insufficient measure. Many of the most important decisions are out of our hands, and much of the garbage related to our individual consumption is created and discarded long before any product reaches us. The market rarely offers us a choice of a daily newspaper printed on recycled paper using nontoxic, biodegradable ink. Nor can we ensure that the dutifully bundled newspapers we place at curbside for recycling will indeed be recycled. Such decisions lie in the hands of publishers, paper manufacturers, politicians, and government bureaucrats.

Take the newspaper itself. Over a twenty-year period, assuming current levels of recycling, the typical American household "consumes" the equivalent of roughly 100 trees in the form of newsprint. Sixty to 65 percent of that newsprint is devoted to advertisements.[15] Though we may never read and have no interest in the ads, we are not given the option of subscribing to a paper without them.

According to the Worldwatch Institute, "most materials used today are discarded after one use—roughly two thirds of all aluminum, three fourths of all steel and paper, and an even higher share of plastic."[16] The physical environment is disrupted to extract the materials involved, vast amounts of garbage are generated, we work extra hours to earn the money to keep replacing what is discarded, and we become beasts of burden endlessly toting replacements from the store to our homes and then out to the garbage. This may be good for the economy and for corporate profits and executive salaries, but it degrades the quality of our living.

Recycling not only reduces the environmental costs of resource extraction, it saves energy as well. Producing steel from scrap requires only a third as much energy as producing it from ore, reduces air pollution by 85 percent, reduces water pollution by 76 percent, and eliminates mining wastes. Making newsprint from recycled paper takes 25 to 60 percent less energy than producing it from virgin wood pulp, while reducing the release of air pollutants by 74 percent and water pollutants by 35 percent. Reuse produces even more dramatic gains. Recycling the glass in a bottle reduces energy consumption by a third, while cleaning and reusing the bottle itself can save as much as 90 percent of the energy required to make a new bottle.[17]

Germany has pioneered the idea of life-cycle product planning and responsibility. Government-mandated programs encourage manufacturers of automobiles and household appliances to assume responsibility for the disassembly, reuse, and recycling of their products. Besides being environmentally sound, this practice relieves the consumer of the burden of disposing of those items at the end of their useful lives.[18] Life-cycle management can be carried out through lease arrangements in which the ownership of the item remains with the manufacturer, which becomes responsible for both maintenance and disposal and thus has an incentive to design products for maximum durability and ease of recycling.

Governments can encourage producers to design their products and packaging to limit disposal by charging them a fee to cover the estimated public cost of eventual disposal. Governments can also require that multisized and -shaped beverage and other containers be replaced with standardized durable glass containers that can be reused many times simply by washing and relabeling.[19]

Individual choices can make a difference. We can reduce the amount of meat in our diets. We can buy a water filter to reduce our dependence on bottled water and soft drinks. We can buy fewer clothes or a more gas-efficient car. There are countless such positive choices to be made. However, we must give more attention to organizing our societies for sustainability so as to make the responsible choices easy and economical.

Sustainable Livelihoods

An important part of the demand for economic growth comes from the carefully cultivated myth that the only way we can keep people employed is to expand aggregate consumption to create jobs at a rate faster than corporations invest in labor-saving technology to eliminate them. We neglect an important alternative—to redefine the problem and concentrate on creating livelihoods rather than jobs.

A job is defined by *Webster's New World Dictionary* as "a specific piece of work, as in one's trade, or done by agreement for pay; anything one has to do; task; chore; duty."[20] A livelihood is defined as "a means of living or of supporting life."[21] A job is a source of money. A livelihood is a means of living. Speaking of jobs evokes images of people working in the factories and fast-food outlets of the world's largest corporations. Speaking of sustainable livelihoods evokes images of people and communities engaged in meeting individual and collective needs in environmentally responsible ways—the vision of a localized system of self-managing communities.

We could be using advances in technology to give everyone more options for good, sustainable living. If we so choose, instead of demanding that those fortunate enough to have jobs sacrifice their family and community lives on the altar of competition while others languish in the ranks of the unemployed, we could be organizing our societies around a twenty- to thirty-hour workweek to assure secure and adequately compensated employment for almost every adult who wants a job. The time thus freed could be devoted to the social economy in activities that meet unmet needs and rebuild a badly tattered social fabric.

The possibilities are extraordinary if we acknowledge that many existing jobs not only are unsatisfying but also involve producing goods and services that are either unnecessary or cause major harm to society and to the environment. This includes a great many of the jobs in the automobile, chemical, packaging, and petroleum industries; most advertising and marketing jobs; the brokers and financial portfolio managers engaged in speculative and other extractive forms of investment; ambulance-chasing lawyers; 14 million arms industry workers worldwide; and the 30 million people employed by the world's military forces.[22]

This leads to a startling fact. Societies would be better off if, instead of paying hundreds of million of people sometimes outrageous amounts to do things that are harmful to the quality of our living, we gave them the same pay to sit home and do nothing. Although far from an optimal solution, it would make more sense than the wholly irrational practice of organizing societies to pay people to do things that result in a net reduction in real wealth and well-being. Why not organize to support them instead to do things that are socially beneficial and environmentally benign, such as providing loving care and attention to children and the elderly, operating community markets and senior citizen centers, educating our young people, counseling drug addicts, providing proper care for the mentally ill, maintaining parks and commons, participating in community crime watch, organizing community social and cultural events, registering voters, cleaning up the environment, replanting forests, doing public-interest political advocacy, caring for community gardens, organizing community recycling programs, and retrofitting homes for energy conservation. Similarly, many of us could use more time for recreation, quiet solitude, and family life and to practice the disciplines and hobbies that keep us physically, mentally, psychologically, and spiritually healthy.

Our problem is not too few jobs, it is an economic structure that creates too much dependence on paid employment and then pays people to do harmful things while neglecting so many activities that are essential to a healthy society. It is instructive to remember that until the last ten to twenty years, most people served society productively in unpaid work in the social economy. In many instances, these societies had a stronger social fabric and offered their members a greater sense of personal security and fulfillment than does our own.

Although initiatives toward creating sustainable livelihood economies may evolve in different ways in response to different circumstances and aspirations, we may infer some of their features from the above principles and examples. For example, in urban areas, they would most likely be organized around local urban villages or neighborhoods that bring residential, work, recreation, and commercial facilities together around sustainable production to meet local needs with a substantial degree of self-reliance. They would feature green spaces and intensive human interaction and seek considerable self-reliance in energy, biomass, and materials production.

Human and environmental productive activities would be melded into localized, closed-loop coproduction processes that recycle sewage, solid waste, and even air through fish ponds, gardens, and green areas to continuously regenerate their own resource inputs. Urban agriculture and aquaculture, repair and reuse, and intensive recycling would provide abundant livelihood opportunities in vocations that increase sustainability. Organizing these activities around neighborhoods that are also largely self-reliant in social services would help renew family and community ties, decentralize administration, and increase the sharing of family responsibilities between men and women. Needs for the transport of people and goods would be reduced. Locally produced foods would be fresh and unpackaged or preserved in reusable containers.

We might find a wide range of traditional and electronic-age cottage industries, many involved in various kinds of recycling, existing side by side with urban agriculture. Family support services such as community-based day care, family counseling, schools, family health services, and multipurpose community centers could become integral neighborhood functions, engaging people in useful and meaningful work within easy walking distance of their homes. Many localities may issue their own local currency to facilitate local transactions and limit the flow of money out of the community. Most adults would divide their time between activities relating to the money economy and those relating to the social economy. We would see a return of the multifunctional home that serves as a center of family and community life and drastically reduces dependence on the automobile and other energy-intensive forms of transportation. We might line our byways with trees rather than billboards. We might limit advertising to product information that is available on demand, only when we want it.

On the path to true social efficiency, we would have ample time for other aspects of living, including recreation, cultural expression, intellectual and spiritual development, and political participation. We might travel to other localities for cultural exchanges. We might maintain friendships and collegial relations with others around the world by videophone. Or we might conference on computer networks to share exotic recipes, ideas on how to organize a local food co-op, or experiences in campaigning to improve public transit service. We might network internationally on citizen advocacy regarding proposed new trade rules. Or we might tune in to the news broadcasts from Russia, India, and Chile to see how people there are reacting to election results in South Africa.

We do have the option of creating healthy societies that allow us to live whole lives. It is time to reclaim our power and get on with that task, as millions of people are already doing.

23 An Awakened Civil Society

Our historic challenge is to add, sift, stir, spice, knead, and otherwise blend ourselves together, over time, into a genuine people's political power.
—James Hightower[1]

We, the people of the world, will mobilize the forces of transnational civil society behind a widely shared agenda that bonds our many social movements in pursuit of just, sustainable, and participatory human societies. In so doing we are forging our own instruments and processes for redefining the nature and meaning of human progress and for transforming those institutions that no longer respond to our needs.
—"The People's Earth Declaration,"
UNCED NGO Forum

January 1, 1994, was the inaugural day of the North American Free Trade Agreement (NAFTA), an agreement intended to complete the integration of the economies of Mexico, Canada, and the United States. Business leaders throughout North America welcomed the new opportunities for corporate expansion afforded by the merger. The indigenous peoples of Chiapas state in southeastern Mexico took a strikingly different view. They had for generations endured similar economic "advances," each time losing more of their lands and finding their livelihood opportunities ever more limited. Calling NAFTA a death sentence for the people of Chiapas, some 4,000 Indians launched an armed rebellion against the Mexican government.

Mexican political analyst Gustavo Esteva has called the Chiapas rebellion the "first revolution of the twenty-first century." Whereas the revolutions of the twentieth century were contests for state power, the struggle of the Chiapas people was for greater local autonomy, economic justice, and political rights within the borders of their own communities.[2] They did not call on their fellow Mexicans to take up arms against the state but rather to join them in a broad social movement calling for the liberation of local spaces from colonization by alien political and economic forces. Their battle cry—"Basta!" (Enough!)—was picked up by popular movements all across Mexico and resonated around the world.

Each day, more people are saying no to the forces of corporate colonialism, reclaiming their spaces, taking back responsibility for their lives, and working to create real-world alternatives to the myths and illusions of economic globalization.

Saying No

Journalist Dai Qing is a courageous and outspoken opponent of the Three Gorges dam in China that threatens to displace 1.2 million people, flood 100,000 hectares of the country's most fertile agricultural land, inundate a magnificent stretch of canyons, and destroy the habitat's endangered species. In her words, "The highest expression of dignity can be summed up in the single word 'No!'"[3]

The democratic legitimacy of the institutions to which we yield power derives from (1) being duly constituted by and accountable to the sovereign people, (2) conducting their operations according to an appropriate code of morals and ethics, and (3) producing desirable consequences for the whole.[4] Most are failing on all three counts, not because the individuals who head them are corrupt, but because these institutions have become too big, too distant, and too captive to special interests. Capturing state power, whether by election or revolution, does not change this. Nor do reforms that simply chip away at the edges of the current structure. This is why elections have become meaningless. We must transform the system itself by reclaiming the power that we have yielded to the corrupted institutions and taking back responsibility for our own lives—exactly what growing millions of people are doing at this moment everywhere on the planet.[5] As this process progresses, we redefine the relationships of power between the global, the national, and the local, and the power of once seemingly invincible institutions evaporates.

In 1986, the Philippine people took to the streets in massive demonstrations to say no to the hated and corrupt Marcos dictatorship. The military sided with the people, Marcos fled the country in disgrace, and democracy was restored with scarcely a shot fired. The world saw an even more dramatic demonstration of this truth in 1989 in Eastern Europe, and in 1991 in the former Soviet Union.

In India, Tasmania, Canada, Thailand, France, Hungary, and elsewhere, people are joining Dai Qing in saying no to dam projects that threaten their homes, livelihoods, and wild places. The women of India's Chipko movement are wrapping themselves around threatened trees to save them from loggers; Penan tribal people of Sarawak, Malaysia, are blockading logging roads with their bodies; and the 1 million strong Future Forest Alliance is organizing protest demonstrations and media campaigns in Canada.

People are mobilizing to protect mangroves in the Ivory Coast, reef systems in Belize, and wildlife in Namibia. They are opposing toxic dumping in the United States and campaigning to protect Antarctica as a natural preserve. Japanese citizens are pressuring Japanese logging companies to change their practices abroad. Germans are calling for an end to foreign aid that destroys primary forests. Indigenous pocket miners, farmers, and fisherfolk in the Philippines are mobilizing to challenge the right of a few powerful mining corporations to destroy the livelihoods of thousands of people.

The ideologues of corporate libertarianism tell us that environmentalism is a middle- or upper-class issue—a luxury that the poor cannot afford. Yet we find with increasing frequency that the most heroic actions to save the environment are being taken by the poor, who know the costs of allowing the plunder of the natural resources upon which their existence depends.

Indigenous peoples are often at the forefront. In Ecuador, they have organized to reclaim their lands, protect the Ecuadorean rain forests from foreign oil companies, and block a government agricultural modernization program that would drive them off their farms. In Peru, they have formed a 300,000-member alliance to initiate projects that combine environmental and indigenous land objectives. National Indian organizations from Peru, Bolivia, Ecuador, Brazil, and Colombia have formed an international alliance representing over a million people to press for Indian land rights. Native Americans blocked a Honeywell corporation plan to create a nuclear weapons testing site in the sacred Black Hills of South Dakota and rejected offers from AMCOR Company to build a 5,000-acre landfill and incinerator on tribal lands. In southern Panama, indigenous peoples have organized to prevent the completion of the Pan-American highway through the tropical forests of their homelands—well aware that the highway would lead to the devastation of their forests, the expropriation of their lands, and the destruction of their culture.

In the Philippines and Colombia, people are saying no to violence, declaring their villages to be zones of peace and telling both government and insurgent combatants to fight their wars elsewhere. The Women's Action Forum in fundamentalist Islamic Pakistan has brought women out from the seclusion of their homes and veils to join in mass public demonstrations to say no to the curtailment of women's rights.

There are costs to saying no. Many of the nonviolent warriors of the Ecological Revolution have suffered public ridicule, threats, loss of jobs, bankrupt businesses, imprisonment, torture, and death at the hands of those who do not share their vision of life-centered societies. They bear the burdens of the political and spiritual awakening that must precede the transformational changes on which our collective future depends.

Creating alternatives, the building blocks of healthy societies, is an important part of saying no. The women of Kenya's Greenbelt movement have set up 1,500 grassroots nurseries and planted over 10 million trees. Other African women are following their lead. The fisherfolk of Kerala state in India have organized to protect their coastal fisheries resources. In the United States the Quinalt Indians on the west coast of Washington State are buying back the lands of their reservation acre by acre to carry out plans for their sustainable management. Nearby, the people of Willapa Bay, a major salmon and oyster fishery, have formed an alliance of environmentalists, loggers, local businesspeople, government, fisherfolk, landowners, and members of the Shoalwater Bay Indian tribe to regenerate their once dynamic and biodiverse ecosystem as the foundation of a prosperous, diversified, and sustainable local economy. In Seattle, Washington, a group of citizen leaders has formed Sustainable Seattle to pioneer the development of indicators of progress toward sustainability.

Japanese women operate a 200,000-household Seikatsu Club Consumers' Cooperative that works with suppliers to assure that they provide safe and healthful products and treat workers and nature properly. The 23,000 members of the Spanish Mondragon Cooperatives grossed $3 billion in sales in 1991 and provide the world with a model of the potential of dynamic worker-owned, community-based enterprises. In hundreds of communities in Canada, Argentina, Australia, New Zealand, the United States, and elsewhere, people are creating their own community currencies—known variously as LETs, green, or time dollars—to free themselves from colonization by the global financial system, revitalize their communities, and build economic self-reliance.[6] Over 7,500 households representing some 20,000 people in thirteen European and North American countries participate in Global Action Plan International (GAP) to support one another and monitor their individual and joint progress toward more sustainable lifestyles. Students in the United States have organized to make their schools advertising-free zones. Five hundred Philippine citizen organizations have formed a National Peace Conference to develop a national peace agenda to end the long-standing armed conflict in their country. In Israel, the Re'ut Sadaka Jewish Arab Youth Movement encourages Arab and Jewish youth to live and study together.

Each such initiative reclaims previously colonized space, advances the rebuilding of human communities and natural ecosystems, and serves as an inspiration for others.

The Power of Citizen Networking

When citizen volunteers organize to oppose powerful institutions that command billions of dollars and access to the most privileged inner sanctums of political power, it seems a highly uneven contest. The institutions of transnational capital are highly visible, their power is concentrated in an identifiable corporate core, and they command enormous amounts of money. Yet their ability to command the life energies of people diminishes quickly if their money flows are restricted. Citizen activists are learning to turn these characteristics into vulnerabilities.

The power of civil society rests with its enormous capacity to rapidly and flexibly network diverse and dispersed individuals and organizations that are motivated by voluntary commitments. Effective citizen networks have many leaders—each able to function independently of the others. The diversity and independence of their members allow them to examine problems from many different perspectives and bring diverse abilities to bear.[7] Their use of the same electronic communications technologies—phone, fax, and computer—that corporations have used to extend their global reach allows them to move quickly and flexibly in joint actions at local, national, and global levels.

The lack of defined structure can make the actions of citizen networks incoherent and difficult to sustain, but it also gives them the ability to surround, infiltrate, and immobilize the most powerful institutions. These same characteristics make them virtually impervious to attacks by the more centralized, money-dependent global institutions of business and finance. Any one node in the network can be immobilized and isolated—key actors have even been assassinated—but a functioning network is able to adjust almost instantaneously. It is much like a hologram that can be reconstructed from any of its parts. Indeed, attacks on citizen networks expose the ill will of the perpetrators, offend moral sensibilities, increase the network's visibility, attract new recruits, and strengthen resolve.

There are many contemporary examples of the ability of such networks to make a difference at both national and global levels. In the

former Soviet Union, grassroots environmentalists held the government accountable for widespread environmental degradation and built
a movement that helped spark the region's democratic transformation.
These groups are now allied under the politically powerful Socio-
Ecological Union to advance a broad environmental and human rights
agenda. In South Korea, the Citizen Coalition for Economic Justice
helped establish democratic rule and now works for economic justice
and environmental sustainability. In Finland, 2,300 committees of the
Village Action Movement have affected the lives of some 500,000 people and restored rural areas to a central place in national life.

A social movement in Sweden called the Natural Step is building a
national consensus around a commitment to make Sweden a model
of sustainability by achieving near 100 percent recycling of metals,
eliminating the release of compounds that do not break down naturally in the environment, maintaining biological diversity, and reducing energy use to levels of sustainable solar capture. Some 10,000
professionals, business executives, farmers, restaurateurs, students, and
government officials are active in sixteen specialized networks developing and carrying out action plans. Forty-nine local governments,
members of the Swedish Farmers Federation, and twenty-two large
Swedish companies are now working to align themselves with these
rigorous objectives.

A broadly based U.S. citizens' alliance of farmer, consumer, environmental, animal welfare, religious, labor, and other public-interest
organizations is working on a broad agenda to transform U.S. agriculture to restore small farms, eliminate the use of toxic chemicals, and
make land management practices sustainable.[8] New initiatives in the
U.S. labor movement—largely spearheaded by women and minority
groups—have more of the community-oriented, participatory, and open
quality of social movements than conventional hierarchically organized
craft or industrial unions and are seeking alliances with small farmers
and small business owners who share a stake in strong local economies.[9]
Local African American groups are reclaiming their power and taking back responsibility for their communities by mobilizing to steer
their young men away from drugs and guns and build more economic
opportunity for African American people.[10]

One of the most dramatic national-scale citizen initiatives is Citizenship Action against Misery and for Life—Brazil's grassroots hunger
movement spearheaded by Herbert "Betinho" de Souza of the Brazilian Institute for Social and Economic Analyses (IBASE). It is an out-
growth of the broadly based Brazilian citizen movement that led to the
1993 impeachment of Fernando Collor, the Brazilian president whose
corruption grew to exceed even the tolerance of Brazil's jaded middle
and upper classes. Once the new government was installed, de Souza

capitalized on his own reputation as a leader of the impeachment movement and the resulting sense of civic empowerment to mobilize Brazilians behind a national commitment to end a national disgrace—32
million of Brazil's 156 million people living in perpetual hunger on
incomes of less than $120 a year in a country with one of the world's
most modern and dynamic economies.[11] A 1994 survey estimated that
some 2.8 million Brazilians, roughly 10 percent of the population over
sixteen years old, were active participants in neighborhood hunger committees made up of workers, students, housewives, businesspeople, art-
ists, and others. Roughly a third of Brazil's adult population has made
some kind of personal contribution to the campaign.[12]

Three key elements make the Brazilian hunger movement distinctive:

1. *The problem is broken down into manageable pieces.* Members of
   the middle and upper classes were admonished to go into their
   immediate neighborhoods, find one person who was hungry,
   and do something about it. An individual feels overwhelmed
   and disempowered by the hunger of 32 million people, but
   doing something about the hunger of one or two people who
   live within a block of home is possible—and deeply fulfilling.
   Each individual has the empowering experience of being able
   to make a difference. When millions of people share this experience, it can create a new civic culture.
2. *It involves direct human engagement.* People are not asked to send
   money to a relief agency so that professional hunger workers
   can feed the needy in some safely distant place. They are challenged to go into their own neighborhoods and build human
   relationships, to allow themselves to be touched by the life of
   a poor and hungry person whom the system has excluded, to
   hear that person's story and share in the burden of his or her
   suffering, and to serve as a bridge to make society whole again.
3. *It builds toward a new political and spiritual consciousness.* People
   are encouraged to reflect on the act of befriending and improving the life of a hungry person as both a political and a
   spiritual experience and as a source of insight into the source
   of the dysfunctions of Brazilian society. Through media pre-
   sentations and local meetings, citizens are led to a growing
   awareness of the dynamics of inequality and exclusion that
   flow from the concentration of economic power in a few
   giant corporations.

International citizen advocacy has come into its own in the past twenty
to thirty years. Global alliances such as Amnesty International have

long been at the forefront of the international struggle to recognize basic human rights. In the late 1960s and early 1970s, the International Planned Parenthood Federation led a global transformation in attitudes toward family planning and a woman's right to birth control.

In the 1980s, while U.S. President Ronald Reagan was characterizing the Soviet Union as the evil empire and Soviet leaders were characterizing Americans as barbaric monsters, thousands of private American and Soviet citizens were engaged through groups such as the Institute for Soviet-American Relations, the Esalan Institute, the Natural Resources Defense Council, and the Context Institute in building foundations for peace, mutual understanding, and democratization.[13] The Philippine Development Forum, with offices in Washington and Manila, has helped block multilateral funding of destructive energy projects, expose toxic wastes at U.S. military bases, and advance creative new funding mechanisms to promote sustainable development in the Philippines. A coalition of Canadian, Mexican, and U.S. groups formed to oppose NAFTA is coordinating citizen proposals for people-centered economic cooperation among the countries of North America. When Honeywell and General Electric fired union organizers at their plants in Juárez and Chihuahua, Mexico, unions in the United States and Canada representing workers employed by these multinationals joined to act against these companies in support of their Mexican counterparts.[14]

In 1979, Malaysian consumer activist Anwar Fazal, then president of the International Organization of Consumer Unions (IOCU), convened the International Baby Food Action Network (IBFAN), an international alliance of citizen advocacy groups, to boycott Nestle products. Responding to evidence that bottle-feeding was causing thousands of infant deaths each year in poor countries, the boycotters demanded that Nestle stop the aggressive promotion of its infant formula product as a modern and nutritious substitute for breast-feeding. Nestle launched a vicious counterattack, which spurred the rapid growth of IBFAN into a coalition of more than 140 citizen groups in seventy countries. As a result of the IBFAN efforts, the World Health Organization issued a code of conduct in 1981 governing the promotion of baby formula, and Nestle made a promise—subsequently dishonored—to follow the code.

Building on the IBFAN experience, the IOCU regional office in Penang, Malaysia, launched other citizen networks to counter threats to human health, safety, and pocketbooks from the activities of transnational corporations dealing in pharmaceuticals, tobacco, toxic wastes, chemical agriculture, biotechnology, and food irradiation. The Third World Network, an important Southern citizen advocacy group led by former university professor Mohammed Idris, was also born in

Penang—making this coastal city a global focal point of citizen resistance to the new colonialism.[15]

The way in which citizen networks with modest resources are able to surround and infiltrate the most powerful international institutions is demonstrated by the "Fifty Years Is Enough" campaign organized by citizen groups on the occasion of the fiftieth anniversary of the World Bank and the International Monetary Fund (IMF). The Bank and the IMF command massive financial resources, leverage the world's largest financial markets, and virtually dictate the policies of many governments. They can mobilize thousands of highly paid staff to generate statistics and policy papers favoring their positions, buy media reach through the world's most prestigious public-relations firms, and co-opt influential nongovernmental organizations (NGOs) with offers of grants, contracts, and foreign travel.

Citizen groups in nearly every country in which these two institutions operate rose to the challenge of this highly unequal contest, even eliciting cooperation from sympathetic staff within these secretive institutions. The Bank and the IMF now are never certain what secret internal documents will find their way into citizen hands and publications or where protest banners, mass demonstrations, op-ed pieces, advertisements, and special issues of citizen journals and newsletters will appear challenging their claims of effectiveness and calling for cuts in their funding. No more than three years ago, the suggestion that the World Bank should be shut down seemed naive and even a bit frivolous. Now the Bank's funding replenishments are in jeopardy, and its closure is discussed as a serious proposal.

This is only a small illustrative sampling of the countless initiatives being undertaken by ordinary people everywhere. Together they represent the awakening of civil society and the emergence of the social and political forces of the Ecological Revolution.

Globalizing Consciousness

Global citizen networking is a crucial part of the process of creating a new globalized human consciousness. In countless forums, people from every corner of the world are meeting to share their experiences with an errant global system and build a cooperative agenda.[16] The United Nations Conference on Environment and Development (UNCED), or Earth Summit, held in Rio de Janeiro in June 1992 was a defining moment in the global citizen dialogue. While the official meetings were going on in the grand and heavily guarded Rio Centro convention center, some 18,000 private citizens of every race, religion, social class, and nationality gathered in tents on a steamy stretch of beachfront on the other side of town for the NGO Global Forum to draft citizen treaties setting agendas for cooperative voluntary action.

The two gatherings could hardly have been more different. The official meetings were tediously formal and tightly programmed; they largely affirmed the status quo and carefully avoided most of the fundamental issues, including planetary limits to economic growth, unaccountable corporate power, and the consequences of economic globalization. The citizen deliberations were chaotic, free-floating, and contentious. They directly confronted the fundamental issues and called for sweeping transformational change. In the end, it was evident that behind the cacophony of discordant voices were important elements of consensus manifesting a new global political, environmental, and spiritual consciousness.

At UNCED, citizen organizations worked largely at the periphery of the official discussions, but the citizen treaty process made a major contribution to putting in place the foundation of a citizen consensus and helped prepare the way for more substantive input to future global meetings. Key elements of the Consensus were synthesized in "The People's Earth Declaration: A Proactive Agenda for the Future" (see the appendix). At subsequent official international conferences, citizen groups have become more familiar with and skilled in dealing with official UN processes—especially key organizations within the women's movement, such as Development Alternatives for Women in a New Era (DAWN) and the Women's Environment and Development Organization (WEDO). By the time of the 1994 International Conference on Population and Development in Cairo, the women's movement demonstrated that it was the first among the citizen movements to truly master the UN meeting process. Working with and through national governments and the UN secretariat, women's groups set the basic frame of the official conference document. Dissenting governments and the Catholic Church were the ones placed in the position of seeking adjustments in the nuances of phrases to which they objected. Bearing a disproportionate share of the human burden of the global human crisis, women are now taking the leadership in crafting a new gender-balanced human development agenda to benefit all people.[17] The women's movement is rapidly emerging as the political vanguard of the Ecological Revolution.

Doing the Possible

We live in an era in which the potential for rapid change on a global scale far exceeds that of any previous period in human history. In a single year, 1988, the environment, which previously had been an issue only for hard-core environmentalists, broke into global consciousness. Environmental concerns became a major issue in a U.S. presidential election, and *Time* magazine named the endangered earth the media event of the year. Four years later, in June 1992, the largest gathering of heads of state, other political leaders, corporations, and citizen organizations in human history took place in Rio de Janeiro to complete agreements protecting the global environment.

Consider the ridicule that would have been heaped on the visionary prophet who dared even in 1988 to predict that by 1991 the Soviet Union would peacefully dissolve itself, Germany would be reunited, the Berlin Wall would be gone, and the leadership of the former "evil empire" would be inviting the United States to help dismantle its nuclear arsenal. What if this same prophet had predicted that in 1993 the Israelis and Palestinians would sign a peace accord? And that in 1994 Nelson Mandela would be elected the president of South Africa in an open multiracial election?[18] Perhaps even more remarkable than the fact that these events occurred at all is that fact that we already take most of them for granted, quickly forgetting what extraordinary events they were and how rapidly impossible dreams are becoming accomplished fact.

Now let's consider a number of possible contemporary predictions in line with the agenda of the Ecological Revolution. Most of us would conclude that anyone foolish enough to predict that any of the following might occur within the next five years had taken leave of his or her senses. Yet in each case, ask just one question before jumping to this conclusion: is it any more preposterous to suggest that this event may occur by the year 2001 than it would have been to suggest the possibility of any of the above-mentioned events happening even as little as three years before their actual occurrence?

- International arms sales will be banned and the world's major armies dismantled in favor of a small unified UN peace-keeping command.
- Japan, the United States, Canada, Germany, and a number of other European countries will levy a 50 percent tax on advertising to finance consumer education on the merits of frugality and research on how to eliminate the growth imperative from the national economy.
- Current national income accounting systems based on returns to business enterprises will be replaced by systems that measure economic performance on the basis of human needs met

and the enhancement or depletion of a country's human, social, and natural capital stock.

- A rigorous international antitrust agreement will be signed by the world's nations, and aggressive implementation of its provisions—combined with a rash of community and worker buyout initiatives—will break up most of the world's larger transnational corporations and convert their components into community- and employee-owned enterprises serving predominantly local markets.

- Massive agrarian reform initiatives will break up corporate and other large agricultural holdings nearly everywhere and convert them into family farms serving local markets, using bio-intensive agricultural methods and recycling organic wastes.

- Ninety percent of the debts of low-income countries will be repudiated or forgiven, and long-term international borrowing will be sharply curtailed.

- A drastically downsized World Bank will be converted into a technical assistance agency melded into the United Nations Development Programme to function under UN auspices as an advisor to countries on how to become less trade dependent and localize their economies.

- The IMF and the General Agreement on Tariffs and Trade–World Trade Organization will be replaced by UN agencies under the authority and supervision of the UN's Economic and Social Council and will be engaged in rewriting international finance and trade policies to support economic localization within a framework of global cooperation.

- Several thousand indigenous cultures previously on the verge of extinction will be revived and flourishing.

- The industrial countries will reduce their per capita consumption of nonrenewable energy by 50 percent, and sales of new gasoline-powered automobiles will fall in the industrial countries by 75 percent with the phase-in of solar conversion and the redesign of urban habitats to facilitate walking, bicycling, and public transit.

- The world's major fisheries will be well on their way to recovery under regimes of sustainable management carried out by resource management cooperatives made up of small-scale family fishing enterprises.

- An international agreement will make the patenting of life-forms illegal, and an international authority will be established, funded by a tax on international capital movements, to purchase rights to the most socially and environmentally beneficial technologies, place them in the public domain, and facilitate access to them by anyone in the world who wishes to put them to beneficial use.

- A number of national and international business organizations representing many of the world's largest corporations will voluntarily accept codes of conduct that include capping executive salaries at a level no greater than twenty times that of the lowest paid worker anywhere within a firm's global production network, reducing nonrenewable energy use to 25 percent of 1995 levels by 2010, and achieving 90 percent product life-cycle recycling by the same year.
- Most countries will eliminate taxes on incomes and basic consumption up to the levels required for a comfortable subsistence in favor of taxes on resource extraction, international movements of money, luxury consumption, upper-level incomes, and inheritances.
- More than half of the world's countries will have policies that convert the productivity gains of mechanization and automation into a twenty-hour workweek and a guaranteed income.
- Most exclusionary fundamentalist religious sects preaching fear and intolerance will fall into obscurity in the face of an ecumenical movement born of the widespread inner spiritual awakening to the unity of life and consciousness.
- Most women and men will be sharing equally in household and voluntary community duties.
- All but 500,000 of the world's refugees will be permanently and peacefully resettled—most in their countries of origin.
- Most of the world will embrace the norm of the two-child family, with the endorsement of the Catholic Church and other major religious bodies.
- Political party structures will be realigned in most countries, and grassroots political movements born of concern for democratic accountability, social justice, and environmental sustainability will be flourishing—with many people from ordinary walks of life contesting and winning election to both local and national office.

Absurdly unrealistic? Yes, but no more so than many of the unlikely advances of the past few years. Am I offering these as predictions? No, but they are among the possibilities that we may wish to include on our agenda for change.

24 Agenda for Change

A political community cannot be healthy if it cannot exercise a significant measure of control over its economic life.
  —*Herman Daly and John Cobb Jr.*[1]

I sympathize, therefore, with those who would minimize, rather than with those who would maximize, economic entanglement between nations. Ideas, knowledge, art, hospitality, travel—these are the things which should of their nature be international. But let goods be homespun whenever it is reasonably and conveniently possible, and above all, let finance be primarily national.
  —*John Maynard Keynes*[2]

There are few rights more fundamental than the right of people to create caring, sustainable communities and to control their own resources, economies, and means of livelihood. These rights in turn depend on their right to choose what cultural values they will embrace, what values their children will be taught, and with whom they will trade. A globalized economy denies these rights by transferring the power to make the relevant choices to global corporations and financial institutions. Economic globalization is in the corporate interest. It is not in the human interest. Who holds the power to decide is a pivotal issue in the Ecological Revolution.

The guiding principles of the Ecological Revolution are actively pro-business and pro-market, but they favor local over global businesses and markets. They recognize the importance of local businesses that provide employment to local people, pay local taxes to maintain local infrastructure and social services, meet local social and environmental standards, participate in the community, and compete fairly with similar businesses in markets that have no dominant players. If a global corporation wishes to make the case that it can offer local people what local enterprise cannot, it should be up to local people to judge the substance of its argument. If defending democracy, human values, and livelihoods is protectionism, then let us all proudly proclaim ourselves to be protectionists.

This chapter deals with specific measures to transform governance to reclaim our colonized political and economic spaces and restore the rights of people. The aim is to limit the power and freedom of the largest corporations in order to restore democracy and the rights and freedoms of people and communities. This requires more than simple reforms.

Reclaiming Our Political Spaces

Political rights belong to people, not to artificial legal entities. As instruments of public policy, corporations should obey the laws decided by the citizenry, not write those laws. Corporations' claim to the same constitutional rights as natural born persons is a gross distortion of the concept of rights. Particularly pernicious is the corporate claim to the First Amendment protection of the right of free speech, on which corporations base their right to lobby and carry out public campaigns on political issues. As Paul Hawken observes, by invoking this right, "corporations achieve precisely what the Bill of Rights was intended to prevent: domination of public thought and discourse."[3]

We must give high priority to legislative and judicial action aimed at establishing the legal principle that corporations are public bodies created to serve public needs and have only those privileges specifically extended to them by their charters or in law. These privileges are properly subject to withdrawal or revision at any time through popular referendum or legislative action. If a corporation persistently seeks to exceed the privileges granted by its charter—such as knowingly selling defective products—or fails to honor its obligations under the law—such as consistently violating laws regarding toxic dumping—it is the right and responsibility of citizens, acting through their government, to disband it. It is no different from their right to abolish any public body that in their judgment no longer serves the public interest or to incarcerate—and even execute—individuals who willfully break the law and cause harm to others.[4]

Shareholders, managers, employees, consumers, and others have every right in their capacity as private citizens to express their political views for or against the corporate interest. They also have the right to form and fund not-for-profit organizations for the purpose of advancing any cause they choose to support in their private capacities using their personal funds. Corporations have no such natural right. They simply do not belong in people's political spaces.

A first step toward removing corporations from the political sphere would be to eliminate all tax exemptions for corporate expenditures related to lobbying, public "education," public charities, or political organizations of any kind. The ultimate goal, however, should be a flat prohibition on for-profit corporations' involvement in any activity intended to influence the political process or to "educate" the public on issues of policy or the public interest. Furthermore, corporate officers should be prohibited by law from acting in their corporate capacities to solicit political contributions or political advocacy efforts from employees, suppliers, or customers.

Corporations' increasingly aggressive use of not-for-profit organizations as fictitious citizen fronts for corporate political lobbying highlights how thin the line is that separates corporate involvement in public education and charitable giving from overt involvement in politics. Even corporate giving to true public charities and the arts has become increasingly suspect. For example, when New York City proposed a sweeping smoking ban in public places in the fall of 1994, the Philip Morris Corporation made known to the many arts organizations it had funded in the city that it expected their support in opposing the ban.

It is only natural that for-profit corporations would align their charitable giving with their own interests. There is little other basis on which they can justify allocating shareholder profits for charitable purposes. If corporations truly care about the communities in which they reside, then let them provide good, secure jobs and safe products, maintain a clean environment, obey the law, and pay their taxes. Let their managers, shareholders, and employees contribute to charitable and educational causes of their choice from their share of the distributed wages, salaries, and profits of the corporation.

Similarly, any nonprofit organization in which 50 percent or more of the trustees are senior officers of corporations with more than $1 billion in total assets should be ineligible for tax-exempt status on the presumption that it is a front organization operated to advance the corporate interest. When nonprofit organizations with corporate boards raise public monies, issue public statements, or make presentations to public bodies, they should be required to identify themselves as such.

Removing corporations from political participation is an essential step toward reclaiming our political spaces. It is not, however, sufficient.

New York Times columnist Russell Baker all too accurately described the 1994 U.S. congressional elections as an auction, more of a bidding war to outspend opponents on negative campaign ads than a contest of vision, issues, and competence.[5] It was part of the trend that has left American voters increasingly disillusioned with democracy and outraged at a government controlled by big-money interests.

If democracy is to survive, reforms must not only get corporations out of politics but also limit the power of big money to influence the voting behavior of ordinary citizens. The ability to spend millions of dollars to saturate the electronic media, especially television, with negative messages about one's opponent has become a key to winning elections. So long as winning an election is excessively expensive and the only sources of adequate funding are powerful financial interests, policy will favor financial interests over the public interest. Setting term limits or voting incumbents out of office will accomplish very little. Three deep and sweeping campaign reforms are necessary.

1. Political advertising on television should be prohibited. It is enormously expensive, often misleading, and rarely informative. Its elimination would dramatically reduce the cost of running a successful campaign and the consequent dependence on special-interest funding. This might improve the quality of the public debate as well.
2. Total campaign expenditures should be limited. Let candidates concentrate on competing to get their messages out as effectively as possible within a set spending limit. It is a better measure of their ability to spend public funds responsibly.
3. Campaign costs should be covered by a combination of public funding and small individual tax-deductible contributions. Political action committees should be abolished, and corporations should be prohibited from making any kind of political contribution or using corporate resources to favor any candidate in a political campaign.

In return for their right to use public airways, television and radio stations should be required to provide exposure for candidates for public office on issues-oriented interview programs and debates on an equal-time basis. Print media might be provided with incentives to give space to substantive issues-oriented articles and op-ed pieces by political candidates on an equal-space basis. Informing the public regarding the views and qualifications of candidates for office is one of the most basic responsibilities of the news media in a democracy, and they should be held accountable for fulfilling it.

With their dominance of the mass media and their growing penetration of the classroom, corporations increasingly control and shape our primary institutions of cultural reproduction, constantly reinforcing the values of consumerism and the basic doctrines of corporate libertarianism—to align mainstream culture with the corporate interest. To reclaim our colonized political spaces, we must reclaim our colonized cultural spaces. Three measures require serious consideration:

1. *Antitrust legislation.* Special antitrust legislation for the media should establish that it is prima facie evidence of monopolistic intent for a single corporation to own more than one major public media outlet, whether it be a newspaper, radio station, TV station, or home cable service. Furthermore the operation of a media outlet should be the primary business of the corporation that owns it. This would ensure that the outlet is not used primarily as a means to advance other corporate interests. No individual should be allowed to have a majority holding in more than one such media corporation. This would enhance the free-speech rights of the public by limiting the ability of a few powerful individuals and corporations to dominate access to the major means of public communication.

2. *Advertising.* In classical market economics, the role of business is to respond to market demand, not create it. Tax deductions for advertising provide a public subsidy for hundreds of billions of dollars a year in corporate advertising aimed at enticing people to buy things that they neither want nor need and creating a consumer culture that is alien to the needs of healthy societies. Advertising, other than purely informative advertising based on verifiable facts, is not in the public interest. Ideally, it should be prohibited. At a minimum, it should not be deductible as an expense and should be taxed at a rate of at least 50 percent. A portion of the proceeds of such a tax should be used to finance consumer education on healthy, satisfying, and sustainable lifestyles. "Product placements" or brand-name plugs in movies and videos should be prohibited. Radio and TV might be partially funded by tax revenues on a matching basis with user subscriptions or contributions. Product information might be provided on a user-fee basis through product directories, including on-demand directories that are accessible through computer services and interactive TV.

3. *Schools.* Schools should be declared advertising-free zones, administration of public schools should remain a public-sector function, and corporate-sponsored teaching modules should be banned from classroom use under the ban on in-school advertising.

Reclaiming our political spaces goes hand in hand with reclaiming our economic spaces.

Reclaiming Our Economic Spaces

The theories of both capitalism and communism acknowledge a basic truth expressed by the popular aphorism, "He who has the gold rules." Communist theory explicitly calls for worker ownership of the means of production. Adam Smith implicitly made the same assumption in his vision of an ideal market economy comprising small farmers and artisans—a circumstance in which owner, manager, and worker are commonly one and the same. Both communism and capitalism have failed to live up to their ideal in practice. Communism vested property rights in a distant state and denied the people any means of holding the state accountable for its exercise of those rights. Capitalism persistently transfers property rights to giant corporations and financial institutions that are largely unaccountable even to their owners.

There is an important structural alternative: a market economy composed primarily, though not exclusively, of family enterprises, small-scale co-ops, worker-owned firms, and neighborhood and municipal corporations. Malaysian consumer activist Bishan Singh calls it the community enterprise economy, as it melds the market forces of the money economy with the community forces of the social economy.[6] Historian and political economist Gar Alperovitz argues that just such a major restructuring of the American economy is already under way:

> [led] . . . by civic-minded entrepreneurs, innovative labor unions and effective local governments. . . . The number of firms now experimenting with worker-ownership approaches 10,000, involving perhaps 12 million people—more than the entire membership of private-sector trade unions. There are also more than 30,000 co-ops, including 4,000 consumer goods co-ops, 13,000 credit unions, nearly 100 cooperative banks and more than 100 cooperative insurance companies. Add to this 1,200 rural utilities and nearly 5,000 housing co-ops, plus another 115 telecommunication and cable co-ops.[7]

A common element of these innovations is that they establish local control of productive assets through institutions that are anchored in and accountable to the community.[8] This tends to make capital patient and rooted, an essential condition of stable, healthy communities. Such initiatives are thus of vital importance in building the foundations of healthy societies, but they are seriously disadvantaged by economic policies and institutions that favor the large, the global, and the predatory. Reclaiming our economic spaces requires that we transform such policies and institutions to shift the advantage in favor of the small and the locally accountable. To do so, we will need to restore the integrity and proper function of our financial institutions and systems, shift the social and environmental costs of production to producers and the users of their products, eliminate subsidies to big business, localize markets, deconcentrate capital ownership, establish corporate accountability, and restore market competition. The term *transform* is used advisedly. If these measures seem to run counter to the current trend toward the big and the global, that is precisely the intent.

0.5 Percent Financial Transactions Tax. A small tax on the purchase and sale of financial instruments such as stocks, bonds, foreign currencies, and derivatives would discourage very short-term speculation and arbitraging and remove an important source of unearned financial profit.

Graduated Surtax on Short-Term Capital Gains. A capital gains surtax would make many forms of speculation unprofitable, stabilize financial markets, and lengthen investment perspectives without penalizing long-term productive investment. The surtax on the sale of an asset held less than a week might be as high as 80 percent, falling to 50 percent on gains from assets held more than a week but less than six months, 35 percent on those held for more than six months but less than three years, and 10 percent on assets held more than three years.[9] This tax might be phased in over a period of several years. It should be additional to any other applicable taxes on income and should be applied to gains retained by financial institutions and investment funds as well as to those passed directly to individual investors. This surtax would have the effect of giving preferential treatment to income earned through productive work compared with the returns from simply holding money.

100 Percent Reserve Requirement on Demand Deposits. As far back as 1948, Henry C. Simmon, founder of the conservative University of Chicago school of economic monetarism, argued for a 100 percent reserve requirement on demand deposits to limit the ability of banks to create money and to give government greater control of the money supply. Many economists have since called for a similar measure.[10] The reserve requirement in the United States currently averages less than

10 percent. Phased in over several years to allow the financial system to adjust, this action would deflate the borrowing pyramid and help restore the connection between the creation of money and the creation of wealth.

Tight Regulation of Financial Derivatives. Many forms of derivatives are basically high-risk gambling instruments that serve primarily to generate fees for the investment houses that package and sell them. Like any other form of gambling, their creation, sale, and purchase should be tightly regulated and heavily taxed. Pension funds and other funds managed as public trusts should be strictly prohibited from trading in instruments so classified and from investing in companies that do. All publicly held corporations that engage in derivatives trading should be required to include a full report each quarter on their derivatives trading activities, report their potential financial exposure on such instruments, and reveal the proportion of their trading that consists of gambling-grade derivatives.

Preferential Treatment of Community Banks. The U.S. banking system was once made up of unitary or community banks that collected local savings deposits, made loans to local businesses, and financed mortgages to expand local home ownership. Successive changes in banking regulations have allowed the former community banks to be colonized by gigantic money-center banks that channel local deposits into the global money system. If the banking system is to serve local economies, the system of community banks must be restored by requiring money-center banks to divest their branches and by tightening community investment laws to require that a substantial majority of the investment portfolio of any bank covered by federal deposit insurance be invested within its service area and that all its investments meet federally mandated standards. The large, global money-center banks that wish to speculate with their depositors' money in risky investments around the world should not enjoy the advantage of federal insurance protection.[11]

Rigorous Enforcement of Antitrust Laws. Vigorous legal action should be taken to break up concentrations of corporate power. Buyout and merger proposals should be subject to intensive and skeptical governmental review, with the burden of proof resting on the proposing party to show that it will advance the human, in contrast to the corporate, interest.

Worker and Community Buyout Options. In most instances, the human interest is best served by patient and rooted capital. To this end, worker and community buyouts of corporate assets should be supported by public policy. For example, before a major corporation is allowed to close a plant or undertake a sale or merger, the affected workers and community should have a legal right of first option to buy out the assets on preferential terms. The terms should reflect the workers' years of personal investment of their labor in the company and the collective investment of the local community in public facilities that have made its local operations possible. In most businesses, there are many investors in addition to the formal shareholders, and this investment should be recognized in the law. Bankruptcy rules should be structured similarly to give employees and communities the option of taking possession, on preferential terms, of the assets of a corporation that has been restructured under bankruptcy proceedings. Similarly, when a company is required to divest parts of its operation under antitrust laws, employees or the community or both should have first option to buy the divested units. Rules governing company pension funds might allow their use by employees to purchase voting control of their firm's assets. Government oversight should ensure that worker and community buyouts are structured so that workers and communities have real control.

Tax Shifting. One of the most basic, but often violated, principles of tax policy is that taxes should be assessed against those activities that contribute to social and environmental dysfunction. Therefore, corporate tax law should be revised to shift taxes from things that benefit society, such as employment—including employer contributions to social security, health care, workers' compensation—in favor of taxing activities that contribute to social and environmental dysfunction, such as resource extraction, packaging, pollution, imports, corporate lobbying, and advertising. Such taxes would cascade up through the system and discourage the use of socially and environmentally harmful products. For example, a tax at the source on coal, oil, gas, and nuclear energy would increase end-user prices and encourage conservation and conversion to solar energy sources, such as solar heating, wind, hydro, photovoltaic, and biomass. Resulting increases in transportation costs would provide a nondiscriminatory natural tariff to encourage the localization of markets. The added cost of automobile commuting would encourage investment in public transit and locating closer to one's work. A tax on pollution emissions would encourage pollution control. A tax on the extraction of virgin materials would encourage conversion to less polluting, less materials-intensive product designs and modes of production and a greater reliance on recycled materials. Assessing manufacturers an amount sufficient to cover estimated disposal costs of their product packaging would discourage unnecessary packaging. Import tariffs would support a strong self-reliant economy.

Annual Profit Payout. Corporate income taxes should be eliminated simultaneously with the introduction of a requirement that corporations pay out their profits each year to their shareholders. Profits would thus be taxed as shareholder income at the shareholder's normal marginal rate. Depreciation would be adjusted for current replacement prices to allow sufficient retention of earnings to cover capital replacement. Research might be expensed in the current year. The double taxation of corporate profits—once to the corporation and once to the shareholder—would be eliminated, along with the deferral of shareholder taxes and the many distortions that the corporate income tax introduces into corporate decision making. If this were carried out universally, corporations would have no incentive to shift profits around the world to the jurisdiction with the lowest tax rate. Interest payments on debt financing would come directly out of profits rather than out of taxes, thus discouraging the use of debt and encouraging greater reliance on equity financing. Many leveraged buyouts that depend on the tax deductability of interest to make them profitable would be discouraged. Corporations would be taxed on specific activities that it is in society's interest to limit—such as the use of carbon fuels, resource extraction, and speculative financial transactions. Such taxes would be difficult to avoid. Corporate expansion would also become more difficult—a step toward keeping markets more competitive—because a company would not be able to grow simply as a consequence of a management decision to reinvest its profits rather than paying them out to shareholders. If a corporation wanted funds to expand, it would need to raise new money in the financial markets and make its case accordingly. Shareholders could, of course, be given the option of rolling over their dividends into additional stock, much like the current U.S. procedure on the taxation of earnings from mutual funds.

Corporate Subsidies. Welfare reform should give top priority to getting dependent corporations off the welfare rolls. Corporate subsidies range from resource depletion allowances to subsidized grazing fees, export subsidies, and tax abatements. Such subsidies should be systematically identified and eliminated, with the possible exception of those needed to establish and nurture locally owned, community-based enterprises.

Intellectual Property. Information is the only resource we have that is nondepletable and can be freely shared without depriving anyone of its use. Every contemporary human invention necessarily builds on the common heritage of human knowledge accumulated over thousands of years and countless generations. This is the information commons of the species. The justifiable purpose of intellectual property right protection is to provide incentives for research and creative contribution, not to create protected information monopolies. Laws relating to intellectual property rights should be reformed to conform to this principle. Such rights should be defined and interpreted narrowly and granted only for the minimum period of time necessary to allow those who have invested in for-profit research to recover their costs and a reasonable profit. The patenting of life-forms or genetic processes, discoveries funded with public monies, or processes or technologies that give the holder effective monopoly control over a type of research or class of products should be precluded by law. As with any common heritage resource, when there is a conflict between an exclusive private interest and a community interest, the community interest should prevail.

As business is localized, it will be possible to localize government as well. As Paul Hawken notes, it is the unwillingness of big business to accept the essential role of governmental regulation that creates the need for big government. Similarly, it is the interference of big business in governance that renders government ineffective. Hawken describes the dynamic:

> Business assumes the role of guardianship vis-à-vis the ecosystem and fails miserably in the task; governance steps in to try to mitigate the damage; business tries to sabotage this regulatory process and nimbly sidesteps those regulations that *are* put on the books; governance ups the ante and thereby becomes a hydra-headed bureaucratic monster choking off economic development while squandering money; business decries "interference in the marketplace" and sets out to redress its grievances by further corrupting the legislative and regulatory process in an attempt to become *de facto* guardian, if not *de jure*.[12]

The bigger our corporations, the greater their power to externalize costs and the greater the need for big government to protect the public interest and to clean up the consequent social and environmental messes. The more we cut our giant corporations down to human scale, the more we will be able to reduce the size of big government.

Addressing extreme inequality in the distribution of economic power is also important to decolonizing economic spaces. As our current experience shows, justice and sustainability are virtually impossible to achieve in an unequal world. Extreme inequality enables the economically powerful to colonize the environmental resources of the weak and thus consume beyond their environmental means. This commonly deprives the economically weak of their basic means of livelihood and delinks the economically strong from the environmental consequences of their actions. The excluded poor respond to their resulting insecurity by having many children—the one thing they can call their own and their only prospective source of care in their hour of need. As the rich expand their consumption and the poor produce more children, the human burden on the planet grows.

A more equitable and secure society limits individual opportunities for overconsumption and reduces the incentive to seek security through having large families. Additional measures toward creating more secure and equitable societies include the following:

Guaranteed Income. An idea long popular with both conservative and progressive economists, a guaranteed income merits serious consideration. It involves guaranteeing every person an income adequate to meet his or her basic needs. The amount would be lower for children than for adults but would be unaffected by a person's other income, wealth, work, gender, or marital status. It would replace social security and existing welfare programs. Since earned income would not reduce the guaranteed payment, there would be little disincentive to work for pay. Indeed, if some people chose not to work at all, this should not be considered a serious problem in labor-surplus societies. Although some wages would no doubt fall, employers might have to pay more to attract workers to unpleasant, menial tasks.[13] It would allow greater scope for those who wish to do unpaid work in the social economy. Such a scheme would be expensive but could be supported in most high-income countries by steep cuts in military spending, corporate subsidies, and existing entitlement programs and by tax increases on upper incomes, luxuries, and the things a sustainable society seeks to discourage. Combined with an adequate program of universal publicly funded health insurance and merit-based public fellowships for higher education, a guaranteed income would greatly increase the personal financial security afforded by more modest incomes. In low-income countries, agrarian reform and other efforts to achieve equitable access to productive natural resources for livelihood production might appropriately substitute for a guaranteed income.

Progressive Income and Consumption Taxes. Taxes on incomes up to the level required to meet basic needs in a comfortable, satisfying, and responsible way should be eliminated, as should sales or value-added taxes on basic food, clothing, shelter, health, personal hygiene, educational, and entertainment or recreational expenditures needed to sustain good living. There should likewise be a sharply graduated tax on incomes above the guaranteed minimum—going as high as 90 percent on top income brackets. Inheritance or trust income should be taxed the same as any other personal income. This would greatly reduce incentives for individuals to seek excessive incomes yet should not discourage anyone from doing socially useful work. Any job that is so distasteful that qualified applicants cannot be attracted for a reasonable compensation of, say, no more than fifteen times the guaranteed minimum income should be restructured to make it more acceptable. If the problem is that a corporation is too big, then it should be broken up. We would simply learn to do without the services of those who require a greater inducement than this to do socially useful work in an effective and efficient manner. There should be a substantial luxury tax on nonessential consumption items that are socially harmful or environmentally wasteful or destructive. Personal charitable contributions, including to family foundations, should be fully tax exempt, thus providing a substantial incentive for individuals with excess incomes to support a strong independent sector as a counter to the power of the state.

Equitable Allocation of Paid Employment. Access to opportunities for paid employment should also be allocated as fairly as possible through measures to reduce the workweek and assure equal employment opportunity regardless of gender, race, or other extraneous considerations.

Such measures must all be phased in over time and adjusted to reflect experience. The idea here is not to provide a prescriptive blueprint but rather to illustrate the kinds of policies that would lead us toward healthier societies. Different approaches will surely be appropriate in different settings, and the administration and funding of such initiatives should be undertaken by the smallest and most local governance units possible. For example, in predominantly agrarian societies with equitable land distribution, a very small guaranteed minimum income might be adequate. The same might be true in stable egalitarian societies in which there are ample employment opportunities for all who wish to work. A guaranteed income is probably most necessary to correct imbalances in societies such as the United States, where there is extreme inequality and a job market in which jobs paying an adequate wage to maintain a decent living have become increasingly scarce.

If we are to manage our economic spaces in the human interest, we will need appropriate accounting tools suited to this purpose. Sixto Roxas, an economist and former international bank executive from the Philippines, explains that conventional national income accounts do not meet this need, because they measure the costs and benefits of economic activity from the standpoint of the firm, not the community. The differences are fundamental. For example, the firm profits by employing the least possible number of workers at the lowest possible wage. The community profits by having its members fully employed at the highest possible wage. The firm may profit by depleting a local forest or mineral resource, while the community is left devastated.

Roxas and his colleagues are developing a community-based accounting system that assesses economic costs and benefits in terms of their consequences for the health of households, communities, and ecosystems.[14] They also record how much of the value generated from local economic activity remains in the community and how much flows out. Thus, if local forests are being clear-cut and the timber and profits are being exported while the community is left with a barren landscape, this shows up as a net loss rather than the net gain recorded by conventional economic accounting. Significant attention is needed to developing and applying such systems as economic management tools.

Localizing the Global System

As we work at the national and subnational levels to reclaim our local political and economic spaces, we must also transform the global system to create a bias toward the local. This does not mean that global institutions will or can be eliminated. Although we can reduce environmental, technological, and economic interdependence, we cannot eliminate it, nor would we want to. Such interdependence is the foundation of the emerging global consciousness that is essential to both our collective survival and our evolutionary potential as a species. Our goal should be to create a multilevel system of institutions through which we can reduce *unnecessary* interdependence and manage the remaining interdependence in ways that maintain a persistent bias in favor of:

- Empowering the local to control and manage local resources to local benefit;
- Making it difficult for any locality to externalize its production or consumption costs beyond its borders; and
- Encouraging cooperation among localities in the search for solutions to shared problems.

A principal mandate of the global and regional institutions in this multilevel system should be to support and protect the efforts of localities to set their own rules of economic engagement, to give preference to local producers using local resources to meet local needs, and to resist the external colonization of their markets and resources. Suggested measures at the global level to create this bias in favor of the human interest include the following:

International Debt Reduction for Low-Income Countries. The poor of low-income countries must be released from the national debt bondage that leaves them defenseless against the colonization of their economies and resources by the global system. This should begin with an orderly process of repudiating, under precedents already established in international law, "odious" debts that were incurred through *ultra vires* contracts (made by a person without proper authority) or used for purposes that were not beneficial to the people of the territory on whose behalf the obligations were incurred. Much of the outstanding international debt of low-income countries could be classified as odious under these principles—including a substantial portion of the debt owed to the multilateral banks.[15] An international convention should be established under which governments of indebted low-income countries can declare such public international debts uncollectible, with the sanction and support of an appropriate international body. In addition, an international fund should be created, as suggested below, to write off the remaining debts in return for agreements that would preclude governments from re-creating them. Most of the private banks with Southern debt exposure have created loan loss reserves to cover nonrepayment. Although they maintain the debts on their books and continue to demand that Southern countries repay them, the banks would not be consequentially harmed, and perhaps would be usefully disciplined, if the debts were not repaid. Repudiation of World Bank and other multilateral bank loans would force these banks to call their governmental guarantees to cover their debts and create pressure to close them—an action recommended below.

International Financial Transactions Tax. A 0.5 percent tax should be collected on all spot transactions in foreign exchange, including foreign exchange deliveries pursuant to futures contracts and options, as proposed by James Tobin, winner of the 1981 Nobel Prize for economics.[16] The 0.5 percent "Tobin" tax on foreign exchange transactions would help dampen speculative international financial movements but would be too small to deter commodity trade or serious international investment commitments. It would increase the weight given by market participants to the long term and give greater autonomy to individual countries in setting domestic monetary policies. The priority for applying the proceeds from this tax should be to establish a debt repayment fund to retire those international debts of low-income countries that cannot be repudiated under legal precedents relating to odious debt. A second use of this tax should be to finance the operations of the United Nations and its specialized agencies.

Regulation of Transnational Trade and Investment. International agreements are needed regarding trade and the standards of conduct for transnational corporations to guarantee the right of countries and localities to manage their external trade relations and to set the rules and standards for businesses operating in their jurisdictions.[17] These agreements should include provision for coordinating antitrust action among participating nations to break up large transnational corporations and take such other actions as required to ensure the competitiveness of international markets. These agreements should also ensure the right of each country and people to set their own rules regarding intellectual property rights within their own jurisdictions, while limiting the ability of any corporation or country to monopolize and withhold beneficial information and technology from other people who might benefit from its use. These agreements should adhere to the basic principle that when transnational corporations participate in a local economy they come only as invited guests, not as occupying forces, and are expected to honor local rules and customs.

Environmental Resources Monitoring. One of the most difficult challenges of balancing economic needs with environmental limits is to make it difficult for localities to colonize the environmental spaces of others, either through cross-boundary discharge of environmental pollutants or through trade. There is an urgent need to develop environmental information systems that make such shifting of environmental burdens visible and thus encourage environmental self-reliance. With an appropriate strengthening of mandate and technical capacities, the United Nations Environmental Programme (UNEP) might coordinate the development and use of appropriate statistical and accounting methods and the negotiation of international agreements on standards, monitoring, and dispute adjudication relating to regional and national cost internalization. Use of such monitoring capacities should be largely decentralized, with each locality, district, nation, and region maintaining its own accounts. When disputes regarding the shifting of environmental burdens cannot be resolved directly through bilateral negotiations, they should be settled through submission to the appropriate judicial bodies, including the International Court of Justice, for adjudication.

Specific attention will be required to restructure the system of global economic governance—in particular the Bretton Woods institutions. It is unworkable to have the functions of global governance divided among a number of independent global agencies with overlapping jurisdictions and conflicting mandates. Under the current arrangement, responsibility for dealing with global finance rests with the International Monetary Fund (IMF). Responsibility for setting and enforcing the rules of international trade and investment is assigned to the World Trade Organization (WTO). The dominant institution in setting development priorities in low-income countries is the World Bank. All three of the Bretton Woods institutions consistently give priority to the corporate interest over the human interest. Responsibility for the coordination of international economic, social, cultural, educational, health, and related matters rests with the Economic and Social Council of the United Nations, which leans more toward the human interest. Although the Bretton Woods institutions are designated specialized agencies of the United Nations, they are far more important and powerful than the other specialized UN agencies and reject any UN effort to coordinate or oversee their activities.

It is time to dismantle the Bretton Woods institutions and consolidate the functions of economic governance under bodies that are fully accountable to the United Nations. Whereas the mandates of the Bretton Woods institutions were to advance economic *globalization*, their successor agencies should be given mandates to advance economic *localization* by carrying out the activities recommended above. The internal governance processes of the successor agencies should be publicly transparent and open to participation by both governmental and citizen oversight organizations.

The World Bank. The World Bank should be closed. Its major function is to make loans to poor countries, which necessarily increases their international indebtedness. So long as the Bank remains in business, Southern economies will remain indebted to the international system. Creating indebtedness is not a useful function, and it is time to acknowledge that the World Bank was a bad idea. Closing it is an essential step toward assuring that as international debts are eliminated, they are not instantly re-created. The same is true of the regional multilateral development banks, which should be closed as well. Once freed from the corrupting influence of debt dependence and the dictates of the multilateral banks, low-income countries will be in a far better position to undertake people-centered structural reforms aimed at decolonizing their economies and moving toward greater self-reliance, environmental sustainability, and economic justice.

The International Monetary Fund (IMF). The IMF might be replaced by a United Nations International Finance Organization (UNIFO) responsible for (1) managing the process of repudiating and writing off the international debts of low-income countries; (2) regulating international financial markets; (3) providing a forum within which governments can coordinate policies aimed at keeping their foreign accounts in balance; (4) coordinating measures to establish enforceable reserve requirements for the lending of quasi-international currencies, such as Eurodollars, in instances when they are not presently regulated by national governments; and (5) collecting and administering the Tobin tax on foreign exchange transactions.

The World Trade Organization (WTO). The WTO should be replaced by a UN Regulatory Agency for Transnational Trade and Investment (UNRATTI). The prime mandate of UNRATTI should be to facilitate the negotiation of agreements relating to the regulation of transnational corporations and trade and to serve as a coordinating forum for governmental actions aimed at enforcing them. The performance of UNRATTI should be assessed in terms of progress toward increased local economic self-reliance and global equity. Transnational corporations should be barred from participating on national delegations to UNRATTI or from making other representations to it, except when they are specifically requested to provide information. In function and purpose, UNRATTI should be nearly the mirror opposite of the GATT–WTO.

Corporate libertarians will doubtless point out that the measures suggested here will significantly interfere with the operations of transnational corporations and financial markets. That, of course, is precisely their intent. Our goal should be to create a system that works well for people. Corporations are only a means of meeting human needs. If, in doing what we believe will best serve our needs, we find useful roles for corporations, then we should by all means make such use of them. But the right to decide must reside with people.

There may also be complaints that these measures will create large global regulatory bodies at a time when the political sentiment is toward reducing governmental regulation. The intention in all instances is to create a framework in which actual regulatory action is taken at the lowest possible level. The function of global- and regional-level institutions is to support the local in such matters. We must keep in mind, however, that it is primarily the existence of powerful global corporations that creates a need for global regulatory bodies of sufficient power to hold them accountable to the public interest. The less obtrusive global corporate power becomes, the less the need for obtrusive global regulatory bodies. By reducing the size and power of global corporations and moving the system toward more rooted and patient capital, we limit the need for international bureaucracies and police powers.

By taking actions such as those suggested above, we can reclaim the power we have yielded to the global system and restore our ability to rebuild our communities and heal the earth as we work to create healthy societies that allow us to experience life in its fullness and diversity. Otherwise, we will continue to live under the tyrannical rule of a global financial system that is leading us in the direction of almost certain social and ecological collapse. We must hold one thought clearly in mind: The global institutions of money have only the power we yield to them. It is our power. We can reclaim it.

Epilogue:
A Choice for Life

*I wonder if we wouldn't become more gracefully produc-
tive by recognizing that we are all living cells within living organisms like cities, bioregions, continents, and the
earth itself. Could we lessen our stress, become healthier
and more whole, if we saw our work as simply helping
these organisms realize their own living wholeness?*
—*Daniel Kemmis, mayor of Missoula, Montana*[1]

*The question I constantly ask myself is, "What are the
creative catalytic linkages that strengthen community and
enable communities of people to exercise social and ecological control on economic and technological processes?"*
—*Vandana Shiva, global networker*[2]

The spiritual and political roots of our crisis run
deep. It is little wonder that a policy discourse
dominated by an economics that takes no account of
either the spiritual or the political remains so unproductive. It is in the discourse of an awakening civil
society that we find a more realistically grounded perspective. It is as if we are rousing from a deep cultural
trance to rediscover neglected political dimensions of
our societies and spiritual dimensions of our being. If
our crisis is a consequence of an excessively partial view
of reality, as I believe it is, then this awakening—by bringing us to a more holistic awareness of who we are—may
lead to long overdue acceptance of essential responsibility for how we use our technical and organizational
capacities.

As science tells the cosmic story, consciousness is
nothing more than an illusion born of chemical reac-
tions. It is a story without meaning or purpose that

leaves us with little reason to restrain our hedonistic impulses. Reading Thomas Berry's *The Dream of the Earth*[3] awakened my own belief that our survival as a species may depend as much as anything on discovering a new story that gives us a reason to live—a story that helps us ask one of the most basic of questions: why?

This question has been very much on my mind the past few years. The basic outlines of what we must do to avoid self-destruction as a species have long seemed clear to many of us. Yet I came to sense that if survival holds no larger meaning for us, avoiding extinction is not a sufficient reason to draw us to the difficult changes we must make. To make a choice for life, we must be drawn by a compelling vision of new possibilities grounded in a sense of meaning.

My own search for such understanding played a major role in my decision to break with my established routines and write this book. Such a search leads inevitably beyond the fact-based world of science into faith and personal subjective experience.

The story I sought remained elusive until late 1993, when an autographed copy of Duane Elgin's *Awakening Earth* arrived unsolicited in my mail. Elgin and I had never met and knew each other only through our writings. His book seemed like a divine gift. The story of the epic unfolding of the human consciousness, as revealed to him during the course of an extended personal meditation, spoke to my own inner being, opening me to a profound sense of the cosmic purpose behind the current human dilemma and the opportunities that lie ahead. It also gave me new hope for the prospects of our success. It deeply influenced the thrust of this book, particularly the concluding chapters.

Elgin's essential message is captured in two brief sentences:

As humanity develops its capacity for reflective consciousness, it enables the universe to achieve self-referencing knowing of itself. Through humanity's awakening, the universe acquires the ability to look back and reflect upon itself—in wonder, awe, and appreciation.[4]

This idea suggests that we inherit through our birth a responsibility far beyond ensuring our own survival. Our wondrous ability to perceive beauty and feel love is an essential aspect of our being, central to our role in a grand, continuously unfolding cosmic event. It is a far more logical thesis than the alternative premise that our experience of consciousness is nothing more than a chance and meaningless event in an otherwise lifeless universe, or that we were given the miracle of life so that we could destroy the fruits of millions of years of evolution on this unique planet. It is an idea that calls on us to accept responsibility for the impact of our actions on the course of evolution and to assume a conscious and responsible role in creating conditions on this planet that advance the continuing evolutionary process.

It suggests as well that our relationship to the larger web of life is neither that of master nor that of servant. Rather, our existence is integral to and inseparable from the universal consciousness that manifests itself through our individual being. This suggests to me that we best serve both the whole and ourselves by experiencing with wonder and joy the awesome beauty of a living universe and by living our own lives to the fullest in relation to self, family, community, the planet, and the cosmos.

It suggests as well that although we are neither higher nor lower than other forms of life, we do have our own distinctive capacities and functions in relation to the whole. It is for us to develop these capacities and discover our intended functions.

We unquestionably have more power and greater freedom than other species on this planet. To our own peril, we have confused this power and freedom with the right to dominate, rather than recognizing that it confers on us only a greater responsibility for the whole. In Elgin's words:

> Our universe is deeply caring but intent upon giving us the precious freedom we need to develop our unique capacity for reflective self-determination. . . . After giving us the priceless gift of existence, the Meta-universe demonstrates its great compassion by not interfering in our choices, whether personal or planetary.[5]

For me, it gives a compelling meaning to the transformation to which I believe the Ecological Revolution is calling us.

Our species, far beyond any other, has been engaged in a continuing process of intellectual, social, and technological evolution toward ever greater species abilities. It is one of the great and mysterious wonders of the cosmos that as each of our developmental stages exhausts itself in preparing for the next, it creates the imperative to break free from the familiar and take an uncertain step into the unknown.

I am among those who believe that we are now being invited to take such a step, to cross the threshold into a new era. A scientific paradigm that largely dismissed consciousness focused our life energies on the task of mastering the secrets of the physical world and on building the technical capabilities that now open vast opportunities to build healthy societies devoted to advancing our social, intellectual, and spiritual growth. We have misused this capacity in many terrible ways and have yet to establish that we have the maturity as a species to use our newfound powers wisely. That same technology, however, gives us the ability to eliminate physical want and deprivation from the world; to give all human beings the freedom to devote a larger portion of their life energies to activities that are more fulfilling than the struggle for daily physical survival; and to bring ourselves into balance with nature.

Both the failures and the successes of the West in the era that is now passing can be traced to imbalances in our image of ourselves and the cosmos. Materialistic monism was critical to achieving our technical mastery, but it led to the development of the material aspect of our societies to the exclusion of the spiritual. Dualism left mind and body divided, each alienated from the other to the detriment of both. I believe that the future of East and West, South and North may now depend on graduating to a coevolutionary perspective that brings together the spiritual and material aspects of our being in a synergistic union to create whole persons, communities, and societies.

Our spiritual awakening may be integral to our political awakening. Alienation from our spiritual nature has left us exposed to manipulation by both the advertisers who turn our longing for spiritual connection into an insatiable quest for money and the political demagogues who connect this quest with the corporate interest. Just as the cultural messages of science would leave us spiritually dead, the ideological doctrines of corporate libertarianism would leave us politically inert.

The Copernican Revolution divided science and religion and initiated an awakening to the potentials of the material side of our existence. The Ecological Revolution now invites us to experience ourselves as spiritually alive and politically active participants in the unfolding exploration of the potentials of a living universe.

As the old assumptions crumble, so too will the old political alignments. Traditional distinctions between Left and Right, liberal and conservative, have lost their meaning. Appeals to a political center are futile posturing by those who fail to recognize the meaning and significance of the challenges we face. The political future belongs to those who have the courage and vision to form new alliances based on ways of thinking that cannot be defined by the old categories.

We must approach this difficult period with the mutual caring and tolerance for diversity that are the essential foundations of the healthy societies we hope to create. Even as we each seek to remain centered in our core values and to build alliances with those who share such values, we must be constantly aware that we are engaged in an act of creation for which there is no blueprint. We are all learners in an unfolding process, requiring that we look with a critical eye and an open mind for the kernel of truth in each idea and the spark of goodness in each person. We are embarking on what may be the most profound change of course in human history, and it requires that we bring to bear the full creative potential of our species.

Appendix
The People's Earth Declaration: A Proactive Agenda for the Future

We, the participants in the International NGO [non-governmental organization] Forum of Global Forum '92, have met in Rio de Janeiro as citizens of planet earth to share our concerns, our dreams, and our plans for creating a new future for our world. We emerge from these deliberations with a profound sense that in the richness of our diversity we share a common vision of a human society grounded in the values of simplicity, love, peace, and reverence for life. We now go forth in solidarity to mobilize the moral and human resources of the civil societies of all nations in a unified social movement committed to the realization of this vision.

The urgency of our commitment is heightened by the choice of the world's political leaders in the official deliberations of the Earth Summit to neglect many of the most fundamental causes of the accelerating ecological and social devastation of our planet. While they engage in the fine tuning of an economic system that serves the short-term interests of the few at the expense of the many, the leadership for more fundamental change has fallen by default to the organizations and movements of civil society. We accept this challenge.

In so doing we wish to remind the world's political and corporate leaders that the authority of the state and the powers of the private corporation are grants extended to these institutions by the sovereign people, by civil society, to serve the collective human interest. It is the people's right to demand that governments and corporations remain accountable to the public will and interest. Yet through a process of global economic integration pressed on the world's people by the G7 governments, the Bretton Woods institutions—the World Bank, International Monetary Fund (IMF), and General Agreement on Tariffs and Trade (GATT)—and transnational corporations, the sovereign right and ability of the world's people to protect their economic, social, cultural, and environmental interests against the growing power of transnational capital is being seriously and rapidly eroded.

This erosion has been only one of the many damaging consequences of a development model grounded in the pursuit of economic growth and consumption to the exclusion of the human and natural interest. Others include the increasing spiritual impoverishment of human society, the economic impoverishment of some 1.2 billion people, the rapidly widening gap between rich and poor, economic racism, institutionalized exploitation of women, the displacement of millions of peoples from their lands and communities, marginalization of the handicapped, and the progressive destruction of the ecological systems that sustain us all.

The path of deepening international debt, structural adjustment, market deregulation, free trade, and the monopolization of intellectual property rights that currently dominates policy thought and action is a path to collective self-destruction, not to sustainable development. We will use our votes, our moral authority, and our purchasing power to remove from positions of authority those who insist on advancing these socially and ecologically destructive policies to serve short-term elite interests.

The Bretton Woods institutions have served as the major instruments by which these destructive policies have been imposed on the world. They constitute a formidable barrier to just and sustainable development. We will work for their transformation or replacement by more suitable institutions. Until they have become fully transparent, publicly accountable, and supportive of the human interest, they must not be allowed to capture control of the sustainability agenda.

The world's military forces survive primarily as instruments to protect elite interests and suppress the civil unrest that results from economic injustice. They further place an unconscionable burden on earth's scarce ecological resources. We will work for their elimination and the transfer of their resources to more beneficial purposes. As a first step we will work to end international arms trade and assistance.

These are realities the official UNCED [United Nations Conference on Environment and Development] process has avoided. They have been among our central concerns.

We have not, however, limited our attention to critique. We have also sought to define our vision for an alternative future and our agenda for its accomplishment. We are diverse in our experience and languages. We seek alternatives for which there are no clear models. The existing dominant development model and its supporting institutions emerged over a period of some 500 years. The two weeks we have spent in deliberations in Rio are only a beginning toward crafting an alternative. We have achieved a broadly shared consensus that the following principles will guide our continuing collective effort.

- The fundamental purpose of economic organization is to meet the community's basic needs, such as for food, shelter, clothing, education, health, and the enjoyment of culture. This purpose must take priority over all other forms of consumption, particularly wasteful and destructive forms of consumption such as consumerism and military spending—both of which must be eliminated without further delay. Other immediate priorities include energy conservation, shifting to reliance on solar energy sources, and converting agriculture to sustainable practices that minimize dependence on non-renewable and ecologically harmful inputs.
- Beyond meeting basic physical needs, the quality of human life depends more on the development of social relationships, creativity, cultural and artistic expression, spirituality, and opportunity to be a productive member of the community than on the ever increasing consumption of material goods. Everyone, including the handicapped, must have a full opportunity to participate in all these forms of development.
- Organizing economic life around decentralized relatively self-reliant local economies that control and manage their own productive resources, provide all people an equitable share in the control and benefits of productive resources, and have the right to safeguard their own environmental and social standards is essential to sustainability. This strengthens attachment to place, encourages environmental stewardship, enhances local food security, and accommodates to distinctive cultural identities. Trade between such local economies, as between nations, should be just and balanced. Where the rights and

interests of the corporation conflict with the rights and interests of the community, the latter must prevail.

- All elements of society, irrespective of gender, class, or ethnic identity, have a right and obligation to participate fully in the life and decisions of the community. The presently poor and disenfranchised, in particular, must become full participants. Women's roles, needs, values and wisdom are especially central to decision-making on the fate of the Earth. There is an urgent need to involve women at all levels of policy making, planning and implementation on an equal basis with men. Gender balance is essential to sustainable development. Indigenous people also bring vital leadership to the task of conserving the earth and its creatures and in creating a new life-affirming global reality. Indigenous wisdom constitutes one of human society's important and irreplaceable resources. The rights and contributions of indigenous people must be recognized.
- While overall population growth is a danger to the health of the planet, growth in the numbers of the world's overconsumers is a more immediate threat than population growth among the poor. Assuring all people the means to meet their basic needs is an essential precondition to stabilizing population. Reproductive freedom and access to comprehensive reproductive health care and family planning are basic human rights.
- Knowledge is humanity's one infinitely expandable resource. Beneficial knowledge in whatever form, including technology, is a part of the collective human heritage and should be freely shared with all who might benefit from it.
- Debt bondage, whether of an individual or a country, is immoral and should be held unenforceable in international and civil law.
- Transparency must be the fundamental premise underlying decision making in all public institutions, including at international levels.

Implementation of these principles toward transformational change will require a massive commitment to education. New understanding, values, and skills are needed at all levels and across all elements of society. We will educate ourselves, our communities, and our nations to this end.

We acknowledge our debt to indigenous wisdom and values. These have greatly enriched our deliberations and will be sources of continuing learning. We will honor this heritage and work to protect the rights of indigenous people.

Our thinking has also been enriched by the teachings of the many religious traditions represented among us. We recognize the central place of spiritual values and spiritual development in the societies we seek to create. We commit ourselves to live by the values of simplicity, love, peace, and reverence for life shared by all religious traditions.

Our efforts in Rio have produced a number of people's treaties to define more specific commitments to one another for action at local, national, and international levels. These treaties are in varying stages of development. All are documents in process. We will further refine them through countless dialogues and negotiations throughout the world as ever larger numbers of people join in our growing movement.

We invite the leaders of business and government to join us in this act of global citizenship. They must, however, know that we no longer wait for them to lead us in dealing with a global reality they have so far chosen to ignore. The time is too short and the stakes too high.

We, the people of the world, will mobilize the forces of transnational civil society behind a widely shared agenda that bonds our many social movements in pursuit of just, sustainable, and participatory human societies. In so doing we are forging our own instruments and processes for redefining the nature and meaning of human progress and for transforming those institutions that no longer respond to our needs. We welcome to our cause all people who share our commitment to peaceful and democratic change in the interest of our living planet and the human societies it sustains.

International NGO Forum
United Nations Conference on Environment and Development
Rio de Janeiro, Brazil
June 12, 1992

Notes

Prologue: A Personal Journey

1. On the occasion of the Liberty Medal Ceremony, Philadelphia, July 4, 1994.
2. This paper is available in monograph form from the Asian NGO Coalition, P.O. Box 3107, QCCPO 1103, Quezon City, Philippines; fax (63-2) 921-5122. It has also been published in a number of other formats and languages, including as a two-part serialization in the Society for International Development journal *Development* (1993, no. 4 and 1994, no. 4).

Chapter 1. From Hope to Crisis

1. Jerry Mander, *In the Absence of the Sacred* (San Francisco: Sierra Club Books, 1991), p. 26.
2. United Nations Development Programme (UNDP), *Human Development Report 1993* (New York: Oxford University Press, 1993), p. 12.
3. UNDP, *Human Development Report 1994* (New York: Oxford University Press, 1994), p. 31.
4. United Nations High Commissioner for Refugees, *The State of the World's Refugees* (New York: Penguin Books, 1993).
5. Gene Stephens, "The Global Crime Wave," *The Futurist*, July–August 1994, 22–28.

6. "Out-of-Wedlock Births up since '83, Report Indicates," *New York Times*, July 20, 1994, pp. A-l, A-16.
7. UNDP, *Human Development Report 1994*, p. 31.
8. UNDP, *Human Development Report 1994*, p. 47.
9. United Nations High Commissioner for Refugees, *State of the World's Refugees*.
10. Gallup poll, June 2, 1990.
11. Harris poll, January 3, 1994.
12. "The New Deal: What Companies and Employees Owe One Another," *Fortune*, June 13, 1994, 44–52.
13. Poll result cited by Robert Reich, U.S. secretary of labor, in a presentation to the Democratic Leadership Council, Washington, D.C., November 22, 1944. The figure for those without college degrees is 68 percent.
14. Kettering Foundation, *Citizens and Politics: A View from Main Street America* (Dayton, Ohio: Kettering Foundation, 1991), pp. iii–iv, as quoted in Stephen Craig, *The Malevolent Leaders: Population Discontent in America* (Boulder, Colo.: Westview Press, 1993), p. 83.
15. Seymour Lipset and William Schneider, *The Confidence Gap: Business, Labor, and Government in the Public Mind* (Baltimore: Johns Hopkins University Press, 1987), p. 410; Elizabeth Hann Hastings and Philip K. Hastings (eds.), *Index to International Public Opinion, 1992–1993* (Westport, Conn.: Greenwood Press, 1994).

Chapter 2. End of the Open Frontier

1. Royal Society of London and the U.S. National Academy of Sciences, *Population Growth, Resource Consumption, and a Sustainable World* (London and Washington, D.C.: Authors, 1992), as cited in Lester R. Brown, "A New Era Unfolds," in Brown, et al., *State of the World 1993* (New York: W. W. Norton, 1993), p. 3.
2. Herman E. Daly, "Sustainable Growth: An Impossibility Theorem," *Development*, no. 3/4 (1990): 45.
3. Originally published in Henry Jarrett (ed.), *Environmental Quality in a Growing Economy* (Baltimore: Johns Hopkins University Press, 1968), pp. 3–14.
4. See the "guiding principles for the creation of healthy twenty-first century societies" enumerated in Chapter 21.
5. Lance Davis and Robert Huttenback, *Mammon and the Pursuit of Empire* (New York: Cambridge University Press, 1986), as cited in Richard Douthwaite, *The Growth Illusion* (Tulsa, Okla.: Council Oak Books, 1993), p. 46.
6. Davis and Huttenback, as cited in Douthwaite, p. 46.
7. These statistics were compiled by William E. Rees and Mathis Wackernagel, "Ecological Footprints and Appropriated Carrying Capacity: Measuring the Natural Capital Requirements of the Human Economy," in A-M Jannson, M. Hammer, C. Folke, and R. Costanza (eds.), *Investing in Natural Capital: The Ecological Economics Approach to Sustainability* (Washington, D.C.: Island Press, 1994), p. 380. Note that 1 hectare equals 2.47 acres. For further documentation of the thesis that human activities now exceed many of the natural limits of the ecosystem, see Robert Goodland, Herman E. Daly, and Salah El Serafy (eds.), *Population, Technology, and Lifestyle: The Transition to Sustainability* (Washington, D.C.: Island Press, 1992), pp. 3–22; Donella H. Meadows, Dennis L. Meadows, and Jørgen Randers, *Beyond the Limits* (Post Mills, Vt.: Chelsea

Green Publishing, 1992); Gerald O. Barney, *Global 2000 Revisited* (Arlington, Va.: Millennium Institute, 1993); and Sandra Postel, "Carrying Capacity: Earth's Bottom Line," in Lester R. Brown et al., *State of the World 1994* (New York: W. W. Norton, 1994), pp. 3–21.

8. Alan Durning, *How Much Is Enough? The Consumer Society and the Future of the Earth* (New York: W. W. Norton, 1992), p. 56.

9. Vandana Shiva, "Homeless in the 'Global Village,'" *Earth Ethics* 5, no. 4 (1994): 3.

10. "Aid for Profit: Japanese DDA in Leyte," *Kabalikat*, September 1990: 8–10.

11. "Pollution and the Poor," *The Economist*, February 15, 1992, 16–17.

12. Peter M. Vitousek et al., "Human Appropriation of the Products of Photosynthesis," *BioScience* 24, no. 6 (1986): 368–73.

13. Rees and Wackernagel, p. 382.

14. Rees and Wackernagel, p. 374.

15. Manus van Brakel and Maria Buitenkamp, *Sustainable Netherlands: A Perspective for Changing Northern Lifestyles* (Amsterdam: Friends of the Earth, 1992).

16. Alex Hittle, *The Dutch Challenge: A Look at How the United States' Consumption Must Change to Achieve Global Sustainability* (Washington, D.C.: Friends of the Earth, 1994).

17. van Brakel and Buitenkamp, p. 6.

18. David Pimentel, Rebecca Harman, Matthew Pacenza, Jason Pecarsky, and Marcia Pimentel, "Natural Resources and an Optimal Human Population," *Population and Environment* 15, no. 5 (1994): 352.

19. Pimentel et al., 364.

20. Pimentel et al., 363.

Chapter 3. The Growth Illusion

1. Mahbub ul Haq, special advisor to the United Nations Development Programme's annual *Human Development Report*, in his Barbara Ward Lecture to the 21st World Conference of the Society for International Development, Mexico City, April 1994.

2. International Chamber of Commerce (ICC), *The Business Charter for Sustainable Development* (Paris: ICC, 1990), as quoted in Paul Ekins, "Sustainability First," in Paul Ekins and Manfred Max-Neef, *Real-Life Economics: Understanding Wealth Creation* (London: Routledge, 1992), p. 415.

3. Jan Tinbergen and Roefie Hueting, "GNP and Market Prices: Wrong Signals for Sustainable Economic Success That Mask Environmental Destruction," in Robert Goodland, Herman E. Daly, and Salah El Serafy (eds.), *Population, Technology, and Lifestyle: The Transition to Sustainability* (Washington, D.C.: Island Press, 1992), pp. 52–62.

4. Tinbergen and Hueting, pp. 52–62.

5. Richard Douthwaite, "The Growth Illusion," in Jonathan Greenberg and William Kistler (eds.), *Buying America Back* (Tulsa, Okla.: Council Oak Books, 1992), pp. 92–96.

6. Paul Ekins (ed.), *The Living Economy* (London: Routledge, 1986), p. 8.

7. Herman E. Daly and John B. Cobb Jr., *For the Common Good: Redirecting the Economy toward Community, the Environment, and a Sustainable Future* (Boston: Beacon Press, 1989), pp. 401–55.

8. UNDP, *Human Development Report, 1991* (New York: Oxford University Press, 1991).
9. Richard Douthwaite, *The Growth Illusion* (Tulsa, Okla.: Council Oak Books, 1993), pp. 96–119.
10. Douthwaite, *The Growth Illusion*, pp. 33–50.
11. Robin Broad and John Cavanagh, *Plundering Paradise* (Berkeley, Calif.: University of California Press, 1993), pp. 24–31.
12. Broad and Cavanagh, pp. 24–31.
13. Eduardo A. Morato, "Far More Destructive Non-Events amidst Us," *Manila Chronicle*, June 18, 1991.
14. Broad and Cavanagh, pp. 61–72.
15. Morato, "Far More Destructive Non-Events amidst Us."
16. See John Young, "Mining the Earth," in Lester R. Brown et al., *State of the World 1992* (New York: W. W. Norton, 1992), p. 111.
17. Edgar Cahn and Jonathan Rowe, *Time Dollars* (Emmaus, Pa.: Rodale Press, 1992).
18. Clarence Shubert, "Creating People-Friendly Cities," *PCDForum Column* no. 72, April 5, 1994.
19. Douthwaite, *The Growth Illusion*, pp. 33–50.
20. Edward McNall Burns, *Western Civilizations: Their History and Their Culture*, 5th ed. (New York: W. W. Norton, 1958), pp. 659–60.
21. Douthwaite, *The Growth Illusion*, pp. 50–56.
22. Bennett Harrison, *Lean and Mean: The Changing Landscape of Corporate Power in the Age of Flexibility* (New York: Basic Books, 1994), pp. 191–92.
23. Robert Goodland, Herman E. Daly, and Salah El Serafy (eds.), *Population, Technology, and Lifestyle: The Transition to Sustainability* (Washington, D.C.: Island Press, 1992), p. xv.
24. Alicia Korten, "Cultivating Disaster: Structural Adjustment and Costa Rican Agriculture," *Multinational Monitor*, July/August 1993, 20–22.
25. Bruce Rich, *Mortgaging the Earth: The World Bank, Environmental Impoverishment, and the Crisis of Development* (Boston: Beacon Press, 1994), p. 155.
26. Clarence Maloney, "Environmental and Project Displacement of Population in India. Part I: Development and Deracination," *University Field Staff International Report*, no. 14 (Indianapolis, Ind.: University Field Staff International, 1990–91), p. 1.
27. Rich, p. 156.
28. *Southeast Asia Regional Consultation on People's Participation in Environmentally Sustainable Development*, vol. 2, *National & Regional Reports* (Manila: Asian NGO Coalition, 1991), pp. 1–2.
29. Walter Hook, "Paving over Bangkok: Development Bank–Funded Highways Will Displace Tens of Thousands," *Sustainable Transport*, no. 2 (September 1993): 7.

Chapter 4. Rise of Corporate Power in America

1. Richard L. Grossman and Frank T. Adams, *Taking Care of Business: Citizenship and the Charter of Incorporation* (Cambridge, Mass.: Charter, Ink, 1993), p. 6.
2. Grossman and Adams, *Taking Care of Business*.

3. Douglas Dowd, *U.S. Capitalist Development since 1776: Of, by, and for Which People?* (Armonk, N.Y.: M. E. Sharpe, 1993), p. 10.
4. Leo Huberman, *We, the People: The Drama of America* (New York: Monthly Review Press, 1960), pp. 50–52.
5. Adam Smith, *An Inquiry into the Nature and Causes of the Wealth of Nations* (1776; New York: Modern Library, 1937), p. 123.
6. Grossman and Adams, p. 3.
7. Grossman and Adams, p. 3.
8. Grossman and Adams, pp. 8–9.
9. Grossman and Adams, pp. 11–12.
10. As quoted in Edwin Merrick Dodd, *American Business Corporations until 1860* (Cambridge, Mass.: Harvard University Press, 1934), p. 130, as cited in Grossman and Adams, p. 13.
11. Harvey Wasserman, *America Born & Reborn* (New York: Collier Books, 1983), p. 84.
12. As quoted in Wasserman, pp. 89–90.
13. Wasserman, p. 90.
14. As quoted in Wasserman, p. 291.
15. As quoted in Wasserman, pp. 92–93.
16. Wasserman, p. 108.
17. Grossman and Adams, p. 21.
18. Grossman and Adams, p. 21.
19. Grossman and Adams, pp. 18–20.
20. Wasserman, p. 110.
21. Grossman and Adams, pp. 18–20.
22. Paul Hawken, *The Ecology of Commerce* (New York: Harper Business, 1993), p. 108.
23. Wasserman, p. 110.
24. Melvyn Dubofsky, *Industrialism and the American Worker, 1865–1920* (Arlington Heights, Ill.: Harlan Davidson, 1975), p. 87.
25. Wasserman, pp. 110–18; Dubofsky, pp. 29–71.
26. Wasserman, pp. 110–18.
27. Wasserman, p. 108.
28. Dubofsky, pp. 72–108.
29. Wasserman, p. 124; Dubofsky, pp. 77–80.
30. Dowd, p. 157.
31. Robert L. Heilbroner, *The Worldly Philosophers* (New York: Simon and Schuster, 1992), pp. 249–50.
32. Wasserman, p. 140.
33. Wasserman, pp. 146–47.
34. Kevin Phillips, *The Politics of Rich and Poor* (New York: Harper Perennial, 1990), pp. 241–42.
35. Walden Bello, with Shea Cunningham and Bill Rau, *Dark Victory: The United States, Structural Adjustment, and Global Poverty* (Oakland, Calif.: Institute for Food and Development Policy, 1994), pp. 4–5.
36. Bello, p. 3.
37. Bello, p. 5.
38. Bello, p. 5.
39. The 1978 figure is from Phillips, p. 239. The 1994 figure is from the annual survey of the world's billionaires by *Forbes*, July 18, 1994, 135.

40. *Forbes*, July 18, 1994, 135.
41. Bello, pp. 5–6.
42. Bello, pp. 3–4.
43. For further development of the autonomous purpose of corporations, see Jerry Mander, "Corporations as Machines," chap. 7 in *In the Absence of the Sacred* (San Francisco: Sierra Club Books, 1991).
44. William Greider, *Who Will Tell the People? The Betrayal of American Democracy* (New York: Simon and Schuster, 1992), p. 331.

Chapter 5. Assault of the Corporate Libertarians

1. "Is Free Trade Passe?" *Economic Perspectives* 1, no. 2 (1987): 131.
2. Gar Alperovitz, "Building a Living Democracy," *Sojourners*, July 1990, 16.
3. Michael Pusey, "Reclaiming the Middle Ground . . . from Right 'Economic Rationalism,'" in Stephen King and Peter Lloyd (eds.), *Economic Rationalism: Dead End or Way Forward?* (New South Wales: Allen & Unwin, 1993), p. 18.
4. Michael Pusey, *Economic Rationalism in Canberra: A Nation-Building State Changes Its Mind* (Sydney: Cambridge University Press, 1991).
5. *Webster's New World Dictionary* (New York: Simon and Schuster, 1980), s.v. "rationalism."
6. David Boaz and Edward H. Crane, *Market Liberalism: A Paradigm for the 21st Century* (Washington, D.C.: Cato Institute, 1993), p. 23.
7. Adam Smith, *An Inquiry into the Nature and Causes of the Wealth of Nations* (1776; New York: Modern Library, 1937), pp. 60–61.
8. Smith, p. 674.
9. A. V. Krebs, *The Corporate Reapers: The Book of Agribusiness* (Washington, D.C.: Essential Books, 1992); and an information sheet titled "America's New 'Centrally Planned' Food Economy," prepared by A. V. Krebs and distributed by Prairie Fire Rural Action, Des Moines, Iowa.
10. Paul Hawken, *The Economy of Commerce* (New York: Harper Business, 1993), p. 95.
11. Neva Goodwin, "Externalities and Economic Power" (paper presented at the fall retreat of the Environmental Grantmakers Association, Bretton Woods, N.H., October 13–15, 1994), p. 2.
12. Smith, p. 423. It should be noted that this is the only reference to the famous invisible hand in Smith's nearly thousand-page manuscript.
13. Smith, p. 700.
14. United Nations Centre for Transnational Corporations (UNCTC), E/C.10/1993/2, March 3, 1993, p. 8; as reported by John Cavanagh in a May 1, 1993, memo.
15. These arguments are developed in much more detail by Herman E. Daly and John B. Cobb Jr., *For the Common Good: Redirecting the Economy toward Community, the Environment, and a Sustainable Future* (Boston: Beacon Press, 1989), pp. 209–35.
16. Goodwin, p. 2.
17. James Stanford, "Continental Economic Integration: Modeling the Impact on Labor," *Annals of the American Academy of Political & Social Science* 526 (March 1993): 92–110.

18. James Stanford, "Free Trade and the Imaginary Worlds of Economic Modelers," *PCDForum Column* no. 45, April 5, 1993.
19. Statistics cited by Richard J. Barnet, "Stateless Corporations: Lords of the Global Economy," *The Nation*, December 19, 1994, 754.
20. Lawrence Summers, internal World Bank memorandum dated December 12, 1991, p. 5. The relevant excerpts from this memo were quoted by *The Economist*, February 8, 1992, p. 62. Summers, a leading proponent of economic rationalism, responded to widespread public criticism of his argument by claiming that he had inserted it into the infamous memo as an ironic counterpoint rather than an actual proposal.
21. "Pollution and the Poor," *The Economist*, February 15, 1992, 16–17.
22. This is a regular theme in the World Bank's *World Development Report* series. See, for example, World Bank, *World Development Report 1992: Development and the Environment* (New York: Oxford University Press, 1992), p. 3.
23. This was the central argument of a paper titled "Comments on Thomas W. Pogge's 'Radical International Inequalities,'" presented by distinguished development economist Paul Streeten at the Panel on Consumption and International Justice of the Conference on Consumption, Global Stewardship and the Good Life, School of Public Affairs, University of Maryland, September 29–October 2, 1994.

Chapter 6. Decline of Democratic Pluralism

1. "Free Trade, up to a Point," *Times* (London), March 5, 1994, p. 18.
2. Francis Fukuyama, *The End of History and the Last Man* (New York: Avon Books, 1992).
3. The following points are drawn from Herman E. Daly and John B. Cobb Jr., *For the Common Good: Redirecting the Economy toward Community, the Environment, and a Sustainable Future* (Boston: Beacon Press, 1989), pp. 49–60.
4. Based on personal correspondence from Marilyn Mehlmann, Swedish Institute for Social Inventions, March 3, 1994.
5. Kenneth Hermele, "The End of the Middle Road: What Happened to the Swedish Model?" *Monthly Review*, March 1993, 14–24.
6. David Vail, "The Past and Future of Swedish Social Democracy: A Reply to Kenneth Hermele," *Monthly Review*, October 1993, 24–31.
7. Hermele, "The End of the Middle Road."
8. Hermele, "The End of the Middle Road."
9. Vail, "The Past and Future of Swedish Social Democracy."
10. Hermele, "The End of the Middle Road."
11. Hermele, "The End of the Middle Road."
12. Vail, "The Past and Future of Swedish Social Democracy."
13. Hermele, "The End of the Middle Road."
14. Hermele, "The End of the Middle Road."
15. Vail, "The Past and Future of Swedish Social Democracy."
16. Larry Diamond, "Beyond Authoritarianism and Totalitarianism: Strategies for Democratization," *The Washington Quarterly* 12, no. 1 (Winter 1989): 141–63.
17. William M. Dugger, *Corporate Hegemony* (New York: Greenwood Press, 1989), pp. 12–15.

18. Dugger, p. 15.
19. Dugger, p. 15.

Chapter 7. Illusions of the Cloud Minders

1. From "The Cloud Minders," *Star Trek*, episode 74, Febuary 28, 1969.
2. Graham Hancock, *Lords of Poverty* (New York: Atlantic Monthly Press, 1989), pp. 38–40.
3. Address by Barber B. Conable to the board of governors of the World Bank and International Finance Corporation, Washington, D.C., September 30, 1986, as quoted in Hancock, p. 38.
4. As reported in Nancy Scheper-Hughes, "The Madness of Hunger," *Why*, no. 14 (Fall 1993): 11.
5. Walter Hook, "Paving over Bangkok," *Sustainable Transport*, no. 2 (September 1993): 7.
6. Hook, 6.
7. UNDP, *Human Development Report 1992* (New York: Oxford University Press, 1992).
8. U.S. data are for families and therefore are not directly comparable with the individual data used by UNDP.
9. Gar Alperovitz, "Building a Living Democracy," *Sojourners*, July 1990, 13.
10. "Executive Pay: The Party Ain't over Yet," *Business Week*, April 16, 1993, 56–64.
11. "Executive Pay."
12. "The Forbes Four Hundred," *Forbes*, October 18, 1993, 110–11.
13. Although net asset values are not directly comparable to gross national product, which is a measure of income, the orders of magnitude are revealing. GNP and population figures are from John W. Wright, *The Universal Almanac, 1994* (Kansas City, Mo.: Andrews and McMeel, 1993).
14. "The Forbes Four Hundred," 111.
15. Lawrence Mishel and Jared Bernstein, *The State of Working America: 1992–93* (Armonk, N.Y.: M. E. Sharpe, 1993), p. 256.
16. Mishel and Berstein, p. 46; based on data from the House of Representatives Ways and Means Committee, 1991. Figures are in 1992 dollars.
17. James M. Clash, "Reversal of Fortunates," *Forbes*, October 18, 1993, 105–6.
18. Eric Konigsberg, "No Hassles: The Ultimate Perk of the Ruling Class Is Freedom from Pesky Details," *Utne Reader*, September/October 1993, 76.
19. James Bennet, "New Ford Chief Hasn't Bought One, Lately," *New York Times*, October 7, 1993, pp. D-1, D-15.
20. "CEO Disease: Egotism Can Breed Corporate Disaster—and the Malady Is Spreading," *Business Week*, April 1, 1991, 52–60.
21. Konigsberg, 76.
22. Richard J. Barnet and John Cavanagh, *Global Dreams: Imperial Corporations and the New World Order* (New York: Simon and Schuster, 1994), pp. 325–29.
23. Barnet and Cavanagh, pp. 325–29. See also Cynthia Enloe, "The Globetrotting Sneaker," *Ms.*, March/April 1995, 10–15.
24. "Eisner Pay Is 68% of Profit," *New York Times*, April 16, 1994, p. 48.
25. "The World's Wealthiest People," *Forbes*, July 5, 1993, pp. 66–111; "The Billionaires," *Forbes*, July 18, 1994, 134–219.
26. Robert B. Reich, *The Work of Nations* (New York: Alfred A. Knopf, 1991), p. 275.

27. Extensive documentation of this trend within the United States is provided by Reich, pp. 268–81.

Chapter 8. Dreaming of Global Empires

1. "A Survey of Multinationals: Everybody's Favorite Monsters," *The Economist*, March 27, 1993, 7.
2. Richard J. Barnet and Ronald E. Muller, *Global Reach: The Power of the Multinational Corporation* (New York: Simon and Schuster, 1974), pp. 13, 15–16, as cited in Howard M. Wachtel, *The Money Mandarins: The Making of a Supranational Economic Order* (Armonk, N.Y.: M. E. Sharpe, 1990), p. 6.
3. Akio Morita, "Toward a New World Economic Order," *Atlantic Monthly*, June 1993, 88.
4. Morita, 92–93.
5. Morita, 93.
6. Morita, 94–95.
7. "Cosmocorp: The Importance of Being Stateless," *Columbia Journal of World Business* 2, no. 6 (November–December 1967), as quoted in Jeff Frieden, "The Trilateral Commission: Economics and Politics in the 1970s," in Holly Sklar (ed.), *Trilateralism: The Trilateral Commission and Elite Planning for World Management* (Boston: South End Press, 1980), pp. 63–64.
8. *GATT–The Environment and the Third World, an Overview* (Berkeley, Calif.: Environmental News Network, 1992), p. 3, as cited in Paul Hawken, *The Ecology of Commerce: A Declaration of Sustainability* (New York: Harper Business, 1993), p. 101.
9. Rosabeth Moss Kanter, "Transcending Business Boundaries: 12,000 World Managers View Change," *Harvard Business Review*, May–June 1991, 151–65.
10. Calculated from global trade and output tables in Lester R. Brown, Hal Kane, and Ed Ayres, *Vital Signs 1993: The Trends That Are Shaping Our Future* (New York: W. W. Norton, 1993).
11. "A Survey of Multinationals," 7.
12. "The Power of the Transnationals," *The Ecologist* 22, no. 4 (July/August 1992): 159.
13. United Nations, *World Investment Report* (New York: United Nations, 1993), pp. 19, 22.
14. As quoted in Gerald Epstein, "Mortgaging America," *World Policy Journal* 8, no. 1 (Winter 1990–91): 29.
15. *Business Week*, May 14, 1990, 99.
16. Robert B. Reich, "Who Is Us?" *Harvard Business Review*, January–February 1990, 54.
17. Andrew Pollack, "G.M. to Make Toyota Cars for Sale in Japan," *New York Times*, April 16, 1993, p. D-1.
18. "The Stateless Corporation" *Business Week*, May 14, 1990, 98.
19. "The Stateless Corporation," 99–102.
20. Michael E. McGrath and Richard W. Hoole, "Manufacturing's New Economies of Scale," *Harvard Business Review*, May–June 1992, 94–102.
21. "A Survey of Multinationals," 8.
22. Office of Technology Assessment, U.S. Congress, *Multinationals and the National Interest: Playing by Different Rules* (Washington, D.C.: U.S. Government Printing Office, 1993), pp. 1–4, 10.

23. Kenichi Ohmae, *The Borderless World: Power and Strategy in the Interlinked Economy* (London: HarperCollins, 1990), p. xii.
24. "U.S. Companies Use Affiliates Abroad to Skirt Sanctions," *New York Times*, December 27, 1993, pp. A-1, D-3.
25. Ohmae, pp. x–xi.
26. Ohmae, p. 19.
27. "Exports Will Fly High, but so Will Imports," *Fortune*, July 25, 1994, 64.
28. Andrew Cohen, "The Downside of 'Development,'" *The Nation*, November 4, 1991, 544–46.
29. This discussion is based on William Greider, *Who Will Tell the People? The Betrayal of American Democracy* (New York: Simon and Schuster, 1992), pp. 378–87; Richard Rothstein, "Continental Drift: NAFTA and Its Aftershocks," *The American Prospect*, no. 12 (Winter 1993): 68–84; Ross Perot and Pat Choate, *Save Your Job, Save Our Country* (New York: Hyperion, 1993), pp. 45–47; and Richard J. Barnet and John Cavanagh, "Creating a Level Playing Field," *Technology Review*, May/June 1994, 23–29.
30. As interviewed by and cited in Greider, p. 383.
31. "The Boom Belt: There's No Speed Limit on Growth along the South's I-85," *Business Week*, September 27, 1993, 98–104.
32. Robert Reich, *The Work of Nations* (New York: Alfred A. Knopf, 1991), p. 281.
33. Reported by Robert Reich in a presentation to the Democratic Leadership Conference televised on C-Span, November 29, 1994.

Chapter 9. Building Elite Consensus

1. Peter Thompson, "Bilderberg and the West," in Holly Sklar (ed.), *Trilateralism: The Trilateral Commission and Elite Planning for World Management* (Boston: South End Press, 1980), p. 158.
2. Felix Rohatyn, "World Capital: The Need and the Risks," *New York Review of Books*, July 14, 1994, 48.
3. Leonard Silk and Mark Silk, *The American Establishment* (New York: Basic Books, 1980), pp. 183–90.
4. The discussion of these events is based on Laurence H. Shoup and William Minter, "Shaping a New World Order: The Council on Foreign Relations' Blueprint for World Hegemony," in Sklar, pp. 135–56.
5. Silk and Silk, pp. 197–98.
6. Shoup and Minter, pp. 135–56.
7. Memorandum E-B32, April 17, 1941, Council on Foreign Relations, War-Peace Studies, NUL, as quoted in Shoup and Minter, pp. 145–46.
8. From Memorandum E-B34, July 24, 1941, as quoted in Shoup and Minter, p. 141.
9. Shoup and Minter, p. 141.
10. Bruce Rich, *Mortgaging the Earth* (Boston: Beacon Press, 1994), pp. 49–56.
11. Thompson, p. 157.
12. Statement by John Pomian (secretary to Joseph Retinger, who was a founder of Bilderberg and its first permanent secretary), as quoted in Thompson, p. 169.
13. Thompson, p. 177.
14. As quoted in Thompson, pp. 177–78.

15. Holly Sklar (ed.), *Trilateralism: The Trilateral Commission and Elite Planning for World Management* (Boston: South End Press, 1980).
16. From descriptive materials provided by the Trilateral Commission.
17. Thompson, p. 176.
18. Thompson, p. 177.
19. From an undated information sheet provided by the Trilateral Commission.

Chapter 10. Buying Out Democracy

1. As quoted in *Justice for Sale: Shortchanging the Public Interest for Private Gain* (Washington, D.C.: Alliance for Justice, 1993), p. 1.
2. As quoted in *Justice for Sale*, pp. 10–11.
3. *Justice for Sale*, pp. 11–12; Mark Megalli and Andy Friedman, *Masks of Deception: Corporate Front Groups in America* (Washington, D.C.: Essential Information, 1991), p. 153.
4. Megalli and Friedman, p. 153.
5. As quoted in *Justice for Sale*, p. 12.
6. *Justice for Sale*.
7. These and other cases are documented in Megalli and Friedman, *Masks of Deception*.
8. Rosemary Brown, "Unveiling Corporate Front Groups," *Co-Op America Quarterly* (Winter 1994): 14. For a published directory of business-sponsored front groups, see Carl Deal, *The Greenpeace Guide to Anti-Environmental Organizations* (Berkeley, Calif.: Odonian Press, 1993); available from Odonian Press, Box 7776, Berkeley, CA 94707, for $5 per copy plus $2 handling per order.
9. William Greider, *Who Will Tell the People? The Betrayal of American Democracy* (New York: Simon and Schuster, 1992), p. 48.
10. *Justice for Sale*, p. 3.
11. Greider, *Who Will Tell the People?*
12. From a descriptive brochure provided by the Business Roundtable.
13. The ratio is based on the 1992 average annual compensation of $3.84 million for the CEOs of major U.S. corporations as reported by *Business Week*, April 16, 1993. Since the Roundtable members are the CEOs of the very largest U.S. corporations, we can presume that their average compensation is higher than the average reported by *Business Week*.
14. Sarah Anderson, John Cavanagh, and Sandra Gross, *NAFTA's Corporate Cadre: An Analysis of the USA*NAFTA State Captains* (Washington, D.C.: Institute for Policy Studies, 1993); available from IPS, 1601 Connecticut Ave. NW, Washington, DC 20009.
15. Greider, p. 35.
16. John Stauber, "Countering the Flack Attack," *Co-op America Quarterly* (Winter 1994): 18.
17. Stauber, p. 18.
18. Greider, pp. 253–54.
19. Greider, p. 270.
20. Pat Choate, "Political Advantage: Japan's Campaign for America," *Harvard Business Review*, September–October 1990, 87–103; "Is Japan 'Buying' U.S. Politics?" *Harvard Business Review*, November–December 1990, 184–98.

Chapter 11. Marketing the World

1. William Leach, *Land of Desire: Merchants, Power, and the Rise of a New American Culture* (New York: Pantheon Books, 1993), p. xiii.
2. Richard J. Barnet and John Cavanagh, "The Sound of Money," *Sojourners*, January 1994, 12.
3. Paul Hawken, *The Ecology of Commerce: A Declaration of Sustainability* (New York: Harper Business, 1993), p. 132.
4. Duane Elgin, *Voluntary Simplicity* (New York: William Morrow, 1993), pp. 50–52.
5. Elgin, pp. 50–52.
6. Leach, p. xv.
7. Leach, pp. 11–12.
8. The statistics and analysis of television are from Jerry Mander, *In the Absence of the Sacred: The Failure of Technology & the Survival of the Indian Nations* (San Francisco, Calif.: Sierra Club Books, 1991), pp. 75–82.
9. Mander, pp. 97–98.
10. As cited in Richard J. Barnet and John Cavanagh, *Global Dreams: Imperial Corporations and the New World Order* (New York: Simon and Schuster, 1994), pp. 171–72.
11. United Nations, *Report on the World Social Situation 1993* (New York: United Nations, 1993), p. 48.
12. Alan Thein Durning, "Can't Live without It," *World·Watch* 6, no. 3 (May–June 1993): 13.
13. Akio Morita, "Toward a New World Economic Order," *Atlantic Monthly*, June 1993.
14. As quoted in Barnett and Cavanagh, "The Sound of Money," 14.
15. Barnet and Cavanagh, "The Sound of Money," 14.
16. Sarah Ferguson, "The Comfort of Being Sad: Kurt Cobain and the Politics of Damage," *Utne Reader*, July/August 1994, 62.
17. *TV Nation*, produced by Michael Moore, NBC television, August 2, 1994.
18. Except as otherwise referenced, information on corporate advertising in the classroom is from Alex Monar, "Corporations in the Classroom," *Co-op America Quarterly* (Winter 1994): 19–20.
19. As quoted in Robert Pear, "Senator, Promoting Student Nutrition, Battles Coca-Cola," *New York Times*, April 26, 1994, p. A-20.
20. "A, B, C, D, Economics," *New York Times*, May 26, 1994, p. A-23.
21. Donella Meadows, "Corporate-Run Schools Are a Threat to Our Way of Life," *Valley News*, October 3, 1992, p. 22; Monar, p. 20.
22. As quoted in Monar, p. 20.
23. Hawken, p. 129.
24. "Empires of the 21st Century?" *Business Week*, February 21, 1994, 19.

Chapter 12. Adjusting the Poor

1. To eleven African heads of state, Libreville, Gabon, May 27, 1993.
2. The ad was placed by the Philippine government in 1975, as quoted in Elizabeth M. Krahmer and Donella H. Meadows, "Money Flows" (draft paper, March 29, 1994), p. 19.

3. Robin Broad, *Unequal Alliance 1979–1986: The World Bank, the International Monetary Fund, and the Philippines* (Berkeley, Calif.: University of California Press, 1988), p. 21.
4. Bruce Rich, "The Cuckoo in the Nest: Fifty Years of Political Meddling by the World Bank," *The Ecologist* 24, no. 1 (January/February 1994): 9.
5. Rich, 9.
6. Rich, 9.
7. Broad, pp. 6–7.
8. Broad, pp. 6–7.
9. Broad, pp. 6–7.
10. Broad, pp. 26–27.
11. Rich, 9–10.
12. Rich, 10.
13. Broad, p. 27.
14. As quoted in Robert W. Oliver, *International Economic Cooperation and the World Bank* (London: Macmillan Press, 1977), p. 160, and cited in Bruce Rich, *Mortgaging the Earth: The World Bank, Environmental Impoverishment, and the Crisis of Development* (Boston: Beacon Press, 1994), p. 59.
15. *World Debt Tables 1992–93: External Finance for Developing Countries* (Washington, D.C.: World Bank, 1992), p. 212.
16. Frances Stewart, "The Many Faces of Adjustment," *World Development* 19, no. 12 (December 1991): 1851.
17. *World Debt Tables 1992–93*, p. 208.
18. Jonathan Cahn, "Challenging the New Imperial Authority: The World Bank and the Democratization of Development," *Harvard Human Rights Journal* 6 (1993): 160.
19. Clay Chandler, "The Growing Urge to Break the Bank," *Washington Post*, June 19, 1994, pp. H-1, H-7.
20. Rich, *Mortgaging the Earth*, p. 77.
21. Senate Committee on Banking and Currency, *Participation of the United States in the International Monetary Fund and the International Bank for Reconstruction and Development*, 79th Cong., 1st sess., 1945, S. Rpt. 452, pt. 2, "Minority Views," p. 9, as quoted in Rich, *Mortgaging the Earth*, p. 62.
22. Senate Committee on Banking and Currency, p. 9, as quoted in Rich, *Mortgaging the Earth*, pp. 61–62.
23. David C. Korten, *Getting to the 21st Century: Voluntary Action and the Global Agenda* (West Hartford, Conn.: Kumarian Press, 1990).
24. Reported by Pratap Chatterjee, "World Bank Failures Soar to 37.5% of Completed Projects in 1991," *Third World Economics*, December 16–31, 1992, p. 2.
25. Reported by Michael Cernea, "Farmer Organizations and Institution Building for Sustainable Development," *Regional Development Dialogue* 8, no. 2 (Summer 1987): 1–19.

Chapter 13. Guaranteeing Corporate Rights

1. Farewell lecture to the World Bank, January 1994.
2. William M. Dugger, *Corporate Hegemony* (New York: Greenwood Press, 1989), pp. ix, xiii.

3. Paul Hawken, *The Ecology of Commerce: A Declaration of Sustainability* (New York: Harper Business, 1993), pp. 99–100.
4. Information on the trade advisory committees is from Tom Hilliard, *Trade Advisory Committees: Privileged Access for Polluters* (Washington, D.C.: Public Citizen's Congress Watch, 1991).
5. U.S. Department of Commerce and Office of the U.S. Trade Representative, *Procedures and Rules for the Industry Advisory Committees for Trade Policy Matters*, (n.d.), p. 3, as cited in Hilliard, p. 9.
6. Hilliard, p. 7.
7. "Government Seeks Advice from Industry on U.S. Trade Policy," *Business America*, January 16, 1989, 9, as cited in Hilliard, p. 7.
8. Hilliard, *Trade Advisory Committees*.
9. As quoted in Mark Ritchie, "GATT, Agriculture and the Environment: The US Double Zero Plan," *The Ecologist* 20, no. 6 (November/December 1990): 217.
10. As cited in "Power: The Central Issue," *The Ecologist* 22, no. 4 (July/August 1992): 159.
11. Cited in Ritchie, p. 216.
12. From a study by Tim Lang for the United Kingdom National Food Alliance, as reported in Tim Lang and Colin Hines, *The New Protectionism: Protecting the Future against Free Trade* (New York: New Press, 1993), pp. 100–103.
13. In an April 24, 1993, interview with *New Scientist* magazine, cited in Natalie Avery, "How Companies Influence Global Food Standards," news release issued by *Third World Network Features*, 87 Cantonment Road, Penang, Malaysia, January 1994, p. 7.
14. Hope Shand, "Patenting the Planet," *Multinational Monitor*, June 1994, 9–13.
15. Shand, 9–13.
16. As quoted in Vandana Shiva, *Monocultures of the Mind: Perspectives on Biodiversity and Biotechnology* (London: Zed Press, 1993), p. 122.
17. Shiva, p. 122.
18. *The Ecologist, Whose Common Future? Reclaiming the Commons* (Philadelphia: New Society Publishers, 1993), pp. 55–56.

Chapter 14. The Money Game

1. "Hot Money," *Business Week*, March 20, 1995, 46.
2. The number of participants is an estimate noted by Representative Henry B. Gonzalez, chair of the House Banking Committee of the U.S. Congress, at a hearing on the derivatives market; cited in Thomas L. Friedman, "International Investors Bet Everything on Anything," *New York Times*, April 17, 1994, sec. 4, p. 1.
3. Diana B. Henriques, "Questions of Conflict Sting Mutual Funds," *New York Times*, August 7, 1994, p. 1.
4. "Another Year in 'Bank Heaven'?" *Business Week*, January 10, 1994, 103.
5. Pension fund figures are from Randy Barber and Teresa Ghilarducci, "Pension Funds, Capital Markets, and the Economic Future," in Gary A. Dymski, Gerald Epstein, and Robert Pollin (eds.), *Transforming the U.S. Financial System: Equity and Efficiency for the 21st Century* (Armonk, N.Y.: M. E. Sharpe, 1993), p. 288.

6. On an average day in July 1993, $1.087 trillion in dollar-based transactions, most of the currency trades, took place on the New York Clearing House Interbank Payments System alone. Jay Mathews, "Putting Currency Trading on Trial," *Washington Post*, August 22, 1993, p. H-1.

7. Joel Kurtzman, *The Death of Money* (New York: Simon and Schuster, 1993), pp. 64, 149.

8. For more detailed nontechnical discussions of the financial economy, see Kurtzman, *The Death of Money*; Howard M. Wachtel, *The Money Mandarins: The Making of a Supranational Economic Order* (Armonk, N.Y.: M. E. Sharpe, 1990); and Roy C. Smith, *The Money Wars: The Rise and Fall of the Great Buyout Boom of the 1980s* (Plume, N.Y.: Truman Talley Books, 1990).

9. The actual rate varies, depending on such things as the total assets of the bank, but it averages a little under 10 percent.

10. *Report of the Presidential Commission on Market Mechanisms* (Washington, D.C.: U.S. Government Printing Office, 1988), p. I–2, as cited in Wachtel, p. 251.

11. Kurtzman, p. 98.

12. Kurtzman, p. 161.

Chapter 15. Predatory Finance

1. The comment was made about a period of currency stability in March 1987, as quoted in Hobart Rowen, "Wielding Jawbone to Protect the Dollar," *Washington Post*, March 15, 1987, p. H-1, and cited in Howard M. Wachtel, *The Money Mandarins: The Making of a Supranational Economic Order* (Armonk, N.Y.: M. E. Sharpe, 1990), p. 269.

2. Joel Kurtzman, *The Death of Money* (New York: Simon and Schuster, 1993), p. 128.

3. Felix Rohatyn, "World Capital: The Need and the Risks," *New York Review of Books*, July 14, 1994, 53.

4. "A Survey of Multinationals: Everybody's Favourite Monsters," *The Economist*, March 27, 1993, 6.

5. Personal communication with J. T. Ross Jackson, president, Gaiacorp, Copenhagen, Denmark.

6. Carol J. Loomis, "Untangling the Derivatives Mess," *Fortune*, March 20, 1995, 50.

7. "Survey: Frontiers of Finance: On the Edge," *The Economist*, October 9, 1993, 4.

8. Saul Hansell, "A Primer on Hedge Funds: Hush-Hush and for the Rich," *New York Times*, April 13, 1994, pp. A-1, D-15.

9. "Excerpts from Soros Testimony," *New York Times*, April 14, 1994, p. D-6.

10. Allen R. Myerson, "When Soros Speaks, World Markets Listen," *New York Times*, June 10, 1993, p. D-1.

11. "Big Winner from Plunge in Sterling," *New York Times*, October 27, 1992, p. D–9.

12. Elizabeth M. Krahmer and Donella H. Meadows, "Money Flows" (prepared for the annual meeting of the Environmental Grantmakers Association, March 24, 1994), p. 48.

13. Jay Mathews, "Putting Currency Trading on Trial," *Washington Post*, August 22, 1993, pp. H-1, H-4.

14. Felix Rohatyn, "World Capital: The Need and the Risks," *New York Review of Books*, July 14, 1994, 51–52.

15. Saul Hansell, "A Bad Bet for P. & G.," *New York Times*, April 14, 1994, p. D-6.

16. Rohatyn, 52.

17. Susan Antilla, "A Concealed Danger for Funds," *New York Times*, April 17, 1994, p. 15.

18. "Today, Orange County: The Muni Mess on Wall Street: How Bad?" *Business Week*, December 19, 1994, 28–30.

19. Saul Ansell, "For Rogue Traders, Yet Another Victim," *New York Times*, February 28, 1995, pp. D1, D8; "The Lesson from Barings' Straits," *Business Week*, March 13, 1995, 30–32; Richard W. Stevenson, "Young Trader's $29 Billion Bet Brings Down a Venerable Firm," *New York Times*, February 28, 1995, pp. A-1, D-9.

20. Sheryl WuDunn, "Tokyo Stocks Plunge on British Firm's Collapse," *New York Times*, February 27, 1995, p. D-1.

21. As cited in Joel Kurtzman, *The Death of Money* (New York: Simon and Schuster, 1993), pp. 89–91.

22. Based on an interview with Christopher Whalen, chief financial officer for Legal Research International, by Russell Mokhiber of the Corporate Crime Reporter, January 19, 1995, distributed via Internet.

23. "The World's Wealthiest People," *Forbes*, July 5, 1993, 66; "The Billionaires," *Forbes*, July 18, 1994, 194–95.

24. "One Year Later: NAFTA Disaster!" Information package prepared and distributed by Public Citizen's Trade Program, Public Citizen, Washington, D.C., March 1995, p. 1.

25. "Austerity and Rates of 92% Fail to Perk Up the Peso," *New York Times*, March 16, 1995, p. D-8.

26. Anthony DePlama, "Mexicans Ask How Far Social Fabric Can Stretch," *New York Times*, March 12, 1995, p. A-1.

27. Allen R. Nyerson, "Peso's Plunge May Cost Thousands of U.S. Jobs," *New York Times*, January 30, 1995, p. D-4.

28. Anthony DePlama, "Crisis in Mexico Deepens Damage in Latin Markets," *New York Times*, January 11, 1995, pp. A-1, D-2.

29. Ralph Nader, testimony on the bailout of the Mexican government before the Senate Banking Committee, U.S. Senate, Washington, D.C., March 9, 1995, p. 4; David E. Sanger, "Dollar Dips as the Peso Falls Again," *New York Times*, March 10, 1995, p. D-1.

30. Harvey D. Shapiro, "After NAFTA: Facing the New Global Economy," *Hemispheres*, March 1995, 74–79.

31. Paul Craig Roberts, "How Clinton Is Bashing the Buck," *Business Week*, August 8, 1994, 14.

32. Mathews, p. H-4.

33. Thomas A. Russo, "Let Wall St. Handle Derivatives Rules," *New York Times*, May 15, 1994, sec. 3, p. 13.

34. As quoted in Mathews, p. H-4.

35. As quoted in Sylvia Nasar, "Jett's Supervisor at Kidder Breaks Silence," *New York Times*, June 26, 1994, pp. D-1, D-14.

36. Sylvia Nasar, "Kidder Scandal Tied to Failure of Supervision," *New York Times*, August 5, 1994, pp. A-1, D-3.

37. As quoted in Thomas J. Lueck, "Incentives of $31 Million Keep Kidder Peabody in New York," *New York Times*, October 30, 1993, pp. 23–24.

Chapter 16. Corporate Cannibalism

1. William M. Dugger, *Corporate Hegemony* (New York: Greenwood Press, 1989), p. x.
2. The meaning of the phrase "creating value" is commonly distorted by corporate libertarians to refer to anything that inflates a price or extracts a profit. I use the term only in reference to adding to the real value of the world's stock of goods, services, and productive assets.
3. Joel Kurtzman, *The Death of Money* (New York: Simon and Schuster, 1993), p. 164.
4. Data compiled by Donald L. Bartlett and James B. Steele, "America: What Went Wrong? Part 8: The Disappearing Pensions," *Philadelphia Inquirer*, October 27, 1991, p. 1-A, as cited in Jonathan Greenberg, "The Hidden Costs of Corporate Takeovers," in Jonathan Greenberg and William Kistler (eds.), *Buying America Back* (Tulsa, Okla.: Council Oak Books, 1992), p. 153.
5. As quoted in "The Power of the Transnationals," *The Ecologist* 22, no. 4 (July/August 1992): 159.
6. Ned Daly, "Ravaging the Redwoods: Charles Hurwitz, Michael Milken and the Cost of Greed," *Multinational Monitor*, September 1994, 12.
7. John Skow, "Redwoods: The Last Stand," *Time*, June 6, 1994, 59.
8. Skow, 59.
9. Daly, 13.
10. As quoted in Susan Faludi, "The Reckoning: Safeway LBO Yields Vast Profits But Exacts a Heavy Human Toll," *Wall Street Journal*, May 16, 1990, p. 1A, and cited in Greenburg, p. 159.
11. Gretchen Morgenson, "The Buyout That Saved Safeway," *Forbes*, November 12, 1990, 88, as cited in Greenberg, p. 155.
12. Greenberg, p. 155.
13. Data compiled by Donald L. Bartlett and James B. Steele, "America: What Went Wrong? Part 3: Shifting Taxes from Them to You," *Philadelphia Inquirer*, October 22, 1991, p. 1-A, as cited in Greenberg, p. 152.
14. Greenberg, p. 151.
15. Greenberg, p. 159.
16. Based on Joseph Pereira, "Split Personality," as reprinted by *Utne Reader*, September/October 1993, 63–66, from the *Wall Street Journal*.
17. As quoted in Pereira, 64.
18. As cited in Ross Perot and Pat Choate, *Save Your Job, Save Our Country: Why NAFTA Must Be Stopped–Now!* (New York: Hyperion, 1993), pp. 52–53.
19. Perot and Choate, pp. 52–53.

Chapter 17. Managed Competition

1. Bennett Harrison, *Lean and Mean: The Changing Landscape of Corporate Power in the Age of Flexibility* (New York: Basic Books, 1993), p. 220.
2. "Let the Good Times Roll—and a Few More Heads," *Business Week*, January 31, 1994, 28–29.

3. "The Rise and Rise of America's Small Firms," *The Economist*, January 21, 1989, 73–74, as quoted in Harrison, p. 13.
4. Based on Harrison, pp. 9–11.
5. "Let the Good Times Roll," 28–29.
6. Harrison, p. 18.
7. Paul Hawken, *The Ecology of Commerce* (New York: HarperCollins, 1993), p. 8.
8. "Executive Pay: The Party Ain't Over Yet," *Business Week*, April 26, 1993, 56–62; "That Eye-Popping Executive Pay: Is Anybody Worth This Much?" *Business Week*, April 25, 1994, 52–58.
9. Brian O'Reilly, "The New Deal: What Companies and Employees Owe One Another," *Fortune*, June 13, 1994, 45.
10. John Naisbitt, *Global Paradox* (New York: William Morrow, 1994), p. 14.
11. "Learning to Survive in the '90s," *Business Week*, January 10, 1994, 95.
12. "Channeling Big Stores' Awesome Clout," *Business Week*, December 21, 1992, 98.
13. Donella Meadows, "Wal-Mart Should Come on Our Terms, Not at Our Expense," *Valley News*, June 12, 1993, p. 26.
14. "Clout! More and More, Retail Giants Rule the Marketplace," *Business Week*, December 21, 1992, 66–73; "Brawls in Toyland," *Business Week*, December 21, 1992, 36–37.
15. "Clout!" 73.
16. This compares 1991 GNP data for countries against total sales of the world's largest corporations for the same year. GNP data are from *The Universal Almanac, 1994* (Kansas City, Mo.: Andrews and McMeel, 1993) supplemented by *The Economist, Book of Vital World Statistics* (New York: Random House, 1990). Aggregate sales data are from tables in *Hoover's Handbook of World Business 1993* (Austin, Tex.: Reference Press, 1993) for the world's 500 largest industrial corporations, the world's 50 largest utilities, the world's 50 largest retailing companies, and the world's 50 largest diversified service companies. Many sources indicate that only forty of the hundred largest economies are corporations. This figure is based on the *Fortune* list of the world's hundred largest "industrial" corporations, which excludes nonindustrial corporations.
17. Hawken, p. 92.
18. Hawken, p. 92.
19. "A Survey of Multinationals: Everybody's Favourite Monsters," *The Economist*, March 27, 1993 (special supplement), 6.
20. Asset figures for commercial banks and financial companies are from *Hoover's Handbook of World Business*, pp. 68, 72.
21. One of the exceptions is Roger Terry, *Putting the American Dream Back Together* (San Francisco: Berrett–Koehler, forthcoming).
22. Adam Smith, *An Inquiry into the Nature and Causes of the Wealth of Nations* (1776; New York: Modern Library, 1937), p. 128.
23. "The Age of Consolidation," *Business Week*, October 14, 1991, 86–94. "Making the Perfect Connection," *WordPerfect Report*, Summer/Fall 1994, p. 2.
24. These estimates are from "A Survey of Multinationals," 17.
25. A. V. Krebs, *The Corporate Reapers: The Book of Agribusiness* (Washington, D.C.: Essential Books, 1992); A. V. Krebs, "America's New 'Centrally Planned' Food Economy" (information sheet distributed by Prairie Fire Rural Action, Des Moines, Iowa).
26. Joan Dye Gussow, "A Nutrition Policy . . . That Leads to a Food Policy . . . That Leads to an Agricultural Policy," *WHY Magazine*, Summer 1993, 25.

27. Krebs, *The Corporate Reapers*, p. 102.
28. Krebs, *The Corporate Reapers*, pp. 372–82.
29. "The Virtual Corporation," *Business Week*, February 8, 1993, 100.
30. "The Virtual Corporation," 100.
31. "The Partners," *Business Week*, February 10, 1992, 102–7.
32. "The Partners," 102–7.
33. "A Survey of Multinationals," 14.
34. *The Economist*, Febuary 6, 1993, 69.

Chapter 18. Race to the Bottom

1. "What's Wrong?" *Business Week*, August 2, 1993, 59.
2. Jeremy Brecher, "Global Village or Global Pillage?" *The Nation*, December 6, 1993, 685–88.
3. Laurie Udesky, "Sweatshops behind the Labels: The 'Social Responsibility' Gap," *The Nation*, May 16, 1994, 666–68.
4. Ms. Diaz's testimony before a hearing of the Subcommittee on Labor-Management Relations, Committee on Education and Labor, U.S. House of Representatives, Wilkes-Barre, Pa., June 7, 1994, as cited in an ad placed in the *New York Times*, June 19, 1994, p. A-23, by the International Ladies Garment Workers Union.
5. Bill Keller, "The Revolution Won, Workers Are Still Unhappy," *New York Times*, July 23, 1994, p. 2.
6. Bill Keller, "In Mandela's South Africa, Foreign Investors Are Few," *New York Times*, August 3, 1994, p. A-1.
7. "Damping Labor's Fires," *Business Week*, August 1, 1994, 40–41.
8. "Damping Labor's Fires," 40–41.
9. "The Wild, Wild East," *Business Week*, December 28, 1992, 50–51.
10. Robert A. Senser, "Outlawing the Crime of Child Slavery," *Freedom Review*, November–December 1993, 29–35.
11. Senser, 29–35.
12. Senser, 29–35.
13. Udesky, 665–68.
14. Robert Levering and Milton Moskowitz, *The 100 Best Companies to Work for in America*, rev. ed. (New York: Penguin Books, 1994), p. 500.
15. "Managing by Values: Is Levi Strauss' Approach Visionary—or Flaky?" *Business Week*, August 1, 1994, 46–52.
16. Levering and Moskowitz, pp. 501–2.
17. "Slash and Earn on the Continent," *Business Week*, May 2, 1994, 45–46.
18. "Europe's Economic Agony," *Business Week*, February 15, 1993, 49.
19. "Rage in the Streets," *Business Week*, April 11, 1994, 46.
20. "Doleful," *The Economist*, October 9, 1993, 17.
21. "Doleful," 17.
22. "Doleful," 17.
23. "Europe's Economic Agony," 48–49.
24. "Land of the Rising Jobless," *Business Week*, January 11, 1993, 47.
25. Michael H. Armacost, "Japan Goes to Business School, *New York Times*, July 28, 1994, p. A-23.
26. "A Bargain Basement Called Japan," *Business Week*, June 27, 1994. 42.

27. David Sanger, "New Japan Access for Wall Street," *New York Times*, January 11, 1995, pp. A-1, D-5.
28. "Wal-Mart Jitters Reach Canada's Stores," *Business Week*, January 31, 1994, 38.
29. "Invasion of the Retail Snatchers," *Business Week*, May 9, 1994, 72.
30. "NAFTA: A Green Light for Red Tape," *Business Week*, July 25, 1994, 48.

Chapter 19. The End of Inefficiency

1. Jeremy Rifkin, *The End of Work* (New York: G. P. Putnam's Sons, 1995), p. xiv.
2. Richard Douthwaite, *The Growth Illusion* (Tulsa, Okla.: Council Oak Publishing, 1993), p. 24.
3. William M. Dugger, *Corporate Hegemony* (New York: Greenwood Press, 1989), p. 13.
4. Brian O'Reilly, "The New Deal: What Companies and Employees Owe One Another," *Fortune*, June 13, 1994, 50.
5. John Burgess, "Debate on Executive Pay Moves across the Atlantic," *International Herald Tribune*, October 24, 1991, Business/Finance section, p. 1.
6. Derek Bok, *The Cost of Talent: How Executives and Professionals Are Paid and How It Affects America* (New York: Free Press, 1993), pp. 108–14.
7. Lee Smith, "Burned-Out Bosses," *Fortune*, July 25, 1994, 44–46.
8. Smith, 44–46.
9. Sarah Lyall, "Publishing Chief Is Out at Viacom," *New York Times*, June 15, 1994, pp. D-1, D-16.
10. Alison Leigh Cowan and John Holusha, "Eastman Kodak Chief Is Ousted by Directors," *New York Times*, August 7, 1993, p. 49.
11. "Getting Rid of the Boss," *The Economist*, February 6, 1993, 13.
12. "The Contingency Work Force," *Fortune*, January 24, 1994, 31.
13. "Planning a Career in a World Without Managers," *Fortune*, March 20, 1995, 72–80.
14. Jaclyn Fierman, "The Perilous New World of Fair Pay," *Fortune*, June 13, 1994, 64.
15. Lawrence Mishel and Jared Bernstein, *The State of Working America 1992–93* (Washington, D.C.: M. E. Sharpe, 1993), pp. 131–34.
16. Jason De Parle, "Sharp Increase along the Borders of Poverty," *New York Times*, March 31, 1994, p. A-1.
17. As summarized in "Lifestyles of the Poor and Working," *Utne Reader*, March/April 1993, 19–20.
18. "Downward Mobility," *Business Week*, March 23, 1992, 57–58.
19. "Bellboys with B.A.," *Time*, November 22, 1993, 36.
20. George J. Church, "Jobs in an Age of Insecurity," *Time*, November 22, 1993, 36.
21. "Lifestyles of the Poor and Working," *Utne Reader*, March/April 1993, 19–20.
22. The Millers' story is reported by Dirk Johnson, "Family Struggles to Make Do after Fall from Middle Class," *New York Times*, March 11, 1994, pp. A-1, A-14.

Chapter 20. People with No Place

1. As quoted in "Development as Enclosure: The Establishment of a Global Economy," *The Ecologist* 22, no. 4 (1992): 131–47
2. Quoted material is from Helena Norberg-Hodge, "The Psychological Road to 'Development,'" *PCDForum Column* no. 62, October 8, 1993. A more detailed account may be found in *Ancient Futures: Learning from Ladakh* (San Francisco: Sierra Club Books, 1991). An excellent video documenting life in Ladakh before and after development is available from the International Society for Ecology and Culture (ISEC), 12 Victoria Square, Clifton, Bristol BS8 4ES, UK; or P.O. Box 9475, Berkeley, CA 94709, USA.
3. For a more detailed account of the history of the land enclosure process, see the special issue of *The Ecologist* 22, no. 4 (July/August 1992) on the theme "Whose Common Future?"
4. "Development as Enclosure: The Establishment of a Global Economy," *The Ecologist* 22, no. 4, (July/August 1992): 134.
5. "Development as Enclosure," 135.
6. "Development as Enclosure," 135.
7. "Development as Enclosure," 135, 137.
8. For a thoroughly documented account of clandestine U.S. political and military interventions throughout the South, see Jonathan Kwitny, *Endless Enemies: The Making of an Unfriendly World* (New York: Congdon & Weed, 1984).
9. Robert D. Kaplan, "The Coming Anarchy," *Atlantic Monthly*, February 1994, 46.
10. Kaplan, 48.
11. Martin van Creveld, *The Transformation of War*, as quoted in Kaplan, 74.
12. United Nations High Commissioner for Refugees, *The State of the World's Refugees* (New York: Penguin Books, 1993).
13. "Two Million Refugees," *New York Times*, July 20, 1994, p. A-18.
14. United Nations High Commissioner for Refugees, foreword, p. iii.
15. Kaplan, 72.

Chapter 21. The Ecological Revolution

1. Willis Harman, *Global Mind Change: The Promise of the Last Years of the Twentieth Century* (Indianapolis, Ind.: Knowledge Systems, 1988).
2. Wangari Maathai, "All We Need Is Will," in *Can the Environment Be Saved without a Radical New Approach to World Development?* (Geneva: CONGO Planning Committee for UNCED, 1992), p. 27.
3. Mary E. Clark, "The Backward Ones," *PCDForum Column* no. 51, June 25, 1993.
4. The following discussion draws on Harman, pp. 34–35; Duane Elgin, *Awakening Earth: Exploring the Evolution of Human Culture and Consciousness* (New York: William Morrow, 1993), pp. 15–16; and personal communications with William Ellis.
5. Edward McNall Burns, *Western Civilizations: Their History and Their Culture*, 5th ed. (New York: W. W. Norton, 1958), p. 520.
6. Harman, p. 12.

7. Burns, p. 521.
8. Jacob Needleman, *Money and the Meaning of Life* (New York: Doubleday, 1991), pp. 40–42.
9. Joe Dominguez and Vicki Robin, *Your Money or Your Life: Transforming Your Relationships with Money and Achieving Financial Independence* (New York: Viking, 1992), p. 54.
10. Dominguez and Robin, p. 54.
11. Fritjof Capra, *The Tao of Physics* (New York: Bantam Books, 1976); Gary Zukav, *The Dancing Wu Li Masters: An Overview of the New Physics* (New York: Bantam Books, 1979). Fritjof Capra, *The Turning Point: Science, Society, and the Rising Culture* (New York: Simon and Schuster, 1982), and Harman, *Global Mind Change,* deal specifically with the implications for society.
12. This thesis is developed in George T. Lock Land, *Grow or Die: The Unifying Principle of Transformation* (New York: Dell, 1973).
13. Arnold Toynbee, *A Study of History,* abridgement of vols. 1–6 by D. D. Somerwell (New York: Oxford University Press, 1947), p. 555.
14. Herman Daly, "Toward Some Operational Principles of Sustainable Development," *Ecological Economics* 2 (1990): 1–6.
15. This scheme is based on James Robertson, *Future Wealth: A New Economics for the 21st Century* (London: Cassell Publishers Limited, 1989).

Chapter 22. Good Living

1. Eknath Easwaran, *The Compassionate Universe: The Power of the Individual to Heal the Environment* (Tomales, Calif.: Nilgiri Press, 1989), pp. 73–74.
2. Mary E. Clark, "The Backward Ones," *PCDForum Column* no. 51, June 25, 1993.
3. Robert D. Putnam, "The Prosperous Community: Social Capital and Public Affairs," *The American Prospect* 13 (Spring 1993): 2.
4. Putnam, 2.
5. Alan Durning, *How Much Is Enough: The Consumer Society and the Future of the Earth* (New York: W. W. Norton, 1992). Durning's terms for the three socioecological classes are consumers, middle income, and poor.
6. Michael Renner, "Assessing the Military's War on the Environment," in Lester R. Brown et al., *State of the World 1991* (New York: W. W. Norton, 1991), p. 139.
7. David Engwicht, *Reclaiming Our Cities and Towns* (Philadelphia: New Society Publishers, 1993), p. 17.
8. Engwicht, pp. 48–51.
9. Engwicht, p. 45.
10. William E. Rees and Mark Roseland, "From Urban Sprawl to Sustainable Human Communities," *PCDForum Column* no. 54, June 25, 1993.
11. Statistics are reported by Marcia D. Lowe, "Reinventing Transport," in Lester R. Brown et al., *State of the World 1994* (New York: W. W. Norton, 1994), pp. 82–84, from a study by the U.S. Federal Highway Commission. For further discussion, see Engwicht, pp. 138–44.
12. Nicholas Albery, Matthew Mezey, and Peter Ratcliffe (eds.), *Social Innovations: A Compendium* (London: Institute for Social Innovations), pp. 92–93.
13. Robyn Williams, foreword to *Reclaiming Our Cities and Towns,* by Engwicht.

14. Application of these concepts to villages in India is developed in detail in Anil Agarwal and Sunita Narain, *Towards Green Villages: A Strategy for Environmentally Sound and Participatory Rural Development* (New Delhi: Centre for Science & Environment, 1989).
15. Alan Thein Durning and Ed Ayres, "The Story of a Newspaper," *World Watch*, November/December 1994, 30–32.
16. Lester R. Brown, Christopher Flavin, and Sandra Postel, *Saving the Planet: How to Shape an Environmentally Sustainable Economy* (New York: W. W. Norton, 1991), p. 65.
17. Brown, Flavin, and Postel, p. 65.
18. Brown, Flavin, and Postel, p. 68.
19. Brown, Flavin, and Postel, p. 70.
20. *Webster's New World Dictionary*, 2d college ed. (New York: Simon and Schuster, 1980), s.v. "job."
21. *Webster's New World Dictionary*, s.v. "livelihood."
22. The armed forces and defense worker estimates are from UNDP, *Human Development Report 1994* (New York: Oxford University Press, 1994), pp. 47, 60.

Chapter 23. An Awakened Civil Society

1. "20 Questions," *Utne Reader*, January–February 1995, 79.
2. Gustavo Esteva, *Proceso*, February 14, 1994, as quoted in "Chiapas and the Americas," *The Nation*, March 28, 1994, 404; Neil Harvey, *Rebellion in Chiapas: Rural Reforms, Campesino Radicalism, and the Limits to Salinismo*, Transformation of Rural Mexico Series no. 5, (San Diego, Calif.: Ejido Reform Research Project, Center for U.S.-Mexican Studies, University of California, 1994), p. 1.
3. "Goldman Environmental Prize: The First Five Years" (San Francisco: Goldman Environmental Foundation, n.d.), p. 34.
4. Based on Willis W. Harman, personal communication, September 9, 1993.
5. I can mention here only a few of the millions of examples. The cases cited here are drawn from sources such as Paul Ekins, *A New World Order: Grassroots Movements for Global Change* (London: Routledge, 1992); *Goldman Environmental Prize: The First Five Years* (San Francisco: Goldman Environmental Foundation, 1994); nominee lists from the "We the Peoples: 50 Communities Awards" sponsored by the Friends of the United Nations, 1151 Wellington Crescent, Winnipeg R3N 0A1, Canada, fax (1-204) 487-0149; Robin Broad and John Cavanagh, *Plundering Paradise: The Struggle for the Environment in the Philippines* (Berkeley, Calif.: University of California Press, 1993); and Julie Fisher, *The Road from Rio: Sustainable Development and the Nongovernmental Movement in the Third World* (Westport, Conn.: Praeger, 1993). Each issue of *The Ecologist* has an excellent center spread on current protest actions around the world. Subscriptions are available from RED Computing, 29A High Street, New Malden, Surrey, KT3 4BY, United Kingdom; fax (44-81) 942-9385. Reviews of social movements in India are provided by Smitu Kothari, "Social Movements and the Redefinition of Democracy," in Philipp Oldenberg (ed.), *India Briefing* (Boulder, Colo.: Westview Press, 1993), pp. 131–62; and Smitu Kothari, "Incompatibility of Sustainability and Development: In Search of Social Justice," *Journal of Public Administration*, July–September 1993, 312–30.

6. Thomas H. Greco Jr., *New Money for Healthy Communities* (Tucson, Ariz.: Thomas H. Greco Jr., 1994); Edgar Cahn and Jonathan Rowe, *Time Dollars* (Emmaus, Pa.: Rodale Press, 1992).

7. These and other network characteristics are discussed in Jessica Lipnack and Jeffrey Stamps, *Networking: People Connecting with People, Linking Ideas and Resources* (Garden City, N.Y.: Doubleday, 1982), pp. 222–28.

8. For a rich inventory of resources on the sustainable agriculture movement in the United States, see *WHY Magazine*, Summer 1993, 24–25.

9. Peter Rachleff, "Seeds of a Labor Resurgency," *The Nation*, February 21, 1994, 226–29.

10. James L. Tyson, "Young Blacks Get Helping Hand from Chicago Marchers," *Christian Science Monitor*, May 13, 1994, p. 1.

11. "Hungry," *The Economist*, July 10, 1993.

12. Further information on Citizenship Action against Misery and for Life is available from IBASE, rua Vicente de Souza, 29-Botafogo, 22251 Rio de Janeiro/RJ, Brazil; fax (55-21) 286-0541.

13. Michael H. Shuman and Hall Harvey, *Security without War: A Post-Cold War Foreign Policy* (Boulder, Colo.: Westview Press, 1993), pp. 90–92; Gloria Duffy, "Transformation in the USSR—The Role of Track-Two Diplomacy," *Surviving Together*, Spring 1993, 3–5; David Ignatius, "Innocence Abroad: The New World of Spyless Coups, *Washington Post*, September 22, 1991, Outlook Section.

14. Rachleff, 226–29.

15. Information on these networks is available from IOCU, P.O. Box 1045, 10830 Penang, Malaysia; fax (60-4) 366-506.

16. Jeremy Brecher, John Brown Childs, and Jill Carter, *Global Visions: Beyond the New World Order* (Boston: South End Press, 1993).

17. Noeleen Heyzer, "Women's Development Agenda for the 21st Century: Unifem as a Vehicle of Change for Sustainable Livelihoods and Women's Empowerment" (address by the director, United Nations Development Fund for Women, to the Third Committee of the General Assembly of Nations, United Nations, December 1994).

18. The presentation of these examples is inspired by a presentation made by Paul Hawken at The Learning Center in New York City.

Chapter 24. Agenda for Change

1. Herman E. Daly and John B. Cobb Jr., *For the Common Good: Redirecting the Economy toward Community, the Environment, and a Sustainable Future* (Boston: Beacon Press, 1989), p. 174.

2. As cited in Daly and Cobb, p. 209.

3. Paul Hawken, *The Ecology of Commerce: A Declaration of Sustainability* (New York: Harper Business, 1993), p. 108.

4. Hawken, p. 120.

5. Russell Baker, "The Big Hog Wallow," *New York Times*, November 1, 1994, p. A27.

6. Bishan Singh, "A Social Economy: The Emerging Scenario for Change," in Tina Liamzon (ed.), *Civil Society and Sustainable Livelihoods Workshop Report* (Rome: Society for International Development, 1994), pp. 29–37.

7. Gar Alperovitz, "Ameristroika Is the Answer," *Washington Post*, December 13, 1992, p. C1.

8. For a partial inventory and assessment of this experience, see Jeff Shavelson, *A Third Way: A Sourcebook: Innovations in Community-Owned Enterprise* (Washington, D.C.: National Center for Economic Alternatives, 1990).

9. See Richard J. Barnet and John Cavanagh, *Global Dreams* (New York: Simon and Schuster, 1994), p. 416.

10. Herman E. Daly and John B. Cobb Jr., *For the Common Good: Redirecting the Economy toward Community, the Environment, and a Sustainable Future*, 2d. ed. (Boston: Beacon Press, 1994), pp. 414–35.

11. See Barnet and Cavanagh, pp. 415–16.

12. Hawken, p. 163.

13. James Robertson, *Benefits and Taxes: A Radical Strategy* (London: New Economics Foundation, March 1994), pp. 12–17. A variant of the guaranteed income, a graduated positive income tax, is proposed by Daly and Cobb, *For the Common Good* (1989), pp. 315–23. These two sources discuss the history of such proposals and the support they have enjoyed from across the political spectrum.

14. Further information is available from Sixto K. Roxas, President, SKR Managers and Advisors, Inc., No. 59 Hillside Loop, Blueridge A, Quezon City, Philippines; fax (63-2) 722-5547. See also Sixto K. Roxas, "Strategies for Community Economic and Social Transformation," in Liamzon, pp. 41–47.

15. See Patricia Adams, *Odious Debts: Loose Lending, Corruption, and the Third World's Environmental Legacy* (London: Earthscan, 1991).

16. James Tobin, "A Tax on International Currency Transactions," in UNDP, *Human Development Report 1994* (New York: Oxford University Press, 1994), p. 70.

17. See Tim Lang and Colin Hines, *The New Protectionism: Protecting the Future against Free Trade* (New York: New Press, 1993), p. 127, for a discussion of positive approaches to protectionism.

Epilogue: A Choice for Life

1. "20 Questions," *Utne Reader*, January–February 1995, 79.

2. "20 Questions," 81.

3. Thomas Berry, *The Dream of the Earth* (San Francisco: Sierra Club Books, 1988).

4. Duane Elgin, *Awakening Earth: Exploring the Evolution of Human Culture and Consciousness* (New York: William Morrow, 1993), p. 18.

5. Elgin, p. 312.

Index

About the Author

DR. DAVID C. KORTEN has over thirty-five years of experience in preeminent business, academic, and international development institutions as well as in contemporary citizen action organizations. He is currently founder and president of The People-Centered Development Forum, a global alliance of organizations and people dedicated to the creation of just, inclusive, and sustainable societies through voluntary citizen action.

Korten earned his M.B.A. and Ph.D. degrees at the Stanford University Graduate School of Business. Trained in economics, organization theory, and business strategy, his early career was devoted to setting up business schools in low income countries—starting with Ethiopia—in the hope that creating a new class of professional business entrepreneurs would be the key to ending poverty. He completed his military service during the Vietnam War as a captain in the U.S. Air Force, serving in Air Force headquarters command and the Office of the Secretary of Defense.

Korten then served for five and a half years as a faculty member of the Harvard University Graduate School of Business and taught students in Harvard's middle management and M.B.A. programs. He also served as Harvard's advisor to the Nicaragua-based Central American Management Institute. He subsequently joined the staff of the Harvard Institute for International Development, where he headed a Ford Foundation-funded project to strengthen the organization and management of national family planning programs.

In the late 1970s, Korten left U.S. academia and moved to Southeast Asia, where he lived for nearly fifteen years, serving first as a Ford Foundation project specialist, and later as Asia regional advisor on development management to the U.S. Agency for International Development (USAID). His work there won him international recognition for his contributions to pioneering the development of powerful strategies for transforming public bureaucracies into responsive support systems dedicated to strengthening community control and management of land, water, and forestry resources.

Disillusioned by the evident inability of USAID and other large official aid donors to apply the approaches that had been proven effective by the nongovernmental Ford Foundation, Korten broke with the official aid system. His last five years in Asia were devoted to working with leaders of Asian nongovernmental organizations on identifying the root causes of development failure in the region and building the capacity of civil society organizations to function as strategic catalysts of national- and global-level change.

Korten came to realize that the crisis of deepening poverty, growing inequality, environmental devastation, and social disintegration he was observing in Asia was also being experienced in nearly every country in the world—including the United States and other "developed" countries. Furthermore he came to the conclusion that the United States was actively promoting—both at home and abroad—the very policies that were deepening the resulting global crisis. For the world to survive, the United States must change. He moved to New York City in 1992 to help advance that change process.

Dr. Korten's publications are required reading in university courses around the world. He has authored or edited numerous books, including *Getting to the 21st Century: Voluntary Action and the Global Agenda*; *Community Management*; *People-Centered Development* (edited with Rudi Klauss); *Bureaucracy and the Poor: Closing the Gap* (edited with Felipe B. Alfonso), all published by Kumarian Press. He contributes regularly to edited books and professional journals, as well as to the publications of countless citizen organizations.

Selected Titles from Berrett-Koehler Publishers

The Age of Participation:
New Governance for the
Workplace and the World
Patricia McLagan and Christo Nel

Economic Insanity:
How Growth-Driven Capitalism Is
Devouring the American Dream
Roger Terry

The End of Bureaucracy and the
Rise of the Intelligent Organization
Gifford and Elizabeth Pinchot

A Higher Standard of Leadership:
Lessons from the Life of Gandhi
Keshavan Nair

Leadership and the New Science:
Learning About Organization
from an Orderly Universe
Margaret J. Wheatley

Merchants of Vision:
People Bringing New Purpose
and Values to Business
James E. Liebig

Putting Democracy to Work:
A Practical Guide for Starting
and Managing Worker-Owned
Businesses
Frank T. Adams and Gary B. Hansen

The Courageous Follower:
Standing Up To and For Our
Leaders
Ira Chaleff

EcoManagement:
The Elmwood Guide to Ecological
Auditing and Sustainable Business
*Ernest Callenbach, Fritjof Capra,
Lenore Goldman, Rüdiger Lutz, and
Sandra Marburg*

The Fourth Wave:
Business in the 21st Century
*Herman Bryant Maynard, Jr., and
Susan E. Mehrtens*

Future Search:
An Action Guide for Finding
Common Ground in
Organizations and Communities
*Marvin R. Weisbord and
Sandra Janoff*

New Traditions in Business:
Spirit and Leadership in the
21st Century
John Renesch, editor

Stewardship:
Choosing Service Over
Self-Interest
Peter Block

Send orders to:

Berrett-Koehler Publishers
San Francisco

155 Montgomery Street
San Francisco, CA 94104-4109 USA
Fax: (415) 362-2512

Or order by phone: 800-929-2929
24 hours a day, 7 days a week (U.S. only)

Selected Titles from Kumarian Press

 KUMARIAN PRESS Books for a World that Works

Bread, Bricks, and Belief:
Communities In Charge of
Their Future
Mary Lean

All Her Paths Are Peace:
Women Pioneers in Peacemaking
Michael Henderson

Summer in the Balkans:
Laughter and Tears after
Communism
Randall Baker

GAZA: Legacy of Occupation —
A Photographer's Journey
Dick Doughty and Mohammed El Aydi

HIV & AIDS:
The Global Inter-Connection
Elizabeth Reid, editor

The Human Farm:
A Tale of Changing Lives and
Changing Lands
Katie Smith

 KUMARIAN PRESS Books on International Development

Getting to the 21st Century:
Voluntary Action and the
Global Agenda
David C. Korten

Down to Earth:
Community Perspectives on Health,
Development, and the Environment
*Bonnie Bradford and
Margaret A. Gwynne, editors*

Promises Not Kept:
The Betrayal of Social Change in
the Third World, Third Edition
John Isbister

The Wealth of Communities:
Stories of Success in Local
Environmental Management
*Charlie Pye-Smith, Grazia Borrini
Feyerabend with Richard Sandbrook*

Democratizing Development:
The Role of Voluntary
Organizations
John Clark

The New World of Microenterprise
Finance: Building Healthy Financial
Institutions for the Poor
*María Otero and
Elisabeth Rhyne, editors*

Intermediary NGOs:
The Supporting Link in
Grassroots Development
Thomas F. Carroll

In Defense of Livelihood:
Comparative Studies on
Environmental Action
*John Friedmann and
Haripriya Rangan, editors*

For a complete catalog, call:
800-289-2664 toll free

KUMARIAN PRESS, INC.

630 Oakwood Avenue, Suite 119   203-953-0214 / inquiries
West Hartford, CT 06110-1529 USA   203-953-8579 / fax
kpbooks@aol.com / e-mail